# LYRICAL MOVEMENTS, HISTORICAL HAUNTINGS

# Lyrical Movements, Historical Hauntings

ON GENDER, COLONIALISM, AND DESIRE

IN MIRAJI'S URDU POETRY

GEETA PATEL

MANOHAR
2005

First published 2001 by Stanford University Press
Reprinted 2005 by arrangement with original publishers.



ISBN 81-7304-652-2

*Published by*
Ajay Kumar Jain *for*
Manohar Publishers & Distributors
4753/23 Ansari Road, Daryaganj
New Delhi 110 002

*Printed at*
Lordosn Publishers Pvt. Ltd.
Delhi 110 007

*Distributed in South Asia by*
FOUNDATION BOOKS
4381/4, Ansari Road
Daryaganj, New Delhi 110 002
and its branches at Mumbai, Hyderabad,
Bangalore, Chennai, Kolkata

*In memory of Akhtarul Iman, whose stories gave Miraji life*

*

Writing like Shahrazad, to prolong the times between life
and death:
for the women in my life,
my mother, my masi, mataji, devi, Alisha, India
and finally Kath

CONTENTS

## ACKNOWLEDGMENTS

Many people and institutions have sustained me in places I have come to call "home" as I worked on this book; among them Columbia University and New York, the University of Iowa and Iowa City, and finally, Wellesley College and Cambridge.

Two people were instrumental in helping me envision and complete this project. One, Akhtarul Iman, gave me access to Miraji's papers and spent many hours of his time imparting wisdom and stories that enriched this work beyond measure. The second, Professor Frances W. Pritchett, my advisor under whose tutelage I first read Miraji and Urdu poetry, kept me to task.

I am grateful to a range of people in the Urdu literary universe who talked to me and sent me papers, poems, and information. Shamsur Rahman Faruqi, in his roles as a reader of my work and as a critic of poetry, gave me seminal insights into Miraji's poetry. Varis Alvi, Zoe Ansari, Baidar Bakht, Jamil Jalibi, Ajmal Kamal, Muhammad Umar Memon, C. M. Naim, and Sultana and her family were forthcoming with articles and tidbits of knowledge. David Lelyveld and Carla Petievich took time to read portions of this work, talk, compare notes, and assist me constantly.

In New York, a group of friends and colleagues—Susham Bedi, Nadine Berardi, Professor Hawley, Eric Huberman—kept me inspired and engaged, giving me encouragement in ways they might not even have envisioned. Professor Riccardi, a member of my committee, took time out to talk as I began my research and encouraged my early pursuit of it. David Rubin, who read the manuscript in its different stages, kept me nourished with tea and cookies. My language teachers, Fran, David, Ted Riccardi,

Jack Hawley, Susham Bedi, and Barbara Miller helped me acquire the tools I needed to read the relevant texts.

In Iowa many people sustained my work. My reading companions and friends—Sabine Gölz, Maureen Robertson, David Stern—offered suggestions, love, homes, and commitment to the project. Their belief in the value of my research kept the devils at bay. Rusty Barcelo, Jeff Cox, Lois Cox and my reading group, Sally Kenney, Kevin Kopelson, Philip Lutgendorf, Teresa Mangum, and Gregory Williams helped me in myriad ways. Papusa Molina gave me a computer, affection, and her time so that I could write the last chapter. To the innumerable librarians and libraries (James Nye, CRL, The National Archives of India, Mumbai University Library at Kalina and at Fort, J. B. Petit Library, Mrs. Vaswani at The Asiatic Society Library, Devashri Mukherjee at The Marg Archives, The Baroda Museum Library, and The Jawaharlal Nehru Memorial Library) who found materials for me, gave me permission to photocopy, and sent me off on new searches I can only give my heartfelt thanks.

At Wellesley my department and its ancillary members—Pat Berman, Ann Congleton, Elena Creef, Alice Friedman, Rosanna Hertz, Lidwein Kaptjiens, Salem Mekuria, Mary-Pat Navins, Katy Park, Susan Reverby—held my hand. I am also indebted to Faculty Awards at Wellesley College for a dissertation grant, which funded the final pieces, and the Barnett Miller Faculty Development Grant and Mildred McAfee Horton Fund, which gave me the means to travel back to India to collect archival materials. Margaret Dodds and Wren Fournier read and reread each piece until it met their exacting standards of writing perfection. Friends, colleagues, and relatives brought me back to the pleasure, the *khalish*, of writing: Ayesha Abraham, Meena Alexander, Anjali Arondekar, Begoña Aretxaga, Paola Bachetta, Lauren Berlant, Margaret Cerullo, Shih-Weh Chen, Lawrence Cohen, Julie Erfani, Marla Erlien, Janet Jakobsen, Jitu Mayor, Leela and Vinodini Mayor, Jose Muñoz, Ann Pellegrini, Anindyo Roy, Kumkum Sangari, Forbes Singer, Katie Stewart, Susanne Vaughn, Minakshi Menon, and Naren Subramanian. Many more, whose names I have not mentioned here, haunt the pages of this book. Helen Tartar, whose willingness to believe, helped this book to be. Marty Brody's lovely music flowed through my translations.

I am very grateful that various members of my family were there as I worked my way through to the end. Sanjay, Leslie, Cami, Frank, and my nieces, my Masi, Titu, Bitu, Neena, Jayashree, and Roma offered unconditional love and affection. My brother Sunil and his office staff, Jayesh Patel, set up all my Baroda excursions, photocopied valiantly, and my father encouraged each trip and sent me materials. Sagar Mama set meetings up for me in Delhi and read the book with a critic's eye. My mother in her role as a field researcher followed material around until it manifested, and in her role as a reader provoked this version of the book into life. Steven Kossak and Evelynn Hammonds, Nancy and John Romano, Juliana and Clarissa stood by my side, and Kath Weston I thank for the endless patience and love, as well as the quick, precise, and exquisite suggestions that helped me finish.

# A NOTE ON TRANSLITERATION

The letters of the Urdu alphabet have been transliterated as follows:

*alif* as: a, i, u, ā
b p t ṭ ṡ
j c ḥ ḳh
d ḍ ż
r ṛ z zh
s sh
ṣ ẓ
t̤ z̤
ʿ gḥ
f q

k g
l m
n
*vā'o* as: v, ū, o, au
h
*baṛī ye* as: y, ī, e, ai
*nūn-e ghunnah* as: ñ
*hamzah* as: '
*iẓāfat* as: -e

*Hindi and Sanskrit words follow their Urdu transliteration.*

# *One* BEGINNINGS

Let the mind lay its listening net
however it will
meaning is elusive, a bird of myth
even in its sure realm of speech.[1]

# INTRODUCTION: JOURNEY TOWARD MIRAJI

Sitting in a classroom at Columbia, in an elegant white room with wooden window frames, I looked around at the small group of fellow graduate students who had come to study modern Urdu poetry with Urdu scholar Fran Pritchett. We had already read selections from two of the three canonical poets of the twentieth century, Faiz Ahmad Faiz (1911–84) and N. M. Rashid (1910–75), their verses having been carefully chosen for variations in poetic texture by Professor Pritchett and Shamsur Rahman Faruqi, one of the foremost Urdu literary critics in India.[2] Fran steered us methodically through the works of Rashid and Faiz, guiding us to multiple, complex readings; she then introduced us to the remaining member of the triumvirate: Miraji (1912–49).[3]

Nothing we had done to that point—neither Faiz's early evocative reworking of conventional Urdu lyric nor Rashid's sparser, terser Arabicized poetry—had prepared me for Miraji. The poems we read—"Samundar kā bulāvā," "Ābgīne ke us pār kī ek shām," "Jātrī," "Taḥrīq" (Call of the sea, A night on the far side of the wine glass, Traveler, and Movement)[4]—were difficult, although not difficult, like Rashid's poems, because of their esoteric vocabulary; in fact, most of Miraji's words were remarkably straightforward. Their language, syntax, and rhythms echoed spoken Hindustani, yet the "ordinary" language in which they were written was offset by their exquisiteness. They were voluptuously and lyrically synaesthetic.[5]

When I read Miraji's poems literally they appeared accessible, but their images eluded easy readings; I got "stuck" in the disjunctures, between the ease with which the words *seemed* available to me and the obstacles I encountered when I tried to make sense of them. I couldn't understand the poems, although I felt they should be fairly clear because their language was close to simple spoken Urdu and their images were concrete. "A Night on the Far Side of the Wine Glass" (henceforth "A Night"), a three-page poem that has haunted me for years, is a case in point:

> Have you ever seen the sparks in a fireplace?
> Laughingly stroking your cheek, painted red
> every finger
> oozes blood.
> A thin sliver of delicate succulent fruit touches
> my tongue, look—
> the simple whiteness of a plain robe crushes dry leaves.

These lines, from the heart of "A Night," flow effortlessly from the page. The texture produced by the light meter in which they are written is sinuously pleasurable, their images so physically vivid and compelling that they can be translated on or into a reader's body even as they are enunciated. They map a sequence of sense and sensation—looking, touching, oozing, feeling with one's tongue, crushing—drawing together anomalous images by connecting a tenuous web of associations—red sparks, red-painted cheek, blood on finger, wet blood, (wet) succulent fruit, delicate succulence on tongue. The question Fran raised about the poem in our class stays with me: Is something actually happening in "A Night," or is it just a marvelously lyrical, delicious piece of whimsy?

The language of classical Urdu poetry, as it is taught in the United States and the Indian subcontinent, is different from spoken Urdu—it is a language that readers and reciters must learn. While spoken Urdu has some continuities with spoken Hindustani, a simple speaking or reading knowledge of it is not enough to understand classical Urdu poetry and poetics.[6] In India and Pakistan some children learn poetry at home by reciting and listening to *shi'r*, while others, like us, learn in a classroom.

My mother, who grew up in Delhi and Lucknow in the 1940s, and her mother, who grew up in Agra in the 1920s and 1930s, were competent in many dialects of Urdu and were fluent in classical Urdu poetry. My grandmother, in fact, was more comfortable with Urdu script than she was with the Hindi script, Nagari. My mother's family spoke Hindustani, a language that resembled literary Urdu and had connections to the "classical" language of Urdu poetry. By the time my mother's generation was in their teens, however, India and Pakistan had been established as separate territories; the advent of partition (in 1947) augmented the development of two state-sponsored languages—Hindi and Urdu. Sarkari, or Indian-government Hindi, relied more on Sanskrit words, while the Urdu taught in Pakistani schools used more Persian and Arabic.

By the time I went to school in Bombay in the 1960s I was thoroughly educated in Sarkari Hindi; the "state" had made it impossible to learn the Urdu script in school. My mother's family still spoke to each other in Hindustani, and it was because of this that I was more at ease with reading turn-of-the-century Hindustani texts than were my classmates, whose families spoke other languages at home. I read a fair amount of Hindi poetry, but, except for movie songs and an occasional mushaira (poetry symposium) (where I was often lost), I was unfamiliar with the history of or idioms peculiar to Urdu poetry.

With Fran Pritchett's help, I finally honed my Urdu script and learned Urdu poetry. She taught us meter, recitation, and exegesis, the careful unpacking of multivalent lines. In a way unusual to American universities, our class simulated the subcontinental practices of poetic competence—we learned poetry by heart and had to choose, recite, and explain our favorite *shi'r*. Some of us, in an excess of devotion to authentic practice, anointed ourselves with a poetic name, or *takhalluṣ*. What we were given in the process was the multivocal, idiomatic pleasure of poetry (*kaifiyat*); we could enjoy brilliant verse, luxuriate in delicate lineages that subtly played on lyric heritage, recognize slight shifts in meaning that various poets gave refrains, sound verse on our tongue at moments when a special *shi'r* was apt. In short, we had been turned into the closest possible American equivalent of subcontinental aficionados of classical Urdu poetry.

So I became familiar with, even took for granted, the need to learn and speak in a specialized linguistic world when reading or reciting poetry. That is why, when I first encountered Miraji, I knew that I needed a new, particular competence in his poetic language and diction; the terms of classical poetry—poetry for which I had a certain linguistic knowledge—did not work for him. I don't mean that some twentieth-century Urdu poetry is *not* classical, for classical poetry as an unchanged genre, as well as a form that incorporates transformed, nontraditional contents, continues to be written and sung. The transcontinental drift of poets like Rashid and the political intonations of poets like Faiz, who have given such genres as the *naẓm* (free verse) public recognition, would belie any assertion that classical poetic modes held supremacy in the middle of the twentieth century. What I want to point out is that in order to comprehend what Rashid and Faiz are trying to say with their poetry, one has to learn a specific poetic language. It may seem obvious to say that one has to learn different "languages" (terms, phrases, meters, and stories) in order to understand certain kinds of poetry. But it appears necessary, here, to state the obvious because the opposite is often believed to be the case, especially for modern (*jadīd*) poetry written in the twentieth century. In the commonly held beliefs about it, modern poetry broke from earlier lyric by refusing to cohere around the covenants and etiquette that ruled nineteenth-century poetic practice.

Faiz is the kind of poet who exemplifies the position that poetry is easily accessible. Poets like him have provided a popularized standard by which a poet like Miraji is judged. On the other hand, Faiz falls into a special category; his poetry is so widely disseminated as recitation and song that its registers have become familiar to many song lovers. His poetry has become publicly comfortable—so much so that the idea that one might have to "learn" it is almost transgressive, on a par with not knowing what Hindi film songs are saying.

## COMPETENCE IN THE OBSCURE

What, then, is different about Miraji? As I began my research, I realized that his poetry was not accessible in the usual ways; I could not simply go to a teacher or to a class or spend some time reading him and expect to become a non-native speaker of his poetic language. As a foreign speaker of Urdu classical poetry, and even of some contemporary poets, I learned languages, developed a competence in them, and made certain regular mistakes that I could then discover (sometimes to my embarrassment) and sort out over time.[7] But when I asked people who had read Miraji what contingencies I should expect when I read him, I was faced with an odd response: almost everyone, with the notable exception of Faruqi Sahib, told me that I had set myself to an impossible task. "He's a difficult poet," I heard over and over. "You're crazy to work on him." When I attempted to move the discussion beyond "He's difficult," however, I was stopped short by the tautology "He's difficult because he's obscure." Fortunately, this did not deter me. Miraji's exquisite poetry, such as "A Night," held me in thrall.

Much of his work seemed a paradox: easy to read yet incomprehensible. I knew that I could not learn to read it simply by asking for help. Before I went further I felt that I had to address what it meant that his poetry was ambiguous to people who had read him. Some of the questions I had to work through were: What exactly was "difficult" about Miraji's poetry? What did the word "difficult" mean when used on Miraji's work? Why did "difficult" lapse into "obscure" when it was applied to Miraji? The first question bears directly on my journey toward this book; the other two questions will be discussed in later chapters.

What makes Miraji's work "difficult" is that it *seems* to be readable; the paradox lies in its *un*readability, despite the fact it is written in the idioms of spoken language. Even though some of the words, sentences, fragments, and phrases that make up a poem evoke (are intertextual with) different poetic traditions, such as Braj and Awadhi mystical poetry or Urdu ghazals, they can be read or heard as simple spoken Urdu, so not knowing what to do with the poems as one reads them is odd and uncomfortable.[8] The obvious alternative to thinking of Miraji's poems as simple written Urdu is to treat them as a separate, marked category—as "Miraji's poetry"—something that *resembles* classical poetry, but for which one has to learn a different language. I, like other readers of his work, learned that this could not be done.[9]

## SEARCHING FOR THE POET

My pursuit of Miraji, encouraged by Fran Pritchett, was fueled by the continuities I found between his poetry and my own competencies in several different lineages of poetry. His work used words, images, and syntax from different Indic traditions—Urdu, Braj, Sanskrit, Bengali; and because he translated poets like Baudelaire, Li Po, and Sappho, he also carried other, non-Indian literary worlds into Urdu. For a comparatist like me, his work was provocative and engaging.

As I worked on translating "A Night," I also began to search for books by Miraji and articles about him. The first piece I read, by the Marxist critic Aijaz Ahmad,[10] had been recommended as "*the* article" by everyone I'd asked in the States. Fran had introduced me to Ahmad's collection of transcreations of Ghalib's ghazals by famous American poets. Like everything else on or by Miraji, the article by Ahmad was not easily available. Then C. M. Naim, one of those who had suggested I read it, found it among his papers. In the interval before it reached me, however, I interviewed Jamil Jalibi, an Urdu literary critic from Pakistan who was compiling Miraji's poetry.

Jalibi, who at the time was traveling around the United States with his wife, agreed to meet me by the Air India terminal at Kennedy Airport in New York. In the murky August heat I met them, surrounded by the ubiquitous, oversized cases and piles of plastic shopping bags stuffed with presents that people traveling to and from the subcontinent often seem to have. After snaking our way through lines of passengers, we collapsed gratefully on sofas in the air-conditioned lounge and I pulled out my tiny tape recorder, setting it on the low table between the three of us.

The first question was asked by Jalibi: had I read Ahmad's article? Not yet, I responded, anxious to ask a question of my own about what he thought of the stories I had heard that Miraji was a sexual deviant. When I'd asked people what they meant when they used phrases like "sexual deviant," I received responses like "He had an Oedipal fixation on his mother," "He was a nymphomaniac," "He masturbated," "He had syphilis." When I would then ask them to be more specific, most of my informants would expand with a description of a habit they considered characteristic of or peculiar to Miraji—he kept silver foil balls in his pants pockets and kneaded them constantly. My information usually ended there.[11]

I wanted Jalibi to comment on this foreshortened narrative that overlaid "deviance" with an idiosyncrasy that "proved" the deviance was real. Miraji's delicate poetry had led me to expect more of him than this. Since Jalibi was writing on Miraji and had told me that he had collected letters and papers from Miraji's friends, I thought he was someone who could fill me in on details about Miraji's life. But we did not have a great deal of time at the airport; we had a brief, capsule discussion on Miraji's poetry but never got around to the many stories about Miraji's life. My search, which circled around the question of the authentic, returning home to find the "real" story, was stymied immediately at an airport where I sat down in the midst of the diaspora.

## FIRST VIEWING

> Lean body, coarse complexion, long, filthy strands of black and white hair so matted together that his head looked like a mound of ashes, a vibrant face, sunken eyes but sharp and twinkling, an expansive voice, a commanding presence, rings on his fingers, in his hand—balls to which he kept adding glittering wrappings from cigarette boxes so that they looked like silver balls, a taste for lying in conversation, a deadly intellect choked with violent thoughts of self-destruction, his imagination replete with the ghosts of obscure physical activities. By the final few years of his life he had crafted himself with such cunning that anyone who looked at him could see anything: an ascetic, a weasely criminal, the poorest factory worker, a walking, wandering corpse.[12]

This was the first portrait I saw of Miraji. The vivid picture Aijaz Ahmad drew on the opening page of his influential article "Mīrājī: Shakh-ṣiyat aur fann" (Miraji: Personality and work) followed me as I read Miraji's poems. Jalibi had given me a few clues—Miraji's papers were the property of another Urdu poet, Akhtarul Iman; he never finished a formal education, but he read voraciously and carefully in the library; he was fascinated by Freud; he did all his own translations of non-Urdu-speaking poets (mainly from English); many poets respected his careful readings of their work. What made me curious was the conflict that emerged between Ahmad's powerfully evocative portrait of a wild young urban man and Jalibi's self-made, curious, library-bound intellectual. Like his poetry, Miraji's body seemed to slip between significations.

I wanted to know more about the poet who was beginning to be a presence in my life. Jalibi told me that Akhtarul Iman would be a good source of material about Miraji, so I went to Fran Pritchett to find out what I could about him. She and Faruqi Sahib told me that Akhtarul Iman lived in Bombay, the city where I had grown up and where my parents still lived. Fran and I debated the possibility of my going to Lahore, where Jalibi said Miraji's brother lived. As an Indian Hindu, however, the intricacies of getting permission to enter Pakistan with a visa for research seemed insurmountable, so we discussed a potential visit to Bombay instead.

As I began to look for work by Miraji, I realized that much of it was out of print and some was still unpublished. I would need access to Akhtarul Iman's collection of Miraji's papers and to Indian libraries if I wanted to write a book that did not just rely on copies of the few books I had managed to scrounge, with Fran's help, from aficionados of Urdu poetry and Urdu literary critics. Faruqi Sahib sent word to me through Fran that meeting with Akhtarul Iman would be useful, but also that he was a recluse who no longer spent time with many people outside of his family.

Fran suggested I talk to my parents. Up to this point, they had not been particularly pleased with my academic choices and would have preferred to see me in a professional school. Once they realized the unlikeliness of this, however, they refused to have much to do with me. But when I called my mother to find out if she would be willing to locate Akhtarul Iman and interview him for me, she was elated by her prospective involvement with my research. She went looking—walking into Urdu bookstores on Muhammad Ali Road (in the Muslim section of Bombay), following leads given to her by poets and bookstore owners apparently bemused by a short, round, older, obviously upper-middle-class Hindu woman who spoke comfortable Urdu asking questions for a daughter working on Urdu poetry in the United States. Her anomalousness provoked curiosity and prompted people to help her. When she called me, excited because she had located Akhtarul Iman, I asked her to see him and to tape an interview with him on my behalf.

Akhtarul Iman was extremely gracious to my mother; she had piqued his interest enough that he invited her to his home to talk. She visited him several times, sharing stories of my life with him and eliciting pieces of information about Miraji. After several trips to his house, he told her that he felt I needed to come to talk to him myself, and that he would be willing to give me access to Miraji's papers if I would come to see him in Bombay.

I first returned to Bombay in the winter of 1989 and then again in the heat of June. I had not been to India for many years. The last time I visited home, my maternal grandmother, to whom I had been very close, was nearing death. In many ways I was her child, an inveterate reader intrigued by verse and philosophy. Now, to return home to gather material for my book was to come back as her child-turned-adult. It would also be the final confirmation that I had repudiated my father's imagined future for me—scientist, technician, businesswoman, preferably married.

Akhtarul Iman proved to be a wonderful contact. He was frail from his recent bypass surgery, but he spent afternoons with my mother and me, having let us join in on his late-morning routines. Sultana, his wife, fed us delicate *bhatorā*, samosas, and hot spicy tea. We sat in his living room, three women surrounding him as he rested on the divan, tired from talking. I was introduced to his children, played word games with his granddaughter, and was initiated into family discussions.

I asked Akhtarul Iman question after question, and he sent me off to talk to other poets in Bombay who had known Miraji. As we grew more familiar with each other, he slowly began showing me the papers that Miraji had left as his legacy—carefully annotated poems, translations, prose pieces, some in square, lined notebooks, some just in piles, and some in hand-bound, string-tied, manuscript form. Exquisitely calligraphed, yellowing frontispieces and tables of contents opened the books of poetry that Miraji had compiled for publication. Lists of poems he had published mingled with short scripts for films, accounts, publishers' booklists, library information sheets, and notes left over from the translations of Braj poetry he had been working on before he died. The farther we traveled into the bags, the more fragile the papers we withdrew. The final set I saw had been shredded into Rorschach blots by worms, among them several versions of "A Night." The papers evoked the details of Miraji's life—libraries, writing, and an obsession for compiling lists.

Akhtarul Iman gave me the lists of poems, written on long, yellowing sheets of paper; they weren't interesting to him because they weren't central to Miraji's poetic corpus. For me, however, they conjured up someone who had spent hour after careful hour writing the names of everything he had ever published, annotating the information with dates and the names of journals. Akhtarul Iman let me take away the rest of the material to copy, and I walked with my mother in the thick Bombay summer to the local market in a small store that sold stationery and comic books, to photocopy volumes of poetry, prose, and the debris of Miraji's life.

When we brought the papers back, Sultana, Iman's wife, would talk to us. I learned about her life with Akhtarul Iman, an itinerant poet-writer. She told me the other side of living in a community of male poets who would come to her house to be fed, to drink, and to talk about poetry. After the initial gentle admonitions of her husband, she became comfortable acceding to my curiosity about her life and regaled us with stories, silencing Akhtarul Iman with soft humor when he interrupted her tales. Sultana gave me valuable access to narratives told by women about the men they lived with and succored. Up to that point, all I had were stories told by men of predominantly male worlds, masculine lineages, and male care. Sultana told me about raucous nights when people fell asleep in her living room. She talked about listening to complicated discussions of poetry and politics that would heat up into arguments fueled by drink. She described the graphic aftermath, walking delicately between strewn bodies, cleaning up cups and vomit. She opened up for me the anxieties of a time when work and money were scarce and friends lived in her house because there was nowhere else to go.

It was because of Sultana that I learned about the ambivalence Miraji left behind. She and Akhtarul Iman had taken care of him for many years in Bombay; they cared deeply for their friend, but they were also angry about his insensitivities. Both spoke with pain of the incredible isolation from his community that Miraji endured before he died. It was clear to me after I talked to Akhtarul Iman and Sultana that Miraji's life played out and continued the contradictions that had characterized his early years. Sultana's stories provoked a retelling of the ordinary, drunk gatherings to which poets were prone, and which had over two generations become identified with the (implicitly though necessarily male) poetic persona. She sent me back to reconsider why what seemed so natural would in the case of Miraji turn into signs of abnormality.

Miraji had lived in several different colonial Indian urban centers—Lahore, Delhi, Poona, and finally, Bombay. As a literary figure, he wrote between poetic traditions—bhakti, courtly Urdu, and Persian. His politics, both anticolonial and apolitical modernist, positioned him centrally and in ancillary relationship to his literary contemporaries. He was credited with being a forefather of the well-placed circle of writers who called themselves the *Ḥalqah-e arbāb-e ẕauq* (Circle of the men of taste), although he was eventually marginalized by many of his cohorts. His name—a woman's name—could have easily placed him in a lineage of poets who took pen names, but the gendered implications of the name, coupled with the dissonance produced by his often "obscure" though beautiful poetry, circumvented his placement in a literary tradition.

The stories of Miraji's life that I have compiled began with Akhtarul Iman's and Sultana's, but they now include a variety of sources. Several collections of Miraji's work and articles about him were made available to me; in addition, I have taped interviews with Jamil Jalibi, Shamsur Rahman Faruqi, Akhtarul Iman, and Sultana, as well as poets like Zoe Ansari, a member of the Marxist Progressive Writers' Association, the organization primarily responsible for Miraji's isolation in Bombay.

Many of the articles on Miraji's life insistently describe him in ways that echo Aijaz Ahmad's depiction of him: a crazy, messy, insane, apolitical, self-absorbed man with peculiar sexual habits. This has become the standard portrait. But other narratives I have collected, both in oral and written form, paint Miraji in a different light—as someone who was excessively kind, meticulous, thoughtful, and politically and intellectually committed. The first chapter, his biography, shall attempt to weave these two paradoxical portraits together in order to draw a more complicated picture of him.[13]

Sitting a little way away from Huzur's Jali in beautiful Medina, lost in meditation, I was asking blessings for my friends as they came to mind, one by one, until no one's name was left unremembered. I was suffused with a strange happiness. My feelings seemed to be dissolving and strings of pearl tears poured from my eyes when suddenly Miraji stood in front of me and said, "You've forgotten me—you didn't pray for me!" I prayed for him right away; he continued to stand before me. When I finished praying and looked up, he was gone and so was everyone else; no one was around; neither Miraji nor anyone else. I was alone, by myself. Just me and Huzur's Jali. I was amazed . . . astonished . . . perplexed. What sort of adventure was this?[1]

# 1. STORIES FROM A CHILDHOOD

## MYTH AND MEMORY

> Telling, a memory of that fabulous angelic love,
> and on the other hand
> the poetry of my disclosure, unfurling language
> and, a friend who gathered my secrets
> became, in the end, my rival.[2]

Zainab Begam had traveled a long way from Kathiawad, Gujarat, where her husband, Mahtābud-din Dār, was stationed. She had come to give birth to her first child in his family home, which was tucked into a tiny lane in Muzang (Muhallah Balucha Muzang), nestled in the heart of Lahore.[3] At five in the morning, on May 25, 1912, Sana' ullah Ḍār—Miraji—was born into a home already bustling with children. Photographs of the house reveal its long brick face shuttered off from the narrow street by heavy wooden doors and barred windows. The weight of the doors is balanced uncertainly on a thin stone sill.[4]

Like many of the details that thicken stories of Miraji into life, descriptions of the place where he was born are rife with contradictions. Inadvertently modulated into anachronism by Anis Nagi in his book *Mīrājī: Ek bhaṭkā hu'ā sha'ir* (Miraji: A poet who lost his way), Muzang becomes overwhelming, cross-hatched by open sewers that flood over during the monsoons. Nagi perhaps projects backward into Miraji's childhood the streets of Muzang familiar to him from late-twentieth-century Lahore. But these streets are familiar to us. They are from another topography, that of colonial Indian cities sketched in the black-and-white photographs from another time. Condensed into Nagi's Muzang are the ghostly outlines of these colonial cityscapes. Literary portraits from the *Imperial Gazetteer*'s description of Lahore, for example, seem to materialize in Nagi's descriptions: "Narrow and tortuous streets as well as lanes, some of them ending in culs-de-sac, and lined by tall houses give [it] a mean and gloomy appearance."[5]

These lanes in Muzang, Lahore, Delhi, or Lucknow could easily have been those whose reiteration dead-ended in E. M. Forster's *Chandrapore*, where fantasy bleeds into desire: "The streets are mean, the temples ineffective, and though a few fine houses exist they are hidden away in gardens or down alleys whose filth deters all but the invited guest." Chandrapore's unsurprisingly tortured Indian geography is offset by the civil station, settled on a rise from which it can look down on and survey the city's "low but indestructible form of life." This other city is a "city of gardens, . . . no city, but a forest sparsely scattered with huts." Unlike the adjectives "abasement, monotony, and excrescence" that liven the Indian city into allegory, the civil station "provokes no emotion"; it neither "charms nor repels." But it produces a kind of sense through the forms its sensibility takes—it is "sensibly planned." English houses, bungalows, are laid out along roads that "intersect at right angles." One can almost visualize their insides widening into verandas. Though Forster literalizes this, the outsideness of the pastoral melting into the angular mathematical regularity of a very civil station, the buildings, the technology of the British colony, need not have been literally outside. Instead, it could easily have been tucked into its dark other, the Indian city, blending almost unobtrusively into the Indian city as university, school, telegraph office, or railway station.

Outside both architectures, outside the mean chaos of India, its jewels hidden by dirt and disuse, and outside the ordered, hypocritical symmetry of the Raj, situated on a mountain, are the Marabar caves. Their hollows suck in water, sound, and meaning. They amplify sounds into rebounding echoes. Their walls, the horizons that cup echoes, are never seen; they are merely imagined as a ghostly limit. Entering them and traversing them are possibilities offered only as the contradictions of violence. The caves become the place around which colonial encounters turn desire corporeal. Desire scratched onto body, whose resolutions take place through law and the resistances of nationalism that crowd streets.

The dirt and disease that Nagi pencils into Miraji's birth place follow the familiar contours of science, criminality, and law—British nineteenth-century depictions of class and future promise. If you are born colonized into the meanness of a place like Muzang, where you are born overwhelms everything else. Where you are born foretells what you will become. Here, there is no possibility of redemption by education; no possibility of leaving-behind by moving up.[6] So Nagi, too, describing Muzang, presages his portrait of the grown poet's insalubriousness, his "night-soiled clothes," his "public masturbation," and his *āvāragī*, his "vagabond ways."

Other voices offer other accounts of Muzang, of the architecture of Indian cities, of their imaginary forms, of the ways that they wind into memory, character, life, and desire. Mrs. Din (who knew the woman Mirajī fell in love with in Lahore), reminiscing to me about the 1930s Lahore of her childhood, says that Muzang at that time, like many city areas, was crowded and animated, houses and shops tightly packed around little winding lanes filled with people. But it was neither dirty, nor mean, nor gloomy.[7]

Lanes, and more particularly city lanes, *galī* and *kūcā*, are the byways of the city of poets, the city that comes alive as poets in the eighteenth and nineteenth centuries dream Urdu verse out of a desire (*ārzū*) that can neither be relinquished nor realized. Lanes echo across lyric moments. Replete with meaning, lanes become one place, furling out of time, where the lover's being comes alive in lavish abjectness. Carrying an *'āshiq*, a lover, toward his beloved, the lane that stops at the beloved's house (*koṭhī*) is resonant with the promise of love. Holding a lover as he waits hopelessly outside, pain and pleasure mingle. The pleasure of pain (*ārzū*) and the pain of pleasure held in abeyance (*tanhā'ī*) blend allegory into the lane's dust, *ḳhāk*, which clothes a lover, shrouding him in despair, dressing him in memories. Real and yet not, stretching between glimpsing and having, hovering between the byways of imagination and the symbolic alleys winding through Delhi or Lucknow or Lahore, these are the lanes that Jur'at (d. 1810), composing poetry in Lucknow, evoked so eloquently in his *shi'r*: "On the dust of your lane, you no longer let me lie stretched, / where you once spread out, alas, carpets to honor me."[8]

Miraji is born into a cross-hatched lineage: Muzang, a noisy space, tightly knotted into an Urdu- and Punjabi-speaking city. Miraji's forefathers migrated for three generations down to rural Punjab from Dogra in Kashmir, and then, when they had accumulated enough capital, moved to Lahore. The poet's father lived a life of quotidian vagrancy as a railway employee. Miraji's lineage is the colonial city's dirt and disease traveling the ways of tightly scripted lanes. It is also the *ḳhāk* layered into the poetry of *galī* and *kūcā*. The poet's lineage foretells both his future *āvāragī*, his wandering, his vagrancy, his aloneness, his dissoluteness, as well as the propriety of his poetic stance. Miraji was born somewhere between the time of the present and the time of the past in the modern. H. lived, as Aijaz Ahmad so aptly puts it, as "an ascetic [a sadhu, a *sant*, a pir], a weaselly criminal, the poorest factory worker, a walking, wandering corpse." Miraji the pir, the *sant*, the sadhu, the *āvārā*, the *maiḳhvār* (wine-loving) poet who is classified as a criminal, menial, vagrant, drunkard, insane under colonial erudition and lore.[9]

Miraji was the eldest child of his father's second wife, Zainab Begam, whom Munshī Mahtābud-din had married in 1910, shortly after the death of his first wife, Hasina Begam. Preceded by two older half brothers, Muhammad Ata' ullah and Muhammad 'Ināyat' ullah, who took him into their care, Miraji was followed by six younger siblings.

The new mother remained with her young son in the "ordinary" multifamily home in Lahore for fifteen months. As was the case with many other employees of the railways, Munshī Mahtābud-din, an assistant engineer on the Bombay Baroda and Central Indian Railway lines, was transferred frequently and transported his growing family with him to new posts, which included stations in Bindiyachal and Halol, Kohistan in Baluchistan, and Sukkur and Karachi in Sindh. While Zainab Begum was recovering from her delivery, Miraji's father was transferred to Godhra near Baroda state. Miraji's mother joined him there with her young son.

## DEATH AND THE NATIONALIST FANTASY

> Ko'ī kahe ye jīvan acchā ko'ī kahe us pār
> dūr ke ḍhol suhāne/sahāne haiñ lo naqd na tīrh udhār.[10]

Little information is available on Miraji's childhood and what little information there is does not draw his childhood into the political events of the day. Perhaps the precursors of this kind of telling, denuded of politics, lie in Miraji's autobiographical article, "Nāmukammal sailf-porṭraiṭ" (Incomplete self-portrait),[11] where childhood is sketched as a series of dreamlike scenes, with its politics coded only in the occasional adjectival color of metaphor. Or perhaps this curious lack of political texture merely follows and repeats critics' beliefs that Miraji's poetry was apolitical. But Miraji's work is imbued with political resonances that do not take the form of dry rhetorical gestures toward a politics that marked itself as such. His poetry reaches for political efficacy through an ethics that arises/arrives with death. And his poetry, using the taste of words lingering on the tongue, using translation as a memorial,[12] dealt again and again with the call that echoed from beyond death to bring authors like Sappho into life:

> Prophecy from another time
> After my life has come and gone, after my death perhaps
> in a spring season
> when a call returned drifts in
> my songs will be heard, once more, the world over![13]

Miraji was a poet who carried and recast nineteenth-century death elegies—Urdu lyric that mourned the dead from 1857 and the ghazal's evocation of death as the longing that pulled a forsaken lover toward it—into twentieth-century idioms. Many of the plot moments and tropes explored in the narratives of the *Titanic* disaster foreshadow those seen in Miraji's historical writing as well as in his lyrics: how Miraji narrated modernity as emerging through the "shipwrecked" orders of things: modernity as the process of remembering after disaster, modernity as the accounting of bodies that lived, and modernity as providing the frames for the ethics of decisions made at the moments between life and death, modernity as the relation between the abject, the dead, and the forgotten from Europe in relation to nationalisms in colonial India. Then there was the matter of character: not who Miraji was, but the way his contemporaries figured him to be, as shipwreck, as the collection of fragments that abounded in death, of the debris that floated up as something was dying.

Thus it is peculiarly apropos that on the day of Miraji's birth the lead story in the *Lahore Tribune* was from Halifax, Nova Scotia, where debris and bits of bodies were still washing in from the *Titanic*, which had sunk when it struck an iceberg. Among the bits and pieces was the body of a two-year-old girl. All the fragments were boarded into hastily nailed wooden crates. Abutting the *Titanic* story was one about the decision of the Indian National Congress to host its next meeting in Bankipur, "Behar" (*sic*). Detritus, the material leftover from the lost ship, a monument to the failure of an unmediated faith in Western technological power, was juxtaposed with an anticolonial movement whose prior political call, *svadeshī*, was to loosen its allegiances to commodities produced in the West, and against a rejuvenated Muslim League angry at the British for not supporting Turkey in the Italian and Balkan wars.[14]

Though the *Tribune* merely settled the *Titanic* alongside forms of indigenous nationalisms, the contiguity of them in the *Tribune* offered the possibility of a kind of seeing that forced the two into an imbricated relationship. The *Tribune* opened a way to allow one to see something about nationalist desires for nations-to-be in colonial settings that could not be seen from the vantage point of the metropole. As a ship sailing the high seas between Southampton, England, and New York City, the *Titanic* was engaged in a transnational venture between two metropolitan sites. At the same time, it sank between national borders—at sea, where national borders did not obtain. The detritus of the ship that floated ashore, and the residue that lay between nations, picked up by newspapers in India, was produced as meanings that perhaps did not entirely "obscure the terrifying impact of the presence" of death. Exploring the forms the meanings took might give us a momentary glance into the person and poetics of Miraji, a writer whose sometimes startling (*acakānā*, *ackāvbharī*, *ajīb*, *anokhī*) work and life repeatedly comes face to face with desire, endings, and the syntax of the finitude of temporalities.[15]

In yet another place on the Indian subcontinent in May 1912, a monthly English periodical, the *Modern Review*, published in Calcutta, also carried a series of vignettes about the death of the *Titanic* and the subsequent transfer of live passengers to the *Carpathia*. The next two issues (June and July) also ran articles on the *Titanic* and its passengers. The stories in the May and June issues were slipped into the notes sections of the periodical; as "miscellany" they did not appear in the table of contents. In the May coverage of the *Titanic* the voices of witnesses, both men and women, blended death and life, life up to the death of the ship and life after the ship went down. The stories in the June periodical, on the other hand, were excerpted from writers in European newspapers and offered commentaries and eulogies only on those who died—specifically, the men who went down with the ship.

The third time the *Titanic* story appeared, in July 1912, it had moved from the notes section to the body of the journal as one of its lead pieces, a story about one of the passengers who died, W. T. Stead, "founder in England of the New Journalism," an eccentric, politically vocal English newspaperman who edited the *Review of Reviews*. Stead believed in a new internationalism, which was based on his "conviction that the English-speaking man was appointed to be, in every continent, the instrument of the world." Stead gathered traveling intellectuals in his living room, and from their casually pointed conversations emerged his trenchant, often subversive reports of Indian news, like the partition of Bengal, supplemented by portraits of Indian figures. Memoralizing this body of Stead's work gives India and Indian nationalism an entry into the sinking of the *Titanic*. This story on Stead moved an event seemingly incidental to the body of Indian nationalism and thus relegated to ephemera, to the body of the *Modern Review*, and the body of Indian nationalism. W. T. Stead, a particular friend of Indian nationalism, became the body whose history allowed an expansion of the narration of the death of this overdetermined ship—from notes into a full-fledged feature that located Indian nationalism through one rendition of the British public (media) sphere.

In the May 1912 issue of the *Modern Review*, the *Titanic*'s demise was covered under subheadings that narrated sentimentality—a litany of pathos and gallantry, separation and valor in the face of death.[16] Cobbled together into a narrative sequence from "accounts furnished by survivors," it begins with "Not a Sob Was Heard"; travels through "Confronted with Disaster," "Pathetic Scenes," "Mr. Stead," and "His Heroic End"; closes with "No Discrimination in Rescue Work" and "Full List of Saved"; and sounds down the final coda, "Splendid Conduct of the Stringmen."

The May tales open with the transfer of passengers from the *Titanic* to the *Carpathia*, ropes swinging the adults into the safe ship, the children swung aboard in bags. A short sentence on the boats that carried people away from the *Titanic*, some full, some part empty, follows upon the transfer. People are swung over the space of terror, swung over death into life and into the space where they are fed a warm breakfast. Silence, "not a sob . . . heard," attends the fullness of feeding.

Boats appear consistently and erratically over the course of these narratives. They navigate terror, sail some people from death to life, leave some people to death as the boats travel toward life. The first passengers into the rescue boats being lowered are men, followed by women who begin to hurry onto the deck of the sinking ship as the captain orders everyone to wear life preservers. Officers, augmented by their drawn arms, organize passengers. The initial response of the passengers is surprise. The sea seems calm, the ship still, the night silent, the ship tilting so slowly, so gently downward that people cannot comprehend the eventual result. The sudden violence of an accidental collision with an iceberg is submerged in repetitive movements that tell still, slowed silence. The only sound accompanying the sinking ship floats out from the ship's saloon, where the band is playing "Nearer My God to Thee."

More people hurry to the deck. Men stand back in absolute silence as ladies climb onto life boats quietly. Some, however, refuse to leave their husbands. As the boats holding women and children leave, dispersing into darkness, men clamber quietly onto remaining life boats. The opening stories, then, are of control, admirable conduct, of perfect quietude, of ideal comportment in the face of impending death.

The stories then move into a different register, in which control is surrendered in the tellings of death. A half-demented passenger offers reports of suicides, a wave knocks the captain down, he comes back to his feet only to be knocked down again as he sinks with the ship. Mr. Stead makes spectral appearances. These stories about the sighting of men going down with their ship begin to be told by named voices. George Braden sees the captain. Barkworth, Mr. Seward, and a steward named Cunningham all talk in turn about the elusive disappearing and reappearing Mr. Stead, who is seen on deck, but not seen there, who may have returned to his stateroom, who probably helped people board life boats, who was helped into a life vest by the steward and then never seen again.

As control is asserted again, names are still specified: Mr. Astor, who helped and died; Mrs. Churchill Candee, the woman who survived, although her legs were broken, and who talked about the men saved from the water; stokers who tried to escape were driven back like sheep, and the discipline was splendid, according to Major Peuchen. The discipline of the narrative then comes apart as statistics are offered up as explanation, as expiation. Numbers. The numbers of people saved and the numbers of those who died, tallied up by class, is settled between two utopian stories. Both these stories, "no discrimination in rescue work," and "all poor women and children saved," are at odds with the numbers in the middle. Those numbers speak the not-to-be-spoken: the largest percentage of women and children who died (fifty percent of the women and sixty percent of the children) were from the third-class section of the boat, the section into which Indians who were traveling alongside British colonials would have implicitly been put. These people, the largest percentage of those who died, probably locked into the body of the ship, whose death is told not in stories but in numbers, allegorize the colonized.

The editorial that concludes this May narrative of sentiment follows on this coda: "the splendid conduct of the stringmen playing (almost to the end) cheerful ragtime, and finishing with "Nearer My God to Thee." The *Titanic* is said to provide a moral lesson. It "show[s] the world that British people and western races generally occupy a dominant place in the world not by mere brute force or superior scientific weapons of destruction, but all by calm courage in facing certain death, by self-sacrifice." "The rich, the strong, the famous could have saved themselves, but preference was given to the weak, and the obscure." This editorial concludes by mourning W. T. Stead, "the fighter, the worker, the hero, the friend and the advocate of the weak and the oppressed all over the world, the promoter of peace." There are no children here.[17]

The stories speak, yet cannot fully voice the terror that sounds with them. Modernity promised by and premised through the *technae* (civil public sphere, industrialization, governmentality) of the British state holds the desire that bolsters a call to an emergent nationalism.[18] The knot of meanings condensed into the sinking of the *Titanic* are overdetermined.[19] But placed here, in India, in an incidental relationship to narratives about colonization, "The Colonization of India" and "Towards Democracy," in the body of the May issue of the *Modern Review*, they do something different. The accident of this incidental placement allows a seeing into the historical that provides an angle for looking at colonization and the call to forms of independence in the colonies.[20] This is a kind of seeing that Walter Benjamin allegorizes in "Theses on the Philosophy of History."[21] Produced through a shock to the teleological narratives of modernity, produced through the tellings of the spaces between life and death, this seeing opens up moments in differential temporalities, in different times.

The body of the *Titanic*, the description of its size, shape, volume, or physical layout, never appears in the *Modern Review*. The *Titanic* becomes a spectral presence in the stories from the May, June, and July issues. In the May issue the editors specifically refuse to retell the "details" of the disaster, which "have appeared in the papers and need not be repeated." "Some passages from the accounts furnished by passengers [on the other hand] deserve prominent insertion." The mass of the sinking ship, the physical debris left over by the ship as it breaks apart, is then consigned to ghostliness, haunting the passengers' accounts. The stories then become scenes, moments when death in time is spoken through affect. The form and matter of their scripting echoes and rebounds with the forms that Miraji's writing will take. In Miraji's work, death comes as a longing, a tired call whose seductive reach stretches across time and eventually absorbs the boat.[22]

These *Titanic* stories articulate a desire in relation to state formations and national formations. In the face of the ghostly sinking of the overwhelming symbol of Western technological superiority ("brute force . . . superior scientific weapons") and hubris, these *Titanic* stories stumble onto something: silence. The stories reiterate something that persists in attempts to gentrify silence into sentiment—valor, bravery, fortitude. That something is also produced as an accompanying sentimental wish, which says that all the poor [unwashed and unnamed] women and children will be saved by those rich strong and famous ones who died with such valor and bravery, in such a silence.

These sentiments and sentimental wishes are those that the editors of the *Modern Review* feel their other (the West) has, and are what the editors want for Indian men who are in the throes of emerging nationalist movements. These qualities are produced in the face of the death of part of what the other is, through a death of a part of what the other has, the apparatus of the state.

The *Titanic* is a mystified thing, a machine which, through its properties, stands in for and can be mistaken for something else. These properties are its magnitude and the technological superiority of the very modernity that made it (and which will give colonized peoples access to nationality through the apparatus of a state that they both want and whose death they must oversee). The narration of the *Titanic*'s death attempts to resolve the mystification bodied in the ship by turning the ship spectral and by turning to those people who lived as well as those who died laboring to save others. But the stories about people also renarrate mystification through a recourse to the numbers of those who lived and died, which then become the statistical enumeration of knowledge, the process and content of whose production provides certainty.[23]

These narratives about death go to the labor of racialized mourning—the work of Westerners coming unto death. But the narratives do not speak other kinds of labor that went into the ship. They do not speak the labor of the *Titanic*'s making, in a Belfast shipyard, in Ireland. Nor do they speak the relationship of that labor to colonization. And they do not speak completely the labor of those laboring in the belly of the ship who had to die so that the ship could move unto its death, those nameless stokers who tried to live and were driven downward to sink with the ship. The musicians (stringmen) whose musical knell punctuates the narrative and finally ends it have "splendid conduct." But their labor situated precisely between the divisions of the ship by class, in the stateroom but never of it, is never completely articulated.

The editorial continues the silent forgetting spoken in the stories—a forgetting that speaks a desire in terror, a nostalgia for a modernity that never quite was and can quite never be. The end of modernity foretold in the specter of this ship that sank is the end of a certain symbolic order. At the same time that ending is necessarily incited, accompanied, and accelerated by the openings of orders like nationalisms and labor movements that carry within them the mirroring fantasies that had permitted modernity to achieve the status of the symbolic. The nationalism that the longer stories accompanying those on the *Titanic* call for would leave the majority of Indians to die. The wish in this narration (in the narrative explication of the numerical) is that an Indian would be given the same chance for life as all those women and children who purportedly lived, and would not be driven downward like the nameless stokers who tried to live. Life is a game of loaded dice for the nationalist who rolls them for life on colonized territory organized in a colonial symbolic, even if that symbolic is seen in the form of the end of an order.

What is left, then, to nationalist movements in the colonies as the state of modernity is brought to its death is a range of stances through which the moments before death can be faced. Those stances, enumerated above, perform bravery. They are those stances possible in the now of a nationalist movement that does not yet have a nation. They allow for a vision, a seeing of decolonization that does not have to defer access to nationalist sentiment and an accompanying colonial masculinity. This is a masculinity produced not through modernization and a narrative of development, but through its failure. The elusiveness of Mr. Stead in the May stories alludes to the elusiveness of the presence of Indian nationalism, while also calling attention to the elusive possibility of a stance of masculinity for colonized subjects.

In June 1912, the *Modern Review* couples the dead men of the *Titanic* with a piece on the death of public-spirited men in India that enumerates, based on an article in the *Christian Register*, the characteristics such men might possess. Public-spiritedness and spirited muscular civility, according to the *Christian Register*, is profoundly social. It is a habit that inhabits those who devote themselves to the amelioration of social circumstances and work exclusively to ensure the well-being of the individual only in relation to the community, to civil and state institutions. The other of a public-spirited man is one whose entire terrain is the personal, the private sphere of domesticity. The latter sort of man enacts the duties of a citizen, but, unlike his public-spirited counterpart, his actions do not fold themselves into a rigorous, dutiful, and responsible relationship to the *socius*.

Miraji was such an other. He became the one whose *āvāragī*, whose life in motion rendered him outside the civil community. He was precisely construed as the unmuscular, uncivil, uncouth, unwashed criminal, someone whose recourse to the poetics of the personal seemed to refuse the proprieties of the public sphere and would forever relegate him to its limits. His death could not be accounted. His call from beyond his death, his stance before terror was the stance of a mystic who holds onto the clarity of terror to see.

The men whose deaths are accorded space in the notes section of the July issue of the *Modern Review* are men who possess public spirit. Public-spiritedness is precisely that stance with which "you face terror" so that the terror you feel at the sudden call of death ceases to be terror. Two qualities, according to M. Capus, one of the two writers quoted in the July issue, embody this stance.

The first quality is French chivalry handed down from the Christian Middle Ages, the root feature of Western civilization which persists through all changes and has "enforced itself on every race." Chivalry is part and parcel of morality. It is enacted through saving women, who are "vowed by nature to submission [and] have become sovereign [*sic*] in the realm of sentiment." Barbarism or immorality attends those worlds that allow women to either "fall from her estate" or "invade other realms." Barbarism, then, is the state of nongrace allocated to Indian men, who must learn Christian chivalry so that they can accede to the moral position of Western men who save their women with such grace.[24]

The second quality is a "modern stoicism," bodied more easily in the upper classes and artists, and rarely found among the people. Stoicism is not merely an attitude toward death, a scorn of death and pain, but a doctrine of action. As action it is a "sublime corrective," indifferent to its results, and done merely for its own sake or for duty. Its lineage, too, is old, but older than that of chivalry, Roman rather than Christian, and spoken in the words of Marcus Aurelius and Epictetus. Photographs of John Jacob Astor and Isidore Strauss punctuate this paean to the chivalrous, stoic deaths of famous men.

The editorial that concludes this paean talks about what gives people access to precisely this form of public-spiritedness. Independent nations have "rights, professions, occupations and activities, which we [the colonized] do not have." These rights come from being a citizen of a modern state and from the performance of activities that form the modern state. Among them are soldiering and the free use of firearms, which give their bearers access to militarized masculinity. Also among them are building ships that are officered by men who indulge in maritime adventures to map the unknown (the terror of the deep) and to hunt science, wealth, and knowledge. Another is the pursuit of medical science and chemistry, the dangers of which train men to face death by disease or explosion. Mountaineering and manly sports bring this litany of modern manly feats to a close—a litany of activities, condensations of the history of political desires, that covers a range of concerns around masculinity and a lack of access to it (a lack of it).

"Western races," then, occupy a dominant place precisely because they are trained/inculcated into the muscularity of/in the doing—of organized "brute" force—and because they indulge in the making—of superior science through its technologies. Laboring bodies moving/driven by/propelled through technology, science, and sport, produce both the state as civil and the citizen as its civilized embodiment. The civil sphere merges with the state. Stances before death are acquired precisely through the labor engaged in making a state as *socius*: whether those stances are the troubling deferrals practiced by capitalists or the captains of ships and industries who died though their power might have helped them live; whether they are the regimental masculinities exercised by sailors with arms who assured flawless loading or a major who drove stokers to their death; whether they are the ambivalent ones, the musicians who fiddled away in an allegorical call to death as the ship went down; or whether they are the renarrated ones of the stokers whose labor hastened the ship to its death. Men who captured the most attention in this telling of death were those who are powerful but whose only power came through their death. They were narrated as chivalrous and stoic, as helping others live. That masculinity, unavailable in India, Western masculinity in this telling, includes godliness and good learning, a kind of muscular capitalist Protestantism.

Indians here tell of themselves as they tell the West. The games mania of the federal, imperial projects in the late nineteenth century appears not in discussions of stoicism (Western representations of itself), but as the editors comment on what they desire. The Indian past is not Roman, not the French chivalric, not one imbued with a Christian male moral stance. The presented forms of a pan-Indian Hindu past that holds unmanly Indians back from access to muscular Christian masculinity are the forms of their religion, past and present, sedimented into a caste system that curtails compassion. Islam, its masculinity rendered from James Mill through Kipling, fades from view.[25] It reappears curiously, as a foretelling of an emergent Khilafat movement (that perhaps tells also the emergence of nationalist bodies that arose from the failure of a volunteer movement in the late nineteenth century), the parodic double of Western masculinity, as political cartoons extracted from papers published in Warsaw, Amsterdam, and Stuttgart.[26] In one cartoon Russia and England stand, swords sheathed at their sides, contemplating a divided Persia. In another, each Western power, guns drawn or spears at attention, surrounds the hapless birds—Turkey, Persia, Egypt, Tunis, Morocco, Tripoli, Anatolia. In the third, Moses stands, holding a tablet that says "Thou Shalt Not Steal" blindly before a comfortably portly gentleman who is wearing a top hat, carrying a walking stick in one hand while his other hand supports and outlines his stomach. Behind them is a hilly penciled-in landscape peopled only by the backs of army troops on the march, weapons up. Science, trade, the technologies of war, adventure, mapping, and Christian morality resonantly at odds with the longing drawn out in the editors' desire for the *technae* of modernity.

Miraji lived and spoke in contention with a desire for this kind of masculinity as the proper stance for a nationalist man who wants a nation. His essays and poetry intersect with the voicings of nationalist movements in India, whether they be the languages of secular nationalism spoken by the congress and the left wing or the more religious refrains of Islamicized or Hinduized nationalisms. Miraji's collections of essays, *Mashriq o maghrib ke naghmeñ* (Songs from the East and from the West) and *Is naẓm meñ* (In these poems), perform several different kinds of desire. In some essays/translations Miraji extracts a pan-Indian past that seems to only appear occasionally in twentieth-century Urdu poetics, a past that incorporates the kind of Bengali, Maithili, Braj Bhasa, and Sanskrit lyric of desire that was permeated by bhakti. For these essays Miraji relies on local "vernacular" sources as well as late Orientalist English translations.[27] In other essays, Miraji extracts the abjected male literary figures in a Western pantheon like Villon, Mallarmé, Baudelaire, D. H. Lawrence, Poe. In yet other essays Miraji turns to poetry written in Chinese, Korean, and Japanese, to establish historical lineages of love lyric that stretched out toward affiliations other than European.[28]

Miraji's cross-cultural groupings establish lineages that entangle writing in Urdu with writings that explore scenes of desire, as well as death and abjection. Some of these lineages disinter the gendered bodies whose sexuality pushes at national sentiment immanent in a masculinity (chivalry, stoicism) established through the salvation of women. "Sappho," the greatest Western woman poet, refuses intransigent, youthful, militarized (and heterosexual) masculinity engendered by a Lesbos wreathed in war, turning instead to sex with her women companions. Sappho's is also the only "patriotic" poetry, written "in Athens' name,"[29] that Miraji translated as exemplifying an acceptable nationalism—the desire of someone considered abject. Miraji's more local groupings of poets enable affiliations that refuse and refute the formalized narration of fame and its allegiances to acceptable nationalized masculinities. Cultural capital, taken on in these essays as a spectral quantity, did not float in the colonies in the forms that colonizers wished to give it. It was articulated, instead, as capital rendered in the abject, and in the detritus of improper responses to modernity.

Through both his own poetry and his life Miraji offers a supplement to the kinds of implicit critiques of nationalized masculinity offered in his essays (through *ruḥ* and *ḳhudi*). The masculine "I" appears in poems such as "Traveler" in ways that can be folded back into Miraji's concerns as an abjected masculine "I." In other poems, Miraji goes instead to an "I" that never takes form as either the masculine or the feminine, provoking comparisons to the Sapphic "I," or to an "i" modulated by the work of Mirabai. In "Love Song of the Clerk," Miraji's only poem that ventures the historical specificities of a laboring body, the clerk's dailiness is spent in the verities of the ordinary—eating the half slice of bread left over from yesterday, walking past carriages and cars on the way to work, extracting a file, listening to the *baqvās* of his boss—and soaked in forlorn desire for a "you," the imagined beloved who he talks to all day, and whose class places him or her outside the clerk's provenance (makes the beloved the inaccessible locus of the clerk's desire).[30] The clerk's body is a body that walks along the street, saturated by longing that must be deferred because of his class. His gaze trained on the places he travels, and the places he works, opens them up to class. His is the masculinity of the petite bourgeoisie, masculinity in the domain of work, that sees itself as incomplete, "half a slice of bread," rendered through what it must hold over for the next day and what it cannot have.

Over the course of his life, Miraji obsessively refused to leave his community of literary travelers even as they attempted to make him a "walking . . . corpse." Miraji's poetic stance fashioned a sort of response to his journeys up to the brink of literary death. He wrote scene after scene of desire, each scene speaking a poetics of the moment, a telling of the time of finitude, a time that drew out moments of desire. These scenes suggested the infinity of the incidental, the accidental meeting, the lambent anguish of lost love, the call from beyond death—of desire at the point of death (*fanā* and *baqā*).[31]

The distortions that inform vision and habits of seeing, the moralities encoded in visionary sight, were often given by Miraji through translation, mirroring, or mimesis. Mirrors appear in poems like "Samundar kā bulāvā" (Call of the sea) and imitation forms the basis of Miraji's critiques on the work of contemporaries. But the mirrors, *ā'inah*, dissolve in the poem. And as he makes clear in his introduction to *Is naẓm meñ*, Miraji demanded of his fellow writers (poets of mimesis) a kind of rigorous attention to imitation especially necessary if the other being imitated was Western. He insisted that practice should be accompanied by a clear understanding of the works that were imitated, that names and works not be taken up merely as rhetorical gestures, that one should be self-conscious about the transformations inherent in colonial mimicry. Miraji's own poetry, in scripting a different kind of seeing with allegiances to earlier Urdu, Sanskrit, Bengali, and Braj lyric, did not produce clear resemblances. Rather, it picked up on attitudes to *naẓar*, looking or viewing, the look or the gaze. It drew on an angular relationship to timed desire.

Miraji's production of his own masculinity had to resist the medical technologies of the modern without completely letting them go. He was interpolated into psychiatric categories that were often used on women—"homosexuality" masquerading as "nymphomania," "hysteria," and so on.[32] Instead of refusing these categories completely and attempting to go to an elsewhere, Miraji played out his own story in those terms. He was neither chivalrous nor stoic. Nor was he public-spirited.

Miraji occupied the space given to women, the space of sentiment (perverse eroticism, domesticated sentimentality, the personal) dissolved into want, wish, and dreamlike fantasies. Miraji's incomplete, fragmentary scenes from his life as well as scenes from his poetry resolve again and again into an "I." Biography woven through with desire was only possible in the space of the personal. A moral, ethical stance was only accountable to public responsibility through the desire of a single person. Miraji did not take recourse in the reasoned moralities threaded through the political, labor, or civil/social worlds. Instead he believed that the arduous struggles of responsibility could only be resolved through desires that came into play when a person was stripped down to an "I," faced down by death or faced by an other one could not have. Miraji lifted those encounters between self, death, and other from a legacy of Sufi and bhakti mysticism, translating backward to resignify what had come to be seen as the violent excesses of delirium and madness, into the ecstatic visionary beside-or-beyond-oneself-ness for which a mystic strove. Neither Miraji's life nor his work allowed for salvation through the saving of another's life. His salvation was through a mystic's difficult skirmishes with love, a journey that might lead somewhere but that also might lead one to lose one's way. As Miraji's says in his *shi'r* with simple, direct clarity:

> The traveler wandering from town to town forgot
> the path to his house. What was mine, what was yours, both
> of the self and of the other, lost,
> then, to memory.[33]

## SCENES FROM AN "INCOMPLETE SELF-PORTRAIT"

While the debris from the *Titanic* demise was floating ashore, accumulating narratives about life and death, Miraji and his family were inaugurating their journey along the railway lines of northwest British India. All the visual memoryscapes in Miraji's incomplete self-portrait condense around the railways. He either tells his stories as scenes that seem to accrue around railway sites or as scenes given to him by traversing landscape available through the railways. The first place Miraji was taken to shortly after his birth was Godhra. When he was six his father moved him and the rest of his family to Halol.

Both places are in Gujarat, and both places had sedimented into them histories of political encounters. Kheda, the site of Gandhi's early campaigns, is nestled in the area delineated by Godhra and Halol (in Vadodara / Baroda State). Jinnah gave a speech in Gujarati around the time that Miraji was taken there to live. Baroda, near Halol, had long been the nucleus of local political unrest. The Ganganath Vidyalaya, settled on the bank of the Narmada River in Baroda, which was the site of agitation between 1900 and 1912, was the home of Narsinhbhai Ishwarbhai Patel, a man who was infamous for his handbook for making bombs, concealed under the title *Vanaspati davao* (Herbal medicines). Aurobindo Ghose had taught in the college at Baroda and he and Tilak (popular local school heroes) formed a kernel of nationalist resistance in the area. Their activities were taken up by Mohanlal Pandya and a group of friends in Kheda who might have been responsible for persuading Gandhi to lead the district in its first no-revenue campaign in 1917–18.[34] Patidar peasant agitations between 1917 and 1934 were provoked perhaps by agricultural depressions between 1899 and 1935 that desiccated the region in a series of severe famines, one around the time that Miraji was born and another when Miraji was about seven years old.[35] Miraji's father, caught up in the political fervor of the time, wrote and staged two plays to raise money for famine relief. Miraji's brother Ata' ullah said that those plays were Miraji's first forays into the arts.[36]

Miraji's father traveled much of the system of railways that traversed northwestern India, and several of the sites at which he worked were notorious in railway history. Sukkur in Sindh was the site of the Lansdowne Bridge (named after the man who was viceroy of India from 1888–94), commemorated with a *burra tomasha* on March 25, 1889. Imagine the British officials sweating in their inappropriate uniforms in the desiccating desert heat, unlocking a heavily decorated padlock designed by J. L. Kipling (principal of the Mayo School of Art in Lahore and Rudyard Kipling's father); the heavy iron gates guarding the bridge entrance swinging open and the group marching across in straggly order to repair for breakfast and toasts.

This bridge, for a short while the longest girder bridge in the world, had drawn derogatory commentary because it could not hide its aesthetic allegiances to a machine age, and because its many engineers experienced so much trouble constructing it. Its modernist steel lines strung tautly, it stretched like a metal trapeze over the Sukkur and Rohri channels, straddling a geological fault. The builders of it had had to swim through floods; survive the dry heat of the summer smothered in dust storms; survey bedrock shelves and a deep chasm sedimented with silt; build a tentative temporary bridge; and finesse giant derrick struts with guy ropes to swing into place at impossible heights. Designed and composed in pieces by engineers in London, the bridge had claimed at least six Indian lives. This bridge offered an angled glimpse into the age of mechanical reproduction: the aura of artisanry in London blueprints dissipated into the productive repetition of steel girders and the impasses of colonial geography. When it was finally completed, the bridge opened a rapid transport system from Lahore to Karachi on the coast. Trains could carry wheat from Punjab fields to a port for shipping.[37]

Halol, too, was a place where imperial financial expediency demanded branch railway lines and a tiny station. The lines running through Halol were segmented into a web of narrow gauge couplings that had initially been funded by princely capital from the Gaekwad of Baroda, part of the Marquess of Dalhousie's scheme, proposed in his 1853 railway minute.[38] Dalhousie, wanting to husband British commercial and military interests, included among his multifaceted prospectus a proposal of marriage: between imperial enterprise (underwritten by mercantile capital) and indigenous princely capital. Or perhaps a more apt phrasing would be that he wanted to husband with a supplement of princely capital. For the railways were primarily to be used, telegraph lines (strung across their length) echoing their length, to support colonial industry and to enforce a grid of colonial controls. It was no accident that Dalhousie, assiduous meticulous architect of colonial technologies, helped birth the system. In the regions of India where Miraji's father had been assigned, railways carted troops; transported cotton after the American Civil War had denuded British mills of their regular supply; extradited wood extracted from Bhil traversed forests, eventually to be turned back into railway ties; and ferried raw ores from mines to smelters.[39] But in the ways that colonialism's architecture sometimes get turned around on itself, Indians who were meant to run screaming from the new technologies disabled and hampered by fear, class, and caste restrictions took to them in droves. They thronged in lines at railway stations to view trains, packed into third-class compartments (some of which were eventually fitted out as double-deckers), and slowed down the supposedly immutable timetables by up to three hours.[40]

The *Illustrated London News* of May 23, 1863, printed an etching of wooden railway cars pulled along the lines in Baroda by two giant Gujarati bullocks. The Gaekwad had the first narrow gauge (two and a half feet), its first rendition a tramway between Myagam and Dhaboi, which was a "feeder line" linked to the Bombay Baroda and Central India mainline.[41] "His Highness," the *London News* reported, "had ordered small engines for this line; but he will probably find animal power better adapted to the traffic, which is exclusively in native passengers and goods. One pair of bullocks will draw five loaded wagons from two to three miles an hour. The passenger trains may be worked either by country ponies or trotting bullocks." By 1914, when Miraji was a child in the Baroda area, the Gaekwad's Baroda State Railways had put down at least three hundred miles of narrow gauge.[42] By 1916, Halol had been established as a British railway colony with lines set in 1911 running back and forth from the Champaner and Pani mines, shuttling mainly manganese, but also limestone, lead, zinc, copper, graphite, feldspar, and so on, to the broad-gauge system that connected Bombay and Delhi.[43] Halol, where Miraji moved when he was six and had just started school, was the site of all of Miraji's early memories of a "normal" childhood, the son of an Indian civil servant "aping" the activities of his parents and friends.

*Scene 1: Halol Games*

Whenever the English engineer visited [Halol] on his rounds [of railway stations], a hunt was arranged for his entertainment. Children, because they are the tiny descendants of monkeys, ape their parents. So, our childhood games also included hunting. The Railway Dak Bungalow was a short distance from our house. This is a description of a particular incident that occurred when the engineer was visiting [us] on his rounds. His son and daughter strolled with my sister, me, and the two sons of our household servants over to the rambling garden [of the Dak Bungalow] to play. Our other companions, the son and daughter of the Bungalow's watchman, were assembled there. The Bhil tribe lives in that area [Halol]. Having graduated from an agricultural livelihood, they are now skilled at pillaging and stealing, as well as driving or beating for game. In that kind of hunting, people sit high up on a raised platform [*macān*] and a line of Bhils flushes animals out [of the forest] with many different noises, surrounds them, and drives them towards the platform. We, too, played at driving game in the Dak Bungalow [garden]. We had designated a tree our "raised platform." The engineer's son and I, pretending to be the Bhils, had wandered away [to find game]. Just then, the servant's daughter ran towards us, and yelled out that Jamuna was a very bad girl—she was sitting on a tree and peeing. I, well versed in the set of rules that ordered my family's behavior, also thought of the act as "bad." However the sensual specialness of that event has since stamped itself on my consciousness. I have just begun to understand the tangled effects of that sensual experience. But at the time, the experience had not only an exotic, provocative seductiveness, but a sense of harmony with nature (as well as carrying a profound moral ambivalence).[44]

*Scene 2: The Mountain Outside My Window in Halol*

Our father was an assistant engineer on a small line there. We lived (in Halol) near the famous ancient historical site of Champaner. The mountain of Pavagadh was four or five miles away. There was a Kali temple at its summit. We could see the mountain from our courtyard. I've written a line: "Who is responsible for the blue mystery of the mountain?" Though the mountain looked as if it were close by, it held a deep indigo mysteriousness for me—the kind of secret whose allure leaves a profound impression on one's mind.

The monsoons lasted for quite a few months in those areas, and for a large portion of the year the sight of the mountain veiled in the smokiness of the rain held a special enchantment.[45] In my imagination the rivers, draped randomly over the mountain's smoothness, turned into chalk streaks. Their sensual and sexual significance has recently become clear to me. The special characteristic of that region was the profusion of snakes [that appeared] during the monsoons. For a child, the dangerousness of snakes was not as significant as their seductiveness, which, like the story of Adam and Eve, snared men's imaginations. These were the important images [for me]—the mountain's smokiness, flowing streams, and colorful snakes.[46]

## STORIES OF DESIRE

Halol is twenty miles from Vadodara, a comfortable distance from what used to be the princely center of Baroda State. The Halol station has been shut down and abandoned by the railways; the lines once connecting it to the mines are severed, those links only detoured now through Champaner and Pani. Few in the city of Vadodara even remember that there was once a station at Halol. But the town that was previously appended to the railway colony is small and bustling, a typical district headquarters, which, though the railway longer passes near it, still feels like a place thrown up to provide sustenance for a large BBCI Railway station.

Abandoned in the 1940s, the Halol station—criss-crossed by lines that angle through a massive, hulking repair shed, a testament to the traffic that once circulated through it—is overshadowed by Pavagadh. Even through a summer haze the starkly sculpted rock hill rises so unexpectedly from flat checkerboard fields that it is easy to understand why Miraji might have been seduced by its power. Its mystery is enhanced by the legends that have accrued around its genesis—invariably, it is said to have dropped to earth. One story, a local addition to the *Ramayana*, gives that right to Hanuman who is said to have lost a portion of Mount Kailash as he flew over the region in a rush to get Himalayan herbs to salve Laksmana's war wounds.[47] Another story attributes the mountain's origin to Parvati. Here, Pavagadh is a Shaktipith, one of the fifty-two places where a part of Parvati's body fell as Shiva danced destruction in the *tanḍava*.[48] Vishvamitra, the sagacious friend of the world, is said to have hunkered down on the mountain to meditate.[49]

The mountain's ridge is a site of pilgrimage. As Miraji says, a tiny Kali (Mahakali) temple, reached by steps carved into the face of the mountain, nestles at its top. The temple is an especially auspicious stop: women travel to it to sing hymns to Kali for the *garbha* danced at Navaratri; it is one of the twelve pilgrimage stops for Jains; Mira *bhajan* (devotional songs) are sung there throughout the year; and the Jama Masjid in nearby Champaner is visited by pilgrims who want special boons from the pir (holy man) buried in one corner of the once magnificent gardens seated before the mosque.[50] Miraji calls Champaner a famous ancient historical site (*masshūr tārīkhī muqām*), and in that phrase is secreted the kind of history, the kind of local tales Miraji alludes to in one of the short richly suggestive prose pieces the poet wrote in the late forties: "History says that into every moment from the distant, secret past is tucked an entire volume of magical stories/tales . . . and then every fantasy, every thought turns to secret itself into memory or step by step becomes history, or goes onto people a drop of water."[51]

The layers of sediment that cushioned the rocks of Champaner and Pavagadh told a long, fractured history of settlement. Situated strategically on a popular trade route between the Surat coast and Madhya Pradesh, and between kingdoms, Champaner had repeatedly been reduced to rubble and then refortified by the Rajput Chauhans, Patai Rawal, Rajput Muslims, and finally and most famously, by the Muslim king Mahmud Begda, who in the 1400s turned it into the capital of his kingdom. Alfonso de Albuquerque, a Portuguese trader traveling in Gujarat in the early 1500s, describes Champaner as "a great city in very fertile country of abundant provisions." Even in its now depleted state the fort hovers, a behemoth, light patterned through the shards of intricately carved *jālī* falling on the ruins of its widely spaced gardens.[52]

In contrast to the fort, the abandoned station at Halol seems almost ephemeral, a mundane memorial to another history of conquest. The land was not transformed by pillaging armies and large-scale rebuilding, but by contracts levied on local Bhils and struck with local rajas. What is left is a legacy of crumbling quotidian buildings now resettled by laborers on the railway line and by the occasional descendants of the Bhils and villagers who had been uprooted when the British turned local jungle into "forests" mined for forest protection and wood. These are the descendants of the people, "tribals," whose history of displacement, disenfranchisement, and resignification under British auspices Miraji packs into his wry irony, rendering politics in another key.[53]

The Bhils "graduated" from a (respectable) agricultural livelihood into (criminal) "vagrancy," he tells us. Children like Miraji imitate them, pretending to be shikar attendants in the colonial games people play and children ape. These locals are the props who enable the game of turning jungle into hunting preserve to come to a successful culmination; they flush out wild animals for a shoot weighted to acquire hunt.[54] Colonial spectacle is the place of Miraji's desire—under its regime he views the mundanity of Jamuna peeing.[55] Under its regimes of propriety he has been taught the rights and wrongs of public displays of bodily infraction, "excess," of the public architecture of class, difference, gender: engineer and assistant engineer's son pretending to be Bhils, servant's daughter exposing Jamuna's infraction as such. Only later, he tells us, can he understand the event's tangled implications. That "bad" was a family code learned to order, that peeing and the call to its exposure was both provocatively seductive and one with the streaks of white water that lit up Pavagadh in the monsoons. In these, the seminal stories of Miraji's desire, Jamuna, mountains, streams, *nāg, nāginī,* and the snake in the garden of Eden come together. And in these, Miraji's origin tales, one begins to see the moments of writing history tightly bound within a sentence or two that he expanded into the enticing, meticulously crafted, political, literary, and historical background offered for the authors whose translations he folded into essays.[56]

When one goes to Halol today, one sees the faint outlines of the world of the railway colony in which Miraji had lived. Beside the tin-roofed repair shed, its wooden door still padlocked, one can see at the other end of a length of entangled lines, the yellow brick station, its waiting courtyard and wrought-iron benches, a blackboard with prices for tickets still scratched on it in white, and the huge water tank perched precariously on wooden scaffolding, Pavagadh fading into the background. A sadhu clothed in white has laid out his mat and bowl under the wide banyan tree that eclipses the station. The railway lines run taut curves past the station, disappearing into thick undergrowth and the mountain in the distance, which seems to be pulled closer by them like a kite skittering out from behind trees tugged by strings no longer seen. The lines running as they do, appearing suddenly out of one dense horizon and dissolving into another, promise a kind of mystery, the enchantment of beyond, enticing to an dreaming child.

Families squat in those government tract houses that have been reduced to a few standing indigo white walls, the architecture of their construction exposed: two rooms, one bricked in, one shaded from the sun by a parodic simulacrum of Muslim Gujarati stone jalis built from crossed wooden slats. Women hunch in the small yards set off in front of each house, husking rice before open-air stoves. In the houses occupied according to railway code by employees, *chārpais* are stacked up against walls. On the edges of the colony are queues of electric blue tube tents, people threshing grain and stretching red saris before they are set to dry in the sun, fat round bales of grass, a goat, a cow, and a Rabari herding his sheep toward the center of the station.

Larger houses still huddle close by. One that Miraji might have lived in is long and cool, yellow on the bottom, dusty white on top, nested back behind tall white walls, its slate yard leading to the kitchen, the servants' quarters and storage shed a short distance away. Trees—thick mango, long-leaved neem, and purple feathery jacaranda—lurch over it. A man, smoking on a *chārpai* hidden in the veranda, says he stayed behind to work on the railway when his family left during the movement for independence. The trees, he says, are a legacy of the British. He still allows children running in rambunctious groups to play in and out of them. Looming between the trees is Pavagadh.

*Scene 3: First Flickers of Desire*

This is a story from the time in my life when I had first begun to feel flickers of physical desire. We had just been transferred to a new place near Multan. Our neighbor, the stationmaster's daughter, brought over a welcoming gift for us. A plate was balanced in her right hand and, holding open the reed mat blinds that covered the door with her left hand, she walked into the room. I was by the door, sitting in a comfortable armchair, reading a book. As she stepped over the threshold and looked around, she realized that I was the only person in the room. When she asked me, I gestured towards the inner room, letting her know that the rest of the inhabitants were inside. She left. But for a moment, as she stood hesitating, my eyes lingered on her with a half-woken dream of desire. She was wearing a thin white shift; she must have been ten or eleven years old. Perhaps because she was on an errand inside the house, she hadn't worn a slip under her clothes. The sun suddenly glimmered through the veil of her clothing and outlined the delicate body inside. This stolen vision, dissolved from deep inside the earth, has come to inhabit my life and poetry in many forms—as clothing.[57]

*Scene 4: Desiccation*

Our travels with our father took us to Kohistan in Baluchistan. But this place did not have the thick, dense scenery of the hot, moist terrain of Hindustan. The changing circumstances of our lives took me to Sindh too, desiccated and barren, inhabited by forbidden beings. Here, the only place worth speaking about was by the sea of Sindh, a spot thirty-seven miles from Karachi—Dabeji's mausoleum. I sat there, many times, by the sea. After a while the ocean's being would appear before me as a demon, prone and still, a creature both repulsive and seductive. The land around Dabeji's tomb, stretched out [in front of me] stripped of all its tall green grass, spotted with dry, spiny brambles, and shriveled, stunted trees. I saw before me, about four or five miles away, the smoky outline of the seashore. At the shore, I'd heard there was a garden, home of Sassi, the beloved of one of Hindustan's most famous lovers—Pannu. I don't know whether the garden really existed or whether it was just a story from local folk legends. However, that place was bathed by hot, fierce winds off the sea.[58]

These, the landscapes of Miraji's childhood, provide an unusual, unexpurgated look into his own production of his primal scenes of sexuality. Miraji used the childhood memories that he designated as his earliest ones to explore and explain the timbre of his adult excursions into sexuality, in both his life and his poetry. Sexuality divorced from a moralizing message was, for him, an important component of the life of every person. He was aware that his work was thought of by many of his readers as primarily sexual, but he felt strongly that sexuality could not be isolated from other aspects of a person's life, that indeed it was part of the complicated pattern of life and could be neither ignored nor excessively highlighted.[59] The critical pieces he wrote exploring poetry, facets of his life, and diverse literary traditions weave sexuality with other threads—community behaviors, social expectations, histories of literary production, and discussions of aesthetics.

Young Sana' ullah's moralizing response to sexual and scatological scenes (they were "bad") presages some of Miraji's later discussions on the moral ambivalence with which sexuality and physical pleasure were treated by his contemporaries. Miraji felt that his desire for women, including the desire recorded in his poetry and in the gesture he made of adopting a woman's name, could be explored in his childhood fascinations with nature and women's clothing.[60] His desire for women, according to him, was always thwarted, never realized. Miraji's lament echoes that of the poet-lover of classical Urdu poetry—insistently spurned, forever yearning, never satisfied. In "Self-Portrait," rather than establishing continuities between his poetic imagery and the earlier poetic traditions he also incorporated into his work (*bhakti*, Urdu ghazals, Sanskrit love poetry), he returns to the stories of his childhood to find precursors of his later imagery. He began his piece with Mirabai and alludes to her later influence on him, but he never goes back to her in these forays into his desire.

In his early work (poetry and prose), looking (*naẓar*) was the mode through which Miraji articulated his sexuality. Held, by his own accounts, from physical consummation of his desire, Miraji moved toward several valences of looking, rather than literal touching, to speak sexuality.[61] Looking, when employed conventionally by him, expressed a desire for someone (or something like a text)—desire that could be potentially realized or averted. In its less conventional sense, looking was in lieu of physical union: merging with beloved or text. Looking in this case replaced touching. When desire was consummated, looking was rendered through pleasure, when repulsed or repudiated, inflected with pain. But Miraji also wrote about the ways in which his expressions of desire (for an object or for its own conclusion), rather than attaching to a woman's body, were routed through obsessive descriptions of scenery, weather, clothing, story. Thus, when looking was the form that "touch"—contact or performance—effectively took, desire could be seen as doubly distanced from body-to-body contact: first, by touching through looking, and second by transmuting bodies into natural or sartorial images.[62] Nature and clothing, nature dissolving into clothing, or nature emanating through clothing, became the processes of fetishization that signified want.[63]

Scenes from Miraji's childhood gave him the language through which his sexuality as an adult found its expression. Halol was the site from which lush metaphors for the "thick, dense" seductive pleasure of looking emanate/exude, while Sindh, with its hot, barren topography, provided/granted/bequeathed him with the language to describe the parched dryness of pain when desire was thwarted.

## EARLY LAHORE YEARS

The last move Miraji made with his family was to Bustan in 1921. A few years later his father was transferred to Sukkur, but by this time his parents had sent Miraji to finish his education in Lahore, where he lived with his half brothers, Ata' ullah and 'Inayat' ullah, in the boarding house attached to MacLagen Engineering College, the school the older boys attended. By the time Miraji came to Lahore in about 1926, the Khilafat movement had ended and alongside it the huge national *satyāgraha* that had convulsed the nation.[64] From April to June 1925, Lahore was unsettled by a massive strike on the northwestern railways, provoked when a union leader was dismissed.

In the meantime, a tradition of writing political poetry in Urdu had been firmly established. There was, of course, Iqbal. But accompanying him were Zafar Ali Khan, Hasrat Mohani (who was later to join the Progressive Writers' Association), Muhammad Ali (Jauhar), and Brij Narayan Chakbast.[65] Political poetry seems to have been written in two registers. One was in a bared form, where the politics sat on the surface of the poem, lodged in its syntax, grammar, and language. Zafar Ali Khan, writing in Lahore in *Zamīndār*, the journal he edited, clothed the nakedness of this kind of lyric in a dry humor, close to the tautness of a political cartoon. One sees his cast of humor, perhaps educed from *Qaṣīdah dar ḥajv* (Odes of satire), in poems like "Līḍar ke nauyyat" (Special quirks of leaders).[66] The other form of political poetry encrypted politics into the language of passion, translating into the world of the ghazal and *gīt*, and of the *naẓm* as it was coming into its own as a formal designation, sentiments that were clearly political. Both forms of writing left their legacies in the verse written by Progressive writers; the second, in addition, came to an unusual fruition in Miraji's work. When in the late thirties and early forties Miraji wrote essays on his contemporaries (Faiz, Rashid, Tajvar Samari), he spoke of both kinds of political lyric as representative of new thought and styles of the time (*zamāne ke naye uslūb o tafakkur*).

After being sent back to Lahore, Miraji entered the ninth grade of Muzang High School, where he met people who were to remain his lifelong friends—Salim Soz, Din Muhammad, Nazir Samari, and Bashir Ahmad. His brother Ata' ullah, a poet whose pen name was Laṭīfī, invited Miraji to join his circle of literary friends; these men, Maḥmud-dīn Tāsīr, Sirājud-din Aḥmad, Niẓāmī, Badrud-din Badr, and Maulavī Ghụlām A'bbas, initiated him into their world. Miraji started writing poetry and prose under the pen name "Sāḥarī" and called his bedroom *Sāḥar ḳhānā* (Sahari's room), although he had used his given name for his first work, a collection of essays that he distributed as a pamphlet to his friends and publicized from Sahar Khana.[67] By age sixteen, in 1926, Miraji had already published—children's fables that appeared in the weekly *Phūl* (Flower).[68]

It was at that time in Lahore that he met the first person he fell in love with, Bashir Chand.[69] Throughout his life he wrote passionate letters to him that evoked the anxious despair of a lover who knew his desire was troubling and unrequited: "My love! I'll tell you truly, the love I've felt for a man and a woman has left me destitute."[70]

While he was working on his matriculation, Miraji met the only other person he is said to have loved—Mira Sen, whom he called his "nemesis." According to N. M. Rashid, who saw her picture, she was a tiny, dark, uninspiring Bengali woman—Rashid thought of her as an unlikely instigator of the lifelong passion Miraji is said to have had for her. Another source of information on Mira Sen, Mrs. Din, who went to college with Mira Sen's sisters, says that the girls, daughters of a Bengali professor who taught in Lahore, were the toast of Lahore. Mira, the most beautiful and the most coveted, was trailed by hosts of entirely enraptured swains. She was also the most publicly intelligent of her siblings, participating in debates where she usually bested her opponents. That she formed the centerpiece of Miraji's desire, and that stories about his attempts to meet her accrued like/as legends is not surprising. These stories, about Miraji's meeting with Mira Sen, form the basis of the "How Miraji Got His Name" tales.

*Miraji Sees Mira Sen: As Nagi Tells It*

The only thing that seems certain about her was that she was a 13- or 14-year-old Bengali girl who lived on Lek Road in Lahore, and Miraji fell in love with her at first sight. Another tale [told] about him was that Mira Sen studied at FC College [Forman Christian College] and Miraji tried to talk to her in front of the YMCA, but she, anxious about him, walked on. What happened to Miraji after that is well known. He first changed his name and then his entire being. He began to wear a mala around his neck, abandoned his home, and for the rest of his life wandered the world. In one of his letters, Miraji writes that he spent 13 years in Mira Sen's servitude. There is a picture of Mira Sen tucked into a newspaper in Miraji's papers. Two letters he wrote to her and never posted were found among his effects. This long imaginary love and emotional connection indicates an extraordinary scene. . . . He felt a kind of madness that manifests [itself] in his poetry. This is the visible face of Miraji's personhood, and one that he held onto.[71]

*Miraji Sees Mira Sen*

Miraji was in a lull between high school and university, studying for the entrance exams. He and his friend Salim Soz were sitting on Punjab University's hockey field one day when two Bengali women—Mira Sen and Protima Das—walked past. Miraji was so smitten with Mira Sen that he stopped studying; as a result, he failed his exams.

Mira Sen was a student at FC College. Trying to get close to her, Miraji would visit their mutual friend at the same school, Muhammad din Farazdaq, whose sitting room was next to Mira Sen's. Miraji would ask his friend to write fiction stories that he could then edit and have published, presumably to gain Mira Sen's attention. When he found out that Mira Sen's friends called her "Miraji," Sana' ullah changed his name to hers.[72]

*Miraji Observes Mira Sen*

One of Miraji's friends lived in a house that shared a wall with Kinnaird College, where Mira Sen went to visit her friends. Miraji and his friends would congregate there, drink, and scrutinize the girls who

> went to Kinnaird through a peephole they had dug into the common wall. Miraji caught sight of Mira Sen, fell in love with her, and began to follow her home.
>
> Only once did he gather the courage to talk to her. Just as she reached home he walked up to her and said, "I have something to say to you." Mira Sen turned to look at him but remained completely silent, her face empty. Then, without a word, she walked into her house. Miraji never tried to talk to her again, but he continued to keep track of her until she left Lahore.[73]

The tautness drawn out between seeing and wanting, the silent conjuring of a beloved's fervor chased down a trail of speculative questioning working through yearning's contradictions—those traces of tenderness, those angled falterings of coy bashfulness—so that the lover could keep hope alive, are plainly and eloquently spoken in the *naẓm* which opens *Sah ātishah* (With fire), the book of poetry Miraji compiled just before his death.[74] Composed in Lahore and written in the cadences of longing pressed into conversation, this *naẓm*, "Āṅkh micolī" (In the blink of an eye), is one of the few whose emotional pulses actually seem to syncopate with details that punctuated and leavened Miraji's life. In its naked language the gaze, the glance, the glimpse, is not assuaged, soothed, or eased by the dense visual iconography of fetishism that Miraji speaks of when he talks about his passion in "Nāmukammal sailf-porṭraiṭ." Instead it voices, simply, and by pulling time apart, so that the moment which is also a movement, a blink, a glimpse, expands to calibrate desire. Reading gestures as measures of time, longing is told in the imaginary exchanges (*guftagū*) that ostensibly took place between Miraji and Mira Sen (or her double, the "any woman" who turned away):

> How I love this woman
> I walk past my house a little way, glimpse her, wish she were here.
> Quickly, how quickly she eludes my glance
> What should I believe, does she abhor me?
> But this! She looked down so soon, so quietly
> What should I believe, does she know my longing
> And this? When our eyes meet, she shuts her door, and

I, destitute, wander.
Never to see her again
Well, yes . . . her friend emerged. Looked me over, went away.
What ought I think, did she come because she was asked?
What did I really witness: their laughter, graceful, sounded that
  moment
when in a quick turn of passion . . .
was it defeat exulting
or a spoor of courage?
What can I expect, what can I presume
does she despise me, or breathe yearning, if she hungers so
why must it take so long? If she hates me so
what must she imagine? Why tease me so,
endlessly? Yes,
I have news of her,
yes, this my love's prayer, absolute, sure, flawless gold its faith. Yes,
how I long
for that girl, who lives so close to my house.

Miraji's complete absorption in Mira Sen apparently persuaded him that he was not interested in attending university. When his father realized this, he set out to find his son a practical, income-generating vocation. Subsequently, Miraji was apprenticed to his father's friend Dr. Nizamuddin and became a skilled homeopath. Although he did not want to pursue medicine as a career, Miraji continued to treat himself, his family, and his friends throughout his life.[75]

## YOUNG LITERATUS IN LAHORE: WILD MAN OR METHODICAL EDITOR?

Following his episode as an apprentice, Miraji began to write poetry in earnest, frequenting local Lahore coffeehouses and other haunts of aspiring writers and poets. As one of the most visible younger literary figures of the late 1920s and early 1930s, he became the nucleus of a coterie of literary neophytes. This was also the period during which he started a habit that was to stay with him all his life: going to the library.[76] One senses, reading the quick edge of curiosity in his essays and the sensual pleasure suffusing his translations, the excitement he felt at hunting down new verse in the library and his taste of delight as he recited it.

In the library he discovered the love lyric of Japanese geishas in a limited edition, three-volume set of love poetry, exquisitely printed, interspersed with boldly etched gold plates and translated by E. Powys Mathers, appositely titled *Eastern Love.* These translations were to stay with him until his death, when he transmuted "Lessons of a Bawd" into the Urdu as *Nigār ḳhānah* (Picture house; or House of portraits). His first translations from this collection included Li Po, Chandidas, and Amaru. In his sojourns to the library Miraji also found e. e. cummings, Cecil Day Lewis, Anna Akhmatova, Alexander Pushkin, Thomas More, the Brontë sisters, Baudelaire, Sappho, D. H. Lawrence, and Freud, and began the massive task of translating them, as well as many other writers, into Urdu. In 1936 or 1937, just as it had come out, he happened upon Charles Mauron's edition of Mallarmé's poetry, translated by Roger Fry:

> This is an anecdote from about 1936 or 1937, when, while studying the literature and poetry of the West I encountered the work of Stephane Mallarmé. Mallarmé is the best known of the Western poets who favor the darkness of ambiguity [*mub-ham*]. I found some of his poems in an English collection. The art critic Roger Fry had translated them in moments of leisure. And after his death they had been published as a book. Mallarmé's pleasure in murkiness can be ascertained by the fact that even when they were translated in English, the poems had to be supplemented by a commentary. This work, of providing a clarifying exegesis, had been done by Roger Fry. But, his sort [of poetry,] the poetry of shadows and innuendo is not new. Following on Momin, Ghalib, too, evinced a similar style. I liked the technique of commentary Roger Fry used, to explain and unfold each poem. So when I translated Mallarmé's poems into Urdu, I wrote an essay to accompany it. And with it I also translated Roger Fry's points of clarity.[77]

But Miraji's family apparently did not approve of his new avocation as poet and translator. Miraji's brother, disgusted with his sibling, sold a sheaf of poems to the paper seller to be used for packaging vegetables. This apocryphal fable is the seminal moment in melodramatic life plots of misunderstood, indigent poets who have to survive every adversity including displacement in a new nationalism which renders them superfluous (fit only for garbage, kachra), and one which tosses them out of the security of a good bourgeoisie household into the streets to roam reciting. The cinematic version of the tale is volunteered in *Pyāsā* (The thirsty man), a film directed Guru Dutt in 1957, with lyrics by the poet Sahir Ludhianavi. Miraji's story, told for the first time by his brother in 1978, mirrors the film, with one major difference. In the film the poet Vijay's work is salvaged by a prostitute, fallen but redeemed by her love for poetry and the poet. Vijay finds an ambivalent fame. Miraji is offered no such salvation. He, unlike Vijay, must surrender his soul to the woman to whom he is in thrall. His tragic tale offers the protagonist no reprieve.

Despite his family's lack of support, Miraji eventually got his first paying job by walking into the offices of *Adabī duniyā* (Literary world), a Lahore magazine of letters. In 1938, soon after he was hired, he was promoted to poetry editor and given a princely salary of thirty rupees a month.[78]

Miraji initiated several innovative projects for the magazine. He wrote terse political pieces and published poems as Vasant Sahay. The journal also printed his translations of international poets and writers, which he framed with long critical essays that advocated a revisionist canon of non-Urdu-speaking authors. This was a formidable project for which he did an enormous amount of background historical research that he folded into minutely detailed essays. To lay the groundwork in the essay "Vidyāpatī aur us ke gīt" (Vidaypati and his songs), Miraji began with a short synopsis on the history of Aryan religion (which followed the general profile of histories current at the time) from which deistic Hinduism focused on Vishnu worship emerged. To this he appended the blurring of Vidyapati's origins—in Bihar, but transferred to Bengal when Vidyapati was absorbed into the Bengali poetic canon as one of its premier poets. To recite Vidyapati—as a Bihari Maithili poet—Miraji extracted him from both the Hindi and Bengali canons into which he had been absorbed, by providing him with a regional historical context that incorporated biography into local royalist historiography. *Rivāyat, gīt, ḥikāyat*—the repeated customary ways of assigning lineage, scribing place and life through story, song, and habit that has lapsed unnoticed into the truths of belief—these Miraji attempted to unravel and unwrap as he essayed archaeologies of knowledge in this and in other, similar work. These pieces introduced an Urdu-reading audience to writers often left off the list of "important" literary figures compiled for school curricula in India—writers he felt had been consistently marginalized at the time they wrote because they postulated or embodied alternative worldviews (including positions on sexuality), or because they came from groups, like women, that he felt had been excised at other moments frm literary canons. Over and over again in his work, taking the Symbolists Mallarmé, Baudelaire, Rimbaud, Poe as exemplary, Miraji examined the politics of canon formation, valuation dissembling as pleasure and aversion, and the exclusions based on them. In these exclusions he saw allegories of the dismissals rehearsed by his colleagues and observed under colonial auspices.[79]

For *Adabī duniyā* Miraji juxtaposed the works of widely recited Urdu writers against those of obscure, or freshly emerging Urdu poets whose work he also laced with critical essays. In pieces from this period, later collected in the volume *Is naẓm meñ* (In this poem), Miraji addressed his concerns to a community of Urdu readers whose scope, he felt, was curbed by the narrow canon they embraced and understood as convention. Scanning the ontologies of influence, Miraji pried apart the places where influence was sutured to imitation. As a cautionary tale on the "proper absorption of influences" Miraji offered and the abject form of a display of access to colonial information, a pitiful simulation of mastery, an incantation of names denuded of knowledge or understanding—"People casually drop the names of Western gentlemen [they use] as examples while they declaim—about whom they know so little, that they don't even know whether [these gentlemen] were poets or novelists."[80] Miraji felt that, as an editor of a major literary magazine, he was under an obligation to broaden the universe of these Urdu readers whom he considered his compatriots by introducing them to alternative, foreign forms of writing that would push at the horizons of form and content. But these interjections had to be tempered by a stern, stoic rigor, and the fullness of a documented history.

The poetic journeys he embarked on in the *naẓm* he composed during this period in Lahore he traveled until his death. He is considered one of the foreparents of *naẓm* as a genre. In Lahore he began searching for idioms to craft *naẓm,* twisting the tightly wound two-string ghazal and pulling it out into the lingering temporality of desire. A moment, a blink of an eye, a quick surge of breath gave him the beginning and the end of a kind of rubber-band time that stretched into the finitude of longing, each upheaval, each subtle movement swelling out to fill temporal space. Ghalib and Mallarmé were his antecedents, their dense ambiguity gifting him a language that layered and turned in on itself, and turned out to draw in allusions from a panoply of lyric tongues. Time strung between poles and then lengthened out and arced around so that the past and present fused. The past in the present, past as present, the present an echo that calls out the past. The past as the present's future. Events suspended between future and past. His translations from earlier poets became his poetry and his poetry filtered into his translations.

The languages of his compositions, which he also found in the work of his contemporaries, brought Braj, Awadhi, Hindi, Maithili back to Urdu. Miraji is notorious for his *gīt,* which have haunted him in the charges leveled against him that he was Hindu and took refuge in a language laden with Hindi words.[81] *Gīt* become the folk. In the long piece on love written for the Lahore radio station, Miraji transmuted his essays into voice. He took love lyrics from Baudelaire, Akhmatova, and Pushkin and tuned them down to sing alongside the sparer, more colloquial forms of *gīt.*

Miraji's "folk" poetry, his *gīt,* were a passion for him, written around the time that a revival of "folk" literary forms like *gīt,* street theater, and tales in local languages was taking place throughout the subcontinent, some of it under socialist auspices.[82] The first phase of the Second World War was under way. Popular sentiment against fascism had by 1936 coalesced into protests (by the Congress, Jawaharlal Nehru, and Krishna Menon) directed at Franco's armed revolt that took over the elected republican government of Spain. In Lucknow, the loosely organized Progressive Writers' Association was preparing for their first conference.[83] Cobbled together with help from friends, relatives, and academics engaged in "Progressive" activities and paid for on a shoestring budget, the conference was held at the Raf'ā-e 'ām. This site had been inaugurated by a long history of political assemblies, including the 1920 one that passed the Khilafat resolution, and an agitation when the theosophist Annie Besant was sent to jail. The Raf'ā-e 'ām had recently reincarnated as a club for bridge players and beer and whisky drinkers, its politics sent into the hinterlands of memory by British legislation reassigning its use. The conference drew together writers from all over India and was a small moment in a huge gathering of different constituencies in Lucknow on April 14, 1936. The Congress held a session at the Motinagar camp, as did the All-India Kissan Sabha in the days immediately preceding the Congress meetings. The Kissan Sabha called for land nationalization, zamindari (landrights holders) abolition, and cooperative agriculture.[84] Jawarharlal Nehru, the Congress president, explicitly used "socialism" as a key solution, but he and Rajindar Prasad battled over socialist amendments;[85] in 1936 the All-India Students Federation was founded; so, it was particularly apropos that the leftist writers' association saw its first session at this historical juncture

On a bare dais, not even concealed under a dhurrie, Munshi Premchand (Dhanpat Rai) delivered the opening paragraph of his address:

> The literature that is being promoted today is mostly of the statical, mystical, and romantic type, which is doing more harm than good. There is a great need for the evolution of popular literature which is in close contact with the naked realities of life, which is free from the dreamy and unreal haze of pure romanticism and which stirs in us our dormant energies to action, to the conscious realization of our backwardness and helplessness and national humiliation. . . . The pen was greater than ever . . . [it had to be put to use] against the tyrannies of form and figures of speech . . . [had] to resurrect our dead literature into something more vibrant, truthful, and inspiring to progress.[86]

The Progressive Manifesto was supplemented by several resolutions: to rescue literature from the moribund conservative classes; to bring the arts into closer touch with people and register the actualities of their life; to ask for a lifting of restrictions on the freedom of thought and expression, which the government had garroted under repressive press laws, the customs act, and the Criminal Law Amendment Act that proscribed Progressive literature.[87] This, then, was the ideological terrain on which Miraji composed his lyrics and in relation to which he wrote his many essays.[88]

### *Walks on the Wild or Methodical Side*

Some of the earliest descriptions of Miraji's strange physical appearance are from this time. His biographers have produced contrasting pictures of him, Dionysian and Apollonian. Unlike portraits of Dr. Jekyll and

Mr. Hyde, however, where one person is transmuted into his/her opposite, the two versions of Miraji almost always run as parallel images. The Dionysian, which is prevalent, appeared in accounts by writers as various as Aijaz Ahmad, Shahid Ahmad Dihlavi, and Bashir Ahmad. The Apollonian persona was described by Yunus Javed of the *Ḥalqah-e arbāb-e ẕauq* (Circle of the men of taste) and by Akhtarul Iman in his stories about the young Miraji. The one biographer who attempted to integrate Miraji's two personae was Sa'dat Hasan Manto. Although Manto focused heavily on Miraji's wild side, his bemusement at Miraji's more regulated, restrained quirks creates a more complex persona.

Shahid Ahmad Dihlavi, who later hired Miraji to work on the journal *Sāqī* (Cupbearer), met Miraji at *Adabī duniyā* in the 1930s. His description of Miraji mirrors those of most writers who have published biographical essays on him. All the essays are caught in scopophilic vertigo sucked in by a fascination with abjection, circling around and around visual cues (enriched by smell), repeated obsessively as a way into the truth of Miraji. The images and the odor that suffuse/drench it becomes a measure of the man: he was extraordinarily disgusting-looking, exuding a grotesque charm that provoked the same ambivalent, morbid curiosity as an overflowing toilet that will not flush. Miraji wrapped himself in an overcoat during the summer's thick heat. His body smelled as though he hadn't washed in several days. Uneven stubble dotted his face. He wore a string of beads around his neck. Black, disheveled hair grew down his back in snaky ringlets and was so long that Dihlavi said the children in Miraji's neighborhood would run behind him down the street yelling *baṛī mem* (self-important lady).[89] Miraji would turn around, grab his hair, hold it out in bunches, and gesture to the children to come to him; they would walk up and fall silent for a few moments before resuming their chant.[90]

The Miraji that Dihlavi drew a portrait of was a wild, demonic, self-absorbed figure. Dihlavi corroborated his belief in Miraji's wildness with an incident to which he was privy: Miraji lived with his extended family in the same neighborhood as a well-known poet, Shaqa Kanvare. Kanvare kept mostly to himself and led a fairly regulated life, leaving for work every morning at the same time and settling down in the evenings for a good read. After about six years he realized that the strange man he had often seen by his house was the same person he knew well as an assistant editor of a journal that frequently published his poems.

One night, Miraji tottered home drunk and began pounding on the door of the house in front of his own. Immediately afterward he managed to enter the outer door of Kanvare's house and rang the bell. Kanvare opened the door and tried to have a conversation, but it ended abruptly when Miraji threw up the eighteen bottles of beer he had swallowed—and the woman on whose door he had initially banged came out screaming. Although this inauspicious encounter did not prevent Kanvare's subsequent friendship with Miraji, it was grist for Dihlavi's mill that Miraji was a thoroughly debauched person, a demon born inadvertently into a perfectly ordinary, perhaps even religious, household.

According to Dihlavi, Miraji's addiction to sensual habits (read masturbation) began when he was very young. He satisfied his wanton desires with prostitutes in Lahore's Hira Mandi, the bāzār Dihlavi believes was the source of the syphilis (never quite proven) that caused Miraji constant physical pain. Miraji tried to alleviate his torment by turning to books, but instead of allowing his mind some respite from his body, his taste in reading exacerbated the problem. His addiction to sensual needs, fueled by his reading, turned him into a case history like those he loved to read. And starting with the works of Havelock Ellis, Freud, and "ubiquitous" Hindus, he then went on to Baudelaire and Edgar Allen Poe. Under the influence of these notorious figures, Miraji lost touch with the clean-living world of his origins. Dihlavi, unlike Nagi, did not birth Miraji into a Muzang that handicapped him, but started Miraji off with a clean slate.

Curiously enough, Dihlavi's unhappy account of Miraji's life follows Miraji's own descriptions up to a point, then diverges dramatically. Miraji laid the blame for his unhappiness on his inability to ever actualize his desire for the people he loved. Following a Freudian turn, Miraji located the origin of his discontent in his childhood, but then his laments, as marked by unrequited passion, returned his autobiography to and aligned him with the lineage and genealogy of the lover from classical Urdu poetry. In contrast, Dihlavi blamed Miraji's unhappiness on excessive alleviation of various unwholesome desires. One can read in Dihlavi's anxiously sanctimonious description of these desires that they were the kind of "fixations" that could be endured and cured or withstood. So, Miraji is to be blamed twice over for falling prey to them: once for wanting it and the second time for not restraining himself. Although Dihlavi would probably be horrified to realize that his analysis of Miraji's malaise followed Freud's and Havelock Ellis's catalogues of perverts and sexual deviants, his allusions to deviance ("masturbation," "nymphomania," "hypersexuality"), which appear to take Miraji's life in a different, more modernist direction, were actually consonant with both Ellis and Freud.

Unlike Dihlavi, when Akhtarul Iman talks about the Miraji he met he reminisces about an Apollonian Miraji—memories that are echoed by other young poets Miraji helped. In 1940 Akhtarul Iman walked into the offices of *Adabī duniyā* with some of his poems. It was then that he noticed Miraji, whom he had heard was collecting the works of little-known poets to be published by the magazine. Akhtarul Iman's recollections, corroborated by other writers to whom Miraji devoted time to discuss their poetry or prose, depict Miraji as an intense, gracious man. He is said to have had a remarkably ferocious intelligence that was evident even when he talked about day-to-day, mundane things. His acute mind was matched by a soft carefulness and courtesy. The image that stayed with them was of a soft-voiced man with a measured pacing—the antithesis of the "wild man" he was later made out to be. He was considered an exemplary critic, and writers who brought him their work remember him giving them gentle but rigorous attention, talking carefully through his critique. Even literati who did not like Miraji's poetry eulogize his oral and written criticism as remarkable for its style, humor, and accessible rigor.[91]

In addition, Miraji was generous with his money; he cared deeply about his friends and would rush to their assistance if they needed anything, sometimes even giving away his pay as soon as he had earned it—to a tongawala, for example, who needed cash for his daughter's wedding and had been telling Miraji about his predicament as he pulled him home.[92]

Unlike the self-absorbed, solipsistic, insane, socially inept person of the more widely circulated stories, the Apollonian Miraji who inhabits these alternative tales is someone who lived in and helped sustain a viable literary community.

### *Triplets, Plato's Chariot, or Freud in Another Key*

Like all the other writers who turned their phrases to resolve Miraji's ambiguities and his incommensurable quirks, Akhtarul Iman, too, attempted his own take on Miraji.[93] Akhtarul Iman had his first face-to-face conversation with Miraji in Delhi after a conference that Miraji had attended. They had met previously through letters. Akhtarul Iman had written a *naẓm* while he was doing his B.A. at Anglo-Arabic College in Lahore, and performed it at several venues where it had been received with a great deal of acclaim. Having been published by *Sāqī* in Delhi, he wanted to get something into *Adabī duniyā*, so he sent the journal his *naẓm*. It was returned with a pleasant note from Miraji. Akhtarul Iman tried again, to the same response. Several years later Akhtarul Iman was in Delhi; Meerut, where he was to complete his M.A., was not a city in which he could survive. Looking for work in Delhi, he ran into the fiction writer Krishan Chandar at a friend's house. Krishan Chandar offered him the chance to coordinate a large literary conference in Delhi as a way of making some money. Miraji was to travel down from Lahore to attend, and had sent a message that he wanted to meet Akhtarul Iman. However, when it was time to actually come to the conference, Akhtarul Iman, insecure about his literary accomplishments, fled to visit his father. When he returned to Delhi he discovered that not only had Miraji not left, but that he still wanted to meet him. The meeting was arranged to take place at N. M. Rashid's house. Akhtarul, waiting inside for Miraji's arrival, heard a rich deep voice: "Has Akhtar come yet?" Then a young, fair man entered. That was the only time they met before Miraji moved in with him in Poona, and a few years later, died while in his custody.[94]

Among Miraji's papers was a complete manuscript for a book he called *Sah ātishah*. Akharul Iman had been left as the de facto executor of Miraji's estate, and as such felt he was under an obligation to ensure that Miraji's manuscript be published. But it took him many years to do so. One constraint was his finances, which could not sustain the cost of taking a book to print. Another was the detritus of pain and rage that Miraji had bequeathed to the friend who cared for him. But before his own death, Akhtarul Iman, struggling to come to terms with the anguish of Miraji's betrayal by his friends and anger at the way Miraji treated him, turned to print for expiation and catharsis, and wrote two pieces on Miraji. One, "Guftanī nā guftanī" (What should or should not be spoken), leaves us with the tale of their history together. The other, "Mīrājī ke āḳhirī lamḥe" (Miraji's final moments) offers what previously Akhtarul Iman had only spoken aloud, his recollections of Miraji's last days.[95]

In "Guftanī nā guftanī" Akhtarul Iman chances his analysis of Miraji, as a prelude to the story of their friendship. Miraji's many faces, like the three balls of gun-metal gray he rolled incessantly between his fingers, could be culled down to three. Three balls, three names, three faces, three personalities: a structuralist triad. One was Sana' ullah; the second was Ḍār; and the third Miraji. Sana' ullah wore heavy earrings, grew his mustaches into long Pathan curls sometimes and shaved them off other times, and was always ready to leaven the hackneyed with humor and laughter. This was his asylum from a life that lagged behind success. Ḍār, plagued by nervousness, lost in sexual illness, constantly in vigil before anxiety, had as his role models Baudelaire and Edgar Allan Poe. He was caught in a hell without alleviation. Miraji was the "super ego," the lord of the symbolic. To him was given the mastery of the universe of literature (complete control over Urdu literary history) and the confident will to bend the course of Urdu poetics, prose, and criticism. He strolled the Urdu literary scene with impunity.[96]

Miraji became one of the main figures in the Lahore literary scene, and it is clear from the poem "Jañgal meñ piknik" (Picnic in the jungle),[97] which he wrote with his friend Qayyum Nazar, that belonging to a community of like-minded, playful writers was important to him. The critical discussion he later wrote about the poem opens with intentional misreadings that depict it as a catalogue (doubling as dictionary) of repeated monotonous words, useful as a playful vocabulary list for children. Readers who long for propriety may be able to sense the poem's music, but will only understand it as meaningless. They, Miraji implies, bring meaning and word so decorously together that each seems to flow naturally from the other without a break. If, however, as Miraji proposes in the piece, one is willing to abdicate oneself to freedom from meaning, and give up the urge to couple word with its signified, one can lose oneself in the visual journeys traveled in the poem.

In this poem words are superfluous, exorbitant, shoving and pulling at each other and the reader. As words double and accrue seemingly senselessly, the question of their meaning appears superfluous. So, says Miraji, allow yourself a luxury. Give up your desire to find sense. Give it up and let the question of meaning go. Indulge yourself, Miraji informs us: let yourself float into the space of the poem and allow its movements to cradle and carry you. All you have to abrogate is the impulse that accompanies signification. What you have to abrogate is that impulse that as it chaperons signification pushes you out of the space of the poem toward the elsewhere of what it means, word by word. If you can let the question of meaning go, then the poem's words will pull you in their wake, to see in another way. You will travel with the eyes (sight-lines) that tour the poem: from the jungle's enclosure down to a richly textured ground (shadows, springs, paths, thorns, motes of dust, insects), and then soar up to branches, parrots, and birds. They move downwards again, to streams, single buds sprouting, clothing you, in closing with a sweep of fragrances and visions. Then this enchanted world dissolves, thinning out into writing, and the abraded tip of a pencil scribbling tiredly on a scrap of paper. The poem finally ends, playfully: with laughing friends, poets gathered to enjoy the poem's musical magic. Sharing the poem takes them into its world and metamorphoses their circle into a throng picnicking in a jungle.

"Jañgal meñ mañgal honā." As the reading of the poem ends it resurrects the question of meaning. Meaning is not found in (the) solitary pursuit of the abstinent extraction of juice from a word. It is discovered in camaraderie, when words are handed around a group, caressed, repeated, doubled, punned. A word can be called out to mean something, not just once, but twice. *Itvār*, the "Sunday" of the title, plays against the word *mañgal*—Tuesday, festive rejoicing—with which Miraji ends his short essay. Tuesday meets Sunday, the week curves around in the promise of a joyous, boisterous celebration in a deserted spot.[98] The pleasure of this small group of listeners—fellow literati—evokes the safe space in which Miraji's poetry had found a home: the *Ḥalqah-e arbāb-e ẓauq*.

### *Circle of the Men of Taste: Miraji in the Mainstream*

One day in the bāzār, two writers exchanging casual information about their lives discussed the idea of beginning a group that would meet regularly to discuss each other's work. Although writers met occasionally through the predominantly Marxist Progressive Writers' Association (PWA), the men, Nazir Ahmad Jami and Sher Mahmud Akhtar, felt they needed to form another, nonpolitical organization.

The Halqa, originally known as the *Bazm-e dāstāngo* (Storytellers' gathering), began modestly in 1939. Its inaugural meeting, held on folding chairs in Sher Mahmud Akhtar's home, Lakshmi Mansion, opened with a story read by Nasim Hijazi.[99] At the next gathering, on the first of October, the name of the fledging organization was changed to *Ḥalqah-e arbāb-e ẕauq*.[100] The Halqa met wherever it could find space, and was chaired by different writers. Each meeting began with one or more readings by poets, fiction writers, and essayists who needed a place to present their work.

One of the mainstays of the Halqa in its early days was Qayyum Nazar, who brought many of his friends with him, among them Miraji, who, along with Yusuf Zafar, became a leading member. Miraji first attended the Halqa on August 25, 1940, but his reputation was so entwined with the group that in popular renditions of the Halqa's history, he is even credited with starting it.[101] Nevertheless, Miraji did affect the Halqa profoundly. Before he arrived, the meetings focused almost exclusively on readings, without accompanying critiques. Miraji transformed it from a group where writers met merely to exchange work and congratulate themselves on their brilliance to one that resembled the laughing gathering of friends he created in "Picnic in the Jungle": trenchantly critical of one another.

The careful close reading of poetry that Miraji did for *Adabī duniyā* became the norm for the Halqa. He brought a style of critique that combined aesthetic appreciation with rigorous analysis. As a critic he was not combative or confrontational; he was unfailingly polite, respectful of and attentive to different perspectives. He also believed in the efficacy of spending time reading and understanding other writers' works as a way of learning about one's own. These characteristics of his, when applied in public communal settings, set the tone for a convivial but effective literary forum that welcomed a variety of literary styles and political positions.

The Halqa grew rapidly through word of mouth, becoming a popular, multivalent literary organization. Contrary to subsequent representations of it as a forum that shut out socialist writers, its records show that members of the Progressive Writers' Association, such as Krishan Chandar, Rajindar Singh Bedi, and Faiz Ahmad Faiz, read alongside writers with very different political and poetic beliefs, like N. M. Rashid and Yusuf Zafar.[102] The Halqa encouraged collaboration between social realist writers of prose and fiction, the more modernist experimental poets who wrote prose poetry, and those poets who were reorienting older forms like the ghazal to political concerns.

Because of the range of literature it produced, the Halqa embodied the world of Urdu literature in the 1940s. The same kinds of stylistic juxtapositions, interchanges, and interactions were also occurring in literary journals located in other urban areas. One of the first such magazines was *Sāqī*, in Delhi. More—*Nigār* (Painting), in Lucknow; *Jama*ʿ (Collection), Delhi; *Adab-e laṭīf* (Literary delights), Lahore; *Humāyūn* (Eminent), Lahore; *Shahkār* (Masterpiece), Lahore; *Dāstān* (Epic), Lahore; *Prīt laṛī* (Beautiful necklace), Amritsar; *Akhbār-e hindūstān* (Newspaper of Hindustan), Lucknow—soon followed.[103]

## DELHI YEARS: THE WILD MAN TAKES HOLD—BEGINNING OF A DECLINE

Radio had its uncertain beginnings in Bombay, in 1926, around the time that it began to be established in Britain. But backed by inadequate private capital, the Bombay and Calcutta stations lapsed into receivership.[104] In the early 1930s the moribund technology was revitalized by the government of India. An assortment of sometimes conflicting explanations were given to bolster this move: fear of guerrilla broadcasts from the Congress that would foment sedition in the 1930s; fears that people, deprived of local stations, would be influenced by Russian and western Asian radio propaganda; enthusiasm for radio as a venue of rural education, radio as a technology that would bring India together as a nation.[105] By 1935, after many rancorous disputes about control, a decision was made to establish a station in Delhi, managed by the Department for Industries and Labor that would reach out to the area between Lahore and Allahabad. It would be run by someone sent out from England and broadcast programs in English and Urdu.[106]

On January 1, 1936, All-India Radio (AIR) in Delhi broadcast for the first time. Under the jurisdiction of Lionel Fielden, sent from the BBC, the newly inaugurated station attempted to attract competent, creative Indians to select and design programs (music, ghazal, poetry, plays) by promoting special, well-paid positions for program assistants.[107] Fielden hired S. S. Niazi as one of the people to fill this post (for music), then recruited A. S. Bokhari from Government College in Lahore as station director.

Soon after he moved to Delhi, Bokhari became the deputy controller of broadcasting, and his brother, Z. A. Bokhari, took over as director.[108]

A. S. Bokhari, in consonance with Fielden's preference for a staff with wide-ranging ideas and interests, invited members of the Lahore literary scene to work for him.[109] Those who migrated to Delhi included Faiz Ahmad Faiz, Sa'dat Hasan Manto, and N. M. Rashid. Miraji, too, was recruited; he apparently arrived in 1941 and, because he had broadcasting experience with All-India Radio in Lahore, was hired by the station as a regular scriptwriter in December 1942.[110]

Miraji moved during one of the most tumultuous periods in colonial history; the war was approaching Indian borders (Singapore fell on February 15, 1942, Rangoon on March 8, Andamans on March 23). The All-India Congress Session at Bombay passed the "Quit India" resolution in August of that year ("for mass struggle on nonviolent lines on the widest possible scale"), which was immediately followed by mass arrests of Congress leaders. The resolution marked the failure of the Cripps Mission. Delhi exploded into *hartaks*, strikes, and clashes with police, as did Bombay, Calcutta, Patna, Lucknow, Kanpur, and Ahmedabad. From August on, the violence spread to rural areas. The British response—brutal reprisals—sent the movement underground: student terrorist attacks against police, army, and communication, and quick forays by groups of peasant saboteurs. The "Quit India" movement was described by Lord Linlithgow, the viceroy, as the "most serious rebellion since that of 1857."[111]

When Miraji arrived in Delhi, he cleaned up his appearance by getting an "English" haircut, trimming his trailing mustaches, and buying a "good" three-piece suit to replace his sweaty overcoat.[112] He also acquired a metal ball the size and shape of a lime and began covering it with the silver foil linings of cigarette boxes. He kept the ball in his pants pocket with a sadhu's seed necklace and a conch shell; the three objects became worry beads for him and he played with them constantly. When asked about these things, which he called "frauds," Miraji would smile secretively but make no reply.[113]

In addition to working as a scriptwriter and news translator for AIR, Miraji also composed twenty-four songs for the station. His assistant, a young man called Visvanandan Bhatnagar, befriended him. Bhatnagar described Miraji as a very strange man with long hair and a deep, rich voice who wore ordinary clothes. His one special characteristic, according to Bhatnagar, echoes Dihlavi: his ability to attract people. All who met Miraji found themselves drawn to him.[114]

Despite his charisma, however, in Delhi Miraji began to lead a less settled life. He began to be depicted as someone accelerating rapidly toward decline, as an almost entirely unregenerate "degenerate" who drowned his frustration in rot-gut alcohol when he found he could not satisfy all of his fantasies. Miraji hated thinking about even the ordinary needs of his body. Bhatnagar would bring food to the recording studio and leave it in a cupboard, hoping that his friend would see it and remember to eat. And he could be equally lax about money. One day, Dihlavi and another friend of Miraji's found him lying unconscious on the road by Andheri bazaar. With the help of a tongawala, they managed to pack him into a vehicle and take him home. Before putting him to bed, they found five hundred rupees crammed into his pockets. The friend took the money home for safekeeping and returned it several days later. Miraji, who in the meantime had forgotten about the money, was puzzled by suddenly being given this huge sum.[115] Unlike the biographical narratives from Lahore, in which Miraji is either a drunken Dionysian wild man or a sedate Apollonian editor, the Delhi stories focus exclusively on Miraji's wild side. There is a great deal more information about his evenings, when he was likely to drink, than there is on his daytime activities, when he worked.

Miraji was fired from his full-time job with AIR after only two years; his friends give two different explanations. One is that he did not get along with his immediate boss, whom he considered a fool. When his boss asked him to revise a radio play he was writing he refused because he felt the revisions would ruin the script. The two argued and Miraji was fired. The other reason given is that he was caught spending the night on the sofa in the office; since AIR had a policy forbidding employees from living on their premises, they fired him.

After he left AIR, Miraji started working a series of jobs, earning, according to Bhatnagar, between 100 and 125 rupees per month, which barely covered his living expenses. He wrote a regular column, "Bāteṅ," for *Sāqī*; wrote *Vidyāpatī*, a play for the station that was broadcast in January 1945, and was an intermittent announcer for the radio.

His sojourn in Delhi proved productive for Miraji, even as it took its toll on him. He started a new circle of the Halqa, drawing into it many of his colleagues from AIR: Rajindar Singh Bedi, Mukhtar Siddiqi, N. M. Rashid, Upendranath Ashk, Patras, Krishan Chandar, Aijaz Husain. All of the books published by him while alive were published in Delhi; three volumes of poetry: *Mīrājī ke gīt* (Miraji's songs), *Gīt hī gīt* (Songs), and *Mīrājī kī naẓmeñ* (Miraji's verse).[116] In "Bāteñ," Miraji tried his hand at a prose unlike anything he had previously risked. The column, with its loose structure, permitted him to muse. He ventured into topical issues and moments of philosophical rumination, infusing suggestive disquisitions on time, history, nature, science, creativity, love, and desire with his mastery over a vast array of sources, and leavening them with pithy anecdotes.

Writing for the radio had brought time into a different kind of focus for him. Radio broadcasts, readings, and recitals highlighted the constraints as well as the sensuality of rendering something within an immutable time frame. Time was marked out. It became a category of containment and pleasure. Its new resolutions filtered into "Bāteñ" and into the poetry (like "Yagānagat" and "Samundar kā bulāvā") he was to write in Bombay.[117]

The translations that had been Miraji's bread and butter in Lahore fell by the wayside, appearing only occasionally in his prose. He also composed fewer poems than he had in Lahore.[118] In *Sah ātishah* Miraji compiled merely seven poems from this time. Most of them seem to attempt the new topics that arrested his attention. "Jañg kā" (The upshot of war), a battle of words between daughter-in-law (*bahū*) and mother-in-law (*sās*), is perhaps an allegory of colonial clashes over the house/nation. "Yahūdī" (Jew) condenses the violence of genocide into the tense lyricism of the hunt. Its language, taken from Krishna bhakti, brings/conveys/conducts the war raging outside India home through its metaphors.

Trying perhaps to voice his ambivalence about his ability to compose lyric, Miraji also wrote about creativity and the conundrums that haunted the process of writing. In "Yāʿnī" (Because . . . , That is to say . . . ), rhymes linger on the travails of writing: "maiñ sochatā hūñ ik naẓm likhūñ / lekin us meñ kyā bāt kaḥūñ," "I want to write a poem, / but what do I say in it?"; "dil kahtā hai maiñ suntā huñ / man māne bhūl yuñ cuntā hūñ," "As my heart speaks to me I listen, / sifting through sensuous forgetting"; "pal ke pal meñ ik naẓm likhūñ / lekin us meñ kyā bāt kahūñ?", "Shall I write in the space opened between one breath and another, / but what do I say in it?" The desired one, poem or beloved, speaks back: "kyuñ socate ho ik naẓm likho / kyuñ apne dil kī bāt kaho, bahtar to yahī hai cup hī raho." Her words read ambiguously. They can be translated as encouragement or as disparaging: "Why think, just write the poem / well, just speak your desire it's probably better, to say nothing"; or "Why do you think you can write a poem / say what's in your heart it's probably better if you say nothing at all."

"Cheḍ" (Tease/teasing) is another conversation poem. The terse dialogue, scripted for two, recalls e. e. cummings, whose work Miraji had translated in Lahore. The published version of the poem in *Sah ātishah* is longer than the one in Miraji's *Sah ātishah* manuscript, which was published in *Tīn rañg*. In this second version, probably meant to be read on the page, desire measured in stripped phrases is filled in with cues to orient a reader as to who is speaking and whether the words are imagined or spoken. In the briefer *Tīn rañg* (or manuscript) version, the cues are peeled away from the poem, and the conversation, standing on its own, only comes alive when it is read aloud.[119]

The one consistent thing about Miraji's life in Delhi, as Bhatnagar tells it, was his evening consumption of alcohol, organized into a meticulous daily ritual. As long as Miraji worked regularly for AIR, he had enough money to pay for his daily brew. But after he lost his job and his income dropped, he began soliciting daily contributions from his friends at about four o'clock. Around five, after he had collected enough money, Miraji would walk quickly to Gol Market near the AIR offices, one hand clutching a bag with an empty bottle in it, slung over his shoulder, the other carrying tin foil balls. At the store he would buy a bottle of cheap local liquor and pour it into the bottle he had carried with him, swallowing his first few sips as he walked out. On days when he had more money, he bought the newspaper to read on the bus he would then take to Lodhi Road. On other days, when he had only enough to pay for the alcohol, he walked instead.[120]

Miraji began borrowing various sums of money. One night an irate creditor found him in a drunken stupor at the AIR studios and beat his face. When Dihlavi asked Miraji why he was bruised, he was told that he had been beaten by someone he didn't know. Miraji's more "sober" friends began circulating stories that he liked to beat himself. Dihlavi said that when Miraji and his friends were drunk they liked to beat people, calling the beatings "omelets."[121]

Miraji pared his luggage down to his books, papers, and the few clothes he carried with him from place to place. He rented a house in Pal Bangash, a neighborhood deep in the heart of Old Delhi, for four months, then took turns living on various friends' floors for two to three months at a time; by 1945, he was using Dihlavi's *Sāqī* address as his permanent one.[122] Miraji's friends in Delhi began to lose patience with him. They stopped lending him money regularly and it became harder for him to find places to stay.

The final episode that led to his move to Bombay with Bhatnagar was financially fueled. Bhatnagar was completely broke, and Miraji wanted money both for himself and for his friend M. A. Latif. Latif was desperate to pay for his marriage and had invited Miraji to visit him in Agra to discuss the situation. Miraji and Bhatnagar decided to borrow the money they needed for themselves and for Latif from the local moneylenders, who were Pathans. The mythic mafioso of Delhi at the time, Pathans lent money at exorbitant rates and threatened their "clients" if they were not paid back promptly. After a short search they found a Pathan who was willing to lend them three hundred rupees. Bhatnagar kept one hundred for himself, while Miraji sent a money order to Latif for one hundred and spent the last hundred on clothes and books.

Bhatnagar was close to the end of a six-year contract as a clerk with AIR; both he and Miraji knew it would be difficult to repay the Pathans, so they decided to leave Delhi for a more lucrative place. They picked Bombay. Many of Miraji's Lahore friends had moved to work in the burgeoning Bombay film industry as script- and songwriters, and Bhatnagar had a close friend there. They felt that, with their contacts, they were more likely to find employment in Bombay than new jobs in Delhi.

With their newly gained expertise at locating Pathans, they managed to find another to lend them an additional hundred rupees to front their trip. Bhatnagar says that they packed their meager belongings in one very large suitcase, bought two train tickets and, after a long overnight train trip, arrived in Bombay at Victoria Terminus on the morning of June 7, 1946.

Bombay at this time was between two political convulsions. As Miraji arrived, the city had just begun quieting after the Indian naval revolt. The revolt had been preceded and perhaps fomented by a smaller uprising: a mob that gathered in January to protest the Indian National Army trials that were then being conducted in Delhi.[123] It began, modestly, around the time that the British delegation to India was to leave. A small deputation of sailors refused to return to their ships after shore leave. Their demands: better treatment for Indians, withdrawal of Indian troops being used against Sukarno in Indonesia, and the release of the Indian Nationalist Army soldiers on trial in Delhi. They were quickly joined by another four thousand men from two other ships. Bombay exploded. Thirty thousand people fought back against a police picket, buildings were set on fire, trains canceled, workers went on strike. The city was under curfew for days as the violence smoldered.[124] April brought police strikes.[125]

Just after Miraji came to Bombay, the Muslim League council met there in July. The Simla conference with the British delegation which proposed a three-tier confederacy had been viewed with disfavor by the Muslim League. In the July gathering, Jinnah declared August 16 a direct-action day to protest the government's and Congress's bad faith. August saw Bombay convulsed by violence again.

Miraji spent his first two days in Bombay with Bhatnagar's friend, Mukhtar; then they parted. Bhatnagar, who was very ill, stayed with his friend for a while, then left for Delhi before fleeing to Ambala, Patiala, and finally Lahore to escape the moneylenders. Miraji moved in with an acquaintance, Nakshab Jarcavi.[126]

## LAST THREE YEARS IN BOMBAY: REALLY MAD OR INSANELY REAL?

> Shakespeare in Elysium—question about the meaning of a passage: "I marvel nothing so much as that men will gird themselves at discovering obscure beauties in an author. Certes the greatest and most pregnant beauties are ever the plainest and most evidently striking; and when two meanings of a passage can in the least ballance [*sic*] our judgements which to prefer, I hold it a matter of unquestionable certainty that neither of them is worth a farthing."
>
> —Henry Fielding, in *A Journey from This World to the Next.* Epigraph intended for Roger Fry's collection of Mallarmé's translations.[127]

One of the best known and more sympathetic portrayals of Miraji was written at a time when there was a dearth of pieces being produced about him, in the 1950s and early 1960s. "Tīn gole" (Three balls), written by Sa'dat Hasan Manto, a novelist who also wrote short stories and scripts, describes his Bombay interactions with the poet. As a paradigmatic biographical ramble, "Three Balls" is, alongside Aijaz Ahmad's piece, one of the main repositories of stories in circulation about Miraji.

Manto had a long-standing acquaintance with Miraji, whom he considered a close friend. They had previously "met" through letters exchanged during Miraji's tenure as an editor at *Adabī duniyā*, arguing by mail about the title of *Mausam kī sharārat* (Seasonal mischief), a story that Miraji had solicited from Manto for the magazine; now, in flat number one, Hans Building, Bombay, the men sat across the table from each other for the first time, continuing their discussion of Manto's fiction that had begun with their correspondence. On the table were three balls wrapped in silver foil that Miraji continuously fondled—the balls that gave the essay its title and became the leitmotif around which Manto organized the stories he told. For Manto, the balls mirrored Miraji's twinkling eyes topped by a matted globe of ashen hair.[128]

Miraji's strange appearance lead Manto to assume that his conversation with Miraji would follow the contours of Miraji's dense, seemingly incomprehensible poetry.[129] He was, therefore, perplexed by the poet's sharp clarity and straightforward intelligence—a conversational style and intellectual demeanor so at odds with appearance. Miraji offered trenchant readings of Manto's work, even though his critiques seemed cursory.

Manto was initially bewildered by the paradox he encountered in Miraji—someone who was simultaneously readable and unreadable.[130] Miraji was accessible in ways that Manto had not envisioned because he had conceived of Miraji, through his poetry, as someone who was essentially incomprehensible. Also, Manto's expectations about Miraji had been colored by N. M. Rashid, another poet who wrote free verse and prose poetry. Manto saw Rashid as the antithesis of Miraji. Rashid's appearance, his prose, and his poetry were all accessible to Manto; he could actually understand them, so he expected the same kind of consistency from Miraji—complete inaccessibility.[131] Manto's confusion over Miraji's paradoxical oddness was what most readers of Miraji, including myself, face: the obscureness of some of his poetry seems to belie the clarity of his prose. This capacity to thwart the expectations of readers who demand coherence across different sites (prose, poetry, body, personality) is echoed so often in narratives about Miraji that it becomes, along with the three balls, a leitmotif, one of Miraji's characteristics. Faiz Ahmad Faiz reiterates Manto's dilemma in his preface to Miraji's essays: Miraji's prose is lucid, his poetry opaque.[132]

The difference between Faiz's and Manto's discussions about the poet is that Faiz confines himself to Miraji's poetry, whereas Manto maps poetry onto biography and personality. The dichotomy maintained by critics between Miraji's poetry and prose parallels the separation by biographers of his personality into Jekyll and Hyde parts. Both are clues to particular anxieties about Miraji, but his work and appearance create discomfort not because the ability to read/not read him are located in two separate, differing places, but because they seem to occur simultaneously. Even his *naẓm* are posited as incomprehensible—not because of an inherent truth, but rather because of the confusion created by obscurity founded in convention. Miraji is "difficult" as a writer or as a person because readings of his work and personality are not stabilized. He invites readings that are not familiar, so readers cannot get from him the certainty they feel with something more obviously familiar.

Many of the stories I heard about Miraji that seem to originate with and refer back to "Three Balls" do not keep sight of the paradoxical person Manto depicted; rather, they simplify Miraji into his "strangeness." In those Dionysian tales about Miraji that followed and relied on Manto's, Miraji became the object of a prurient desire for simple oddity; descriptions of Miraji in "Three Balls" provided a basis for later narratives in which Miraji was depicted as merely odd. Miraji's balls were the first signal and signifier of his "strangeness," but more signs rapidly followed: holy (Hindu) beads, long sinuous hair, and "French-cut" beard, all described in the biography penned by Manto. Unlike other biographers, however, Manto did not confine Miraji to a compendium of odd traits. Miraji's life-on-the-fringe paralleled his compatriots' who, like him, owned just one set of clothes that had to be stripped off at the launderer's to be washed. But Miraji, unlike his compatriots, exuded a quality of dervishness. For Manto, he was a mad saint whose strangeness was not merely attributable to bohemian worldliness (unlike other poets who shared the same characteristics); rather, it epitomized a kind of monkish austerity, an otherworldliness. Indeed, the spectral appearance Miraji made to his friend Yusuf Zafar at Mecca—although anomalous because Miraji was not a conventionally religious figure but a mystic alienated from religious conventions and institutions—was in keeping with his "monkishness."

Manto's evocation of Miraji stands in direct contradiction to Aijaz Ahmad's, not in the details, but in the relationship of story to person. The two biographers, at narrative poles from each other in explanations of their "subject's" peculiar habits, echo other storytellers. According to Ahmad, Miraji constructed stories about himself, lived them, and eventually by default and in confusion, collapsed story and self, actually *becoming* the stories he circulated. In contrast, Manto's stories were manifestations of the way Miraji really was; there was no discrepancy or distance between story and person. To Manto, Miraji was not the self-conscious, self-absorbed orchestrator of narratives about some lifestyle he then aspired to live; he was not a poseur saint, a man of the world in disguise, imitating his fellow poets who felt they had to look and act the part of wild bohemians—he was the "real thing." In short, one biographer depicts a wild man who, in a desperate attempt to make himself over as one, eventually forgot that he was *not* one and so betrayed his "true nature." [133] The other tells stories of a wild man who, in his wildness, remained true to his "authentic self." [134]

The two biographers resort to two entirely different taxonomies as they convert details into character. For Manto, Miraji is a dervish, a poet whose lineage stretches back into the eighteenth century, lost in *junūn*, the ecstatic madness of love and longing. For Ahmad, Miraji is merely a multiply signified disreputable man dressing up in the gestures codified in and elaborated by twentieth-century taxonomies of insanity, criminality, homelessness, and labor/class.

### *Bombay Stories: Poona Beginnings*

Miraji had been in Bombay for just a few weeks when Akhtarul Iman invited him to the mountains in Poona, where Iman had moved in 1944 to work at Shalimar Pictures as a scriptwriter. Shalimar was a small studio constantly on the verge of bankruptcy, so Akhtarul Iman and Miraji toyed with the idea of starting a small production company that would fill the niche Shalimar's closing would open. Both men traveled by train to Hyderabad for the big Progressive Writers' Association meeting in 1945 to elicit financing for their scheme.[135] The meeting was a difficult one for Miraji, not only because they found no funding, but also because it was the first time he was publicly ostracized by the community of writers to which he felt he belonged. At the meeting, several writers called for a resolution to condemn and disbar writers like Miraji, Manto, and Ismat Chughtai, whose writings were considered "obscene" and thus thought to contravene the aims of the PWA. Fortunately, a group of famous poets and fiction writers lobbied against the resolution and it was not passed. But from that point on, however, Miraji was fair game at Association meetings in Bombay.

*Onto Bombay*

Miraji was a difficult guest: he got drunk, peed out the window, and apparently also threw up regularly, upsetting Akhtarul Iman's servant with whom Miraji was left when Akhtarul Iman visited Bombay. So after nine to ten months Akhtarul Iman suggested he move to Bombay and stay with his friends, Mulk Raj Anand and Mohan Saigal, in Dadar (then the outskirts of the city). An argument over Mani Rabadi, a young actress, disrupted the arrangement and Miraji had to move again, this time to Esplanade Mansions in the Fort area in the heart of Bombay. He was given a script to write by Mulk Raj Anand and lived off that money for a little while.

Meanwhile, Shalimar Pictures finally closed after the main producer left for Pakistan as a result of partition. In the heat of the riots, Akhtarul Iman moved to Bombay. He was offered a house in Kala Ghoda by a friend who migrated to Pakistan. Akhtarul Iman offered the house to Madhusudan and Miraji, who lived together for a while. At that time Akhtarul Iman married Sultana Ali, whom he had met several years earlier when Sultana was thirteen and he and Miraji had visited Sultana's uncle, Asaf Ali, in Delhi. When her family fled Delhi for Pakistan in 1947, Akhtarul Iman wrote to her sister to send Sultana, who traveled to Bombay to be married. Following their wedding, the couple found a room in an apartment, where their first child was born. Akhtarul Iman's marriage prompted him to look for a permanent job; with help from his friends David and Anjum Naqvi, who had contacts in the film world, he was hired by Filmistan as a scriptwriter on a regular contract. With his new job, Akhtarul Iman began earning enough money to support his young family and move them from their single room to a new, small house they bought in Bandra. Akhtarul Iman settled Miraji in with his new family[136] because he was concerned about Miraji's failing health when Miraji had stopped eating and his body had become depleted by diarrhea.

That finances concerned Miraji is evident from the anxious budgets he kept drawing up; stories of his cavalier attitude toward money are both verified and belied by the careful budgets he endlessly scribbled with seeming carelessness on small pieces of paper, left among his effects when he died. Although he was not willing to compromise his principles to make the money he needed to survive, Miraji did make several attempts to earn an income. He sent a collection of his ghazals, *naẓm*, and *gīt* to Qayyum Nazar, a publication that raised enough money to support himself and Akhtarul Iman for several months. Akhtarul Iman also arranged for Miraji to interview with a movie producer who was looking for a writer. At the meeting, Miraji was asked to write a treatment for a script, but he was so incensed at having to generate writing on the spot like a trained animal that he scribbled a short poem and thrust it back at his interviewer. He did not get the job.

Although much of his life in Bombay was confused and confusing, Miraji established a regular, rigorous daily routine around his writing, reviving stories about the methodical editor of Lahore. Again he went to the library every day to read, find new books, or work on his poetry. Sheets of marked-up, annotated book advertisements and catalogues from local libraries and bookstores testify to his ongoing curiosity about a wide range of authors. He continued to write *naẓm*, and also took lessons to learn the words, rhythms, and meters of medieval Braj and Awadhi bhakti poetry in order to translate it into Urdu.

Miraji was almost obsessively particular about his poetry, scripting and signing each poem with a meticulous hand. He held onto early versions of his work even when he had a final draft. He kept updated lists of poems: where they were published and when, charts of poems collected into books and the categories into which they fell, alternatives for future manuscripts.

The poems he wrote in Bombay are some of his most lushly textured, densely synaesthetic, and beautiful, while also being among his most elegantly nuanced and simple. They roam the geography of desire and the terrain of philosophical speculation and certainty.

His papers also contain short schematic treatments of scripts he was trying to sell. Miraji revived his translations, embarking on three major projects—two on mystical poetry and a third on the complicated relationship between sexual and social mores and practices. As he familiarized himself with bhakti poetry, Miraji translated a set of poems attributed to Mirabai,[137] compiling them into a manuscript and drawing the frontispiece intended for publication. He also began translating the *Rubaiyāt* of Omar Khayyam; scrawled sideways on random pieces of paper, however, they were never polished like the verses of Mirabai. And he returned to *Eastern Love*, the anthology that had so inspired him. Miraji's drafts of *Nigār ḳhānah* (House of Portraits), a book about Malati, a young prostitute being introduced to the seamier side of her trade, originally written in Sanskrit by Damodar Gupta, are translated in the script of a large, casual hand that is at odds with the particular neatness of his other work.[138]

Miraji even made one foray into the movies with a walk-on part as a Brahmin priest, or pujari. Stills from the movie are among the few pictures of him at this time. One, a close-up, captures his ascetic tautness—wide jaws, narrow mouth draped by bushy mustache under sharply delineated nose. The slight frown settled between deep-set eyes evokes the sense of a capacity for intense concentration. A zigzag bandanna is tied a-tilt the top of his shoulder-length disheveled hair; hoop earrings hang from elongated, jutting ears; necklaces circle his lean throat—one with a small locket, the other a double string of beads.

In a second photo he sits cross-legged, bereft of his bandanna, framed by a hanging cloth. Skeletal arms extend forward, his hands hidden by a pujari's accoutrements—burning incense, fruit, flowers on metal plate, water pitcher—in front of him. The edge of the dhoti he wears peeks above the flat surface hosting the priestly paraphernalia. A mandala is drawn on his narrow chest. In the background, at the edge of the photograph, squats a *chārpai*, a frayed covering tossed over it.

The final picture of Miraji, taken just before his death, shows a more restrained, cleaned-up version of the movie pujari. Wearing a starched white shirt, wild curls pomaded into place, he stares out from a flat gray background. The movie stills embody the Miraji his biographers have chosen to depict, name, and identify—an emaciated, intense, ascetic figure. This photograph returns Miraji, from the figure cloaked in fantasy that one sees evoked by the movie stills, back to the ordinary.[139]

Just as Akhtarul Iman and his family were gaining financial stability, the producer of the movie Akhtarul Iman was writing the script for insulted him; he tore up his contract in front of the producer and stormed out of the studio. Sultana said that this early time in Bombay was one of their most difficult periods. She had left Delhi to live as a young bride in a foreign city, bereft of her familial support network. She and her husband had just purchased a house and needed enough money for a baby and a dependent—Miraji. No longer assured of a constant income, they had to survive on the scattered offers for writing that came her husband's way.

In another attempt to raise money, Miraji and Akhtarul Iman started, with the financial backing of a young entrepreneur named Nigam, the bimonthly literary journal *Ḳhayāl* (Thought). Sixty-seven issues of it were published. Akhtarul Iman says that he paid Miraji one hundred rupees a month for his services as chief editor.[140] The fairly extensive "board of advisors" the three men put together for the journal included several members of the Progressive Writers' Association—among them, Zoe Ansari. The all-out war that the Bombay chapter of the Association had declared on Miraji after the Hyderabad meetings resonated in gatherings of the journal board.[141] When, at Akhtarul Iman's behest, I asked Zoe Ansari about Miraji, he talked about the remorse he felt when he remembered his own treatment of Miraji before he died.[142] Miraji's translation of *Nigār ḳhānah* was serialized in several early issues of *Ḳhayāl*. When the first installment of Miraji's translation appeared in the journal, it incited the ire of the PWA in Bombay, which then devoted a meeting to Miraji's "pointless" reactionary text. Following a heated discussion, the members decided to demand that the translation no longer be published by *Ḳhayāl* and asked Zoe Ansari to hand in his resignation from the board if the journal continued to serialize the translation. Zoe said that, in retrospect, he believed the active exclusion and anger against Miraji was a direct reflection of Miraji's unofficial banishment from Bombay's literary scene.

The next meeting of *Ḳhayāl* was at Akhtarul Iman's house. Zoe Ansari attacked Miraji, insulted his work, and insisted that the journal refuse to publish Miraji thereafter. Miraji was apparently very gracious. He questioned Zoe gently about his criticisms and tried to engage him in a conversation about what had made him so furious. The room fell silent as the two men conversed, one more and more heated, the other quietly patient. As the conversation drew to a close, Miraji indicated that if Zoe felt so strongly about the piece, the journal should not continue to serialize it. Zoe told me that he was appalled by his own cruelty during that discussion. Years later, he still regretted his part in ostracizing Miraji, preventing the publication of his work, and cutting off Miraji's access to a community from which he obviously drew sustenance. Zoe's greatest remorse was over his own refusal to acknowledge Miraji's remarkable capacity to encourage and support even violent, violating discussions about his work without rancor or retaliation. But at the time Miraji was, to him, merely a deviant.[143]

This form of ostracism was difficult for Miraji. When he first appeared on Lahore's literary scene, he was the hub of a network of literati. During that period, poets of many different literary and political persuasions shared common spaces where they exchanged work and engaged in critiques of one another's writing, the Halqa being one such site. Over the years, Miraji's literary community stood in for his family, because unlike many other poets, he had not created a conventional family by marriage to replace his family in Lahore; instead, his friends and compatriots supported and sustained him. Akhtarul Iman said that during this time, as Miraji began to feel the loss of his alternate family of friends, he fantasized about returning to Lahore to visit his mother, whom he loved dearly. He applied for a passport and kept it with him, always hoping that he would see her. Although he never managed to collect enough money to pay for a ticket, until his death he held onto the possibility that he might return.

It is important to remember that Miraji's ostracism was not necessarily "personal," although the rhetoric in which it was couched might lead one to believe that such was the case. But he was not the only writer subjected to this kind of treatment by the PWA—Manto and Ismat Chughtai were also persecuted. The harassment constituted a systematic exclusion and marginalization by the organization of particular kinds of writing, and the modes through which the exclusion occurred and the rhetoric that was used to underpin the strategies of exclusion intersected with those employed by the state.[144] That Manto and Ismat Chughtai were recipients of the same kind of treatment allows one to think about Miraji's situation in the context of a more extensive set of shifts in the literary world. Unlike Lahore in the 1930s, when the demarcations of literary stances were not so acute, the late 1940s produced sharp divisions between differing political and literary positions. Miraji made it clear by his behavior at meetings that he did not endorse or follow those demarcations. The boundaries the PWA established for those writers who belonged and those who did not were marked by their attitudes to writers like Manto, Chughtai, and Miraji. Inevitably these boundaries were negotiated in terms of writing about sexuality; that is, the PWA used their "sexual" themes as the reason for their exclusion. That three writers, whose writing differed as greatly from each other as theirs did, were chosen to mark the limits of inclusion for literary communities that considered themselves central says more about those limits than it does about the position of any one writer in relation to an imaginary center.

The rhetoric that was deployed in the 1940s to eject Miraji from the literary community to which he felt he belonged had certain ramifications on the stories that were told about him and those that were considered by his biographers to be paradigmatic. One example is the insistence on telling the story about Mira Sen as the only love story in Miraji's life, an act that effectively, though inadvertently, suppressed others. In a way, the Mira Sen stories become allegorical, explaining Miraji's name and his inability to find a conventional married relationship. At the same time, the Mira Sen tales resonate with the unrequited love that is "conventional" for classical Urdu poetry, thus provoking the same questions about the simultaneity of convention and the repudiation of it that haunts all of the stories about Miraji.

Although he played a part in the circulation of the Mira Sen stories as exemplary of his life, Miraji also told others that would, if added to the tales of thwarted love, produce a slightly different picture of his desires. The other love stories come from two different times in Miraji's life. One I have told before—Miraji's attraction to Bashir in Lahore, to whom Miraji wrote letters as he was also writing to Mira Sen. Another was told to me by Akhtarul Iman when I asked him about an autographed photograph of an actress we came across as we went through Miraji's papers together.

One afternoon in Bombay, Miraji had gone to the home of a friend

(Akhtarul Iman would not disclose the friend's name) to discuss poetry. An actress, Mani Rabadi, in whom Miraji's friend was "interested"—possibly even in love with—happened to be there. The three sat drinking tea and talking. Mani Rabadi began to haunt Miraji's imagination; he tried to pursue her, but without success. She never occupied his fantasy life in the way that Mira or Bashir did, but he developed an obsession for her and kept her photograph with him until he died.[145]

## CONCLUSION: TALES FROM THE CRYPT

### *Premature Burial*

"Where did he die? How?" I asked Akhtarul Iman.[146] I had been offered stories that had been circulated over and over, turned into hagiography, those that had appeared in writing and now in interviews. They began with Miraji's literary birth in Lahore and rapidly descended into descriptions of his degeneration. In his last weeks Miraji was remembered by many people as a body in decay—his difference articulated as disintegration. He became a body that peed and vomited in public places, a body that deteriorated into mania. Miraji was described to me in his final moments as a drunk by Shahid Ahmad Dihlavi; a junkie high on bhang by Manto; a person whose death seemed imminent when he could not control his urge to excrete by Akhtarul Iman. I wanted to hasten the telling of those stories of ever-impending death, to propel them toward conclusion.

The room was thick with the premonsoon heat as I asked questions of Akhtarul Iman, who, tired and ill, was stretched on a divan across from me and my mother in his rectangular Bombay drawing room, his face reflecting the yellow wide-weave cotton of the divan. He responded in his quiet, modulated voice.

"[Miraji] was so ill when we decided to put him into Bombay Hospital . . . he couldn't even make it to the bathroom. Sultana had to clean up after him all the time. His doctor was a fan of his, read a lot of his poetry. It was so ironic that the same doctor was probably responsible for his death. . . .

"He was reading a biography of Baudelaire when he died."

In my imagination I placed Miraji in a monastic garret; a stark, unadorned hospital room. I visualized a pallet, a steel frame, a square headboard constructed from metal tubes. Miraji was emaciated, flattened against a thin, hard, cotton mattress. As the afternoon heat dissipated into cool clamminess, I attenuated the body I saw in photographs to suit the image that occupied the fantasy.

"Did you know that he had electroshock therapy?" Akhtarul Iman asked.

"Why? Aren't electroshock treatments for the insane?" I heard the metallic edge of anxiety in my voice.

"Well, he was so, so sick. The doctor thought that it was the best thing. No one really knew what to do; it seemed right. He was such a difficult patient. He wasn't going to live long. His intestines were perforated and his liver was completely gone. He would steal food, have people hide food for him while he was in the hospital, and drink, too. Then he bit his nurse on her hand. I tried to tell him not to do it. I said to him, humoring him, wanting him to stop, 'Don't do it, she's pretty.' But it didn't work.

"Miraji didn't want the treatments; he begged and begged us not to allow them. He was afraid he would never be able to write again if he had shock therapy. He died the first time he was given the shocks. The very first time. The doctor told me that Miraji was so terrified they had to strap him down to a stretcher to get him out of his room to give him the shock therapy that killed him."

"How did you hear about his death?" I asked, biting lightly into the spicy sharp *bhatorā* that Sultana had placed in front of me. My mother touched my arm. I had forgotten that she was in the room with me, sitting on the sofa. The tape squealed and snapped to a halt. I flipped it over, clicked the recorder to restart.

"I was drinking tea, just like this, with Sultana. The hospital called and I was told that Miraji had died, during his first therapy. I remember the time—it was four o'clock on November third or the second, 1949. I told the hospital to dispose of the body. But I called back the next day. I took possession of Miraji's body and arranged for a funeral for that day, November third. Then I called everyone I knew, poets and writers, to attend the funeral.

"Do you know, no one wanted to come. I couldn't even find pallbearers. None of the people he had known, all those people, not one wanted to join me to carry Miraji's coffin to the grave. Eventually I found three other people: Krishan Chandar, Mahindarnath, and Nigam. We—two Hindus and two Muslims—carried him to his grave. Miraji was buried at the Marine Lines Graveyard. His grave doesn't have a headstone. You'll never find it."

"Why didn't anyone come to Miraji's funeral?"

Akhtarul Iman's voice trembled and tightened with grief and rage as we closed our conversation on Miraji's death. "Bombay was responsible for his demise. He was ostracized here. The way he was treated was terrible. It still makes me angry that everyone abandoned him.

"This is the legacy I want to leave behind. You know that I had a difficult time with him, but I would have never wanted this, that his body, his grave have no meaning. If I say nothing more, I'd like you to tell people about what his end, the loneliness was like. . . . That no one wanted to carry his corpse to rest and no one attended the funeral."

*Dying Twice*

> . . . a death given, the gift of a death that arrives in one way but not another.[147]

> Love sees no difference (Love's glance sees nothing between) between life and death
> the one who we live to see,
> she, faithless heathen, brings us to our death.
>
> Muhabbat meñ nahiñ hai farq jīne aur marne kā
> usī ko dekh kar jīte haiñ, jis kāfir par dam nikle.[148]

The following is the account of Miraji's death that Akhtarul Iman committed to print. It now stands as the authoritative version. My translation condenses Akhtarul Iman's essay, but holds onto his language.[149]

> After Miraji moved in with me, he stopped producing blood almost entirely. He put himself on homeopathy for two or three months. I badly wanted him to try other medicines, but my proposals made him furious. He kept on getting worse. I had to overcome my response to his rage. At last, in desperation, I, on the advice of some doctors, got him to agree to other remedies. Only after I went over it time and again, did he finally accept that without medicines he would never be able to move around easily; he believed that if he were mobile, he might return to Lahore for proper care.

Some doctors I consulted had Miraji start a course of liver injections. He tried to get a permit [to go to Lahore], even took photographs of himself. Whenever he felt slightly healthier, and it was suggested to him that he go to the permit office, he would put off the trip. The liver injections help, they do not cure. I have no idea where he got this, but he came to believe fervently that the more he ate, the faster he would recover, and the more effective the injections would be. We turned into adversaries. I would recommend abstinence, moderation. He would slip off to the food vendors in the market downstairs and glut himself on everything that had been forbidden him. I would offer injunctions to the sick, tell my wife to keep an eye on him; she'd soothe him, he'd get angry, consume the food that had been cooked at home and then order up a parcel of apples to eat. His illness was in its final stages.

I quickly admitted him to a hospital in Bandra. But there he brought the other patients and the people working in the local restaurant around to his way of seeing, and persuaded patients who were in better health than him to give up their meals to him.

When Dr. Faruqi, the chief resident, and I found this out we were furious. We transferred him to King Edward Memorial Hospital. After a few days there, his mental state began to deteriorate. Dr. Kirodar called on an expert psychologist, who put Miraji in analysis. But Miraji refused to divulge most of his history. When I confronted him, he got angry at me, saying, "Akhtar! Listen, these people want to extract my complexes, steal my complexes from me. I don't want to let them. I won't let it happen. If I lose them, how can I write, what will I write. They are the substance of my creativity."

I tried and tried to convince him, but he remained adamant. Dr. Kirdar felt that electroshock therapy might work better. But there was no opportunity to try it.

Miraji needed blood transfusions; Mahindarnath gave him blood, but the possibility of workable cures was fading, and the transfusion was wasted. It did not help Miraji.

I went to visit him at the hospital every day. My wife often came along. Madhusudan and Mahindarnath would come. He would complain to each person in turn—I am being given this, but not given that. We did everything we could to save him, but he refused to come along.

It was the night of November third. I was eating dinner. A telegram arrived from the hospital. I abandoned my food, and rushed to the hospital with Nijam Naqvi and my brother-in-law. I gazed at Miraji's corpse. On his face was dignity, love, innocence, composure, peace, tranquility. I could not believe that he was gone.

Miraji will never leave us. He'll stay with us; write letters to you when he comes back, stop suddenly while strolling along to phone a newspaper office. I went there myself the next day and tried hard, but partisanship had taken them over, the thick cloaking dust of fantasized animosity had hidden their humanness from them.

You must have known how many people attended Miraji's funeral, held in such a crowded city like Bombay: just four. My brother-in-law, Madhusudan, Prem, and I. Miraji was buried in the Marine Lines Graveyard.

His books, his papers, his essays, finished and unfinished. These few things he left behind. They are with me. I had them brought to me from Fort. His famous books are in the Halqa's caretaking. Miraji penned in every book himself, "for the *Ḥalqah-e arbāb-e ẕauq*." When I was able, I sent those books off.

Qayyum! You didn't get to see him before he died. He was so reduced, looking at him was painful. He'd pray: "God, if you won't give Miraji his health, grant him death. At least he won't have to suffer so."

His face, hands, feet, back were coated in inflamed tumors. In his last days he read *Defeat of Baudelaire*. He had taken the book with him to the hospital. It kept him company until he died.

I want to write a complete, full, book on him, replete with details. *Ḳhayāl*, the journal, died with Miraji."

Akhtarul Iman died in 1994.

# *Two* LITERARY MOVEMENTS: MARGINS AND CENTERS

Ḥaqīqat parastī jadīd pasandī [1]

Loving reality, liking newness

# 2. THE TERMS OF THE ENCOUNTER: MIRAJI AND THE PROGRESSIVE WRITERS' ASSOCIATION

When Miraji first appeared on the literary scene in Lahore as a young avant-garde poet, the literary milieu of Urdu was in flux. The newly emerging Progressive movement, solidified through the Progressive Writers' Association (PWA), was to become the most viable literary organization of the 1930s and 1940s. Although its tenets had Marxist undertones, not all of its members were explicitly communist; in this early stage, when its membership was not determined by political affiliation, many Urdu writers, like N. M. Rashid, Manto, and Akhtarul Iman, were still connected with it.

Miraji can be seen as a "member" of several different groups, and his membership in any one group does not automatically exclude him from any other. Although he was gradually marginalized within a community that came to consider itself *the* dominant literary community in Urdu, he can be said to belong to a world of poets suffused with cultural capital that can be fit into an economically determined class structure. As a paid editor on nationally recognized magazines and journals, and as an occasional employee of All-India Radio in Delhi, Miraji can also be considered part of the urban indigenous colonial elite. His place in any of these categories—"cultural" community, economic class, colonial elite—is not fixed, but changes both with his personal history and the historical transformation of the communities in which he participated. Because of his family history, Miraji started out middle class, but once he left home he repudiated most of the conventions that would have codified him as a member of that class—property of any kind, stable housing, a wife, or associations with his extended family. So the position to which he can be assigned varies, depending on perspective and historical location. He is simultaneously marginal *and* privileged, as much a part of a gallery of indigent colonial rogues as a member of a colonial elite.

In the 1930s and early 1940s, when Miraji lived and worked in Lahore as the editor of the literary journal *Adabī duniyā*, he was at the zenith of his influence. As the nucleus of a great deal of literary activity, his literary prose, criticism, and poetry were more widely disseminated and central to this community than to any subsequent one. He helped bring to prominence an informal circle of writers who met to read, recite, and discuss Urdu literature—the *Ḥalqah-e arbāb-e ẕauq*.[2] The membership of the Halqa intersected with that of the PWA and included among its attendees such Progressive writers as Krishan Chandar and Rajindar Singh Bedi; indeed, the range of writers who attended its sessions points to the shifting boundaries of the literary community and the multiple allegiances of its members. Over time, and with the approach of independence, the modernists (*jadīdiyāt*) embodied by the Halqa separated out from the Progressives (*taraqqī pasand*) who belonged almost exclusively to the PWA. But when the organizations were first formed, their members floated between the two, participating actively in both. Their attendances seemed to satisfy the promises and alliances formed through friendship and respect. Members collaborated over the vexed terrain of what constituted *jadīdiyāt* and *tāzagī*, newness in its most expansive literary sense, grappling sometimes together and sometimes separately with *taḥrīk-e taraqqī* (the movement of progress). In his analyses of *jadīdiyāt*, Miraji uses *taraqqī* and newness in this looser sense, not giving over to the movements' names, and holds *haqīqat parast* (social realist) aside to describe writers he felt were in thrall to a certain project of mimesis. But when the history of the Halqa (or of the PWA) is told in retrospect, different narrators describe the membership—and thus the aims of the organization—differently, and anachronistically, based on their own historical entanglements with it. Some Progressives see the Halqa as an organization that was formed in opposition to the PWA, while writers like Rashid see it as a composite, loosely organized, nonaffiliationist group.[3]

The domain in which I place Miraji is a fluid one, formed at the intersections of local/pan-Indian, explicitly/implicitly colonial, and social formations/institutional structures. I wish to define "local" here very specifically and in contradistinction to "local" understood as the geographically mapped locale, the neighborhood that one can point to along a spatial axis. This use of "local" places a group in terms of its geographic location,[4] local group, local community, and is usually contrasted with alliances formed across wider spaces, whether these be literal or fantasmatic. I write of Miraji as though he "belonged" to a specialized (local) community of self-defined urban literati who produced work in Urdu. If "local" is linguistically defined in opposition to rather than in conflation with geography, then people who share language, write in it, publish in it, and form an imagined community across space, across cities, across different locales, can perhaps be said to partake of a local community. This community is local, precisely because it is not the same as the national (multilingual/dominant lingual). As a participant in a group of people who published across South Asia in Urdu, who struggled to settle the civilities of literary societies, who transformed the texture of their common language in print, radio, and film, then Miraji can be considered part of a localized elite community.

Though Urdu writers during this time wrote in Urdu literary journals produced for general, "popular" consumption, in considering this group and Miraji as a part of it, I will be looking at them as their own implied audience that formed a partially closed, semipermeable literary network. In my reading of articles that Miraji published in a range of journals from *Adabī duniyā* to *Sāqī*, I find that the questions raised and issues addressed were targeted at a specialized Urdu literati audience. The journals might have been freely available, but they appeared to speak to and for a specific group. Miraji and the Urdu writers with whom he fraternized from the late 1930s to the middle 1940s also belonged to self-selecting literary clubs like the *Ḥalqah-e arbāb-e ẕauq* in Lahore and Delhi, which relied on word-of-mouth dissemination of their activities and whose new members were explicitly brought to meetings and introduced by the constituted membership. Although these clubs might represent themselves as open, they were, in practice, closed, bound within the intimate alliances that brought them into being and expanded their memberships.[5]

Writing for and publishing in journals, publishing books, and the conversations and readings in the provenance of literary clubs occurred under colonial conditions. The above venues responded to these conditions and had been palimpsestically imprinted by long histories of translation from and into English, by a long history of transformed education, but they were not explicitly conducted for the British. The production of text and voice in these venues was *indirectly* responsive to colonial conditions, unlike the material produced for radio stations, for example, which conformed more obviously to the exigencies of a colonial institution. So my use of the term "local" also identifies the locale or locality in which a group of people operated in terms of their relationship to British institutions. "Local" conditions, then, are those in which a group or groups acted, performed, and produced material ostensibly for themselves, with the British operating at the margins of that production.

Alongside this kind of "localized" activity, many members of the Halqa and organizations like the Progressive Writers' Association were also working and writing for institutions that were explicitly colonial and pan-Indian, although the hierarchy of control and conditions of production were more complicated than an attenuated reading of a colonial institution might warrant.[6] Miraji and other members of his circle wrote to and for and traveled between and settled in a series of urban centers: Lahore, Delhi, Bombay, and Hyderabad. These itinerant, diasporic intellectuals followed patronage systems and worked for British-funded institutions like All-India Radio in Delhi, as well as various indigenously funded ones like the film industry in Poona and Bombay.[7]

Before I continue the discussion on Miraji, it would be useful to focus on the group called the Progressives, to delineate some of their explicit aims and strategies. In addition, I would like to discuss the ways in which Miraji, as an ancillary member of this community, allied and differentiated himself from them, and how his position contributed to his marginalization.

## THE PROGRESSIVES

In this section I will outline the contours of the literary movement aligned with the Progressive Writers' Association, focusing mainly on the

Urdu chapter of the organization. This movement provided a context for Miraji, who, as a writer, was both included in and subsequently marginalized by the Progressives, so my discussion of the Urdu chapter of the movement is oriented/angled toward situating Miraji.

I am concerned here with the modes through which a literary "movement" comes to be fixed and marked off, the ways in which discourses of authorization get cemented as "value" as a community forms. I concentrate, in other words, on questions of who is authorized to speak in the name of a movement as a "Progressive," which rhetorical strategies embolden this speaking, how the movement is defined, and who controls its definition. Therefore, I also deal with the concomitant procedures for inclusion in and exclusion from a literary movement while it is in the process of formation. My interest lies in the "problem" areas, the nodes around which discussions take place, where questions on value get asked and how they are seemingly resolved or supposedly abandoned—the relationship of a writer to politics, form to content, language to objects of study, mimesis to representation, past to present.

As the movement became more and more central to the performance of literary activity in Urdu, the practices of that one community became norms specified for literary activity in general. The issue of assigning value to a literary work tied simultaneously into questions of reading and writing. Certain strategies for reading became ordinary, seemed inevitable. Works were written and read in conformity with those norms—this, despite the ways that writing always exceeded the proprieties enacted in readings of them.

The process of canon formation is often aligned with the language of colonization and state formation. Urdu canons have formed and reconstituted themselves as matrices of transformation shifting through disjunct alliances. Literature had to come into view in the spacings between "literature" as all forms of textuality; literature as those forms of textuality that told and embodied national "racialized" character; genres of textuality that were marked off into a particular domain that constituted the literary as against sorts of writing and speaking that were sent off, for example, into the historical, the improperly lyrical or mythic, the religious (poetry, fiction, theater, etc.).[8] Along with this, Orientalists like Sir William Jones figured texts that were carried "home" from the colonies in translation as booty, in relation to their transformatory worth, excess capital, their value told by their ability to buy/enact change. Jones began the process of discriminating texts from one another based on erratic and necessary (racinated) criteria of worth. Some of his criteria, offered Anglicist-Utilitarians like James Mill and Thomas Macaulay the guidelines to distinguish what they believed could be salvaged and what could not, and the gauges that began to determine what might fall into different "fields" or perhaps what might determine textures of writing (both valorized and disenfranchised): science, law, mythos, history, poetry.[9] Since the eighteenth century, forms of Urdu prose commentaries and collections developed and disbursed within limited "publics," the community of writers and composers in the know, "prescriptive guidelines for judging the correctness and aesthetic status of the language."[10] By the mid-nineteenth century this collation of proper writing, and its right, rigorous corrections, *iṣlāḥ*, had been taken into a different realm by Altaf Husain Hali and Azad. Correction was organized around the intent of writing: to reform the populace at large and Muslim communities in particular. Hali and Azad spoke to the problem of the poetic, taking recourse in some of the critiques that had been handed down through figures like Mill and Macaulay. They were aware of new forms of patronage that institutionalized forms of knowing and knowledge (through the vernaculars), as well as told the proper, the civil, the civilized through law and through state formations (what was deemed immoral, and hence improper was that which fell into the provenance of the illegal). Canonization began to accrue the rhetoric of "pathologization" in the twentieth century.

Miraji, someone who struggled with questions of exclusion, was also someone who, through his essays on poetry (like eighteenth-century commentators, and Hali and Azad), helped draw the contours of a canon of literature in Urdu. By the time he began writing and composing, literary canons in Urdu had clearly demarcated conditions for inclusion that resembled some of the ways in which the literary is now conceived: as poetry, as fiction, as theater, as folk song, and so on. The shifts in what fitted into the canon, as well as who was pulled into the canon, continued to account for the relationship between the literary (writing, recitation, and radio broadcasts) and national formations to be, as well as state-mandated (through law) regulations of the proper, the civil, the ordinary, and the abnormal. Improvement of the *socius*, the newly voting future citizen, the colonized who needed salvation—as the mandates that ought to summon literary works into being, and that began to be instituted in those forms in the nineteenth century—persevered into the twentieth.

Exclusion from the community of Progressives became synonymous with punishment and exile. The processes of exclusion from a community of writers echo the structures of trials and pogroms. Works were understood as activities and were to be fitted into a moral and formal taxonomy that reigned supreme. When works could not be made to conform, the machinery of rejection labeled, libeled, and ejected them—and occasionally expulsed the writer at the same time.[11] The machinery of ejection was organized around certain rhetorical alliances, legal, psychological, medical that were deployed against either the work or the writer. The rhetoric deployed, however, did not necessarily offer the set of circumstances that pushed the work or the writer out.

The PWA grew into one of the most extensive pan-Indian literary organizations; with chapters in many states, it addressed the concerns of languages as diverse as Gujarati and Malayalam. In June 1939, just a year after the PWA's inaugural conference in Lucknow, G. T. Madkholkar's presidential address at the first Madhya Pradesh Marathi Conference echoed Premchand's: "the purpose of literature is not entertainment and repetition of experience, but enlightenment and new experience."[12] The incredible proliferation of "socialist influenced literature" from the 1930s on attests to the success of the PWA: In Marathi (P. Deshpande, Mama Varerkar), Sindhi (Lekhraj Kishin Chand, essayist M. V. Malkani), Oriya (Ananda Patnaik, Kalindi Charan Panigrahi, Mayadhar Mansingh), Malayalam (K. Damodaran, P. Keshav Dev), Telegu (Sri Sri, N. C. Ranga).[13] Hindi fiction saw loosely socialist writing by Ramnarayan Pathak and Sanat Vin; and the Chayavad movement in poetry pressed by the *pratigvādīs* (Progressives) saw new poetry by Nirala in 1938 and by Sumitranandan Pant.[14]

The most influential chapter of the organization was the Urdu chapter, called, not surprisingly, the Urdu Progressive Writers' Association; indeed, many accounts of the Progressive movement conflate the Urdu chapter with the entire movement. At its inception, the concerns of many PWA members overlapped with extant political organizations like the Indian National Congress (Congress) and the Communist Party of India (CPI). Although the PWA was not affiliated with any one political organization, many of its members were active members of the Communist Party of

India, and as the movement aged and expanded, its ties to the Communist Party grew—so much so that it was eventually called "the most important front organization created for specific professional groups by the Communist Party of India."[15] Ahmad Ali, who had been involved with the PWA in its early stages, has said that the shift toward a more explicitly communist alignment occurred between 1931 and 1939. He located one important moment of this shift in the Village Poets Convention on May 14–15, 1938. At that meeting the problems and differences between what he called the political faction (associated with the CPI) and the nonpolitical faction (noncommunist) created an explicit rupture in the organization.[16]

The exact connections between the PWA and CPI were/are, I think, not important. What I do think is important is that the representation of the PWA, in tandem with its self-representation, points to the integral connections made by them between literary and political activity in India in the 1930s and 1940s. The understanding and definition of "the literary" and its conjunctions with "the political" were being disputed in the 1930s. In the process, the meanings of "political" and "literary" turned into contested fields. The agon over the meanings was won in the late 1930s by the PWA, enabling it to control and patrol the signification of the two areas and force them into essentialized categories.[17] This is not to say that the two categories (political and literary) were directly synonymous or completely mapped onto one another. Indeed, not all literati defined themselves as politically active and many politicos were certainly not engaged in literary production. Nevertheless the two activities were intimately connected, and a particular definition of political engagement through literature came to be one of the theoretical credos of a major—if not *the* major—literary movement in Urdu.

## HISTORY OF THE PWA: SPECIFICS

Aag dekho, pānī dekho aur añgāre dekho

Whenever histories of the PWA are written, the beginnings of the movement are located in a set of events: the publication of a controversial collection of short stories called *Añgāre* (Embers) and the overwhelming response to it.[18] *Añgāre* was written, edited, and published by a group of four writers—Sajjad Zahir, Ahmad Ali, Rashid Jahan, and Mahmud uz-Zafar—who were credited with the inception of the PWA, and who continued to be involved with the movement to varying degrees. The collection was published in 1932 or 1933 with funds provided by Sajjad Zahir.[19] Although it seems that the writers were aware that their collection would provoke a response from conservative Muslims, they did not anticipate the extent of that reaction. *Añgāre* incited a widespread outcry from many quarters, both religious and secular. Even writers who believed that the response of religious leaders to the collection was unfortunately excessive subscribed to the same critique of *Añgāre*: that it was "nakedly vulgar," that it lampooned daily social evils, that it elaborated psychological depravities. It was eventually banned ("every copy forfeited") by the Uttar Pradesh (UP) state government, under section 295A of the Indian penal code (Act XLV 1860): "Whoever with deliberate and malicious intention of outraging the religious feelings of any class of His Majesty's subjects, by words, either spoken or written, or by visible representations insults or attempts to insult the religion or the religious beliefs of that class, shall be punished with imprisonment of either description for a term which may extend to two years, or with fine, or with both." The police department notice on March 15, 1933, sites the four authors, the publisher (Zahir again), and the printer, Mirza Muhammad Jawal, and the book is registered in May of that quarter on the list of proscribed publications for UP under section 99A, along with Congress bulletins in English and Hindi; an Urdu poster; copies of the Hindi news sheet "Shankh Nad," and a Hindi short story collection, "Samar yātrā aur anya kahāniyāñ."[20] *Añgāre* was pulled from shelves for "hurting the religious susceptibilities of a section of a community" even as the second civil disobedience movement was winding down; repression against it having escalated and become much more methodical.

Some of the stories in the collection, Ahmad Ali's and Sajjad Zahir's, are said to violate the accepted formal and technical norms of fiction established for Urdu (primarily by Munshi Premchand) because they were written as stream of consciousness and interior monologues. Zahir's story "Nīñd nahīñ ātī" (Sleep does not come)—which takes a reader into the protagonist's mind with a string of alliterative drumming sounds that is followed by "darkness, darkness, darkness. My eyes opened a moment later, the whiteness of the pillowcase dark, but not entirely black . . ."—simulates the lambent measures one sees in Miraji's poetry. But such transgressions of the formal, technical rules for fiction writing were not the main focus of the criticism. The reaction to *Añgāre* seems to have stemmed in part from a conservative Muslim community's response to a particularly egregious segment in the story *Jannat kī baṣārat* (Vision of heaven).

This story by Zahir lampoons sanctimonious religious propriety, depicting the predicament of a pious Maulana who, having spurned the sexual advances of his young nubile wife (by invoking a litany of corrupt seductresses like Eve and Zulaikha), falls asleep to a dream of a paradise populated by voluptuously naked houris offered him by God and wakes up to his wife's laughter to find that the houri he is fondling is in fact the Koran. Like some of Zahir's other stories, this one also turns toward the night. Darkness bares that part of a self which has been repudiated during a day regulated by the repetition of rules (play with *sijdah*) that order morality. Dreams in that dark embody the return to desires cloaked by propriety and held at bay. The Koran that gifts the Maulana with thc list of temptresses he uses to ward off sex (in its proper place) also grants him a heaven that releases his pleasure in an improper place.

The responses to *Añgāre* mirrored the intimacies portrayed in it. Irate readers delved into feeling to craft recriminations. One traces his journey into moral certainty starting with his first sighting of the book in the university book depot. He opens the troubling book diligently and finds his mind melting into fire and his eyes closing/shutting down. He takes to his bed in a turmoil, darkness shadowing his heart's flurried anxiety. As his mind and heart stills to silence he frames a response: the book cannot damage Islam (which is the light that fights tyranny), but the authors need stern guidance bolstered by self-recognizance. The book is mired in trivialities, but it should be banned. Possessing it is a crime, and Islam must be paid obeisance.[21] The subsequent valuation of the book and the way it has been read is framed by rebuttals like this one.[22]

Although the book has been given a preeminent/primordial place in the PWA's history, the priority it is accorded is undermined by phrases like "not a great piece of literature."[23] This kind of qualification continues to control the way *Añgāre* is read, even when it is described in "pro-Progressive" literary histories, and provides more information about the norms for judging "good" literature that were subscribed to by literati during this period than it serves as a "universal" critical tool through which one can read the book.

On April 5, 1933, five months after *Añgāre* was published, Mahmud uz-Zafar and Ahmad Ali retaliated. "In Defense of 'Angarey' [*sic*]: Shall We Submit to Gagging," their article in the *Leader*, a journal out of Allahabad, took on the virulence of the attacks against them:

> The book . . . raised a storm in Moslem circles . . . a shameless attack on Islam and everything decent in society. . . . [An author] believes that his ideas are sturdy enough to fight their own way . . . the world is not composed of madmen and hooligans . . . that is why he takes all the trouble to give some order and sequence to his ideas and put them in a simple and intelligent way. . . . I am surprised to find . . . that an author cannot take all this for granted, that what he says in straightforward language is met with furious and unintelligent abuse and even threats of violence, and all this from those very people whom he had all along considered would be the best qualified by their training and professions to give him the most intelligent hearing. . . . If their [theologians, professors, public men and journalists] reply to new ideas is a resort to scurrilous abuse or to violence or to gagging, it augurs ill for the society they pretend to lead. . . . Socrates was put to death . . . Christ was crucified . . . Mohammad forced to flee . . . It was a matter of opinion whether the Socratic aspect of life was correct. . . . We are supposed to consider today that both opinions and facts should receive the serious and intelligent attention . . . of our friends or our opponents. It is a matter of opinion whether the theist or the atheistic aspect of the world is correct, it is matter of fact that our women are oppressed and our sexual practices are out of harmony with the requirements of our social life. Yet these opinions and the revelation of these facts must remain sealed. . . . A doctor of medicine is supposed to be a man of authority in his line, yet nobody minds whether we prefer modern scientific medicine, or Ayurvedic, or even our own quack remedies. Moreover we are allowed to express our opinions freely about these things in the medical line . . . to practice the most grotesque of operations on friends and relatives. But a doctor of theology is a different person altogether. Nobody is allowed to question his profession or his practices. . . . Sajjad Zaheer . . . is concerned chiefly

> with a criticism and a satire of the current Moslem conceptions, life and practices. His attack is directed primarily against the intolerable theological burden that is imposed from childhood upon the average Moslem in this country—a burden that leads to a contortion and a cramping, an internal torture of the inquisitive or speculative mind and the vital vigorous body, of both man and woman. Ahmad Ali essays into the realm of poverty, . . . especially the poverty of the Moslem woman, and with imagination and admirable boldness breaks through the veils of convention to expose the stark and loathsome reality. Rashid Jehan, who is also a doctor of medicine, drawing on her practical experience, also portrays vividly the ghastly plight of the woman behind the pardah. . . . The standard criticism leveled against the book so far, is in our opinion extraordinarily low . . . bears out the judgement of the authors that present-day Moslem society is ignorant, rotten and decaying. In the peroration of one "review" we are reminded of the Rajpal and the Rangila Rasool case . . . resort[ing] to rough play [and not answering us directly, prove] that religion is ultimately based not on intelligent consent but on abject fear of force. . . . The authors of this book do not wish to make any apology for it. . . . They only wish to defend "the right of launching it and all other vessels like it" . . . stand for the right of free criticism and free expression in all matters of the highest importance to the human race in general and the Indian people in particular. They have chosen the particular field of Islam, not because they bear it any special malice, but because, being born into that particular society, they felt themselves better qualified to speak for that alone. They were more sure of their ground there, but they hope that others of other faiths will come forward and boldly express their opinions, exposing the contradictions and the injustice in their own systems. . . . [T]he time has come . . . to struggle for the right of freedom of expression. Our practical proposal is the formation immediately of a League of Progressive authors, which should bring forth similar collections from time to time, both in English and in the various vernaculars.[24]

This was the first occasion that "Progressive" writers were named in a public forum. The implicit terms of engagement between the authors of *Añgāre* and their critics elucidate the nexus of topics that later became the explicit platform of the PWA. The discussion took place over the definition of "appropriate" literary activity. In publishing *Añgāre* and defending it under the "right of free expression," the writers were calling for their right to define literary activity. The battle was conducted over both the meaning of literary activity and authority; that is, what it was and who would patrol the boundaries and enforce the rules. The call by the writers of *Añgāre* was for new reading strategies with different methods and terms for evaluating and validating literature so that "new" literary materials—of the sort produced by them—could be included in a canon.

As Ahmad Ali's and Mahmud uz-Zafar's letter to the editor makes clear, the extreme reaction over the collection indicates it transgressed more that one condition for literary activity: not only did *Añgāre* violate the formal expectations of fiction, it also violated ideas about who had the socially sanctioned authority to engage in criticism of religious institutions. Because some of the stories in *Añgāre* focused on protagonists whose stories mediated between the social and religious, they reinscribed the place in which literary activity occurred and to whom it was addressed. Fantasy and Islam crept into the crevices of the personal.

The writers were considered "self-consciously" radical because of their polemical, derogatory commentary on entrenched institutions suffused by Islam, like marriage; both areas (religion and marriage) had been parceled off by the colonial state into the realm of the personal or the domestic in which the state was not supposed to legally interfere. *Añgāre*'s literary activity infiltrated and impinged upon a socioreligious sphere. The stories burrowed deep into the crevices where the social and religious seeped into the intimately personal: the self as well as the area designated personal by the colonial state. Literature, by excavating the "ignorant, rotten, and decaying" failures of Muslim society, was called to the work of redemption. These failures were visible to the writers because they possessed expertise that enabled clear sightlines. Authority to speak and the ability to see right were conferred either by birth and upbringing (the four authors were Muslim and therefore intimately qualified to speak on behalf of Islam) or by education (which inculcated them in the *technae* of the modern: Jahan was a doctor).

Publishing *Añgāre* had socioreligious consequences; it tore at the vulnerabilities of religious feeling. The language of the response by the government of UP and the character of the other agencies that responded, like the government and the Central Standing Committee of the All-India Shia Conference, made this clear.[25] The government was committed to non-interference in the matter of religion precisely because it felt that "no offense [such as interference] was more likely to lead to tumult, to sanguinary outrage, even to armed insurrection,"[26] and already harried by civil unrest, clamped down on the collection. The "pregnant dangers" of religious excitement which offered an "incitement to revolt" could only be "averted by a firm adherence to the *true principles of tolerance*."[27] Paradoxically, government rhetoric, a euphemism for "interference" in the matters of a community's private affairs when those matters posed a threat to civil order, enforced a kind of religious order in the guise of "principles of tolerance" by clamping down on religious disorder.

Even a superficial perusal of the institutions that implemented sanctions against *Añgāre* reveals that in this instance the boundaries of literature were patrolled by outside agents and institutions that were engaged in different endeavors, like the Shia standing committee and the colonial state. These institutions and people leveled charges and provided the impetus to proscribe what was unacceptable to them. For the fledgling Progressive movement, authority to legislate their activity was invested outside the movement. Why? I think it was because literary activity was visibly straying into areas that were not conventionally associated with it. I will be addressing this issue in greater depth later in this chapter, but I would like to state here that vehemently *secular* literatures, as exemplified by the writers of the *Añgāre* collection, began to arrogate unto themselves the rights of socio-religious reformers, while challenging the conventions of change associated with transformation of literature. These rights had been, until then (with exceptions like Premchand), the provenance of figures who functioned between literary, social, and religious universes.

As the PWA grew into a more authoritative institution, its practices were generally sanctioned, and its members began controlling the parameters of literary acceptability. Sites that had once been contested for them, or by others who saw them as infringing in places they ought not have been, became normative. Attempts by external agencies, like the state, to proscribe the literary activity of the movement still occurred, but they did not have the force of the response to *Añgāre*. These later proscriptions took a more conventional political form; they were usually directed at journals that published Progressive authors who were considered communists. It was a function of its growing power that the movement no longer had to account for either critiques, which could be trivialized, or critics, who were called "uninformed, ignorant" and their charges "silly."[28]

Whatever the outcome of the battle between the writers of *Añgāre* and their detractors, and whatever this battle portended for the movement, the outcry seemed excessive even to people at the time. Why was there such a pitched battle over a piece of literature that has, in retrospect, been judged wanting by the movement? The book was publicly burned and the authors were condemned at public meetings, their lives threatened with retributions that included stoning and hanging. According to Ali, "Bourgeois families hurried to disassociate themselves from us and denied acquaintance with us."[29] The *Hindustan Times* reported: "The Central Standing Committee of the All-India Shia Conference, [Lucknow] strongly condemns the heart-rending and filthy pamphlet . . . which has wounded the feelings of the entire Muslim Community by ridiculing God and his Prophets and which is extremely objectionable from the standpoints of both religion and morality. The Committee further strongly urges upon the attention of the U.P. Government that the book be proscribed."[30]

If one examines, however facilely and with whatever motives, prior critiques of religious activity, one will find that sanctimoniousness, hierarchies, and injustices are not unusual or limited to *Añgāre*. Almost all religious reform movements angle their critiques at similar targets in order to justify their own "new" programs.[31] Two writers contingently affiliated with the PWA, Ansari and Ahmad Ali, position their agendas in the context of the works of earlier, unambiguously religious reformers, Kabir and Shah Waliullah. So why the rabid response to *Añgāre*? In addition to explanations I have already given, I think that the offenses committed by the authors of the collection were coded or concealed in occasional sentences that I have encountered in Ahmad Ali's and Carlo Coppola's accounts of this period: "Sajjad Zah[i]r who returned to London";[32] the authors were "anti-God and anti-Muslim." The writers were lampooned in the public press, satirized as English heathens who had chosen to malign Islam.[33]

One explanation for the ferocity of the response is located in the differences between other critiques of religion and this one. Earlier religious reforms were proposed within the framework or the context of that specific religion, so those analyses did not take the reformers away from established religious praxis but returned them to an "enlightened" form of it.[34] In this case, the reforms implied a rejection of religion in general or of Islam in particular: "members of other faiths . . . will come forward exposing the contradictions and injustice [of their faiths]." The responses of the writers of *Añgāre* to religion as moribund and decadent were formulated in terms of a new secularism. Implicit in the response is the ascendancy of new paradigms for change—paradigms that emerged out of a "Western" critique of Indian religions and relied on a particular set of codes for constructing "Western" superiority. The notion of "Western *secular* superiority" was written into the agenda advocated by the authors of *Añgāre*. "The [W]est is ascendant because of a more modern outlook, rationalism, and technological advancement, scientific inquiry rather than spiritual acquiescence in known phenomena."[35] Theology and opinion were posed against science and fact. Unintelligent abuse, violence, and unsustained scurrilous charges were posed against civilized disagreement conducted in the civil sphere by people who ought to be in the know. Religion and religious superstition was treated as inimical to reasonable consent.

Since the nineteenth century, the charge of pro-English sentiment had been levied against reformers of literature who implicitly or explicitly endorsed Western education or ideas: Hali was excoriated for supporting Sayyid Ahmad Khan, and Azad had been criticized for his support of English in the speech on the reform of Urdu poetry he gave on May 9, 1894, before the Anjuman-e Punjab.[36] The authors of *Añgāre* had stepped onto the same minefield by publishing their collection. They had effectively appropriated and spoken from a series of positions that their community associated with Western critiques/critics (including the critique that had been folded into the legislation levied against the book). The caricatures of the *Añgāre* four explicitly iterated their pro-Western bent—Zahir was outfitted in Western clothes, his name rewritten in a parody of a Western gesture. Precisely because the four were relatively powerless, their move into a "westernized" slot, in the context of the colonial power written into that position, elicited the displaced anger and rancor that could not be directed at the British.[37]

Ironically it was the same British who ostensibly produced the *Añgāre* four that were called upon to take up the cause of religion against the infidels. The Shia standing committee went to the apparatus of the civil state, assemblies, newspapers, the court, and the police, to marshal the full force of that very legislation in support of religion (and against the *Añgāre* four) which was underpinned by the positions (espoused by the *Añgāre* four) they wished to shut down. And the four had deployed against them, in the form of the law, precisely those beliefs in the freedom of speech and the principles of tolerance that they were fighting to uphold.

Another issue that made the authors of *Añgāre* a special target was the presence of Rashid Jahan in the group. As a woman writing alongside a group of men, she was at many levels resistant to the options available to women. As Carlo Coppola says, "Much of the vilification of the press was directed at her because she was a woman. In Progressive families she became the symbol of the emancipated woman; in conservative homes an example of all the worst that can occur if a woman is educated, not kept in pardah, and allowed to pursue a career."[38]

Rashid Jahan's behavior as a literary figure obviously doubly violated codes for a *pardah nashīn*, woman under *pardah*: refusing to live under *pardah* she also made its violences the targets of her critique. But she also transgressed the expectations for "women reformers." She operated entirely on her own, freely choosing to cooperate with a group of men who were not her relatives. Her work as a member of the *Añgāre* group was framed by a much more subversive "masculinized" discourse and, to some extent, was mediated through it. The men who were her mediators and mentors were not the men who conventionally provided women reformers support and entry into the world outside the zenana, that is, men from the same family: fathers, husbands, and brothers. She was a socialist who chose her own compatriots. As a result, she was much more the social equal of men than she would have been had they been family members with whom she would have played, to some extent, a subordinate role. Of the *Añgāre* group, she was the only one who had had a complete education in the Western sciences. As a doctor, she epitomized both someone transformed by the West, who subscribed to the rhetoric of rationality, and someone who had the authority to speak with a westernized voice. She was the self-sufficient exemplar of the transition from "tradition" (the domestic/private) to "modernity" (the public/civil sphere), while also performing as a mediator for other women in the process of making that crossing.

As a writer, however, she was circumscribed, constrained to the domestic universe occupied by women. She wrote about the zenana. Her critique too, of the zenana, and the plots she allotted to women in her stories were architecturally limited. Rashid Jahan's biographers draw her as a woman who straddled the zenana, the inside world behind *pardah* (the world of women) and the outside, the world beyond the zenana—the world of men. And even though she was not conventional herself, Jahan continued to adhere to those literary conventions that permitted male protagonists fluidity while confining women. Usually her women are portrayed at the moment when they know they want to leave but cannot journey from zenana-dweller to outside-inside traveler by themselves. They need their passage facilitated by men.

## *AÑGĀRE* ACTIVITY

What, then, was literary activity as exemplified by *Añgāre*? This question is useful because some of the general concerns expressed through the book, such as literature as social action, continued to be espoused by the PWA, although some were transferred to the sphere of the sacrilegious as the movement evolved. The collection heralded a call for "literature" as "social action," and the connections were manifold: literary activity was considered social because it was examined *as* a social activity in its capacity as a social institution and because it scrutinized behaviors and practices that fell under the purview of the social; and social action as social change was believed to occur through literature. Literature was a forum in which social institutions, like marriage, could be subjected to a polemical, overt, explicit critique with an accompanying programmatic agenda for improvement. An implicit critique of social institutions was carried out through the mimetic representation of them in literary works. In other words, literature, as a mode through which "life" was reflected, could, by reflecting the "horrendous" conditions of "daily existence," expose these conditions.[39] In the process, areas that the authors of *Añgāre* felt were under *pardah*, like sexuality and sexual experience, were targeted for disclosure and laid bare. The authors of *Añgāre* wanted the freedom to explore the themes of their choice in whatever manner they chose. But the activity they participated in was not self-reflexive. Their critique did not engage their own literary production as one tempered by their participation in colonial institutions subscribing to colonial discourses; it was outwardly directed at the institutions, norms, and practices of their community. Indeed, the critique by the *Añgāre* four is a limited one, especially when directed at marriage.

Unlike some of the stories written by the three men, however, where the hub of the story is male desire and women are merely signifiers through which men play out or speak about their own desire, Rashid Jahan's pieces focus on marriage and address the conditions under which women live. In the one-act play *Parde ke pīche* (Behind the veil/curtain), Muhammadi Begam, the female protagonist despairing under pressure from her husband to produce a male heir, has been bearing children year after year: "itnī guzar gayī, jo bāqī hai kisī naḥ kisī ṭarah guzār degā, merā dil to duniyā se ab aisā akḍā gayā hai, agar un choṭe baccoñ kā ḳhayāl naḥ hotā to ḳhudā ki kisam maiñ zaḥar khā letī."[40] With her health deteriorating, her brother's wife calls in a woman doctor who details the implications of this type of physical abuse, subtly suggesting that Muhammadi Begum resort to birth control. The play ends with a vignette in which the long-awaited son abuses his sisters; the nurse harassed by his spoilt recalcitrance complains: "begam sahibaḥ! baḍe munne miyāñ naḥīñ mānate, jab kamre meñ āte haiñ baccoñ ko satate haiñ, ab khelne nahīñ dete!" (Begum, the boy never listens to me, whenever he comes into the room he upsets the other children, he never lets them play!).[41]

The doctor exemplifies the position of reason, making what appears to be the "rational" suggestion to the protagonist under the circumstances. So the doctor's voice, the voice of a westernized practitioner of an "art," functions synecdocally as the voice of "reason." Against it the playwright enacts the performance of a woman who embodies her own collaboration with a system that uses her to perpetuate it. By including the scene between brother and sisters, Jahan plays with an implicit critique of the stance she endorses, that the position of women will change if they follow the call of "reason" and obey the exigencies of "modern" medicine.

Like the play, the story "Dillī kī sair" (Sightseeing trip to Delhi) addresses the impress of the intransigent anatomy—the institution of marriage—in which women live. Jahan directs her rhetoric of change at the effects of that frame on women. In *Behind the Veil*, she displaces the modification onto women's bodies without proposing any mutations in the skeleton and sinews, in the social relationships and protocols, that might provoke the problems. She suggests that the way of combating this sort of physical abuse is by using contraceptives, thereby supplying contraception as a remedy to the disease of continuous childbirth, without really looking at any of the social mores that make the "production" of a son such a necessity.

In both "Sightseeing Trip to Delhi" and *Behind the Veil* the marriage plot is left intact and sacrosanct. Through the women in both stories a critique is leveled at the conditions they face, but the narratives allotted to them are in no way rescinded or transformed. The women remain the ground on which very specialized narratives of change and modernization are plotted. They are allowed a restrained voice that speaks stories of complaint and lament, but because their voices are quite clearly restricted to their own domain and hidden behind *pardah*, they are effectively contained.[42]

## PRACTICES OF EXCLUSION

What I find illuminating, given the subsequent history of the PWA and the evolution of the language of excoriation by the movement, is that some reactions to the book targeted the explicit sexuality of two stories, "Jannat kī baṣārat" (Vision of heaven) and "Dulārī" (Beloved), written by Sajjad Zahir, the member of the group most closely tied to the PWA as it grew. The language used against the collection included such words as "obscene, morally depraved, base, filthy and foul, trash, shameless."[43] Indeed, the forms the response to *Añgāre* took foreshadows the high moral ground and almost religious fervor of the words and practices of exclusion used by the PWA in the late 1930s and 1940s when they wanted to criticize, condemn, and expel poets like Miraji and short-story writers like Manto and Ismat Chughtai from the movement.[44]

Later, the call that was made by the writers of *Añgāre* to "speak freely" about sexuality, to use sexuality as the angle through which they aimed a critique at other issues, was no longer considered viable by the movement. Sexuality became instead the area hedged in by constraints; the norms of good literature were mapped onto those for depicting sexuality. The charges leveled by the PWA against bad literature (literature whose improprieties denied it a place in the canon) were, among others, directed at the particular ways in which "sexuality" was explored by certain authors like Miraji, Ismat Chughtai, and Manto. So the movement's own evolving strategies of exclusion resembled the format of the responses (in the form of the law, and of medicine) to the first major collection of writing attributed to the newly forming Progressive movement. The conservative Muslim response to *Añgāre* was digested by the PWA and shaped, over time, into the barbs they themselves shafted against those they wished to remove from their ranks.

"Sexuality" is thus, for both the critics responding to *Añgāre* and the later theoreticians of the PWA, a problem area. It is an area hedged in by controls, an area around which proscriptions are written and prescriptions enacted. Its leaky subversions are dammed in and erratically transformed from acts, something identified as a peculiarity contained in a work, to a statement about a person—the truth about a writer's being.

In the later criticism by the PWA, in the early 1940s, discussions around sexuality continued to provide the language of exclusion or of the possibility of excision, the language in which the meaning of "deviance" was written. Naming a literary piece "excessively sexual" was a way of devalorizing it as well as labeling it deviant.[45] Occasionally the label was then metonymized to stand in for a writer's entire oeuvre and finally to stand in for the writer. This was more the case with Miraji and Manto than with Ismat Chughtai.

The naming and control of "deviance," whether that was applied to a single work, an entire oeuvre or a person, is central to the narrative history of the "normal." Constructing categories for deviance constructed and stabilized what stood for the "normal." Both needed to circulate with restrictions written into the "abnormal" position so that the "abnormal" would stay in place and could be kept there. The determinations of both normalcy and its aberrations were based on the language of the law, of psychiatry, and of medicine. Aberrations were called out as obscenity, insanity, and disease.[46]

I would like to suggest that the marking off of sexuality as a "problem," where both fear and repression were couched in terms of a "moral" response to implied or explicit depictions of sexuality, had its correspondences with the circumscription of the Indian-British encounters by the British. In *Race, Sex, and Class Under the Raj*, Kenneth Ballhatchett suggests that the British felt "there was a deep fear of disorder if sexual behavior escaped control."[47] "Excessive" sexuality was the power ascribed to the "abnormal," the "other." As power, it was particularly virulent because of its polluting (miscegenating) seductive potential.[48] The restraints against excessive sexuality often took the form of taboos enacted through rituals of purification and cleansing.

The kinds of controls the British ordered to circumscribe sexual activity between Indians and the British, like the "lock hospitals," had their counterparts in the literary controls on sexuality maintained by the PWA. The British built "lock hospitals" not just to regulate sexuality but to regulate diseases caused by sexual encounters between Indian women and British soldiers. Their mission was to offer remedies for or to cleanse the danger infecting the body politic through people's bodies.[49] The 1886 memorandum by the then surgeon general in Bombay, Dr. W. J. Moore, explicitly addresses the "disorders of body and mind" (masturbation, mercenary love, and venereal disease) that visit the young man who cannot marry and reach that "high moral standard required for repression of physiological natural instincts."[50] The schemes proposed (ensuring that prostitutes were available, housing them in *lal bazaars* [designated red-light areas in markets that serviced military encampments or cantonments], registering them, examining them, and holding them in lock hospitals) followed the systems instituted by the Contagious Diseases Acts in Britain between 1864 and 1886.

The types of sexual encounters that brought soldiers to the lock hospitals were those that transgressed the white-white "norm." Circumscribing the arenas in which sexuality was permitted "free reign" and controlling diseases in these instances allowed the transgressive encounters to move into the purview of colonial jurisdiction. Regulating sexuality by regulating sexual interactions and disease produced a vision of normal sexuality that could be cleaned up and brought under the medical and legal supervision of a colonial state. What had eventually been rendered circumspect in this seemingly natural redrawing of the architecture of cantonments to include a detour toward a regulated sexuality, and in cleaning (disinfecting) Indian women's bodies so that they could be bought safely to satisfy the wandering lust/needs of British soldiers, was the possibility of homosexuality between two soldiers: both British or one British and one Indian.[51]

But the kinds of controls established by the PWA were not isomorphous with those decreed by the British. One area of difference is that the PWA responded to the textual expression of sexuality between two or more Indians, whereas the British usually concerned themselves more directly with proscriptions on the social manifestations of a complex of sexual relations between colonizer and colonized. One of the few exceptions that reinforced the differences between the British and the PWA was N. M. Rashid, whose stark lyric fleshed out colonialism as a series of encounters between Western women and the East. In one early poem, colonial desire is told through the desire of an English woman seeking herself in Indian social landscapes. Another poem turns to violence: the rape of a European woman by an Indian man plays out a fantasy of retribution. The British restrictions were, like those of the PWA, also sometimes enacted in a literary form, plotted as anticipation and impossibilities in the work of Forster and Kipling, but the acceptable narratives, plots, and personae from English fiction and Urdu poetry and fiction obviously could not and did not map comfortably onto one another.

How is sexuality encoded in texts? What are the textual registers of "normative" sexual relations? Although the form of the ghazal repudiated the kind of relationships incarnated in it, they continued to be normative representations of sexuality. Sexuality in the ghazal is poeticized as sexual failure or unrequited desire. Critics like Sadiq, writing about "love" in twentieth-century poetry, would probably not acknowledge the antecedents of their position. It is clear, however, that when they discuss representations of "abnormal" sexuality, they subscribe to an iconography, elicited from the language of the ghazal, of appropriate sexual behavior for the persona of the poet in that genre as a vilified, maligned, unsuccessful lover. The gender of the always-out-of-reach beloved was never settled; the beloved could be a young man, an older courtesan, or someone whose gender was not really pertinent. Representation of sexuality that did not conform to this form was then considered "inappropriate" or deviant. In "The Feminine Voice in the Urdu Ghazal," Carla Petievich writes about the history of the standardization of the ghazal. Her article clarifies what any aficionado of the ghazal ought to recognize as familiar—that many of the sexual encounters in it elaborate desire between two men. This is a point Petievich explores at some length because she is concerned with the ways in which the male-female relationship gets elided in the long history of Urdu poetry.[52] But by the mid-nineteenth century, literary reformers like Altaf Husain Hali, discussing lyric even as the British were institutionalizing *lal bazaars* and lock hospitals, turn to the law to regulate the proprieties of the ghazal: "The claims of every age are different . . . if we follow words of obscenity and shamelessness . . . from the great poets of Iran and India . . . we will be judged according to the law. . . . we must leave our elder's follies aside because of the possibility of punishment . . . but also because of wisdom and morality."[53] The legal restrictions and customs established by the state begin to set the limits of the literary possible, its legislated claims on morality impinge on writing, historical analysis, and the rules of criticism.

One sees here a shift from *junūn* to madness, lovesickness to nymphomania/madness as a medical condition, and the legal then becomes both the external limit (law/state) and the internal limit (absorbed into the quotidian as morality). As the external limit it is called upon to legislate the internal (patrol the communities' norms for morality/propriety): that is when morality is violated the sanctions applied to extract the immoral from the community are twofold. First the community turns to itself as operating in the civil sphere—meetings, printing articles, and so on. Then the community (formed perhaps in a demand for legislative recourse) demands that the law, now the external arbiter of the public sphere (which has within it as legislation fear of the restless public sphere), extrude the imposter. Sanctions are established both through community and the "law." What is immoral is metaphorized through Western (imposter, outsider)—the West (law as outsider/Western) is then called upon to expel what or who is designated implicitly as the representative of the West from the community. That which has been expelled absorbs into itself the terms of its expulsion, and transmutes those terms into the rules for morality/propriety and uses those rules to expel the improper from within itself.

Habermas argues that the public sphere (as bourgeois ideal) emerges through critical public discourses in public institutions (civil society) that set the public's interests against the states'.[54] In colonial settings, the colonial state's interventions into the performance of daily moralities, as daily and as a certain kind of opinion/conduct, inculcate the etiquette of civility, which is then disseminated through civil/public institutions (assemblies, magazines, etc., bourgeois also in relation to a colonial economy, law, habitus). This dissemination establishes a more insidious relationship, that is simultaneously more explicit, between civil society, public interest, and the state. The state is then called to intercede on behalf of the public when it is divided against itself. Divisions within the public prolong the jurisdictions established by the law into the public sphere or into civil society as the realm of the civilized. What the state establishes as obscene is also what PWA members want to fight over "as obscene," as something they themselves believe (despite the chasms of difference between members and the state.) State, here, is not a given, self-complete thing. State appears as states: the colonial state and those who are engaged in the struggles to take it over.

Rules for expulsion obey moralities coded in terms of temporality. With Hali the archaic conventions that were once acceptable must be excised, so that we have a clean-living present. With the *Añgāre* discussions, conventions that come from modernity must be excised so that the community can return to a clean-living past. With the PWA the past must be excised, so that we can turn to a clean-living future. In each case—the past, present, and future—what is identified as belonging to each time frame or temporality is produced in the present.

One very explicit attempt by the PWA to control the depiction and representation of sexuality is the case of Ismat Chughtai.[55] Chughtai was a young woman writer who, in the late 1930s, wrote "Liḥāf" (The quilt), a short story about a sexual relationship between two women living in a zenana—a *bahu*, Begam Jan, and her masseur-companion, Rubbu. Rubbu begins providing the young bride solace when it becomes clear that the hobby of the man the Begum Jan recently married was keeping boys like other men "keep pigeons." The begum's new husband kept "boys, young, fair-complexioned, slender-waisted," boys with "tight-calves, supple-waisted boys in sheer, perfumed shirts eating up syrupy-rich puddings."[56]

The story is told as a flashback by the young girl who witnessed the relationship between the two women. The girl has been sent by her mother to stay with her friend while the mother is on holiday, in the hope that the begum will retrain her child, who has been displaying gender-discordant behavior like climbing trees and beating up boys. The child is put into Begum Jan's bedroom to sleep and thus given intimate access to the relationship. She is an ambivalent spectator who unwittingly and uncomprehendingly enters the circle of the begum's desire and, for a short time, becomes the focus of it. Her reaction to the begum plays out her ambivalence. The begum—her sexuality drawn and positioned between young male preadolescence and the white smooth voluptuousness of a mature sensuous woman—was quite clearly an object of the child's fascinated desiring gaze: "I used to wish that I could just sit and look at her for hours. . . . The most captivating feature of her face was her lips. They were usually tinted red, a light down over the upper one. Long hair tousled at the temples. Sometimes her face would suddenly take on a strange look, like that of an immature boy."[57] Rubbu and the child compete for the begum's attention, and Rubbu is sent away on an excuse. The begum's attention turns toward the child, who finds herself inadvertently servicing the woman who had once been her inaccessible focus of her desire. Rubbu returns and the quilt in the begum's bedroom, under which the women writhe, takes on the attributes of the sinister, and embodies the child's fearful, apprehensive, violating incursion into sexuality.[58]

Chughtai transgressed many boundaries with "Quilt." As a woman writer she took up female sexuality, which until then had been the domain of men. She set the stage (behind the *pardah* that lifts to open the story) on which anyone who could read Urdu was free to the view the spectacle of female sexuality. Furthermore, she situated the sexual not in a place outside the home, where it could be regulated by men, but rather moved it into the domain of the domestic, familiar, and until then, desexualized zenana, where it could be relegated.[59] She opened up a peephole into the sacred space of the household, the space that was hidden from the gaze of the outside, a bedroom in the women's quarters, the zenana.[60] As an unmarried woman, someone who should have been safely ensconced behind *pardah* in the zenana, someone who should have had no access to information about sexuality—let alone have disclosed it to the public—she allowed an audience access to the desire of other inaccessible women like her, thereby exceeding what was permitted her.

The story created an immense uproar when it was published in *Adab-e laṭīf* (Literary delights), and Chughtai received dozens of threatening letters. Although the PWA tried to enact sanctions against her at one of their meetings (in Hyderabad), she was supported at the time by some writers from the PWA, including Krishan Chandar. The response she received did not stop her writing, but it certainly muted one of her modes of expression. In an interview with Carlo Coppola in the 1970s, Chughtai made it clear that she did not have any idea she would provoke that kind of reaction, and in retrospect she was very sorry that she had written the story.[61]

But "Quilt" was not the first instance of representation of female-female sexuality in Urdu. There was a precedent for it, in *rekhtī*, a form of poetry in which women appear to speak to other women. But *rekhtī*, which was performed by men in occasional drag for an audience of men as well as courtesans, was explicitly sexual, graphically physical, framed as a sort of parody of the ghazal, and was produced by men for the titillation of other men and "public" women. *Rekhtī*, poetry in "lesbian" drag, was a socially sanctioned form of "transgressive sexuality."[62] Its performances took place away from the home; as a performance it was closed, self-contained, and private and can perhaps be understood as a genre of cross-dressed vaudeville. In fact it is represented as "bad" Urdu poetry: as Urdu poetry that transgressed the kind of sexual and gender proprieties that define court poetry.

In the process of writing her story, Chughtai transgressed the gendered boundaries of *rekhtī* performance—exclusively *by* men *for* men or *for* women whose lives and work were set outside the limits of the zenana. Not only are men ancillary to Chughtai's zenana, they are eventually excised from both the sexual fantasies of women and the sexual activity of women. Her zenana, which ought to have been the "chastity belt" of the house, the sexually sacrosanct portion of the home where women were ostensibly hidden away to keep them from sexual encounters with men, is instead a den of iniquity where men are not needed. Her story plays out the danger implicit in sexual segregation, that it could turn into sexual separatism: if women were kept apart from men, they would turn sexually to each other. Her story unearths the romance of gender secreted in the anger directed against it: sexual difference does not necessarily produce heterosexuality. The most conventional contained form of sexual difference, a heterosexual marriage, protected from desecration (of public spectacle) by the veils of the zenana, can turn out to be other than itself.

Chughtai's most heinous crime, her most egregious violation, however, was that she seemed so utterly innocent about her designs—"I thought . . . that this was something that only women did. I thought that men always went to prostitutes, but because girls can't go to prostitutes, they do this."[63] So, although she goes on to call the sexuality depicted in her story a "perversion," her initial voicing of her intentions does not code her story as "abnormal."

The position Miraji takes to represent sexuality in his poetry echoes Chughtai's innocence. Although most of the poetry in which he depicts sexuality is about fairly straightforward sexual transactions between men and women, his poetry, too, has been called "abnormal."[64] The melancholic laments of desire in his work, the images sifted out so that they became the repetitive focus of a reader's gaze, recall the poetics of the ghazal. Instead, his work has been called to task for its pathological insistence on loss, its voyeurism, and its fetishism. But Miraji refused to pathologize his own position. He affronted what had come to be the quotidian customs for depicting "normal" sexuality. By doing so, he unpacked the apparent arbitrariness of the conventions used to portray "appropriate" and "deviant" sexual behavior, and slipped subversive interjections into the codes for "normal" and "abnormal."[65]

The case of Miraji and "male" writers like Manto, who digressed from the norms of representation, and the case of Ismat Chughtai, a "female" writer who offended the conventions of representation, are not exactly similar. One of the most important differences is the issue of gender: how the "real" gender of the author is transposed onto their work.

Chughtai enacted a double violation by writing about sexuality as a woman and simultaneously changing the "language" of sexuality. Unlike her male counterparts, she had to repudiate her position and never wrote a story like "Quilt" again, though she continued to compose stories in a Freudian key. The restraints that bound her after she wrote the story were more confining than those that tied Miraji and Manto, who, though contained by the critical discourse surrounding their work, continued writing as they had. If placed in a system of inclusions and exclusions, it is clear that Manto's and Miraji's work often provided the limits for what became central to a particular kind of literary canon; their "marginality" and "difference" operated "normally" to produce and reinforce the "normative." Chughtai, however, had a different relationship to the normative. Her work, conducted at the margins, circulated with a gap, the moment of repudiation written into her position.

Gender might work here to figure in interesting ways the couplings between body and work/act. Miraji's body is refigured (metonymized) in terms of his work—he becomes insane, his body decrepit and degenerating. Manto displays a milder version of bodily decrepitude: he is not insane, just drunk. Chughtai never has her body coded by her work. Her work stands as acts separated from analyses of her being, her person, and her self. Not that the bodies of the men were not in trouble. But what is curious in this triangulation between Miraji, Manto, and Chughtai is that an immutable causal connection is drawn between unsettled work and unsettled self as unsettled body for the men but not for the woman. Biology provides a kind of naturalness, a natural truth.

## MEETINGS, TABOOS, AND NEW CRITICAL NORMS

About a year after the publication of *Aṅgāre*, a series of informal meetings in London in 1934 and 1935 held under the auspices of the Communist Party by a group of Indian students that included Zahir, Jyoti Ghosh, Pramod Sengupta, Mahmud din Tasir, and Mulk Raj Anand are associated with the inception of the PWA. Out of these meetings came the first manifesto of the association,[66] which was published in 1936 in the *Left Review*. The first official meeting of the PWA in India took place in Lucknow on April 9–10, 1936, in conjunction with a convention held by the Indian National Congress. The All-India Progressive Writers' Association (AIPWA) and the Urdu Progressive Writers' Association (UPWA) followed this meeting with an entire series, two for the AIPWA and four for the UPWA, in the 1930s and 1940s.

The meetings were important not just as fora in which standards for literary activity were established and disseminated as manifestos, and proclamations, but as sites in which endorsements by national personae took place. The roster of speakers and attendees included luminaries as diverse as Nehru, Tagore, Premchand, Hasrat Mohani, Kaka Sahib Kalelkar, Pant, and Sarojini Naidu. Their endorsements facilitated the acceptance of the PWA by both the nationalist elite and the established literary elite, which reinforced its position as the preeminent literary organization and placed it within established power networks.

The meetings, like any meeting held for a discipline, were arenas in which the community of literati established its rules and performed the social hierarchies of the discipline. At these meetings the canon that was forming, along with the theoretical criteria by which it was identified, was both articulated and disseminated, and the people who were given authority to speak for the community were presented. The meetings provided the space for official discussions on reclassification, circulation, and production of literature as a valuable cultural commodity and of its concomitant social power, including the profit and power from mediating their circulation.

By the late 1930s, as the PWA grew and defined its boundaries more explicitly, the social dynamics of meetings, in concert with the talks, served as the means through which the organization was civilized and the heretics called out. The agenda established by the UPWA at their gatherings had literary and social ramifications that affected the conditions of literary production on a larger scale, in that the disciplining of writers who were excommunicated occurred outside of the UPWA meetings. At what I call the "mock trials" of writers, the regulatory function of the gatherings brought communal attention to "certain contested aspects of social behavior"; through these conflicts individuals took sides on moral imperatives and constraints, often against their own personal preferences. Even if defendants won their trials, the controls against them continued to be enacted.[67]

For example, in October 1945, during the meeting in Hyderabad, Deccan, a resolution against "obscenity" in literature was proposed by Dr. Abdul Alim. The main focus of the meeting (which Miraji attended) was Ismat Chughtai, but since I have only superficially followed the impact on her of that particular discussion at the UPWA, I will focus on the effect it had on Miraji, with whom I am more familiar. Although the proposition was rejected by the organization because of the opposition of major literati (Hasrat Mohani and Qazi Abdul Ghaffar) to it,[68] the terms suggested by the proposal were nonetheless put into effect in Bombay after the meeting. For a poet like Miraji, the long-term repercussions of the PWA's pogroms were severe. His oeuvre was marginalized and, as I have suggested elsewhere, his canon read through the critical framework provided for it by the "Progressives." Many of his friends were Progressives who slowly abandoned him during his last years; indeed, the social ostracism that accompanied Miraji's literary one was nearly complete by the time he died in 1949.[69]

Another series of events integral to the histories written about the PWA was the production of theoretical "theocratic" materials by the Progressives. These assumed several forms and included speeches given by luminaries who presided over various meetings. Premchand's speeches, for example, were sometimes published in *Hans* (Swan), the journal he edited. The materials published under the auspices of the PWA also included three versions of the manifesto for the PWA. One was written in London in 1934, the second was a reissue of the London manifesto published by Premchand in *Hans* the same year,[70] and the third was produced at the first Indian meeting of the PWA in Lucknow.

The highlights of the theoretical oeuvre of the Progressives included early seminal essays by writers like Akhtar Husain Raipuri, who wrote "Adab aur zindagī" (Literature and life) and published it in July 1935 in the journal *Urdu*, even before *Añgāre* was written.[71] Because Raipuri was a young student, this article was not given the status it might have received. Nevertheless, it is important because its historical analysis provided the basic plot for subsequent narratives of literary history, including those by Miraji.

Several Progressive journals were published under the auspices of the UPWA: *Kālim* (Speaker), which was later banned; *Nayā adab* (New literature), which was established with funds from the CPI in 1939; and finally, *New Indian Literature*. The first three issues of *Nayā adab* laid the theoretical foundations of the movement. One of the first topics the journal addressed was the definition of the term "Progressive" (*taraqqiyāt*). In defining the term, the UPWA laid claim to it, made it central to a discourse about literary value, and established their particular delimitation of its use in the context of the formation of a literary movement. *Taraqqiyāt*, as change (*tabdīl*) oriented toward a new literary future, had been seminal to Urdu criticism from the nineteenth century on: the UPWA's claim on it had to translate it into their tenets. Even Miraji, who at the time was being jettisoned by the PWA, felt the need to define "Progressive" in conjunction with and against the other definitions.[72]

The articles written in the late 1930s and 1940s made it clear that concerns of the movement had diverged from those espoused by the writers of *Angāre*. One major shift involved the position and role of "tradition" in relation to the production of "new" literature. As the domains of tradition were being reorganized in tandem with modernity, the attitude toward "tradition" clearly changed over the course of the first ten years of the PWA: "tradition" was no longer something to be completely repudiated, as the writers of *Angāre* had seemed to suggest; rather, it was something with which the PWA saw themselves in selective alignment.[73]

This period in the movement's history, the late 1930s, seems to be one in which many limits were instituted. While the struggle to possess the word "Progressive" was occurring, the PWA appeared to be becoming more politically consistent, even breaking off from it factions that did not conform to the central beliefs of the movement. One breach in the PWA was between the "political" (*siyāsī/taraqqi pasand*) and "creative" (*jadīdiyāt*) writers, which carried with it other oppositions that ordered the taxonomies weaving through the rhetorical strategies of the PWA during this period—between public, social, historical, material on one hand and private, individual, psychological/mystical, and linguistic on the other. The first set of categories came to be associated with a valorized politicized literary stance (socialist realist, *ḥaqīqat parast*), and the second set with a devalued "depoliticized" (modernist, *jadīdiyāt*) one. As the PWA took the meaning of the word "Progressive" (as political) over, poets and fiction writers who were assigned a negative value or those who wrote from positions perceived as private, individual, and so forth, were considered "apolitical," and the PWA felt justified to condemn these writers specifically because they wrote private, privatized, apolitical pieces.

This had ramifications for critics like Miraji, who emphasized the ways that "realities" were represented through discursive operations magnetized by desire.[74] Since political engagement, as it was defined by the Progressives, excluded a self-reflexive focus on language in use and expressly embargoed the domain of desire (turned it over to the private as self-indulgent), Miraji's particular forms of political engagement could not be thought of as such. His questions about hegemony, specially pertinent when scrutinizing popular literature—his contemporaries' complicity with and dependence upon British literary practices—were not understood as "political" questions. The most pervasive and insidious forms of imperialist ideologies—the bodies, the stories, the narrative twists and turns, the moral filters, the legacies of salvation and redemption that represented the colonized—thus went unremarked by the PWA. This is not to say that Miraji himself did not subscribe to colonial literary practices. The part the British played in his essay on new poetry, "Nayī shāʿirī kī buniyādeñ" (The fundamentals of new verse) is a case in point. Nevertheless, he did voice some important concerns about complicity and politicization at the time in which he wrote that are now common currency among "historic" historians, if not literary historians, and that had not been addressed before because of the way in which "political" was constructed.

What, then, was the conceptual architecture that the "Progressives" used to speak about literature and literary activity? As mentioned above in my discussion of *Añgāre*, literature was connected to social action by the PWA. In the accounts from this time it appeared that there were at least two ways in which literature and social action came together. The first coupling between them is that literary activity was considered labor (*ʿamal*) in, of, and for the *socius* (*samāj*) as political (*siyāsī*); it had social consequences (*maqṣad*) and was performed in social spaces (*māḥaul*). The second bond between literature and social action is that literature reflected social conditions. For the PWA this particular property of literary activity as reflective (as mirror, *āʾinah*) was a necessary component of their understanding of literary activity as exemplary social action. Integral to their stance was a form of temporality, a "philosophy of history" current at the time, with particular notions of "past," or "tradition," and its connection to the "present."[75] The connections drawn between past and present—the past metamorphosed into the present, the past resolutely pulled apart from the present—underwent a change in the late 1930s.

For Akhtar Husain Raipuri, a self-professed Marxist historian, and the other writers who echoed him, the (hi)story of literature was written through the structural differences in literary activity between past, present, and utopian future (*māẓī*, *hāl*, and *mustaqbil*).[76] Raipuri turned to political economy (capitalism, *saramāyah*), to the economic (*maʿāshī*, *iqtiṣādī*), the material (*māddī*): to write a linear modes-of-production narrative assigned to the three temporal spaces.[77] The past was feudal, a time of Oriental despotism, its ornamented poetry funded by a royal, moneyed elite (*ṭabaqah-e amīr*). The present is capitalist, and its literature is created to satisfy a middle class or bourgeoisie emerging with industrialization (*mashīnī*), post 1857.[78] The future is a utopian egalitarian one with literature, freed from the constraints of politics, wealth, and self-absorption (*siyāsiyat, daulat, ḳhud ʿarẓī*) produced within a classless society (*insāniyat kī vaḥdat*).[79]

Though presocial, state-of-nature "origins" appear merely as a moment, as a strange contractual attraction that mediates desire and fear to assure that one's material needs were met, in Raipuri's essay, Raipuri did not focus on them, unlike Miraji, who subscribed to some of the conceptual forms from the modes-of-production narrative while also creating a prolonged myth of "origins." Raipuri's fascination with the presocial coheres around the answers to (Marxist) materialist questions: How are elements (iron, wheat) transformed to ameliorate human desires and needs (*insānīyat-e arzū*)?[80] What are the historical ruptures (like the Battle of Plassey, and 1857) that turn forms of labor from those frayed ones (*farsūdah tarīqoñ*) woven into Asian agricultural feudal organizations to those turned efficient by the use of machinery?[81] Raipuri's questions thread the implements of agriculture (*ṭraikṭar*), the instruments of war (spears to machine-guns), stories evoking and telling desire (earlier *apsara* and *rakshasa* stories become courtesans of cinema and robot *rakshasas*) into the process of constructing a factory—as a building, fabricated from capital, drawn by design and encasing laboring bodies hitched to machines and through whom the entrepreneur's capital is turned solid.[82] This dense narrative grounds Raipuri's descriptions of the movements of value and worth and progress.

So, the accounts of literary history produced by the Progressives, including Raipuri's, decipher literary works through an understanding of the sociopolitical conditions of their production as material. The historical accounts resolve a fantasy of an egalitarian future into a time line that pulls a piece of the past apart from the desired future and refigures that piece as its opposite. These accounts "resonate" with the allegory of the "Fall" and the concurrent move toward deferred redemption.[83] This allegorical conversion carries within it the rhetoric of justification that enables the British "mission" to India.[84] The transition from redemption to fall or from fall to redemption also dovetails into the language of modernization. Some of the Anglican and Utilitarian (as against the early Orientalist) accounts of the condition of the Indian subcontinent depict an explicitly Hindu India of the present as fallen—"dark, chaotic, and unwieldy mired in sin and despotism."[85] Orientalist versions, also folded into some nineteenth-century nationalist ones, offer a past that has at least one moment not mired in sin and despotism, which can be rejuvenated in the present (with a little help) to extend redemption in the future.[86] Redemption comes in the guise of and at the hands of "sturdy legions of British administrators and missionaries" ordained to "modernize" India, eradicate "ignorance," and mediate between past and future.[87] To be redeemed the colonized must first be given the gift of sight proffered through a very particular colonial (missionary of government) education. This new sight, sort of like the rose glasses of a historical consciousness, translates and gathers together diffuse moments scattered in time into history—which will grant the colonized a new vision of themselves.

A fantasy this generic and unconflicted is seldom present in its pure, untrammeled form in literary accounts, biographies, or letters. The literary products allied with the colonial enterprise in its various guises are littered with partly concealed acknowledgments of the duplicity of the enterprise. By the 1920s, even missionaries who tried to circumvent the heresy of duplicity had to explicitly situate themselves in the context of ambivalence about the imperial mission. The vestiges of the allegory of redemption remain not only in colonial writing about India but also in Indian narratives about change as modernization. The allegory of fall-to-redemption, blended from the historical materialism of Marx and the historical visionary analysis of Utilitarian-colonial writing, surfaces in the writing of the Progressives, and even in Miraji's histories struggles with a "will to completion." In Raipuri's work, the will to completion as perfection is adjourned to a utopian future.[88]

### PAST

> I whiled away my youth's time weeping, as I aged I closed my eyes
> So, nights I lost to waking, and as morning awoke, I slept.[89]

Looking at the narratives of the PWA, in the manifestos and in the work of theorists like Raipuri, the past is represented in two ways. One, articulated by Ahmad Ali, plays out the dynamics between remote, or originary, and the near past as the fall from vitality to degeneracy: "Past activity had led to complacency, the one-time vitality of life to effeteness, moral responsibility to love of pleasure, universal brotherhood to sectarianism and regionalism. The concept of progress had become atrophied. The spirit of inquiry was lost."[90] This position reverberates between constructions of Indian history posed as secular, where the idyllic Hindu past falls under the violence of the Muslim conquests, and Muslim accounts of the degeneration of a utopian Muslim past into an Islamic world now fossilized.[91] Against them is Raipuri's more Leftist-secular version in which the entire past is "fallen"; but since his descriptions focus on the desired conditions of production for literature they do not carry the same allegorical conceits.[92]

For Raipuri, the production of literature in the "past" is analyzed as social labor (*samājī ʿaml*). Literature, namely forms of the lyric like ghazal and Sanskrit *shlokā*, was a commodity produced for a nobility and was recited in courts by a group of people (*ʿālim, adīb*) for whom its manufacture was a profession. As such, its "antiquated, withered, and limited, pathetic" topoi reflected the social conditions for its production and exchange: "mauẓūaʿat-e adab baḥut hī fasurdaḥ aur maḥdūd haiñ."[93] Still, it was a culturally viable and valuable commodity that was sold to ornament the elite, and the fastidious preoccupation with this kind of decorative activity produced linguistic elegance, turns of phrase, and plays of metaphor.[94] This linguistic activity, because it embodied the "past," flaunted its obsessions but could never comment on them; hence it was apolitical. Another kind of literature produced at the same time was rather different. Instead of being mired in a certain form of life (that of the elite), it disengaged itself from life completely, and oriented itself toward a negation of life, toward death in life. This kind of literature was said to be captivated with spiritualism and/or mysticism, the noms de plume of forms of "unworldly" religious discipline and hence also apolitical.[95] One exception was Kabir and the bhakti poets. According to Raipuri, Kabir was unusual, "like a mole on a white expanse of face," because his was truly a poetry of the masses, not relying on the allegiance of the elite. His wry, folksy commentary on life's material afflictions foreshadowed the form of literature that Raipuri saw as having value. However, Kabir too was stricken by the symptomology of asceticism: versifying toward/for/unto death.[96]

The analyses of the literature of the past, when focused on Urdu, stress that it flowered in the period of decline of the feudal Mughal civilization. The ghazal as a beautiful woman is the identifying trope or icon for this period. It is clear that this analysis of literature as "reflecting" the conditions of the period and location of its production does not in any way mark off literature as a product with a special insight into social conditions. Any other artistic commodity or aesthetic genre that filled an analogous niche, like painting, could have been used to arrive at similar conclusions.

The Progressives saw themselves as privileged commentators on what they construed as their past. It was a position that allowed them to critique *their* tradition in a language that was contrary to the common rule.[97] It is also clear that the voice with which they spoke and the stances they espoused were privileged precisely *because* they were consonant with a dominant version of and critique of that "past." Their particular investigations were angled through the terms they valorized and endorsed, and viewed simultaneously and paradoxically as peculiar to them as well as universal—that is, science, rationality, change as progress.[98]

Theirs was also a gendered position, a masculinized one. A ramification of that gendering was played out in the case of Rashid Jahan. As a woman writer, Rashid Jahan scripted her critique explicitly through the ordinary codes used to depict the exploitation of women. If one interjects her biography into her literary oeuvre, she, as a woman doctor, CPI member, and someone who functioned as a member of a largely male group, was the site of ambivalence. Indeed, her narratives exhibit the ambivalence of the position from which "women" or people in "feminized" positions spoke. The story "Sightseeing Trip to Delhi" and the plays to which I refer, *Behind the Veil/Curtain* and *Woman* (*ʿaurat*), make it clear that for her women protagonists, socialization into a "feminization" was conducted within the confines of a home, specifically behind *pardah* in the zenana, where women were acclimatized to seclusion. Men and women, husbands, brothers, mothers-in-law, and aunts all participated in socializing male and female children. But boys, unlike girls, were socialized both within their home—to some extent in the zenana—and outside their home.

Transgressive women in some of Jahan's work were often contained within and therefore curtailed by the zenana. Whether they ventured out or they stayed they were given the luxury of a litany of lament, but their plaints were largely ineffectual. In "Sightseeing Trip to Delhi," the tale of a protagonist's miserable journey with her husband to Delhi—where she is abandoned at the railway station—is nestled in a ritual of reproach. The woman tells the story to a gathering of women who share a language in which to complain about their treatment by their husbands. But the assumption that underpins the exchanges of stories about abuse is that nothing will/can be done about them.[99]

In instances when change is actually suggested or enacted, the impetus for it and the rhetorical possibilities it offers are brought to the zenana from the outside by figures like the woman doctor in *Behind the Veil/Curtain* or the male cousins in *Woman.* These characters, with ties to the "outside," bring their access to and control of systems that apparently legislate the world outside the zenana. Mediating between the zenana and the rest of the world, these figures play a role that Jahan herself plays, both as a woman doctor servicing women in the zenana and as a woman writer who exposes the conditions within. The two systems of knowledge/power available to the mediators—medicine and the legal system—are considered products of westernization. And even as she was advocating their potential, at least one, the legal system was deployed against Rashid Jahan when she published "Sightseeing Trip to Delhi" and *Behind the Veil/Curtain* in *Añgāre.*

The ability to actually bring change to the zenana is explicitly gendered. The changes the woman doctor can suggest to the woman suffering the trauma of excessive childbirth is to use birth control, a solution restricted to the body of the woman. The doctor in the story does not actually use the phrase "birth control"; rather, the phrase is implied by the context in which she speaks. The doctor, called in by the patient's sister-in-law, does not recommend any modifications to the architecture of feminine normalization; for example, she does not suggest that the woman leave her husband. The story closes with a dystopian vision of the future—a scene in which the lineage of abuse continues at the hands of the woman's long-awaited son.

The two male cousins in *Woman*, on the other hand, perform a different kind of service than women mediators: they are able to help their female cousin to transform her life-plot. Because she has given him no children, her husband is to remarry and bring his new wife to live in the home that she owns. The cousins are her conduit to medical advice; her medical records are taken by them to a doctor who then informs her through her cousins that she is fertile and it is her husband who is unable to have children. Her cousins also give her, through a lawyer they know, entry to the legal system so that she can obtain a divorce. Her body never walks out of the zenana, never meets the doctor or lawyer: her transactions are *pardah nashīn*, conducted through male mediators.

In these stories, as in life, dealings on behalf of an "abused" woman are more likely to result in a substantial mutation of their life-plot if men negotiate with other men than if women negotiate with men or with other women. Unlike the doctor's offer of care to her patient, the two male cousins give their cousin a way out of her dilemma that would allow her to leave the abusive situation rather than merely stanch the wound with a bandage. Tellingly, the most successful agents of change in these stories are *westernized* men who are willing to give their women relatives access to outside systems and to help them negotiate between the zenana and the outside.

What, then, is the role of a literary figure as exemplified by the literati in the PWA? And where does this leave Rashid Jahan as a literary figure encircled by a phalanx of men in newly forming male-dominated institutions? Clearly, Rashid Jahan is somewhat of an anomaly; her ambivalent relationship to her power is written into her stories through women mediators who live and work in male hierarchies. But the role she plays is consonant with, though more curtailed than, those played by her male counterparts in the PWA. So what of a poet like Miraji? What was his role as a literary figure?

## LITERARY FIGURES

> So I turned to the Garden of Love
> That so many sweet flowers bore;
> And saw it filled with graves.
>
> —William Blake

> Prem kī phulvārī ko samjhe kalī kalī muskān
> āñkh uṭhā kar pal bhar dekhā marghaṭ thā sthān.
>
> —Miraji's translation of Blake[100]

The idealized literary figure, the exemplary literateur, the privileged commentator for his world, according to the PWA at the time, was a messenger (*paighambar*) endowed with second sight who spoke in the rhythms of prophecy. He saw the contours of his universe in so complete a material way that he was able to lay out the full conditions of its crisis or its demise/death and predict its future. Premchand alludes to this messianism secreted into the literary when he says that in the present time, literature, like religion in the past, is the basis for man's moral salvation.[101] Raipuri's essay lays the same terms out, as did the work of the *Añgāre* collective and Premchand's address to the first Indian meeting of the PWA. Such an ideal figure, according to Premchand, sees the degradation of the past and present, understands the causes (*maqāṣid, asbāb*) for the conditions of decay, and strives to remove them.

It is the hallmark of prophetic discourse, literary or religious, that its redemptive message, tailored to the sociopolitical universe in which it is produced, responds to the rhetorical conventions for depicting "crisis," the condition of the present produced by the circumstances of the past, for which future redemption is proposed. Prophecy, for PWA members, was a secular genre and redemption was to be found in education, a mode of learning and seeing right, which was "revelation." The writer is a messianac activist in this schema; he is someone concerned with "changing" the sociopolitical conditions of the time. "Change" then becomes a marked word, as does "newness," and the disquisitions around the two meld.

The writer as a prophet, a standard-bearer, opens up for his followers the path to changing their sociopolitical circumstances. He has to show them the path, through a clear, and distinct, and photographic vision of the present. His vision, saturated with a yearning for certainty, materializes through an analysis of the economic conditions of the present. The stern propriety of this vision repudiates aesthetics, here perceived as a field mired in style, whose sumptuary indulgences are likely to lead one astray and backward into the provenance of a past that must be left behind. The temporality of this visionary politics is stretched out into a longing for a future. The future, along with the past, must take shape in the present. Though this present is told through "crisis," it also nurtures within it the possibilities of the future.

The figure of the artist/prophet synchronizes with other redemptive figures from the late nineteenth to the middle of the twentieth century in northern India's history—religious reformers, political prophets like Gandhi, whose discourse on political change operated at the intersection of social and religious reform, and finally, ubiquitous colonial stereotypes charged with the mission of colonizing the heathens. The continuity between indigenous elite reformers like Raja Ram Mohun Roy and British reformers was discussed by revisionist historiographers of this period.[102]

## LITERARY ACTIVITY: *ADAB AUR ʿALĀ*

As it began to formalize its beliefs, how would the PWA describe the literary activity of its members? So far, I have said that in the PWA's annals, ideal literary figures of their present are prophetic with a special understanding of literary history and a redemptive message for the future. Literary history, in the PWA's scenario, is plotted as a "fall" into crisis. The work of idealized literary figures is to understand and isolate the problems of the past and to offer solutions for the future through literary activity. Literary figures engender sociopolitical change through literature. Certain kinds of critiques and certain kinds of change are valorized over others; critiques and change that focus on material rather than discursive conditions for existence or literary production are thought of as superior.[103] This form of critique comes to be considered "political," while a discursive critique was labeled "apolitical." Calling literature "apolitical" was a way of situating it on the margins of literary activity. Alongside this strategy for exclusion from the PWA was another, more polemical, one—labeling a piece of literature "obscene."

I would like to return for a moment to the question I posed earlier on literary figures: what was the role of writers like Miraji? He and Manto, the two men who continued to write the kind of literature that irked Progressives, despite the sanctions against them, were not merely ordinary dissenters; they could not just be marginalized and ignored. Because these troublesome figures were considered "good" writers, they were actively expelled from the center of the Urdu literary universe as construed by the

Progressives. In addition, the literary habits ascribed to them were naturalized into measurable "traits" so that they were considered embodiments of them. They came to be represented as the epitome of the abnormal—drunk, dissolute, and verging on insanity.

What, then, was exemplary literary activity? As I have suggested, the PWA's understanding of the immediate "past" is a period of stasis and degeneracy, while the "present" is a period of constant transformation. What does this imply, for the PWA, about exemplary literary activity of the present, a time when old mores (ideas that slip into old beliefs and into institutions) are no longer viable and a new society is forming: "Radical changes are taking place. . . . Fixed ideas and old beliefs, social and political institutions are being challenged. Out of the present turmoil and conflict a new society is arising."[104] Literature is bound up with the down-and-dirty production of a new sociopolitical order: the hand-to-hand combat between the "moribund and doomed to decay," wrestling to prolong its life, and the "Progressive spirit" that is taking place on the pages of literary texts. This literature of the present must speak the needs, desires, death, and life of the common people (*avām*) who are to form the new social order and must speak to a wider audience than the literature of the past. The manifesto asks writers to "Bring art to the common people, and register the actualities of life."[105] The attenuation of the common proposed by the manifesto was prolonged by Raipuri into a list that stretched from color and lineage through community into the nation-to-be: *rang o nasl aur qaumiyat o vaṭaniyat.*[106] Here the common and the national are elongated through the extrapolation of other more localized categories that may or may not map easily onto them. Premchand was rigorous in his address to the first meeting of the PWA—he asked his compatriots to change aesthetic standards and through them change measures (*m'aiyār*) of value so that the standards of people who hitherto had not been included in literary activity would become the "normal" rules of aesthetic judgment. He also made the call for literature to become an agent of social chage.[107]

To address through literature the concerns of an audience that the PWA considered victims of oppression—urban and rural poor, and women[108]—meant, as it did for the writers of *Añgāre*, that literature ought to reflect their conditions and propose solutions. There were several assumptions in this belief. One was an assumption about the concerns or the intent of this particular audience, that this unwieldy set of people wanted to see themselves reflected as products of an oppressive system and also wanted this kind of literature produced for their consumption to be used to alleviate their condition. Here the "people" became an other whose lives must be rendered clearly and distinctly, in a prose that registered the daily grammar, the intonations, the inflections of the languages they used. Another assumption was that literature produced by the Progressives was capable of clearly reflecting the conditions of oppression. This meant that the life of these others, whose oppression served as literary material, could be easily, transparently rendered. Finally, unlike the literature of the past, the writing produced by the PWA was considered by them (although not necessarily by anyone else) as an idealized form of social action capable of transcending the conditions of its production. In other words, it was not limited by the allegiances of the social position of the group that produced it, which was primarily middle class and for whom the objects of their literary endeavors were precisely that—objects.

One of the issues that arose in this context at a meeting of the PWA was whether the PWA, as a primarily middle-class organization, was actually capable of speaking for people who were of the "proletariat."[109] Could middle-class writers relate to peasants and workers? If the places occupied by the writer as mediator were thickened, so that they were also subjected to a review, what might ensue? What were the ethical questions enmeshed in this kind of mediation: between subject (writer) and object (representation/reader) who were not analogous in power? In other words, the kind of question that was raised by the Subaltern Studies Collective which was: what are the implications of a group of privileged men speaking for and representing groups that have been designated "underprivileged subalterns"?[110] The interim provisional resolutions to these questions were almost banal. The PWA decided at the meeting held with the *Amritsar kisān sabhā* (Amritsar Farmers Organization) at Jallianwala Bagh in the summer of 1937 that they did not need to share someone's life to know it, but that a better understanding of the conditions of peasant life was necessary. This was the beginning of a turn toward folk literature for some writers. The banality of one coterie of responses to the question of language was offset by the political urgency of another group of questions about language that the Progressives took on: the Hindi-Urdu controversy.[111]

## LITERATURE AND LIFE

Adab aur zindagī, adab aur ā'īnādārī
adab kyā hai? Adab barā'e adab yā adab barā'e zindagī?

*What is art? Art for art or art for life?*[112]

Progressives believed that literature could be brought closer to "life" by reflecting "life." The call in the late 1930s was not quite for social realism but a clarion summoning writers to a "reflection theory of literature." The depiction of the conditions of a group of people came to be called the portrayal of all life. This mimetic turn in the ideal literature of the present was contrasted to the literature of the past, which was considered nonmimetic, a pure linguistic play. In the past, Premchand said, a story was a story and life was life.[113] In the present, however, Raipuri said, literature was a translation of life, and life and literature ought to have the same aims. Value was measured, in however seemingly diaphanous a way, through the geopolitics of intimacy between literature and life.[114]

Allied to the mimetic turn was a developing conception of what constituted a social fact and a theory of language in which language transparently displayed those social facts. Mimesis seemed to promise a photographic rigor, bringing literature and life together with a visual closeness that was so familiar that language as mediating medium seemed to dissolve away. Social fact came to stand for social reality, and the portrayal of particular groups came to represent the social "real" (*ḥaqīqat*) as truth. But mimetic turned into a mimetic fallacy. The demand for mimesis so infected literary critical language that readers obscured the complex relationship between mimesis as the form in which prophecy was rendered in the work of the Progressives and earlier disciplines of representation (like religious desire and prophetic poetry). The hope carried alongside photographic likenesses, that they bring immediate access and clarity, apparently overtook readers, so that they forgot to record or remember the process of sifting and collating by which certain images became exemplary or typical and hence the truth.[115] Critics also forgot for a moment in their quest for political polemical lucidity the fissures produced by traumas of modernization, whose reverberations they wanted portrayed in fiction, and which could not be offered in smoothly translucent prose.

Mimesis had a long, tortured history that wended its way through nineteenth-century Urdu criticism. It traversed arguments and agreements over educational practices; and battles over the pastoral/natural, over the primacy of an uninflected puritan prose, over the seductions that had to be harnessed and turned toward freedom—the nation-to-be, the land, through reworkings of familiar "older" forms of poetry. These were quite clearly tensions in the work of certain Progressive poets like Faiz, tensions that Coppola explores to some extent in his dissertation on the Progressive movement in Urdu literature. The representation of the poet's persona in Faiz's lyric, for example, often continued to follow some rules of the ghazal: the poet continued to be a lover, the object of his desire still a lover, so the representation of "reality" was poeticized in accordance with rules living past the nineteenth century.[116] Faiz's work, like the work of poets writing in languages other than Urdu, went to the interventionary spaces and introverted temporalities of desire; angling the longing cadences of nostalgia toward new fidelities: *mujhse pahlī sī muhabbat mere mehbūb na mañg.* The beloved sometimes became the nation not quite yet, became the land, language, the *qaum, rang, nasl, vaṭan.*

One of Miraji's criticisms of the Progressives was that as *ḥaqīqat parastī* (reality-loving) poets they hinged on a different conception of the role of language in representation than they imagined for themselves. He took seriously Raipuri's contention that literature was a translation of life, and opened it up for rigorous speculation. Literary language was not merely a transparent medium but a medium of translation. And what if translation were not a form of channeling where the body of the host evaporated, but one where the materiality of the host's history offered a conduit that reshaped the product? So, Miraji conceived of literary language not as pellucid, but as ringed and thickened by the messiness of its imbrications in the "real."[117] His criticism of the Progressives as *ḥaqīqat parastī* was not based on their need to represent reality "through the lives of the down-trodden, women, and workers," but rather, it was based on the dearth of tropes available to them for their depiction of *ḥaqīqat* as mirror image. For Miraji, the mirror image (as literary text) only gave readers information about what had been placed before it. At the same time, he spoke about text as reflection and text as translation into a mirror that opened up a space in time between what was before the mirror and the image caught in it.[118] That space was dense with desire—seduction, loss, nostalgia, anguish, pleasure—for the truth of the stuff/self in front of the mirror, for the image/self seen in the mirror, for the way forks and cusps of light resolved into images, for the shapes and edges of the mirror's surface.[119] All these dissolved, blurred, and sharpened, their outlines metastasized and flowed through the material of language.[120] Language was an artifact, a materialization whose dimensions could be transformed by a writer curious about its uses elsewhere. Such a writer might also then alter representation: the shapes that stood before the mirror whose images turned into truth. In order to expand the possibilities of representation (that might even challenge the primacy of the visual) for his *ḥaqīqat parast* colleagues, Miraji wanted to translate, and introduce them to writers like Baudelaire, who he felt imbued reality with desire; he focused on the evocative limber grief and loss written into similar depictions of reality, and whose uses of language, image, tropes, and modes of representation might supplement those of the Progressives.

Ye fitnah admī kī ḳhānāh-e vīrānī ko kyā kam hai
hu'e tum dost jis ke, dushman uskā āsmān kyoṅ ho?[1]

When you set out to mischief you ravage my home,
why bother with the sky as an enemy, with you as a friend?

# 3. MIRAJI'S RESPONSE TO THE PROGRESSIVES

What was Miraji's relationship to the Progressives? Where is he placed, and how? When these questions were posed in Chapter 2, Miraji was situated in a position of privileged marginality. That is, he was read into the dominant twentieth-century Urdu tradition as a "troublesome" member, even though his interaction with it was not consistent over his thirty years of literary activity.

When he first sauntered onto the literary scene of Lahore in the early 1930s, Miraji was considered a young, rising star, an avid advocate of the Urdu avant-garde.[2] But the Progressives were also emerging as a literary force, and as they began to accumulate influence and demarcate the arena of literary activity and mediate value, Miraji, along with other writers, was relegated to the margins of the Urdu literary world. Although measures (*mʿaiyār*) had been set up to cull the so-called "normative" literary community and the canon created by the Progressives, the system proved permeable. Works that were antithetical to the new norms for literary and critical activity like Miraji's poetry or Manto's short stories continued to be produced even as the norms were being put in place, thereby providing the impetus to create yet more controls on the new canon that were specifically formed to fit the characteristics of the works of the authors who were being marginalized.

## MIRAJI AND THE PROGRESSIVES

Some of Miraji's ties to the Progressives can be seen in his language. He deployed the same root vocabulary and accepted the preeminence of certain terms while writing literary history and criticism—"change," "newness," "progress" (*tabdīl, jadīdiyāt, taraqqi*)—but he deliberately enmeshed them in his own iconoclastic explorations, against the way they had been applied by other literary critics. Nevertheless, he did not disengage himself from the common, accepted literary language and, like other writers whose works exceeded the scheme of controls that accompanied their production, he continued to operate within its limits. Miraji also shared with the Progressives structural elements in the story they both told of their literary pasts, coalitions between history and modernity, and the iconography for representing the "past" or "tradition." Both Miraji and the Progressives materialize time synecdocally to figure a relationship with it. For example, the most obvious concatenations between Miraji and certain narratives written by Progressives, like Raipuri, is that they both anthropomorphized the ghazal and feminized it when it was used to represent the past literary tradition. Through this allegorical and therefore bodied past, ghazal as sumptuously ornamented beloved, Miraji and Raipuri ventured over the limen of desire where the body of writing fields its attractions and repulsions to a feminized past.

Some of the differences between Miraji and the Progressives lie in Miraji's particular resignification of key terms he shares with the Progressives. His essay on new poetry, "Nayī shāʿirī kī buniyādeṅ" (The fundamentals of new verse),[3] opens:

> Some people have begun to call free verse in Urdu new verse. I am not among them. Some people, coming at free verse through its content [topics]—women and workers—have begun to call that free verse. It's as though life's political, economic, or sexual aspects in their view are the unformed issues of new poetry. I don't say this either. I believe that even if it is written in meter, lyric can be considered free verse if it shuns noisy effects and is constructed to describe, think about, or express some issue. A new poet is someone who extricates himself from the bonds of convention to create his personhood [poetic self] by revealing a feeling-thought or a desire.

The above paragraph illustrates the rhetorical strategies Miraji used in his work. He wrapped himself, his use of a term, his particular reading of a poem, in other uses or readings. These gestures of inclusion served to draw in readers with assumptions different than his, and once they had been enticed, to convince them of the validity of his own view by showing them that his use of certain terms was much more broad-based than others. The contrast between readings showed off his use or his reading. According to this portion of *shā'irī*, other proponents of new verse see it either in terms of a single formal shift that released meter and rhyme from previous constraints, or in terms of a formal shift that released verse to explore new topics, like women and workers. Promulgators of new verse (the Progressives) believed that through these topics certain "life" issues could be explored.

As Miraji begins to lay out his own position—"In my view"—he gives readers strategies for judging previous opinions. In the next two sentences, when he says that his kind of new poet "abandons noisy or vocal effects" and "extricates himself from . . . conventions," he leads the reader around again to recollect the examples he gave them of poets created by prior critics, who are then read as merely interested in provoking controversy (*hañgāmah*) while mired in the conventional. *His* definition of new poetry is poetry that blends feeling and thought to completely express what goes on inside a person—"a feeling-thought or desire"—and suits form and language to the issue at hand. Such a poet, rather than resorting to the conventionality of the formal to assess his affiliations to newness and thus to the measures of value, turns form to his own use.

The differences I have outlined between Miraji and some of the mainline 1930s Progressives are structured around their relative positions to dominant modes of reading. It is clear that Miraji was marginalized through the way he was read. During his lifetime he had to confront readings of his work by mainline Progressives as "obscene poetry"; he had to provide other readers an alternative framework within which it could be read—not just to create alternative readings but to be read at all. By laying out the ground for new practices of reading, Miraji tried to pry open a space in which his poetry could be read as other than obscene.

Because my limited time in India made it difficult for me to collect all of my own material from writers in Bombay, I commissioned my mother to conduct some interviews for me. She came back with the tapes, a slightly embarrassed cast to her face. I asked her what was bothering her and she said hesitantly, as though afraid I would be angry, that she'd been asked why her daughter was writing on this poet: his poetry was so sexual, so obscene. People did not stop giving me or my mother information, however, despite the question she had been faced with; in fact I think they were even more helpful once they found I was serious. But what the incident made abundantly clear was the charged significance of certain judgments. I asked my mother whether she'd been given examples of Miraji's poetry to support the accusation, but realized even as I asked her that the use of a word like "sexual" in front of her, a sedate-looking, middle-class housewife, was an automatic conversation stopper; it was such a scandalous charge that she could not retaliate with repartee. Were the interviews not being conducted for me, she would not have, as she did, continued them. She certainly would not have gone out of her way to read Miraji's poetry once she heard that it was "sexual." I read her some poems and talked them over with her, discussed multiple significations and readings, but felt unsatisfied.

Calling a poem "sexual" was a way of taking it out of literary circulation, turning it into the provenance of aficionados shielded by their professional knowledge, and perverts. Calling a poem sexual relegated it to the domain of the legal and psychological in the present, or the domain of what ought to have been forgotten, from the past. Once something was labeled "sexual" it also stopped the reading dead, as I discovered when I asked poets questions about optional readings of such poems. They simply weren't interested, and took recourse in tautology: the poem was obscene because it was sexual and it was "just sexual" therefore it was obscene. It brought home to me the absolute necessity Miraji faced of creating reading strategies that would slip out of those provided for his poetry by the Progressives. It also brought into view the circularity of the assigning value, where the terms of assessment were the assumptions on which value was based.

When I reread Miraji's essay on new verse in the context of my recent experiences and his own critical piece analyzing his poem "Picnic in the Jungle" (in *Is naẓm meñ*), it became clear that a part of *New Verse*'s agenda was indeed to provide readers with strategies for reading. In their solicitous mindfulness to the features of each poem, and in their deployment of analytic frameworks suited to each poem's concerns, Miraji's readings differed from the dominant ones endorsed by the Progressives. Translation, too, became very important for Miraji as he rendered a range of poets from Baudelaire to Li Po. These other poets gave Urdu readers alternatives to their own canon as well as access to the conventional Western canon that was the tool kit of affiliations with which every recipient of English education was equipped.

A concern Miraji shared with the Progressives was their common understanding of audiences, both readers and listeners, as protean. In order to speak about reorienting poetry to attract and attend to the needs of new audiences, or to infer that differently composed audiences were making new sets of demands on writers, as both Miraji and Ansari did, they assumed that audiences changed with different historical circumstances. Ansari's protean audiences, whose taxonomies were determined by their economic resources, needs, and their relationship to capital, changed over time from "traditional" royal elite patrons of Sanskrit *kāvya* and the ghazal and the plebeian, humbler audience of bhakti poetry, to the homogeneous proletarian or the homogenous middle-class ones of the 1930s. In Miraji's work this schema transmuted into a more complex notion of multiple audience perspectives (*naẓariyah*). Although Miraji never sifts out audience response as an independent category of literary criticism, in many of his essays that were close readings of single contemporary poems, particularly those in *Is naẓm meñ*, he wends his way through several reading options before arriving at his own, and his rhetoric of persuasion is directed at those other readings.[4]

In *Is naẓm meñ*, Miraji assesses changes in canon formation in response to the shifting desires of different audiences. In his discussion of poetry written prior to the twentieth century, rather than saying that the production of poetry was affected by audiences, he said that he saw audiences influence the assimilation of poetry into a mainstream. So, for Miraji, poetry that did not fit the canon had always been produced. His explanation for why it was not included in the canon at the time of its production is that people did not have the requisite tools for reading it. Tools that were available might bend under the pressure of political shifts, or transmute as the poem was transported to new places. And eventually, even a poem that had once been transparently readable might turn opaque. As audiences were reconstituted (including the Progressives as an audience) they made different demands, read with different presuppositions and biases, and assembled new languages of criticism. With a change in audience, the kind of poetry that was canonized, including poetry that made up the canon from another time or another place, might be transformed.

Miraji's depiction of shifts in audience response looks at audiences not as solipsistic and self-generating but, like the Progressives' analysis of the same phenomena, as produced and refigured under sociopolitical constraints.[5] Literary universes were, for him—as for the Progressives—contingent upon extraliterary events. Under the influence of British rule, shifts in socioeconomic power from Muslim courts to British-dominated institutions opened up the control of Urdu culture that had been, until then, the provenance of the courts. According to Miraji, this moved the audience from a carefully demarcated and patrolled urban court culture to one that was more broad-based. As a member, however marginal, of an elite cadre who defined the canon, he and his compatriots couldn't question or even see that even if the audience had expanded, a cadre no more egalitarian than the old court culture still made the canonical choices and formulated the codes for reading poetry.[6]

Since Miraji chooses a range of sometimes incompatible writers upon which to comment, and tailors readings to the writer's piece, even if he came up with his version of an apposite reading for a poem in his show-and-tell readings, his appraisals could never be threaded easily into a unitary strand, nor could the reading frameworks he uses. The modes he deployed include, for example, reading through gendered colonial desire, through collisions and collusions of genre, through historical materialist analyses. In this refusal to come up with a single reading or grid he is very different from the Progressives. As the Progressive movement gathered steam and was regularized and ordered, it set itself to create a uniform frame of reference for writing, as well as reading, poetry and prose. As a result, everyone (including Miraji) who did not fit the frame was marginalized from *the* literary culture. When Miraji appears to create a unitary position for himself, in those moments when he signifies contested concepts like "progress" and "newness," the position he creates is quite clearly a position that he sees as peculiar to himself rather than as a definition for an entire movement. So he still leaves open the possibility that others might hold antagonistic or just different opinions than him.

As a member of a group of literati who wrote and worked as both literary and political figures, Miraji operated at the limits of both the local and pan-Indian discourses about politics as well as literature. With very little money, Miraji was economically marginal; also in both the literary and economic modes through which he has been constructed and elided, Miraji simultaneously fell into the category of "subaltern."[7] Aijaz Ahmad, who has written a hegemonic frame narrative about Miraji—the narrative one is referred to, albeit with certain reservations about its "Freudian slant," when one investigates Miraji—portrays him either as chameleon "subaltern," self-consciously configured between a range of stereotypical male "subaltern" roles, or as constantly shifting between personae. Although, when he published his article "Miraji: Personality and Work" in *Saverā* (Dawn) Ahmad would not have used the term "subaltern" on Miraji, and possibly might not use it as a designation had he written the article more recently, I think it is worth noting that Ahmad does use the descriptive categories of laborer, yogi, and sadhu on Miraji. Ahmad's categories are formed at the intersection of the signifiers of economic status and the signifiers of dislocation based on medical, psychological, and criminal taxonomies, as well as on earlier rules for cataloguing poetic personae. Since I do not wish to take it on here, I have also left intact in my statement above the problematic designations of and juxtaposition of constructed, fictive personalities and a "real," "authentic" "self" that Ahmad maintains in his analysis of Miraji's "personality."

I would like to propose here that, through rewriting work attributed to Miraji and the space he occupied in relation to a group of intellectuals, the categories of indigenous colonial groups Guha proposed were always in slippage. The way he configured himself with respect to them and the language in which he was read by them were not completely visible or contained within the parameters set up by a particular political polemic. This polemic still informs literary discourse and the language of historiography.[8] So, too, the narratives of resistance were not visible when read through this polemic.

## MIRAJI'S PROSE

As I look at writings by Miraji, I will address discursive formations, stretching the language in which he wrote to account for its materialization into other fields, and will offer some conclusions about how the pieces respond to the circumstances that attended their production or appearance.

Discursive formations are important for two reasons. This kind of project is particularly appropriate for critics like Miraji who focus on the language—linguistic formations and literary lineages—of contemporaries and the ways in which these were unwittingly hedged in by established modes of speaking and assigning value. Furthermore, discursive formations are places where the power of the state is inadvertently vested and displayed through representations of it. In the case of Miraji's essays, the representations of the state, of the community in relation to the state, and of self-representations are those exchanged or circulated within a community that, in this particular mode, is not overtly, directly, or primarily responsive to colonial demands.[9] What this kind of analysis opens to view are the spaces where effects of the power of a colonial state or an affirmative ideology appear to be concealed, not just as complicated narratives in which the state figures but in an iconography of tropes through which the descriptions of the state have become naturalized. In Miraji's work, the representations of the state as an agent of Progressive modernization are undercut by his representation of the condition of his literary community. His description of his community as one marked by profound uncertainty and powerlessness conflicts with and contradicts the cliched valorization of the state. These two narratives do not run in tandem, but disrupt one another.[10]

By the time of Miraji's death, the bulk of his prose had been marginalized in an Urdu canon controlled by the Progressives. The reception of his work, its evaluation, the interpretation of specific poems, and the reciprocities between his prose writings and poetry were affected by the complex interaction of his work with the policies and interpretative responses of the Progressives who dominated the literary scene toward the end of his life and for about twenty years after his death.[11] Miraji's entire oeuvre, as has already been indicated, was shaped and shorn by critics to fit a biography in which he appeared as a drunk, dissolute poet whose narcissistic desire disengaged him from political activity. Read through the valences of this biographizing and a set of particular categories for exclusion and inclusion with measures and rules for political engagement to which these essays did not all conform, marginalization resulted even within Miraji's opus. The parameters for inclusion relied on a materialist language of political engagement, one that asked for an explicit critique of the material conditions—economic and political—of the colonial situation. Since Miraji did not write exclusively in this language, his critique of the discourse of his literary political milieu was considered apolitical; he was thought of as speaking in "purely aesthetic" and transcendental categories—as providing merely a reverie on the condition of modern "Man"—and was, thus, defanged. Even when he was rejuvenated in the work of critics and poets like Wazir Agha or N. M. Rashid, the terms of his rejuvenation never question the reading of him as apolitical. The work discussed here will be mediated by my reading of him, which, as a counterpoint to earlier readings, will concentrate on his essays as work that explores the compromised conditions of literary production in a colonial universe, and which offer occasionally subversive rewritings of certain facets of this production.

Since I will be looking primarily at narratives, the forms collusion and subversion take are discursive ones. I address the narratives as both compromised by the neocolonial representations of the state and resistant to precisely those representations, so there is no pristine set of representations in which an uncompromised dominant position is possible.[12] All of Miraji's work, and particularly that which I discuss here, is impressed by the profound ambivalence that marks similar literary artifacts produced under colonial conditions. Moments of subversion and resistance are constantly folded into, among other things, the iconography of the representation of the colonial state. This iconography is shaped by colonial justifications of their continued and "necessary" presence in India and by the rhetoric of Progressive modernization under the aegis of British rule.[13] I will also treat some of his essays as pieces of discursive subversion directed at the implicit rather than the explicit terms of engagement with colonialism: at hegemonies, at the places of naturalization where people had come to believe in something as plainly true, at those places where desires coagulated. In most of the essays he wrote, Miraji did not explicitly critique the colonial state; rather, some of his critique was directed at the modes through which his own literary contemporaries had come to speak a language in a way that now seemed ordinary—by repetitively imitating the semiotics, genres, vocabulary, grammar, and syntax associated with British writers.

Miraji asked his contemporaries to self-reflexively engage and confront their relationship with and connections to British codes in terms of what they wrote and how they wrote, and not to blindly emulate or imitate what they thought the British did.[14] In addition, he attempted to disengage his contemporaries from a set of filiative literary authorities that were exclusively British and to provide for them alternative literary figures as references and affiliative networks.[15]

The context he provided for the alternative networks—the act of writing on and of translating the work of various men and women poets, thereby introducing into the Urdu canon figures who had not been available in the same way prior to his production—is one piece of a performance of discursive resistance. In the process, Miraji rewrote what he targeted as the authorizing canon or canon of authorities for Urdu literature.[16] His irregular affiliative lineages, traveling through male and female writers, ravaged filiations as patrimonial property lines that inhered in the past constructed as it was up to that point.[17] His translations highlighted *translation* as a colonial apparatus aimed at reeducation, and his essays displayed historical consciousness as a technology that refined/sieved historical remembering through repudiation and forgetting.

## THROUGH THE LYRIC TO MYTH AND HISTORY: *AFSĀNE, SHĀʿIRĪ AUR TĀRĪḴH*

> A historical materialist cannot do without the notion of a present which is not a transition, but in which time stands still and has come to a stop. For this notion defines the present in which he himself is writing history. Historicism gives the "eternal" image of the past; historical materialism supplies a unique experience with the past. The historical materialist leaves it to others to be drained by the whore called "once upon a time" in historicism's bordello. He remains in control of his powers, man enough to blast open the continuum of history.[18]

In the essay considered below, "Nayī shāʿirī kī buniyādeṅ," Miraji disentangled himself from other critics who shared the criteria of "newness" as a basis for assigning value to a literary project. "Newness" in this essay became the badge of honor awarded when a poem fit the criteria for inclusion in the canon. Though Miraji attempted to draw lines between himself and others on how he assessed his contemporaries and tallied up their newness, he had to first seduce the people he saw as his interlocuters. But the diversions of enticement he ventured were not simple, for he too believed at least a little in what he tried to distance himself from. And though the rhetoric his contemporaries might have used was sternly proper, the pull of fiction and lyric moved them to create improper things. They, like Miraji, created things anointed as new, but with allegiances that ran contrary to assignments of value. As Miraji wrote to them, for them, and to entice them, he slipped and slid like them as he fashioned the dense webbing that wove together new and old; past, present, and future; history and historical materialism; the things to be kept, things to be left, and things to be consigned to a future that may or may not ever come.

Newness can rise like a phoenix from the ashes of the old. It can reappear time and again as time recycles itself. It can glow suddenly out from the past as the past curves forward and back. It can be held in abeyance for a future promised and always awaited, never quite delivered. It can be a missive misdirected to an unknown address. It can materialize as nostalgia's ghost. All these show up in Miraji's corpus. Many of them resonate with his elaborations here.

## THE FABULOUS STORIES: *AFSĀNE AUR HIKĀYAT*

Miraji's descriptions of and exhortations to the audience for Urdu literature engage facets of the narratives he writes for his world. In his essays he writes out three parallel tales, moving from the mythic to the historical. The stories are culled from three different portions of the essay on new verse and form the bulk of it.[19] They are framed in discussions of words central to Urdu literary discourse and literary judgment: newness (*nayī*), change (*tabdīl*), and Progressive (*taraqqī*). The stories are as follows:

### *1. The Myth*

New forms, new topics, new gestures of speaking—in new lyric their arrival is intimately bound up, in a certain way, with the wants of the inside and the urgencies of the outside.

The needs of the first humans were limited. Therefore, their poetry walked on the same limited paths. Let's say that their sight could seek poetics within the circle of their necessities. Filling his stomach, he [the first man] found pleasure in moments of forgetfulness/repose with his *hamdam shabānah* [soul-mate night (feminized)], collecting food to fill his stomach and feel fear. Fear of the *maẓāhir-e fiṭrat* [spectacles of nature] and fear of *hamjins* [own species (masculinized)] enemies. These were the very things that birth the stuff of poetry. For the first humans poetry was the intermediary space stretched out between the parallel lines of desire and fear. As they [humans] traveled through stages of progress, and as they acquired the means for civilization and housing, the star of human imagination [*taḳhayyul*] spread, flying in its own splendor, and from its ignited dust/cinders, became the Milky Way in a sky of thought. The arrival of civilization and housing didn't just offer a kind of literary satisfaction given through desire and attraction, but after this moment the intellect began traveling on every kind of creative and uncreative path, and at the same time began to wonder about which point he [the intellect] would make his next destination.

*2. The Fable (Mediating Narrative)*

Art is the interpreter/translator [*tarjumān*] of many identities. And identities put life on display. It is evident that our life these days definitely changes, if not every month, then every year. . . .

Today, science's inventors have brought each thing close to every other thing. But human beings have been separated from each other. It's as though the previous blinding facts [*āñkh ojhal vālī bāt ab nahīn rahī*] are no longer viable. But the straightforwardness necessary for knowing one another, the depth of which is no longer possible to achieve, is not in our constitutions, or at the very least is disappearing. This is the reason why art, while coming closer to life, also remains distant from it. This was also how it was in the past. But it had another form. In the past, a bed of flowers had been spread out for a long time on the consecrated ground of the royal household of Urdu poetry. A beautiful woman [*sundarī*] was sitting on it, adorned [*singār*] with sixteen pieces of jewelry. The people who lived in the simile fanned her with the fly-whisks of metaphor. The people who strolled in and out of the palace were the few hand-picked men who were able to fire up their hearts and bathe their eyes in the beautiful splendor of that restless radiant woman. Not just anyone had the courage to enter this formidable, aloof, and untouchable gathering. Only the courageous were emboldened by courtliness to enter the royal gathering: they were those versed in the niceties of literature, and only they could utter the proper sounds of praise when they listened to others; only they could go there. . . .

After this, a besieging storm crossed the seven seas and arrived. The hurricane of Western culture, organization, and education struck. It picked up dried twigs and leaves. But in its glory it also brought rain to help new buds sprout. Now, slowly, new voices could be heard.

Some said: art should be brought closer to life.

Some said: we cannot carry goods over from our assets.

Some spoke out and said: we know only two things—purity and integrity.

And the commotion of each kind of music created turbulence. New waves seethed out of the turbulence. Which [the waves] produced new stages for life's journey. But whose smokiness is like a forgetfulness. The sort of forgetfulness in which only a few [people] can see the right road and travel on it.

This was the quality of the new poetry of the time. And the new poet stands at a crossroads from which many roads leave, to the right, to the left, to the front, and to the back. But he doesn't really know which road he has picked. What importance the experiences of the past have for him. For how long he has to stand this way. . . .

The old supports on the basis of which people passed their entire lives in the dilemmas of a domestic existence no longer remain with him. He is now all alone and on a quest for help. Sometimes he imagines the wrong things as a support. Sometimes even when he reaches a real support, he doesn't know what happened. And the main reason for this is when a new edifice has to be adorned, it must be poured into a new mold.

### *3. The History*

The causes of this upheaval were located in the murky time of 1857. When for the first time, the connections between social and political norms were splintered and space created for new codes. Let's say that a gap of a few generations had already formed between new young poets and the older generations. They [older generations] saw that time of intellectual turmoil as a pulse.

But history and genealogical memory come together and make the time of its past its experience. Other than this, a person's intelligence is made up from its fusion with the past and future. The past molds his basic affairs. The future investigates each movement it makes, and those aspirations become intentions, reach fruition in the future, and make its identity visible.

When we bring the past of today's poets before us, from a political perspective, then, along with the suppressed ideas which emerge out of the complete desecration of the local government, we see elements which augment the life of new political movements. These were the strong repressions of the first downfall. They took on a political cast and, at odds with the entire fabric of the country, gave birth to new aspirations and created a desire for progress and freedom in all walks of life.

When we look at the life of a poet from a social perspective, we see more than one thing taking place. New education came even as the distances in the cities were closed. And the frog in the well began to think that there was life outside his species and his society. Which was an unyielding space that, because of its intensity, twisted earlier ideas. Education and commerce introduced him to new presences. And the map of a domestic existence began to be erased. Far away from his home he began to feel the dimensions of alienation. That feeling spread in every direction. . . . Superficiality became the norm, and a lack of responsibility grew. New, young poets began to write. But the desire to write the kind of poetry that one needs knowledge for, came later.

These three stories intertwine in various ways. The mythic story is a generic description of the movements of modernization. The players in the myth are human beings and the events that occur in the story generic events are dehistoricized and divorced of cultural details. The historical narrative is located in Miraji's own world, the world of urban Urdu literati. In the essay on new poetry, the shift from myth to history is mediated through a story of the violent impact of the British, "the hurricane of Western culture, organization, and education," on Miraji's cultural universe. The mediating story or historical fable provides the liaison between interactions described in terms of a ubiquitous person residing in a universal /abstract community and his responses to his world, and one that describes the history of shifts enacted by a particularly constituted community rendered in detail. All three stories tell of the movement in a literary tradition and the outgrowth of new literary forms, and all three locate the causes for the movement in (re)formations of the *socius*. The three—myth, fable, and history—map onto one another, and in their reiteration of similar trajectories within differently depicted contexts, read as allegories of each other. Mapping the three stories onto one another as mutual allegorical conceits weaves them together, so that they cannot be easily isolated, one from another, to establish Benjamin's separation between the historical (as fable) and the historical materialist (as history): between "the 'eternal' image of the past" and a "unique experience of the past."

This shift, from myth to history, both substantiates the validity of each kind of narrative and disturbs the privilege or prestige of any one—each story must have the others to survive and be read. The history makes specific, iterating in historical time and moving into the present moment of Miraji's literary circumstances, the generic mythos of "humankind." The myth endorses the historical descriptions by underpinning the historical and moving it into the dimension of the timeless or into the places of out-of-time. But this dichotomization of history and myth is disordered by the way the myth is read. The myth ought to be a shared story of a community that tells its origins, but is instead read as Miraji's peculiarly personal "specific" account of human concerns. The historical narrative, which could have been read as Miraji's own retelling of his time, becomes "generic" and the point of convergence for commonalities between him, his audience, and the knotted place of common cultural tale-telling. The juxtaposition of mythic and historical pulls the historical into the mythic, so the historical narrative, too, becomes a form of cultural tale-telling, a collective fiction that relies on nodal points of information whose veracity would have to be taken on faith and are a part of a body of exchanged and shared beliefs. The imbrication of myth and history offered a counterclaim to James Mill's earnestly believed proposition that the mythic and the historical must be kept apart, and that the separation between them constituted the truly modern sense of the historical.[20]

The residue from the myth Miraji tells, disengaged from the historical narrative that accompanies it, becomes one of the modes through which Miraji's work is read. N. M. Rashid, in an interview with Carlo Coppola, said of Miraji: "He calls him (Man) back to Nature where his primitive self used to be. . . . His poetry symbolizes the eternal quest of Man . . . for the discovery of the lost self."[21] Rashid's analysis of Miraji's project is problematic, because in it he sees Miraji's work functioning in an entirely different discursive and symbolic space from that of Miraji's contemporaries, and thus not political. But Rashid's analysis is useful for a reader like me, because it demarcates the theoretical place in critical writing in and on Urdu literature that is both apolitical and perceived as "belonging" to Miraji, as Miraji's provenance, and as identified with him.[22] Critical positions like Rashid's, which lose or forget the body of Miraji's essay, so that they can remember it metonymically, only through one part, are ironic precisely in relation to what the stories venture. The entire prose piece could be thought of as a kind of voyage of loss and memory, toward loss and about loss, where loss becomes an ambivalent form of liberation in another key.

The three stories map onto one another in several ways. They share plot fixtures and transformatory elements that echo or draw upon a particular narrative of change. Like the neo-Victorian companionate marriage fantasy that continues to underwrite fictional and polemical narratives about family relationships in the new modern of early-twentieth-century South Asia, a "narrative of change" is the structural fixture on which histories are built. In Miraji's essays this "narrative of change" displays archetypal patterns that conform to the exigencies of colonial circumstances. But these patterns are modulated by the context in which they appear. And unlike most narratives of change scripted for a colonized world they do not possess a moral telos.

Temporality takes curious turns in the three stories. In the first and the second stories its apparition is not as historical time. Rather it is embedded in space, embedded into the architectures of transformation, told in images that toll the movement of time. In the third story temporality begins to be spoken as date, as 1857, the date of a rupture, haunted by the bodies that died in war. This is the conventionalized representation of historical time. Into it is folded the possibility of sequences that date: of dates that render events, locate them, and spatialize them.

All the narratives are bipolar, bisected into disjunctive halves organized around change. The first half is the "past" of the story, and the second the "present." The two portions are bound to each other through the moment of transformation or the point at which change begins to occur. The details in the second half of each narrative are constituted through that change.

In the next section of this chapter, I will look at the myth, the mediating narrative, and the history, to see what forms the patterns take in both the first and second part of each narrative. In the process, I will also examine the various tropes that are deployed in the writing of each narrative.

## THE PAST: "ONCE UPON A TIME"

In the first portion of each narrative Miraji describes the originary moment of the story—the moment when the story starts is the "once upon a time" section of each. Here Miraji lays out the concepts that define the "past" for him. This part of each story is configured spatially rather than temporally. It is not described as a series of time-bound transitions but rather as a theater in which a set of repeating transactions takes place. The space forms a closed system pared down to the bare necessities of an endlessly circulating, fixed pattern of transactions between a predetermined cast of actors. The system is self-generating and solipsistic. The location of each theatric engagement provides the conventions, props, and actors for it. All three are located in "natural" sites: the mythic in a generic "state of nature," the mediating narrative in a garden, and the opening of the final historical narrative in a "well." All three sites are literary markers that call up a network of intertextual associations, which Miraji manipulates metaphorically in each narrative.

In the myth, the cast of actors consists of a protagonist (a male human being), and a group of ancillary characters (others like him, a female, feminized spectacles of nature, and food). The interaction of the protagonist with the other characters is depicted as two dichotomous primordial emotional transactions, desire and fear. The protagonist's emotions are pulled out of him at the cusp of responses to various stimuli, including other men (*hamjins*) like him.

The myth moves from desire to fear. Desire hugs need close by it. So as the body's hunger is filled, the body feels pleasure. After pleasuring itself, the body moves outward to night, the time of love, which gives repose/

tranquility and finally, toward fear. For Miraji, forgetfulness, *farāghat*, the feeling provoked by night, is the feeling that anchors the poetics of desire as love. It allows the self release. It permits the self to lose itself in a restful point of stillness, while contemplating an other that is textured differently. *Farāghat* also means gap or space, a hiatus in time and from movement, which mediates between desire and fear. Desire drags the self inward and precedes fear, the emotion through which the self pushes invasive others away. The movement, from in to out, with a break between, modulates the rhythm of the narrative. The story travels from establishing a "self" for the protagonist, through a short space of respite, to his interactions with an "other."[23]

Poetry follows close behind need; arising with the opening sentence, and living only in the space already marked off for it—the limits established by need.[24] As the myth progresses, and the emotional covenants struck by the first human come to encompass both desire and fear, the borders that cradle poetry change.[25] Poetry comes to be produced in the infinite space tucked into and stretched out between these two emotions. Miraji choreographs the cast to enact the emotional covenants between them.

The second story, which intercedes between the mythic and the historical, opens with a garden, the garden of love—one of the common topoi for the ghazal, and the topos (*mazmūn*) that is called upon from the mid-nineteenth century on, when critics want to reform the ghazal. People who enter this garden gather around the beloved. In Miraji's tale, the ghazal turns into the beloved, the object of desire poeticized in it: a beautiful woman/beloved who sits on a bed of flowers, "adorned with sixteen pieces of jewelry," and holds an entire culture in thrall.[26] The bed of flowers and the ghazal are cultural cites/sites that come to stand for the obstinate refusal of the past to change. The beloved must be repudiated or lost, and her spell broken for change to occur. Miraji's use of the ghazal/beloved as the nucleus around which a carefully patrolled literary universe revolves and as a marker of a particular representation of the past is consonant with similar positions taken by his contemporaries.[27] As in the poem by Faiz, "Don't ask me now, beloved, for the love we once had," tensions between a past that must be left behind along with the elite who create it, and a present that attempts to repudiate this culture but must hold onto it to create, are explored through a poet's relationship to the figure of his beloved.

"Frogs in a well," the opening trope of the last narrative, is a reference to the cloistered *pardah nashīn* women who lived in the zenana, the female sanctum sanctorum of the house. The language of the zenana is the venue through which Miraji can speak about a shift from a shuttered domestic existence to a more expansive one. The well is transformed from a closed linguistic universe, inexorably circling its own circumference, to one with permeable and fluid boundaries. Miraji masculinizes the feminized trope of the well/zenana when he puts it to his own uses. It provides him entree into the discourse of social science, the "perspective of the social," in which the language of modernization is detoured through the bodies of women. Women as signifiers of social change on the subcontinent and as pawns moved on a chessboard of tradition and modernity give Miraji the images for a particular description of modernization.[28]

## CHANGE

The second half of each narrative is defined through change (*tabdīl*). This is the portion of all three that is a litany of temporally ordered events. What, then, is change in these narratives? How is it figured and brought about? How are the results depicted and assessed? Miraji's position on change both conforms to and diverges in significant ways from the cliched notion of "progress," supposedly introduced to the Indian subcontinent by the British. In all three narratives, change comes about with the inexorable move from a fixed, self-circulating past to a present that is constantly in transition.[29] Change then begins to occur at a particular point, sometimes impelled by an event like 1857, and from that moment it becomes the organizational principle for the rest of the narrative. Change, for Miraji, is linear, and unidirectional, though nonteleological. A culture that changes is one that moves inexorably from a simple organization to complex socio-political and literary structures.

Edifices are the icons of change in the narratives; they play their way through all three. In the mythic narrative, change is figured in terms of an outgrowth of "housing." In the other two narratives, change calls for new molds to be poured and structures built. In all three stories Miraji dismantles the initial, carefully choreographed relationships so that the symbolic, taking the form of new institutions, edifices, and buildings, can be constructed.[30] The language of construction provides the signifiers of a colonial code. The positive side of the balance-sheet approach to writing imperial history hinges on the enumeration of edifices. The edifices, trains, schools, and bureaucratic institutions—the apparatus of new *technae*, law, medicine, and science—become the material detritus of a civilizing force. N. M. Rashid wrote Miraji a letter in response to an article on Rashid's verse in which Miraji contended that Rashid was too influenced by British sources.[31] In this letter written in the 1940s, Rashid attempted to point out the fallacy of Miraji's position on the British. Rashid tried to justify his own reliance on British literary sources and in his defense tallies the edifices built by a colonial administration. Ironically, in the process of defending himself, Rashid accuses Miraji of deleting precisely the same edifices that are scattered over Miraji's own historical narratives of the period.

Change, in Miraji's understanding of it, is not produced from within the originary spaces with which his narratives open. These spaces are just the breeding grounds on which change occurs. Neither the conditions that define these spaces nor the actors that perform in them provide the impetus for change or the elements that define the changes that subsequently occur. Although gender does provide some of the tropes through which change is figured. In Miraji's fatalistic, deterministic model, change is brokered by an external force or agent of change that "sweeps in" and creates the conditions for new structures to be built. Change is instituted through a colonial language. It is not in the power of the people who are changing to invoke change—it occurs despite them. So the historical conditions under which Miraji wrote provided the language with which he wrote out a story of change or "progress."

Where, then, does the language to figure the agent/s of change come from? The description of the British in Miraji's narratives plays off the erotics of domination and desire that Miraji explores in the mythic narrative. The British are figured in tropes that are used by Miraji in his "mythic" narrative, where he lays out two emotional transactions between a male protagonist and his world—desire and fear.[32] Two sets of affiliations transgress and traverse the dichotomy between desire and fear. The first is the affiliation of the name of the beloved and night with spectacles of nature (*fiṭrat ke maẓāhir*). Night, the feminized personification of nature, stands on the side of desire, while spectacles of nature (also feminized but not personified) stand on the side of fear. Nature is domesticated in two ways: one is through its personification as a beloved, which allows the protagonist to absorb it and lose himself through desire; the other is something that can be looked at but not personified or appropriated and so creates fear. Another thread tying desire to fear in the myth is *ham* (own), which appears on either side of the divide, too. When nature falls into the provenance of desire, it becomes the *hamdam* (own-breath or own-life) of the protagonist. When nature is spectacle, it is aligned with another *ham*, the *hamjins* (own-species), who also inspires fear in the protagonist.

The British are described as a natural phenomenon—a "besieging storm . . . a hurricane of Western culture. . . ." They are an uncontrollable natural force, but a masculinized one rather than the feminized ones that can be domesticated either through desire or in terms of fear.[33] Miraji's perspective on the relationship between colonizer and colonized parts company perhaps from a comparable relationship posed by colonizers in that, for Miraji, emotion is not included in his representations of the British. For a poet whose primary narratives hinge on connections established through affect/emotion or the imagination, it is significant that neither desire nor fear play into his depiction of the British. The British are not available as either objects or agents of desire. Why? What does this allow and what discursive purposes does his representation of the British serve?

In fact, his representation has several ramifications. Represented as a masculine natural force that sweeps away everything before it, the British remain in a position of complete authority, although as a disengaged agent of change. They become seemingly disinterested agents of the objective, agents who bring science and commerce, which transform the ways in which things and people are bonded together, separating them inexorably without desire or fear to serve as a glue. In constructing them as a force with whom no emotional connections have been made, Miraji can slide out of the travails of complicity that desire would call up. Without desire or fear to bind him in a complicitous knot with a colonizer, Miraji as a poet can walk away and create a canon. He can play god. He is not fastened by the entrapping ropes that a clearly visible emotional tie with a colonizer would throw around him. Ironically, because he cuts himself off from desire in his literal depiction of the British, he can also linger on hegemony as that force whose work is done apart from the *visible* strings of desire: the forms of speech, want, pleasure, desire, the turns of phrase, the quotidian habits, that are secreted into the details of the ordinary that come to be normal. "Those Western ideas/thoughts seem to have had an impact on literary and artistic *technae*, specially those which occasion custom or fashion, these, if one considers the issue of creativity, and looks at daily things, and at daily habits, have brought new modes."

## THE CROSSROADS: *MUB-HAM CAURĀSTE*

Miraji's account of change is an ambivalent one. He is caught between his clichéd valorization of progress and the disenfranchising implications of a particular type of progress. He speaks of change as a process that destroys a world of the past in order to build new, raw, and perhaps superficial, artistic, social, and political structures that replace the ones from the past. His historical account of his world is infected by the implications of severing connections to the past and established, though contained and fixed, modes (*ḍhaṅg*, *uslūb*) of functioning.

> And the causes of this upheaval begin in the murky [*mub-ham*] era of 1857. When from the point of view of social and political norms, earlier connections began to be dispersed and space was made for a new order. One could perhaps say this: that a gap of a few generations had already been established between the current young poets and those older/respected men. Who had seen that time of intellectual turmoil as a pulse. But history and genealogical memories [*naslī yādeṅ*] coming together [*mil kar*] make the past era [what has gone by, *guzarā hu'ā zamānā*] its proof; other than this, a person's intelligence is made by bringing together past, present, and future. The past molds his fundamental affairs. Present/time investigates each movement of itself, and those very aspirations, become intentions, and reach completion in the future, to make/render individuality visible.

History, then, and genealogical memories (Miraji might mean forms of chronicle-making here) come together in a certain way. They have in common what they do with a past together: they turn to what has transpired to find proof of what they say or write in the present. History and genealogical memories, counterposed against a single person's intelligence, are collective forms of record. History is one kind of collective public record of the passing of time and genealogical memory another. Perhaps history is the more abstract collective social production of remembering, and *naslī yādeñ*, in its Arabic connotations twined around begetting, birthing, unraveling, progeny, procreation, reproduction, and messily mixed up with sex, the more embodied version of community memory. But both come together in making what has gone by the locus of proof. Alongside the work they do, and the way they grasp at time as it goes by, is the work done in a person's mind, the work done by his intellect. For a single person the past lays the groundwork for what is special/peculiar to him (*buniyādī k̲h̲aṣāʾiṣ*). It is the mold into which forms are to be poured. The present checks, looks, sights, thinks through movement. And the future is the time in which what is merely aspiration in the present becomes itself, and in so doing exposes, reveals, or brings the individual into view as himself. However, all these ruminations on time are qualified by a "but," hitched to a *lekin*. This *lekin* points to what ought to be and cannot, will not, quite be.

What halts the trajectory of time is the way that the past is cut off and the movement of time is torn by certain sorts of change. These are the changes wrought by the building of the orders of modernity that also form the architecture of the colonial symbolic: commerce, education, *technae*.[34] All three stories feature variants on this building. In the myth, civilization, progress, the stuff of modernity, heralds a new age. Between this age, and the past in nature, is an undefined inexplicable hiatus. In the fable, the British arrive as a hurricane that sweeps away, decimates. In the history, 1857 is the time of the rupture, when "earlier connections began to be dispersed." Myth, fable, history, all allegories for each other, weave the modern into the colonial. All tell of the break between past and future common to the advent of modernity, and which commits modernity to the ascendance of colonialism.[35]

People trapped in the process of change are, according to Miraji, marked by forgetting as a loss of memory (*yād nahīn* rather than *farāg̱ẖat*, forgetfulness as repose). In replacing the old with the new, they have lost their connection to a prior tradition so utterly that they are left without the sense of which language they speak or read. Without a past, and without established modes of communication, however limited and fixed, people cannot even conceptualize their present and do not have the ability to project a future. They have no idea what their trajectory might be. They are trapped in the dilemma of "progress," a dilemma which signals the incompleteness of, or perhaps the temporary failure of, modernity (difficulties perhaps allegorized by the *Titanic*). The trope Miraji uses to embody this condition of trauma, characterized by an obscured sight-line, and by an inability to read time, is the "crossroads." The metaphor of the crossroads at which Urdu poets stand allows Miraji to describe Urdu poetry as both replete with choices and haunted by ambivalence.[36]

> And the new poet stands at a crossroads from which many roads leave, to the right, to the left, to the front, and to the back. But he doesn't really know which road he has picked. What importance the experiences of the past have for him. For how long he must stand this way. . . .
>
> The old supports on the basis of which people passed their entire lives in the dilemmas of a domestic existence no longer remain with him. He is now all alone and on a quest for help.

Colonialism maps onto modernity to fracture time, pull it apart, and disperse it in different directions. A poet standing in the midst of this messiness has only an endlessly circulating present under his control. The place at which he stands, the crossroads, offer no solution, for they are not marked by directionals, no name, no mileposts, no arrows pointing to a place. Nothing on them indicates where they go in space or where they might lead in time. This fluidity offers infinite possibility, but one that is meaningless without anchors that tell one whether something was a possibility in the past, was an event in the past, or will be a possibility in the future.

Miraji's position seems to be a reformulation of a deterministic model of choice for a colonized poet living under colonial control and writing his history as a colonial history. His circumstances—past, present, and future, he seems to imply—are completely determined by forces outside his control. His choices, according to him, are so completely mediated by an incomprehensible environment that any choice he makes can never be understood by him or explained to another.

## THE ALTERNATIVE

> In this state, the new poet began to swerve/totter/flinch. This was the root/basic rule of the world, that whoever is beaten or has an accident, they must be pushed/shoved over by her [the world], so that they have the strength to refuse [*manaḥ ke bal kareñ*].[37]

How does one recover from this traumatic beating or traumatic accident? Miraji offers one solution at the close of his essay:

> But we will have to await this time with hope. A time when the warp and woof [nerves and sinews] of life's political, social, and personal dealings no longer need to be disentangled [set properly]. In that kind of time, we will hold onto an empathetic way of seeing [sympathetic sight-line], while paying close attention to this truth of new poetry—that, despite its expansive, extensive possibilities, it is still experimental. It is the kind of experiment for which it is both improper and meaningless to hope for a quick/speedy culmination/resolution/sense of completeness, and whose future really promises a glorious vision/visionariness.
>
> These successes, or possibilities, are in the hands of the new poets. If they contemplate every side of every issue intently through their hearts, and pay careful attention to it, think hard upon it with affection and sincerity, and move forward with a collective heart or will, then whatever befalls them, the field [of possibilities] will sit within their grasp [will remain in their hands].

Miraji's solution calls for a certain kind of vision, one that demands a rigorous scrutiny that brings the heart together with the mind. To see into a future built out of a past that has destroyed, one needs the sight-lines offered by a desiring intellect. It is precisely this desiring intellect that Miraji evokes in a series of translations and essays he published in *Adabī duniyā* in the 1930s.[38] The passage to the crossroads is paved with dismantled literary lineages replaced by new ones picked by someone else. Rather than lying (down) and dying, Miraji made a call for a self-reflexive construction of new literary affiliations. In an attempt to give birth to this new network, Miraji wrote a series of essays to accompany translations into Urdu of the work of several transnational literary figures.[39] These essays provided an alternative to both a dismantled Urdu literary heritage and the filiative lineages from British literature that Miraji believed produced aborted literary children in Urdu poetry.

Through the essays, Miraji performed two tasks. He introduced the Urdu literati of his time to a range of voices, from Sappho to Lawrence. In writing them, he refocuses the modes through which Europeans were represented to Indians. Miraji did not automatically valorize the writers he introduced in his essays; rather, he attempted to construct his own historical frame for them. This frame provided him the space for reformulating the uncertain unequal balances of colonial relationships. The Europeans about whom he wrote, among them the French Symbolists and Heine, were presented in a conflicted relationship with their world. They had been consigned to forms of abjection. He discussed them in terms of the ambivalence with which they were read by their cultures. He framed them with the silences that he felt surrounded them—the attempt by Europeans to silence their own by excluding them from the Western canon, and the legal proscriptions as well as the silent reception of their initial publications, or in the case of Sappho, the way they had been over time consigned to amorality and obscurity.

He read Europe, the hegemonic culture, in the context of its own shortcomings. His essays portrayed the blindness of European culture and its initial conflictual relationship with writers it later canonized. What Miraji turned on Europe was the language of progress—darkness to light—that he felt was being used on Urdu literature.[40] His essay on Li Po gave him the opportunity to exercise similar strategies, providing him the opportunity to emphasize and denounce the relative barbarity of Europe at the time when Li Po wrote. One of the few British writers Miraji included in his new canon of references for Urdu poets was D. H. Lawrence. In his essay on Lawrence, without extensive analysis, Miraji insisted that the Briton was a paradigmatic example of the influence of the East on British literature. Although it is as absurd as any of the allegations by anxious defenders of the Western canon, Miraji's assertion takes the same form, and with it he frames his narrative on Lawrence with a statement of faith that provides the very language through which the poet himself ought to be read.

## BAUDELAIRE: THE TROUBLED MASTER OF THE MODERN

*Strange Familiars*

I took my tranquility on a walk
and chose my roads by their angled slant.
What I glimpsed I sighted from a tower's height.
The city's glory seen so, from here
to those places of rest, what do I imagine
hold those gestures of hell for me: jails, whorehouses, hospital.

Those places of rest bloom like the flowers of evil.
You know well, Satan, the cause of my discomfort.
You know well, this knowing: that I could not come here
eyes found on the road, alchemize
tears into flowers.

I, the old and worn heart, a hedonist
there, my faith tested, on arrival.
Far away, I thirsted, my heart's vagrancy.
Whose hellish beauty brings me to my youth.

My heart clings to you,
your familiarity, O dishonored city
dream that sleep, heavy with wet shadows
on your expanse bares the day's first light, a wave gathering
your body, clothed with the plain dress of night's color

prey and death-dealer, hunting the pleasures of their own forms/being
the blind never come, to the humility of their degraded familiars.[41]

Baudelaire's work becomes a leitmotif in Miraji's work and life, a leitmotif that appears in the guise of translation. Over the course of his life, Miraji wrote about Baudelaire several times, carrying Baudelaire's poetry in translation over from his early essay on Baudelaire written in Lahore, to those for "Bāteṅ" published in *Sāqī* while he lived in Delhi, to pieces he wrote in *Kitāb-e pareshān* during the period immediately preceding his death in Bombay.[42] We are told that when Miraji died, he died with a book about Baudelaire at hand. What was it about this poet, whom Miraji called "the ascetic priest of the whore houses," that so enticed Miraji?[43]

Miraji's first essay on Baudelaire, "*Cārls Baudela'ir,*" was published in *Adabī duniyā* in the 1930s, and was included in the collection *Mashriq o magḥrib ke naghmeṅ*. The conditions for writing it are clearly articulated in the opening sections of the essay: Baudelaire's life and writing needed to be translated into Urdu to fill out the skirt of Urdu poetry, by bringing to it a poet who divulged the horror of a certain life played out during a particular historical period, while he was completely absorbed in the contours of that horror.

Baudelaire was useful to those *ḥaqīqat parast* poets who were themselves enamored of a "reality" that they had translated through the bodies of victims, slaves, and the cheapened lives of criminals and sinners. Baudelaire was useful precisely because the horror he expressed through his poetry was not one merely felt by him while he contemplated the disintegration of another's life, but the necessary emotion that told his own lived experience. This timbre of dread that Baudelaire offered, that it not be an anesthetized response to another's pain, would, Miraji believed, provide a necessary option to the contemplative distance with which the Progressives seemed to view and then represent the subjects of their literary endeavors.

Baudelaire was also useful because the experience of horror that he laid out so exquisitely in his writing was not reflection, not mimesis, but one that was alchemized as it detoured through the intellect, *fikr o gḥaur*, through imagination, *taḳhayyul*, *ḳhayāl* (the imaginary), and through the rigorous contemplation, *taṣavvur*, of emotion. Miraji believed that mimesis in Baudelaire was undercut by a desire that could never be consummated or fulfilled—desire for another person, desire for oneself—desire contoured in a Blakean cityscape. Despite the fact that Baudelaire's desire did not quite ever arrive at completeness, or resolution, this sort of desire pushed the writer toward himself, making that aesthetic separation between writer and signified, which Miraji felt modulated mimesis, impossible. Baudelaire, as Miraji depicted him, rarely furnished the others (or the self as other) who inhabited his poetry as objects of disinterested knowledge (a prerequisite of mimesis). This complex interweaving of emotion and intellect, when rendered through technique—craft, skill, *fann*—turned into poetry. Miraji gave his contemporaries their own precursors through which to contemplate these moments in Baudelaire: Iqbal, who produced aim, movements in particular directions, but ones that were not supposed to arrive at destinations, and Ghalib. Miraji brought Baudelaire and Ghalib together, because though both were very different in kind, both lived in the lyric tension between longing that pulled inward and outward and the crafted play with language, sign as symbol, that pulled poetry askew through *fikr*. In Miraji's encapsulation of Ghalib's work in Ghalib's voice to describe the sympathy between Ghalib and Baudelaire, "pleasure can never be birthed without the capable elegance of ghazal"—*baqadr-e żauq nahīn ṭarf-e tangnā-e g̣hazal.*

Baudelaire's aesthetic project, though detouring around mimesis, mimed the requirements Miraji laid out at the end of "Nayī shāʿirī" for a poet who needed to live through his conditions of loss and failure in the face of the trauma of forgetting his past. Baudelaire was the poet of memory as sudden, of history as something that flashes up at a moment of danger. It was this Baudelaire of *tārīḳh* and *infirādī ḥāfiẓah* (of history and personal memory) that Miraji returned to at the end of his own life to invoke in "Bāteñ."[44] This Baudelaire of Miraji's was someone who went to the flesh as the pliant thickness through which memory was bodied, "a circle of hair, half the world; for a time that lingers long, let me feel my hair's perfume // let me nestle, bury my face in its dense heaviness; as a thirsty man, perhaps, who pours his face in to the spring, as though the spring were a scented handkerchief; let me slap it back and forth as it flows off my hand, so that memories will shake off, and sprinkle into the wind."[45] Different forms of remembering—those evoked by history, desire (for food, for visions), and personal ones—and which ones offered lines of sight that were true, and which false, how was one to know (and was that the appropriate question to ask)?[46]

What Baudelaire did for Miraji was to bring the body to seeing. In this formulation, Baudelaire offered a visionary embodiedness to poets who wanted to represent what they saw in ways that removed their body (a face buried, the flesh that remembered) from the telos of seeing. This Baudelaire is somewhat akin and somewhat different from Benjamin's Baudelaire, who sees "the experience which presented itself to [his] Baudelaire's eyes in its undistorted version."[47]

Miraji's Baudelaire also gifted to writers crafting poetry under colonial auspices the material embodiments of modernity's spectrality which accrued around memory, trauma, and the self. The conditions of modernity, as Baudelaire told them, were not dressed up and covered over, but displayed in their naked exactitude. Seeing, in the poem "Strange Familiars" that inaugurates this section of the present chapter, requires the production of lines of sight, but not as something thrown out from a still, unremarked place. These lines of sight are described, brought into the body of the poem as the "I" looks: roads chosen for their angled slant, a tower that permits glimpses of the city's glory. Sightings of the modern may be from distances that incline subjects in a particular way in relation to what is seen, but those distances are sited, placed tangibly. For example, the tower becomes the moment of the archaic, perhaps a position from which archers lined up to kill, and so displays the city's glories. But this possible archaic takes vision over and triangles it to the buildings of modernity which are jails, whorehouses, hospitals where the eyes rest and restore themselves. The eyes that see have to be found, picked up from a road, and their seeing is not straight: sight becomes the place of ironic, reversed alchemy that transfers across substance, transmuting glory into prisons, and tears into flowers. The specter takes shape, turns into flesh as something other than itself. Seeing, therefore, is a gift, held out to those who see through colonialism's vision; it is not transparent, and its transparency (producing the mimetic) must be alchemized into forms of (perhaps incomplete) incorporation.[48]

Baudelaire, in Miraji's telling of him, embodied a very particular relationship to English colonialism. His work was the culmination of the new in the modern, and it followed a European teleology. Baudelaire was the necessary inheritor of the poetic legacy carried over from Greek and Roman masters like Plato and Plutarch, Aflātūn and Plūtark. It was Baudelaire, and not English writers, who brought to Europe the transitional poetics of the modern, to expand the vocabulary and syntax of modernity's imaginary and symbolic. The British, who were, in their usual way, oblivious to the genius living close by, needed Baudelaire, in translation, so that they too could begin to partake of the richness he had wrought.[49] But Baudelaire himself turned to translation as he wrote. One site of translation that was incorporated into Baudelaire's work was his translation of Edgar Allan Poe from English. Another site of translation, whose influence Miraji left open, was the translation of Calcutta and the humid density of the Indian colony that Miraji claimed Baudelaire visited as a youth in 1841, into Baudelaire's poetry. In his essay on Baudelaire, Miraji pushed Baudelaire into completing the journey to Calcutta, which Baudelaire had aborted in Mauritius/Reunion. Baudelaire's journey to India becomes the first stopping point in the poet's ceaseless *āvāragī*, wandering, and one on which he chose to embark.[50] Baudelaire's journey becomes Miraji's translated desire to take the poet over into the subcontinent.

By turning to Baudelaire to explore translation as a form of reading and writing, and as the place where desire was given substance, Miraji interjected back into translation the reader, "envisaged as [those] to whom the reading of lyric poetry would present difficulties," who had been left as though blank in Benjamin's discussion of translation.[51] For Baudelaire was a poet who created his reading public, "probably one of the first poets of the new poets of the West, who selected his readers (those he addressed, the *mukhātib*) carefully, and in the process expanded the definition of the addressee. His poetry was written for his *żāt*, for his species or his race."[52] The reader, the person to whom a translation might be directed, was in the terrain of colonial translation, a dense site of racialized desire. Miraji revisits the triangulation of text, reader, and writer in his second essay on Baudelaire, where the text triangulates between two parallel lines of desire (those emanating from the reader, and those from the writer), forcing their meeting in peculiar ways.

The project of colonial translation, around the time that Miraji had Baudelaire visiting India, was organized around texts translated from English into vernacular. These translations were expected to transform, to imbue the colonized subject with the proprieties of English manhood.[53] Transposing Baudelaire onto this project of translation revealed the improprieties of its intent. Baudelaire was, after all, the kind of dissolute subject whose translation into Indian vernaculars would heighten rather than alleviate the dissoluteness of the colonized. And if Baudelaire was the one poet who could bring to English what it really ought to know about the Satanic (Blakean) forms taken by modernity, then the proprieties that colonial translation wanted to gift the colonized were lies.

Translation had a another valence in Baudelaire. Translation in Miraji's version of it is never merely conducted neatly between one language and another. Its forms are *pecā*. Incarnations of translated text twist and turn between multiple discourses, between languages that do not map, even uneasily. Translations go back and forth between so many incommensurate worlds of speaking and doing, thick with power, dense with the anguish of hate and unrequited desire, that one has no sense where might they have once begun. Miraji turns to Baudelaire's supposed sojourn in Calcutta to explore the possibility that the anguish, rage, and dissoluteness that Baudelaire brought to his dark spiritual transactions with modernity might have come from Calcutta. Calcutta might have been the precursor of Jeanne Duval, the half black, half white lover who Baudelaire took up with when he returned to Paris from his trip abroad. In demanding (in a historical error) that Baudelaire arrive at the place, Calcutta, he refused to reach, Miraji asks for a reading of Duval that can be interposed with colonial, British desire, fear and hatred for bodies that are made to slide between Africa and India (Mauritius).[54] But Miraji's narrative begins Baudelaire's journey to Calcutta with Baudelaire's negotiations with his two fathers (the proper and the improper one).[55]

Baudelaire's life gives Miraji the material for reading his poetry. The linchpin event of Baudelaire's life, according to Miraji, is the primordial rupture that occurred in Baudelaire's youth. Baudelaire had had an idyllic childhood, saturated with sexuality for his mother. In a letter to his mother, Baudelaire reminisces about his feelings for her: "In the days of my childhood, there was a time when my heart was full of a kind of severe, excessive love for you. . . . This was a time when my entire being clung to you. And you were entirely mine. You were both a friend to me and a kind of idol I could worship."[56] Baudelaire's father, who was consigned to the background of his memories, died. His mother remarried a soldier diplomat, versed in the niceties of bourgeois masculinity: material comfort, soldierly deportment, the regularized order of middle-class propriety. Baudelaire hated his new father for stealing his mother away; he hated him with a passion that drove him to *āvāragī*, to dissolute wandering. This stepfather, wanting to inculcate his own sense of order in Baudelaire, restricted Baudelaire's access to his inheritance from his dead father. Baudelaire writes to his mother about this break with his past and the hunger that pulled him to vagrancy: "As that time came to a close, I remembered it with fresh violence."[57] "Sometimes . . . I stay in bed for three days. . . . I have no freshly washed clothes, no food to eat. The only things that sustain me are wine and alcohol. All my pain is washed away in their substance, but my life does not seem to improve."[58]

This rent in the fabric of Baudelaire's life, that tore the imaginary, taking it to an illegitimate symbolic, and sent the poet to the vagrancy of a concerted refusal of all that symbolic represented, gave Baudelaire a peculiar insight into the dark side of modernity. Baudelaire lived a life between an absent father, a mother he left, and a stepfather. In this, Baudelaire's triangulated desires figured the impossible configurations of colonial modernity. But those desires did not produce the proper man. Instead, Baudelaire lived the life of an indolent hedonist, fueling his vision into the underbelly of the city of newness with wine and opium. He became the utterly improper man, whose refusals of propriety allowed him to see with the "eye picked up at the side of road," and through a darkened spirituality, "alchemize tears into flowers."[59] Baudelaire becomes the poet who, following on the heels of Dostoyevsky, brings together

> a congregation of contraries. Where the excesses of purity and darkness wind around each other unmanageably. The eyes of their forebears [looking upon them] overflow with the enticements and desire of their completely indecent, unseemly words. . . . It is as though [in their work] darkness and light are coupled in the human world of the seen, in the way in which they necessarily and properly come together in the world beyond sight. Two pleasures who wish, hand in hand, you may call them whatever you will: good and evil, freely creative and necessarily ordered faculties, old and new, worshipping the ancients and the call to revolution.[60]

But the language of longing, love, and hate that organizes the ordered chaos of modernity that Baudelaire views with such palpable intensity might well have come from his traumatic encounter (imagined for him by Miraji) with a colonial other. Miraji describes the first journey he sends Baudelaire on, into the heart of his darkness:

> In 1841 his inheritance allowed him a trip to India, and he reached Calcutta. His stay here was a little less than a year. One reason might have been that at a really young, unripe age, he obtained the visual capital that allowed his nature to transform. Also, it is clear from the events of his life, that the dark savory beauty of the sea of Bengal had

> a striking effect on his unformed mind. He must have seen a temple dedicated to Kali, the goddess of darkness. And the story of the *devī-mātā* [goddess mother], that philosophical rumination on injury long concealed in it, with the fullness of its seductive enchanted secrets, stole into his heart like a magical figure, giving its years of suppressed lonely personhood a gift of natural darkness that revitalized and awoke those suppressions in a fresh untouched mode. We must also remember that he came, a dweller of a cold nation. His sexual defenses had not yet been completely formed. And they could not repel different forms of air and water. He had to stay in the sort of country that was not merely not cold, but whose humid warmth and hot wet wind drove the being of a person bred in Europe to extreme disgust and displeasure. The sharp excessive heat of places like India and Africa don't just turn such people towards bodily dis-ease, but also troubles and disturbs them to such an extent that their souls are utterly tormented. This acute feeling matures from the world and causes them to turn away in revolt from the immortality of life, but also gives them new avenues to explore in their social universe, such that they begin a search for the enticements of an excited wailing lament.
>
> For Baudelaire, sexual indulgences were not new things. But in a new world, racial allurements were visible in a new heightened color. In close proximity with Kali Devi and her stories what desires might he have felt. In that dark seductive spicy beauty what enticements was he shown? The proper reply to this is not available to us, we can only approximate it and see its gestures [in his work]. For Indians [unlike for Baudelaire], the dark seduction and beauty is alluring to community, nation, and religion. If you are dark, then the people you love will also look the same, dark. Because the beloved is the imaginary reflection of the lover.[61]

The dynamic of seepage, incorporation and externalization, repulsion; of pleasure and despair; and "revolt from the immortality of life"—all of this sends "dwellers of cold nations on a search for the enticements of their own voice, ecstatic and mourning." Baudelaire, pushed by Miraji to conclude a journey he never completed, is sent off to accrue "visual capital," to see the possible origins of what might have led him to write as he did, signifying a black body, moving it in response to his desires, the doubled ecstatic and mourning search for a beauty between black and white. In Jeanne Duval, Miraji's Baudelaire finds something that never was, bought with capital borrowed from other colonial journeys, "the dark savory beauty of the sea of Bengal, the power translated across another differential" of "Kali, the goddess of darkness." In Miraji's translation, Baudelaire's poem "The Song of Darkness" produces Jeanne Duval as the fetish (nature as fetish / desire) that stands in for modernity's ruptures (generating responses: attraction, repulsion / mourning, excitement). Jeanne Duval "merely allows Baudelaire a necessary capacity, never permitted speech," signified over and over, and "her lustrous secret" embodies and provokes a search:

> The dark heart of hate
> when all roads close
> the gift of grief it bears. . . . [62]
>
> Her every word is tainted black
> she face of darkness appears before me, night's soul in hand.
> Her eyes hidden in a cave's thick dark, whose lustrous secrets, whose glances angled like lightening, tear open night's veil.[63]

The journey that Baudelaire was sent on by Miraji may have allowed him to translate himself, and his racialization into the European modern, through his significations of a dark lover. The stories offered in a colonial context, of the dark goddess's trials with death, transmuted through the horror of dealing with a bodily trauma that infected the cold body of Europe with warmth, may have been the genesis of Baudelaire's repeated evocations of the trauma of separation from the imaginary and entry into the step-symbolic. But this trauma is an alchemized version of that very trauma that Miraji describes over and over again in his essay on new poetry. And the colonizer is not immune to it. And the colonizer learns how to speak it only through the cleaved longing of his own desire, gifted to him through the visit he is forced to make to the dense, spicy, hot, contrary worlds of Asia and Africa. So to speak modernity's abysses (and abjections) one might well have to trade in those desires acquired under the auspices of colonial power, translating these desires through a doubly racialized, mis-mapped body, once one returned to the metropole.

What kind of lesson does this enforced journey offer a poet writing about the worlds of their own abject, in the vernacular, in the colony, in the fractured space of their own modernity? Perhaps that the semiotics that the colonized deploy to describe the crowd of the abject (whose lives incarnate modernity) are necessarily given to them through their own racialization. Perhaps that colonialism and modernity share the same proper stepfathers, who must be set aside if one is to repudiate their influence. Perhaps that modernity and colonialism are intimately woven together through the dark edges of desire. Perhaps that what poets who write back from the spaces of colonization consider their own reflection of their own world is likely to be the translation, albeit a new one, of an insane translation. This insane translation could only be done by Westerners who had to be made to finish their journeys (against their own detours back to their cold world) to the world of heat to garner through repulsion as attraction their spiritual visions of the spoilage of modernity. And perhaps that the colonized consider in their reflection of themselves an accounting of a desire, now denied them, that sees and remembers in its own image of darkness, an unspoiled love. But memory here must be aroused through the body, through synaesthesia, smell, touch, feel, sound, however visualized and however spectralized.

To go to Baudelaire as the exemplary alternative offered by Miraji to his compatriots, caught as they are in the terrifying loss of memory that attends modernity and the advent of colonialism, is to go to Miraji's truncated, transmuted translation of the epitaph, written by someone whom he thought of as an exemplary translator of Baudelaire onto the English scene—Swinburne on Baudelaire's death in 1867:

> Oh my brother
> in the old season of your songs,
> you saw those secrets, that grief, that anguish
> which is denied us.
> The harsh tautness of love's knife flame
> at a place at night
> where no one has dared breathe til now
> the petals of sweet love's poisonous buds
> bloomed for your delicate gaze.
> No one else even glimpsed them.
> The secret treasure of time's ripe fertility
> its faults which have no astronomy

those things leached clean of happiness.
Two places, where with the eyes of a grieving soul
as it turns in sleep, turns from the dust motes
of strange dreams and weeps,
on each face you glimpsed a shadow so
you saw that what people gather in a garden
bloom only as thorn.[64]

# *Three* SELF, LANGUAGE, AND MASCULINITY

Aur us musāfiroñ kī talāsh rahtī hai jo us kī ḳhvāhishāt-e nafsānī aur ẓarūriyāt-e jismānī ko pūrā kar sakeñ.

And through the passage of time we chase those voyagers who can consummate their longing soul and their carnal /embodied compulsions.[1]

# 4. EPIGRAM FOR LONGING SOULS AND COMPELLED BODIES: WHITHER MASCULINITY?

Many of Miraji's prose poems (*naẓm*) shape into lyric form the themes elaborated in his prose pieces and translations: the conflicts and conjunctions that arise when metaphysics and poetics in Urdu are renegotiated by the influx of new ideas about self and poetry. His explorations address the limits, forms, and textures of modes of signification as they come to be established, their power to assign meaning, and their subsequent effects on both poetic voicing and critical readings. In some of his poems Miraji examines the ambivalences associated with shifting sensibilities, when poetic systems, construed as previously secure, are no longer in absolute control, and the place and portrayal of the male lyrical subject (the protagonist of a poem, the "I" who writes, the "I" who reads, the "I" to whom a poem seems to be addressed) are simultaneously reconstrued. This lyrical subject is not exactly congruent with the name Miraji, the signature appended to each poem, which is female and must be kept at a remove so that this lyrical subject can be held to its maleness.

The two poems of Miraji's that most clearly capture the catches of a single voice in syncopation with entrenched movements of signification are "Traveler" (Jātrī) and "Call of the Sea" (Samundar kā bulāvā). These poems fall into a looser category of "journey" poems, which chart the travails of voyages sometimes conducted in relation to another person, object, or place. In them, a psyche (personhood) travels through an episteme, through memory, through the ambivalent possibility of creativity. The precursors to Miraji's journey poems were the first lyrics about love gone awry that he wrote in Lahore. Initially published in journals like *Romān* (Romance), *Sāqī* (Cupbearer), *Navā'e vaqt* (Voice of the age), and *Avāz* (Sound), they were later collected in his book *Sah ātishah*.[2] These early poems, like "Āñkh micholī" (In the blink of an eye) and "Ummīd" (Hope), which enunciate incompleteness, speak of the ambiguous consolations of desire in held in abeyance, and play with time, memory, and the frisson of writing, and bare those metaphors, tropes, images, and those struggles with instituted protocols, subjects, and scenes that Miraji turned to later in the "Call of the Sea" and in "Traveler."

A much younger poem than "Call of the Sea," "Traveler" was written in 1941 and first published in the collection *Mīrājī kī naẓmeñ*, and it establishes the contours of a male subject, the "I" who begins to speak in the space of the poem, in both the context of and confrontation with existing poetic practices. The lyrical male subject who emerges as a feeling, thinking self over the course of the poem is delineated through the form and texture of tropes that come primarily from the corpus of Urdu, Persian, and Braj mystical poetry, and that have been used to articulate pilgrimages toward the divine. As the subject comes into being (standing in the present while events come and go in the narrative past), he negotiates with the poetics of the past, which order the journeys of his compatriots: voiced as a call and its response. The arbitration closes with the lyrical subject in an untenable situation, where he no longer has adequate access to the systems of signification that framed the voice he claimed and then assumed over the course of the poem: "I'm just a parched, leafless, colorless desert in which it is not possible for me to say . . ." (ḳhashk, be barg, be rañg ṣaḥarā hai, jis meñ ye mumkin nahīñ hai kahūñ . . .)[3]

The subject in "Call of the Sea" engages with the particular poetics of signification that hold a poetic universe together while delimiting the interpretative sphere within which poems were read; therefore, they do not require negotiation. Unlike "Traveler," the concrete making of the subject is not investigated, since its disposition is assumed. And, also unlike "Traveler," the gender of the subject is never completely revealed—it is subtly veiled in a grammar that allows it to be spoken indirectly until the closing stanzas of the poem. The lyrical subject forms itself in response (*ṣadā*) to a call (*nidā*) out of the past, which throws up scenarios from the language of Urdu poetry that represent assemblages of signification: "there is a rose garden." As the poem progresses, the subject asserts successively greater control over the linguistic spaces that are given, even though it eventually turns away from them. This poem, too, ends in the dissolution of all systems of signification, but from a very different perspective than that of "Traveler," where the subject is in a position of abandonment and loss, realizing that both his voice and his ability to read himself are no longer cupped between his hands: "every beautiful thing I owned has turned into a flowing gust that my hand cannot contain" (voh sab bahtā sā jhoṅkā hai jise hāth mere nahīṅ rok sakte). By contrast, the subject's voice in "The Call of the Sea" is mirrored back at him; he does not feel as though he will lose his ability to speak. Ultimately, however, the self-reflexive position of the subject is not maintained, for although he finally speaks directly and as a male "I" and thereby wrests control over his own signification, his position is immediately destabilized when his primacy is undercut with "then my voice must be a mirror, and only I am tired of calling" (to phir ye nidā ā'inā hai, faqt maiṅ thakā huṅ).

In poems where both language and self are addressed, one becomes the focus of the poetic narrative while the other either informs the terms of the frame or patterns the text. While crafting his language and carving for himself a linguistic world to which he is integral, Miraji also renders a metaphysics of the self. The journey the protagonist makes in "Traveler" is described through tropes; it is a journey into himself, a journey through which his self assumes a concrete, consolidated shape. In order to follow the protagonist, to chase him through the poem, the audience has to apprehend/grasp the figural language used by the poet, although neither the systems of signification nor the lyrical subject are completely stable.

## WHAT CAN BE RUBBED OUT CANNOT DIE: CONSTRUCTION OF THE "SELF"

Jo miṭ saktī hai, mar nahīṅ saktī: dillī ke nām[4]

As Miraji makes clear in his essays, the search for a new poetic language and for new ways of construing the self did not begin with him; rather, the renegotiation of both poetry and self-identity began with the incursion of norms that leaked both directly and tangentially from colonial assumptions about poetry and personhood. Indeed, one ideologically constructed battle over the language and purpose of poetry appeared in the late nineteenth century, with Altaf Husain Hali's *Muqaddamah-e shiʿr o shāʿirī* (Introduction to poetry and poetics). Hali's struggle in all his work was to make the vernacular, Urdu, adequate to the task of writing a new poetry, *nayī shāʿirī*, and with it, scripting a new kind of selfhood. To do so, Urdu had to be refitted so it could translate into itself from English. But before that was possible, a portion of the language, and the literature in which it spoke, had to be seized, mournfully, from its antecedents—Arabic, Persian (and perhaps even Sanskrit)—and turned, sometimes with trepidation and sometimes with elation, to face English.[5]

Hali (1837–1914) lived in a tumultuous period of Indo-Islamic history, when north Indian literati faced the loss of established institutions of patronage in the major urban centers of north India. The decimation of Delhi in the holocaust of 1857 became the turning point that Urdu writers returned to over and over to poeticize the British investment of themselves as the country's major political and economic force, a move that had sociopolitical as well as emotional repercussions for Indian Muslims.[6]

Taẓkirah dillī marḥūm kā, ai dost ne cheḍ
nah sunā jā'egā ham se, ye afsānah hargiz
. . .
chipe chipe pai haiñ yāñ, gohar-e tah-e ḳhāk
dafan hogā kahīñ itnā, nah ḳhizānah hargiz
. . .
miṭ gaye tere miṭne ke nishān bhī ab to
. . .
ai falak us se zyādāh, nah miṭnā hargiz

voh to bhūle the hameñ, ham bhī unheñ bhūl ga'e

shāʿirī mar cukī, ab zindah nah hogī hargiz
yād kar kar ke jī nah kaḍhānā hargiz
. . .
Ġhālib o sheftā o nayyar o āzād o zauq
ab dikhā'egā ye shakaleñ na zamānā hargiz . . .[7]

Remembering, describing Delhi in its death, O friend, please don't
tantalize me
I can't bear to listen to it, I can bear the story no longer
. . .
With every step here, one walks over a layer of dust veiling pearls
never buried, not even the vestige of stored treasure
. . .
The very traces of the debris of your death have been effaced
. . .
O heaven, can one be erased more thoroughly than this

Poetry has died, it can never be brought to life again

Don't uproot my soul by remembering it over and over
Those whom we forgot, they forgot us too
. . .
Ghalib and Shefta, Nayyar, Azad and Zauq
Time will never unveil these faces again . . .

In "Nauḥah-e dillī" (Lament for Delhi), Hali turns to the *marśiyah* (elegy), the form conventionally used to speak about the death of a person (especially, in Urdu, Hazrat Husain at Karbala), to voice his unbearable grief at the death of its time. The destruction of Delhi after 1857 offers him an occasion for mourning. But Delhi is merely a metonymy, the embodied place that allows Hali to mourn for everything he has lost. And what he has lost is profound. He has lost an entire time of writing. The time when the *marśiyah*, and the ghazal, and the *qaṣīdah* were written by poets like Ghalib and Shefta, Nayyar, Azad, and Zauq.

Hali speaks of his loss directly and indirectly. He communicates his loss by speaking to a friend who partakes of it. In the opening lines of the *marśiyah*, Hali begs a friend not to remind him, begs him not to repeat the death of Delhi. And not to reiterate death, not to share death is to bring another death. It is to call for the death of a death: "miṭ gaye tere miṭne ke nishān bhī ab to." But this call not to share death also brings that death back again and again. In line after line, Hali goes over what he wants to remember, and yet, not remember: the double rubbing out of memory through death and its erasure, through killing with its traces effaced. Hali remembers here what he wants to forget: as he forgets, he is also forgotten by those whom he forgets: "voh to bhūle the hameñ, ham bhī unheñ bhul ga'e." Hali's past erases him (as its future) as he erases it.

With these lines, Hali mourns the demise and extermination of a city. Through them, Hali grieves the death of an era, the death of a certain poetics, the death of his past, and his own death in the eyes of his poetic forebears, as he forgets those that have died. In other places, at other times, Hali's mourning is transmuted into a pragmatic recognition of the need for new alliances, allegiances, and patronage/wealth. In the *Musaddas*, for example, Hali turns to the Europeans—"voh qaumeñ jo sab rāheñ ṭai kar cuke haiñ / żaḳhīre har ik jins ke bhar cuke haiñ" (those people who have established and traveled every road / who have availed themselves of every kind of treasure)[8]—to give him something to replace the deaths that haunt him. Somewhere in this double movement, between his mourning and his pragmatism, between a past and a future, is the kind of poetics and the kind of self that Hali wanted to forge, in the present, for his community.

Hali was born immediately after the questions of education, language, patronage, and their imbrication with the cultivation of a civilized self appeared to have been settled in British India. He was born in 1837, two years after the now notorious Minute on education had been crafted by Thomas Babbington Macaulay under the aegis of Lord William Henry Cavendish Bentinck, the governor-general of India from 1828 to 1835. By the time Hali wrote his lament for Delhi, in 1874, the illnesses unto death that he mourned for had been long past, provoked by layers of reorganization under successive British administrations.

At the heart of Hali's present lies translation, *tarjumah*. Translation makes a new man of Hali, someone who speaks of himself as translated into something different through the operations of translation. Hali's narration of himself is toward a desire fueled by *tarjumah*. After 1857, the second job that he gets is with the Punjab Government Book Depot. There, Hali is put to the task of correcting (*iṣlāḥ*) Urdu translations done from English. This labor infuses in him an affinity for English, one that would not have occurred prior to 1857. The value of Eastern and Persian literature gradually diminishes in his eyes. At the same time, he is encouraged to pursue a new kind of poetry by Colonel Holroyd, the director of public instruction in the Punjab, and by Muhammad Husain Azad. In 1874 Hali recites four *maṡnavī*, at the symposium organized by Azad in Lahore. Hali's reformist zeal, to clean up Urdu poetry and to reform his *qaum*, his community, can be said to date from this point.[9]

This abbreviated narration of a few chosen incidents in Hali's life seems to have an inevitable movement, but what propelled them to their conclusion? What are the conditions under which it seems inevitable that Hali wants to transform Urdu, turning toward English and away from Persian to do so? How does one even begin to comprehend the hiatus between Hali's severe mourning for his past and the passion that drove him to a rejuvenated future?

Hali became the vernacular, and incomplete, version of the kind of person called for by Macaulay in his *Minute on Education*.[10] The much-cited exact quote from Macaulay's February 2, 1835, minute is: "We must at present do our best to form a class who may be interpreters between us and the millions whom we govern—a class of persons Indian in blood and color, but English in tastes, in opinions, in morals and in intellect. To that class we may leave it to refine the vernacular dialects of the country, to enrich those dialects with the terms of science borrowed from the western nomenclature, and to render them by degrees fit vehicles for conveying knowledge to the great mass of the population."[11] But this sort of person, also described below, was proposed early in Bentinck's tenure, years before Macaulay arrived in India. A version of it appears in a piece of writing sent by the Court of Directors to the Bengal government on the education of Indians, dated September 29, 1830, two years after Bentinck's arrival in Calcutta. This section of the discussion speaks specifically about law, because law comes to occupy a predominant place in queries about education, and so issues that are addressed to law may be said to stand as suggestions for other areas:

> . . . the exertions you are now making for the instruction of natives . . . as being calculated to raise up a class of persons qualified by their intelligence and morality for high employments in the civil administration of India. As a means of bringing about this most desirable object we rely chiefly on their becoming through a familiarity with European literature and science imbued with the ideas and feelings of civilized Europe, on the general cultivation of their understandings, and specifically on their instruction in the principles of morals and general jurisprudence . . . with respect to the education of natives. . . .

> That more complete education which is to commence by a thorough study of the English language can be placed within the reach of a very small proportion of the natives of India. But intelligent natives who have been thus educated may as teachers in colleges and schools, or as writers or translators of useful books, contribute in an eminent degree to the more general extension among the countrymen of a portion of the acquirements which they have themselves gained, and may communicate in some degree to the native literature and to the minds of the native community that improved spirit which it is to be hoped they will themselves have imbibed from the influence of European ideas and sentiments. You should cause it to be generally known, that every qualified native who will zealously devote himself to this task will be held in high honor by you; that every assistance and encouragement, pecuniary or otherwise, which the case may require, will be liberally afforded, and that no service which it is in the power of a native to render to the British government will be more highly acceptable.[12]

The call made above was to produce a buffer zone of natives (*sic*) like Hali, qualified by intelligence and morality, who would mediate between British administrators and the millions of unlettered Indians they ruled. These buffer folk were to be inculcated in ideas and feelings commencing in Europe, and in this way were to be instructed in principles and morals. Thus emboldened, they as administrators, teachers in college, writers and translators of texts, would serve as a conduit for British beliefs and codes. The notion of a buffer zone, which saw its culmination under Bentinck's short but far-reaching governance, had its precursors in bureaucratic groupings institutionalized at the beginning of the nineteenth century under Lord Wellesley (1789–1805) and later under the Marquess of Hastings (1813–23). Organizations of power under Wellesley and Hastings incorporated stratified rule—between levels of British officers and between British and Indians. In the stratification, and the explicit separation of the British from Indians through the practices of rule, lay the beginnings of the "buffer zone."[13]

The first articulation of the education of a group of people to certain ends is spoken as a part of an initiative embraced in section 43 of the

Charter Act of 1813, and in the emendation of the East India Company charter by the British Parliament—"a sum was set apart for the revival and promotion of literature and the encouragement of the learned natives of India, and for the introduction and promotion of a knowledge of the sciences among the inhabitants of the British territories."[14] The charter of 1813 opened South Asia up to mercantile investment other than that of the East India Company, and also allowed missionaries to conduct their activities on the subcontinent. Like all such documents produced under British auspices, its language and the arguments that accompanied its passing were stressed by ambiguities. These returned to some of the initiatives introduced in the charter: education, investment, and morality.[15]

The money set aside for education could be considered blood money, offered in reparation for what were deemed British excesses.[16] Excesses had come up before in the 1786–94 impeachments and could be attributed to several factors: dereliction of British authority, delegation of British authority to Indian sycophants, and a sense of insecurity about remaining in power.[17] Insecurity was mediated by a desire to possess, and extract: "discover what could be obtained from . . . Asiatic subjects."[18] And over a very attenuated period of time, this desire to extract was turned into a desire to benefit both the colonizer and the colonized, so that the colonizer could "continue to hold the advantages . . . at first derived from [the natives]. [T]heir happiness was [now] committed to our [British] care."[19] Narrations, like these, of colonial projects, naturalized the good that accrued to colonial subjects and set up a hierarchy between ruler and ruled that had to be maintained so that the colonized, "those committed to our care," could receive the good bestowed upon them by beneficent rulers. These narrations also incorporated into this seemingly neutral good (happiness) the continued extraction of goods, "(continue to hold) advantage," as a part of the equation of payment for kind.

Some of the links between extraction, control, redemption, and salvation through gifting knowledge were first made under Warren Hastings (1772–85), the mercantile maverick administrator whose impeachment in 1786 had provoked the parliamentary discussions on the abuse of colonial power. Orientalism, the promotion of Oriental learning to understand and so rule the natives more efficiently, had been advocated by Hastings in the eighteenth century as ad hoc official policy.[20] This period saw the "assimilation of colonial administrators to a native way of life."[21] But slipping into nativeness needed knowledge that was held by natives. And enabling this movement toward nativeness was a complex process of extraction and displacement.[22] Knowledge was culled by a series of colonial administrators, like Sir William Jones, who gathered oral information and collated it into texts.[23] These texts were then printed as well as translated, and a portion of them returned to the locals to revitalize the knowledge that the British believed that the locals had lost. Texts, notably those on law and language, were also used as references, to alleviate the possibility that the locals, who tended toward deceit (*sic*), might have the upper hand in determining decisions.[24] The excess, that which had not been used up in the colonies, was detoured back to the metropole to infuse a new life into poetry there:

> Our European poetry has subsisted too long on the perpetual repetition of the same images, and insistent allusions to the same fables: . . . if the principle writings of the Asiatics . . . and if the languages of the Eastern nations were studied in our great seminaries of learning, where every other branch of knowledge is taught to perfection, a new and ample field would be opened for speculation; we should have a more extensive insight into the history of the human mind; we should be furnished with a new set of images and similitudes; . . . which future scholars might explain, and future poets might imitate.[25]

The capital that accrued in colonial archives was sent off to the metropole to infuse only what was lying still, sedimented there, so it could move again, revive, to recirculate freshly and freely. That which supposedly circulated on its own strength, on the other hand, lay outside of this need for infusion. Reading this description of circulation as transfusion, one forgets, as one must, that healthy European bodies too might have relied on mercantile capital, from trading posts, to vitalize them. One also partly forgets, at the same time, that underlying this portion of various humanist projects[26] of accumulation, translation, and salvation was a conglomerate of interpenetrating structures of control and rule that put texts to use to consolidate power and accrue mercantile capital.[27] Jones, engaged in the multifarious, almost rapacious, enterprise of amassing an archive—ranging from botany, zoology, geography, mathematics, music, theater, epic, poetry, and religion—was occasionally quite explicit about this as one of the features of his project. In "The Second Anniversary Discourse," delivered on February 24, 1785 (four months prior to his charge to the grand jury), before the Asiatic Society in Calcutta, he said:

> We have a still nearer interest in knowing all former modes of ruling these inestimable provinces, on the prosperity of which so much of our national welfare, and individual benefit, seems to depend[,] . . . but the natural productions of these territories, especially in the vegetable and mineral systems, are momentous objects of research to an imperial, but which is a character of equal dignity, a commercial, people.[28]

Though Orientalists like Jones can be said to value the archive they sought in the East—they saw value in it; gave it value as differential; and recirculated its value in the metropole—they were also so clearly ambivalent about the value of certain sections of the archive that they had to sift them. In the decades of struggle over education following the charter of 1813, the Orientalists came into conflict with the Anglicists as well as with the Utilitarians. The Anglicists (and those Utilitarians who supported them on certain matters of education) felt that the money decreed for education by the charter act ought to be spent on promoting English education, teaching English literature and science in English, and it ought not to be trifled away on education in Indian classical languages or on translating Indian texts. Orientalists like H. H. Wilson continued to believe that Indian texts must be translated, that Indians must be taught their own classical languages in educational institutions devoted to this task, and that the money allocated for education in literature had to be turned to this end. The two groups argued over worth: what was Oriental literature worth? Was it worth the money expended on teaching and translating it? Or was that money best spent on publishing English texts "imbued with the ideas and feelings of civilized Europe"? Macaulay offered a numeral rendering of worth as percentage return accruing to the Book Society in Calcutta: 20 percent. The Orientalists lost out. They lost out partly because they shared certain beliefs with the Anglicists and the Utilitarians. One belief was that both felt that native character needed rejuvenation. Another was the sad state of affairs of knowledge production in South Asia. Both sides concurred that South Asian science was bankrupt.[29] Jones had promulgated this belief many years before. He was quite clear about the forms in which access to such knowledge was apportioned between Europeans and Asiatics. "Reason and Taste," he says, "are the grand prerogatives of European minds, while the Asiatics have soared to a loftier imagination." Though one might glean some value from Asiatic texts on mineralogy and its medical applications, and that too only at the instigation of authorities like Bernier,[30] "we can expect nothing so important form the works of Hindu or Muselman physicians. . . . Permit me to now add a few words on the Sciences, properly so named; in which it must be admitted, that the Asiatics, if compared to our western nations, are mere children."[31] Reason and taste are given to Europeans, and imagination to those mere children, Asiatics, who in the provenance of medicine and science had to be taught by European teachers.[32] The Anglicists/Utilitarians picked up on this shortfall and turned it to their own ends; they inserted their claims into space opened up between reason/taste and imagination.[33]

By 1833, the battle between the Orientalists and Anglicists/Utilitarians over proper education, teaching natives to wean them away from their slovenly habits and erratic character, had been firmly joined.[34] And the battle was couched in precisely those terms: a battle. C. E. Trevelyan (one of Macaulay's supporters, who had written a letter in support of him to the governor-general) writes on April 30, 1834, that

> the last stronghold of the old system [he had been fighting for seven years] has been taken, and tho' some outworks remain, . . . the citadel has been vanquished, and they [the Orientalists] must soon surrender at discretion. The great principle of English education has been established. The foundation stone of the old edifice of Sanskrit and Arabic learning has been taken away.[35]

The struggle between the Orientalists and Anglicists had clearly been long-drawn. Into its purview fell the anxiety about rule, the feeling that the natives, despite outward compliance, were inwardly disaffected.[36] Sir Charles Metcalf, writing a minute on the future government of India in 1829, says:

> We have ceased to be the wonder that we were to the natives, the charm which once encompassed us has been dissolved, and our subjects have the leisure to enquire why they have been subdued. . . .

> [T]hese speculations are not devoid of foundation, they are useful in directing our minds to the contemplation of the real nature of our power, and in preventing a delusive belief of its impregnability. Our greatest danger is not from a Russian invasion [from the outside], but from the fading of the impression of our invincibility from the minds of the native inhabitants of India. The disaffection, which would willingly root us out, exists abundantly. The concurrence of circumstances sufficient to call it into general action may at any time happen. . . . But as long as we retain possession, we are bound to do all the good in our power to our subjects. Although the hope of gaining their attachment be utterly vain, we may often mitigate and neutralize their disaffection. . . . Even however under a certainty of permanent disaffection our duty towards the governed is the same. We are bound to give them the best government in our power.[37]

The question of the "real nature of British power," allied to the awareness of the fading of its impression in the minds of the natives, was one addressed over and over under Bentinck's tenure. Governmentality—ascertaining what form governance ought to take;[38] who ought to govern; British relationships to the ruling princes; the organization of the armed forces[39]—was obviously an issue as certain reforms were being implemented. Threading through the struggles over the army was the memory of the sepoy mutiny in Madras, in 1806, when Bentinck had held the governorship there. Bentinck's term in Calcutta, too, began inauspiciously. He reduced the half-*batta* allowance paid out to officer cadres of the Bengal army stationed at the major cantonments and incited the ire of British officers. Bentinck was also faced with transacting business with, and sometimes having to conciliate, a growing and vociferous Bengali bourgeoisie.[40]

Some of the battles over the forms that power should assume were conducted in the language of dominance. However, these articulations never settled easily into the architecture of dominance. "The fading impression of invincibility," how one addressed and redressed it, was never very far from these discussions. And hovering alongside it was the issue of hegemony: how to mitigate and neutralize the disaffection of native-subjects and assure their (preferably effortless) consent. Transforming how natives saw and what natives desired cleaved to the fissures and fractures, the anxieties over rule, the crevices that opened up even when coherent segments were put together in response to perceived cracks.[41] The projects of neutralizing almost always performed their own neutralizing, civilizing moves by returning to cite disinterest ("We are bound to give them the best government in our power") and thus concealing the labor that disinterest performed to consolidate interests and make them work.

The schemes that attempted to mitigate native alienation assumed several imbricated configurations. These schemes obviously assumed a new, overdetermined form after 1857, when the question of alienation was no longer a question. One set of proposals was organized around cultivating the self of the potentially alienated Indian, turning him, through education, into a person more amenable to Englishness. Cosying up to cultivation were the ever-present, long-standing invocations of morality: the moral character of those under subjugation and the morality displayed by their behavior, as well as the morality inculcated in them by native classical languages, literatures, and religious texts (the three were sometimes folded into one another, and occasionally kept apart in exegeses on the "moral").[42]

One option posed by secularists to transform moral character and behavior was through English literature and European ideas. These became exemplary modes through which character could be given shape and the person, so redirected, became an ideal administrator with "good character, habits of business, of application, of sound judgement."[43] But the post-1835 transmutations of native selves through education did not just require them to turn to English and away from Indian classical languages; that turn was to be made to effect a certain purpose: the reconfiguration of the vernaculars, so that they would be adequate to accommodate the material to be translated into them. Translation moved to the fore; learning English became instrumental. It would "communicate that improved spirit which it is to be hoped they will themselves have imbibed." It would inculcate civility as well as create new languages in which and through which to rule. But translated texts needed to be preceded by translated people, and English was one way to implement this bodily translation. As Kerr puts it, "There was a tendency to believe that if books were only translated into the language of the people, they would certainly be read, and all good effects would follow, without considering that the people themselves required to be 'translated,' so to speak, before they could understand and appreciate the books."[44] Vernaculars, as against classical languages, were the form of the local that would enable a percolation of Englishness down to the masses. Vernaculars were the languages that would enable hegemony. They created those conditions for the right kind of administrator, "qualified by intelligence and morality."

Macaulay, aided by Trevelyan, initiated this move toward the vernaculars in his minute. For him the choice between Oriental languages and English was made because the vernaculars, or as he called them, the dialects, needed improvement. He used the Russians as his case in point: they, and their dialects, were transformed when English was chosen over local beliefs, histories, and knowledge:

> The dialects commonly spoken among the natives of India contain neither Literary nor scientific information, and are, moreover so poor and rude that, until they are enriched from some other quarter, it will not be easy to translate any valuable work into them. It seems to be admitted on all sides that the intellectual improvement of those classes of the people who have the means of pursuing higher studies can at present be effected only by means of some language not vernacular amongst them.
>
> What then shall this language be? One half of the Committee maintain that it should be the English. The other half strongly recommend the Arabic and Sanscrit [*sic*].[45]

"The preparation of class-books in the Vernacular languages, was one of the first objects that engaged the attention of the friends of Native education,"[46] says Kerr, principal of Hoogly College, in 1852. But the impetus afforded vernacular and translations that had begun under the auspices of the Calcutta School Book Society long before Macaulay entered the scene of Indian education was undercut immediately after the 1835 minute. Because there was such a push toward English education at that point, though the education committee had explicitly stated that vernacular literature was "the ultimate object to which their efforts must be directed," little was done on the vernaculars. The committee's failings incited complaints in 1841 that they had "ceased from all active patronage of the vernacular."[47]

Vernaculars were revived as the focus of an educational impetus by Lord Auckland (governor-general, 1836–42), who was viceroy in 1841, the year he gathered together a subcommittee to assess the situation.[48] By 1841, a Vernacular Society, encouraged by the government of the Northwest Provinces, had been formed in Delhi to supply text books to local government colleges. In 1851, Mr. Boutros became the principal of Delhi College and seriously considered making Urdu the medium of instruction. For this he needed text books, and to this end he began a society for "the promotion of knowledge in India through the medium of the Vernacular language."[49] He was the society's first chair, and in his list of books to be translated into Urdu—alongside Mill on political economy, Bentham on jurisprudence, Coombe on physiology, and Plutarch's *Lives*—was a set of selections, in English, of Urdu poetry. This process of educating in the vernacular continued and mimed what had gone on before: it transferred out into English translation knowledge that was then selected and given back in a retranslation, judiciously augmented by appropriate European knowledge. It was no accident that one of the text books chosen for translation into Urdu was Macnaghten's *Principles of Hindu and Mahomedan Law*.[50]

Teaching in the vernacular became a particular kind of necessity after the government of northwest India was placed under a different regime in Agra in 1835 under Sir Charles Metcalfe, and after the annexation of Punjab in 1849. Punjab and the Northwest Provinces were considered quite different from Bengal, the people of those regions judged more "isolated, detached," and the areas less densely populated.[51] The government at Agra picked up a plan that had been suggested by Mr. W. Adam in two reports written between 1835 and 1838. Adam called for an educational renewal, which he believed would raise the characters of the natives (*sic*), by extending and improving on the schools that were already in place and that were run by locals, and augmenting these schools with an Anglo-vernacular school in every district. Adam wanted to bring informal education under the purview of the government and to institutionalize it, adding new class books and teachers, superintending bodies of examiners and inspectors, and organizing forms of enumeration and extraction to fund the innovations.[52]

The Northwest Provinces and Punjab had a different kind of population than Bengal and Calcutta. Because their contact with the English was not as extensive as Bengalis, not only were they less amenable to Englishness given to them in English, but they—the masses of the real India, the village—would not be able to learn English with the same dexterous fluidity. These masses presented colonial educators and administrators with the problem of filtration/diffusion on a large scale, and of the business of controlling alien bodies less in contact with and therefore less under the supervision of the English. By 1852, illustrations of the failure of diffusion sallied forth in response. The Calcutta or British-educated native (mimic-man) who came home to the village spoke two languages: the language of daily intercourse and the language of his translated self. This self was rendered incomprehensible to his friends and family, who saw his translation as caricature. As a source of humor, the mimic-man failed in his project, to allure his friends and family to the British way of things. By then, this caricature had an alternate. James Thomason, in the Northwest Provinces, had already provided another model for the translated man: the recycled village school teacher, who educated students in the vernacular and sent them out to learn Englishness, so that they, never far from their vernacular village origins, could return to replace him and proceed to percolate Englishness downward.[53]

Thomason's ostensible project was to bring teaching and knowledge to bear on the ordinary affairs of the rural masses, to teach them to read the transformations in the codification of their own property. Rural subjects had to be made literate in the systems that organized their lives. Even as they were written up in registers that revealed (and produced) the status of their property, they had to read their names and the delineations of their land so that the correctness of the registers could be maintained. James Thomason contracted education as a necessary supplement to colonial administration. He, following upon Adams, institutionalized the local forms of teaching entirely, while offering this institutionalization, and its collateral detouring of the local through the colonial, as a benefit offered by a beneficent government.[54]

Sir Charles Wood's education dispatch of 1854 picked up on Thomason's work, and projected it into a policy for the colony at large. It extended education to the masses and tied it to its utilitarianness, stating unequivocally in paragraph 10:

> We have also received most satisfactory evidence of the high attainments in English literature and European science, which have been acquired of late years by some of the natives of India. But this success

> has been confined to but a small number of persons; and we are desirous of extending far more widely the means of acquiring general European knowledge, of a less high order, but of such a character as may be practically useful to the people of India in their different spheres of life. To attain this end it is necessary, for the reasons which we have given above, that they should be made familiar with the works of European authors, and with the results of the thought and labour of Europeans on the subjects of every description upon which knowledge is to be imparted to them; and to extend the means of imparting this knowledge must be the object of any general system of education.[55]

Allied to the issue of employable education that also ensured a diffusion of morality through practical and vernacular education was the place of employment for those who had been so educated. Hardinge, whose tenure preceded Wood's education dispatch, had already attempted to give an impetus to diffusion through work, by scripting a resolution in 1844 that required departments to give preferential treatment to candidates with certain qualifications. Hardinge's proposal called for affirmative action for candidates who were bolstered by moral teachings provided through English literature: names were published in annual reports and lists were garnered and followed up assiduously.[56] His suggestions met with a great deal of resistance from missionary schools, and from officers who refused the connections he made between literature and morality, but they were successful "in a silent sense." They drew attention to the importance of morality (introduced and cemented through a certain kind of education) as a prerequisite for public office.[57] Hardinge's proposal, like Macaulay's minute, continued the support given to English by Bentinck, who had attempted to introduce English as the lingua franca of all official matters and had also encountered some resistance.[58] Hardinge's resolution, like Wood's, offered an economic advantage. It would cut costs by employing natives who were cheaper to educate and hire, and cut costs by producing imperial subjects invested in industriousness and morality, who would serve the imperium honestly and not abscond with money. Kerr, commenting on the resolution, offered a rhetorical response: "It may be asked, are the educated Natives more likely to prove 'honest men,' and consequently more useful servants of the State, than the rest of their countrymen? I believe they are. . . . At our Colleges and Schools they acquire, to some extent, the habit of truthfulness. English principles are to a certain extent engrafted in their hearts."[59]

What were the kinds of imperial subjects that were to be produced after Bentinck began his forays into transforming education? It is clear from the *Minute on Education*, and the discursive engagements facilitating it, that Bentinck and Macaulay wanted the reproduction of bourgeoisie subjects. When Bentinck came to his work as governor-general in Calcutta, the local middle classes had already been portrayed as losing their allegiance to Englishness. In a way they were too English, questioning policies, skeptical, described as inhabiting spaces that had lost the morality engendered by local religions. Being Indian, however, did not permit them the possibility of living in moral spaces, because they lived in worlds organized by the immorality proposed by Indian texts, prejudicial religious documents, offering groveling superstition, irregular logic, metaphysics that recycled the imaginary. Englishness had to intervene in the local, transforming it. At the same time Englishness had given to Indians—in a way that deferred, held at bay, what Englishness had to offer—a skepticism that would lead to rebellious interventions.

Bentinck's tenure coincided with an emergence of active working-class movements in Britain. By 1833, Peter Gaskell had written *The Manufacturing Population of England*, the point at which, E. P. Thompson notes, one was to

> step into a world in which the working-class presence can be felt in every county in England, and in most fields of life. The new class consciousness of working people, . . . was a consciousness of the identity of interests between working men of the most diverse occupations and levels of attainment . . . [as well as] a consciousness of the identity of the interests of the working class, . . . as against those of other classes.[60]

Bentinck's tenure, and the 1833 renewal of the East India Company's charter, which called for settlement and pulled back on a certain form of mercantile trade, brought with it an awareness of a fuller movement into an industrial economy, which needed both docile colonial workers (management and labor), unlike those at home, and an expanded base of colonial consumers. The push to the vernaculars is an instance of this awareness.

What the minute called for, with its emphasis on changing the vernaculars (giving vernaculars a kind of status, even as they had to be thought of as inadequate) was a sort of colonial middle-class man, who had an allegiance to Britishness, while maintaining his distance from it and maintaining a bodily connection to Indianness. He was to be Indian in blood and color—he would know himself as Indian through the vernaculars, in other words. He was to be a translated Indian, English in taste, opinions, morals, and intellect: not quite English in intellect, or he would rebel, but quite English in taste and opinions, so he would want to buy English. His morals had to incorporate his desire to be an honest administrator, and so ensure the clear flow of colonial capital, and to disengage his desire to rebel (to which he would be led if he were genuinely skeptical), which would hamper the flow of capital, detouring it toward extraneous expenses. The study of English literature, which allowed the administration to hold to a piece of its pledge to stay neutral on religion, promised to ensure a proper, nonrebellious morality on the part of the colonized. The question of the morality of a colonized bourgeoisie at this historical juncture imbricates it with the formation of a more vociferous working class in England.

The vernaculars were paid close attention at moments in the 1830s when there were new sets of subjects, both rural and urban, from the Northwest Provinces who had to be accommodated, at the same time at which the Chartist movement in Britain was beginning to take form.[61] Adam's reports coincided with this movement. An emphasis on the vernaculars and on local, rural schooling took account of transformations that had to engender both the new rural subjects and urban subjects. As colonial bureaucracies were extending their reach into expanded rural terrains, vernaculars became the places where selves were to be transformed. Changing them attempted to ensure subjects that were properly subjugated. Money was lent to the project of change, prizes given to new writing in vernacular in the Northwest Provinces, and grants offered for translations into them. Subjects translated into the vernacular did not mimic Englishness, they kept their blood and color, and would always be read and raced and nationalized as Indian. But Englishness was engrafted *into* them, through a transfusion of Englishness.[62] The double, mixed metaphors from science portrayed the work that vernaculars were to do, and were to continue to do post-1857. In 1867, a group of Indian, Hindu, and Muslim members of the British Indian Association, Northwest Provinces, writing to the viceroy to propose vernacular as a medium of instruction (and in the long term endorse modifications of the Calcutta university system), make their argument by ensuring that vernaculars would spread English knowledge in a more extensive fashion.[63] Folded into their proposal are the requisite apologias and apologues: "the country as a whole is in a state of uncivilized ignorance; needs a change for the better in the ideas and morals of the people; giving the vernaculars life does not mean a revival of Asiatic learning, because in the face of European research Asiatic learning has either proved false and erroneous, or has changed, or has become obsolete." This proposition, or rather request, by the colonized, heralded a new kind of vernacular, and it was suggested by already translated subjects, who wanted the lessons learned from translation to percolate down their community through diffused translations.

How were community and self constructed in relation to one another? One of the effects promised by the demand to make government more efficient, after Hardinge's mandate to consider education a necessary qualification of public service and the need, after 1857, to make workers more trustworthy, was to begin to fracture the kinds of community allegiances through which jobs had been ensured to members. Regular supervision; competitive recruitment; records of connections to break the power of cliques; the 1869 circular that established communal and caste quotas; mandating educational qualifications like police officer literacy tests in 1860 and university entrance exams for *taḥṣīldār* (revenue officers) in the 1890s: all worked toward this end.[64] People were to be picked not by their contacts, but on the basis of a certain kind of self and self-worth produced by a system that attempted to make education and English (or vernaculars percolated through Englishness) a part of systems of governance.[65]

Documents produced after 1857 attest to the refusal of Muslims to enter this system of education.[66] The various reasons given were pique, processed through a religion which propagated a tenaciousness to the memory and custom of forefathers (unlike the more supple Hinduism); speculation; and fraud, preaching of sedition by the Koran, "which proclaimed the duty of war against heretics." The difficulty Muslims had in entering British schooling was magnified in proportion to the amount of English and European science taught. One exception to this was Sir Sayyid Ahmad Khan.[67]

These reasons given for the shortfall in Muslim educated bodies are obviously cycled through the presuppositions of the writer of the document, who believes that Hindus are better than Muslims, that education can corrupt and destroy but that its modernity rejuvenates. Another account, also written after 1857, suggests a compendium of reasons offered by the Report of the Commission of Education in India in the early 1880s: the Muslim love of the profession of arms; the unfriendliness between British and Muslims; the coldness of the government toward Muslims manifested in textbooks whose tone is hostile to Islam. If asked, a Muslim himself might venture pride of race, memory of a past superiority, religious fears, and an unnatural attachment to Islamic learning.[68] The report also discusses the factors which led to the "decadence and ruin of Muhammadan families." Among these were the ouster of Persian as the official language, the substitution of English and vernacular, English as the exam language for appointments to the civil service (in 1864), the use of Nagari instead of Persian in Bihar courts.[69] The trauma revealed in Hali's poem mourning Delhi lurks between the lines of these seemingly straightforward lists of reasons and lists of statistics. Nestled in the lists, too, is the history of British anger against Muslims after 1857, and spoken in them is what kind of Muslim subject was not the sort whose absence at school had to be counted. These lists are a record of those Muslims who stay apart from British institutions, the fear of whom must be accounted for in them.

These are the northern Indian Muslims who initially refused to conform to the strictures of British rule after 1857. Their rejection of British-imposed conditions, however, ensured their exclusion from the spheres of political and commercial power, even though prior to this Indian Muslims had been the ruling elite. Access to power had been different under the Mughals. Although, as with the British, conformity with its ways was an essential prerequisite for entry into the upper echelons of power, they relied much more overtly on connections formed through birth and lineage rather than through education. David Lelyveld, a historian of Muslim India, describes the apparatus of the Mughal empire as having as its basic principle a society composed of "conflicting segments that could only be brought into harmony by virtue of their subordination to the apex of the system, namely, the ruling dynasty."[70] These segments were defined by some concept of common ancestry, but they were not simple, separate units; there was a wide array of overlapping circles of social identity that came into focus according to the occasion.[71] The connecting tissue between the various segments was a complex network of relations and "ritual ties of loyalty analogous to kinship relations."[72] Lelyveld describes the ruling elite—which actually included both Muslims and non-Muslims—as subscribing to a very specialized set of cultural values that were "centered on the Persian language" and inspired by the "courtly styles of Safavid Iran."[73] This group of people were called *sharīf.* Lelyveld points out that although the word *sharīf* had religious associations in other Islamic regions, in Muslim India it indicated "respectability in terms of cosmopolitan Mughal criteria."[74] *Sharāfat,* the quality that identified the *ashrāf,* or *sharīf* people, was ideally derived through birth; when it was gained in other ways, the person was "quickly redefined in the vocabulary of honorable descent."[75] So, being considered one of the *ashrāf* meant that one belonged to an appropriate lineage—usually one affiliated with power. *Sharāfat* was also a term associated with character, connoting a system of behavior and established moral value, a signifier of a ruling elite that separated them from their servitors. A *sharīf* man was defined as

> one of dignified temperament, self-confident but not overly aggressive, appreciative of good literature, music and art, but not flamboyant, familiar with mystical experience, but hardly immersed in it. Sharīf social relations involved a pose of deference, but were above all a matter of virtuosity within the highly restricted bounds of etiquette.[76]

It is evident from Carla Petievich's study on the distinctions drawn in the late nineteenth century between two different schools of Urdu poetry in northern India—Dihlavi from Delhi and Lakhnavi from Lucknow—that there was an intimate relationship between poetry and the negotiation for and the assigning of power and value, both politically and in terms of the literary as a mode of social expression. In fact, Petievich states that the characteristics of a *sharīf* man "directly echo many of the terms in which the ghazal is discussed in literary criticism." Poetry also played a crucial role in North Indian identifications, a fact that is supported by venerated scholar Aziz Ahmad's assertion, "The cultural [*sic*] expression of Islamic India is best reflected in its literature."[77]

In her concluding chapter, Petievich speaks of the difference between the Delhi and Lucknow schools in terms of their relative possession of qualities associated at this time with *sharāfat*. It is clear from her description that these qualities were responsive to, and in fact incorporated, certain westernized ideas, such as straightforward simplicity and accessibility.[78] By the 1860s, some Muslims had begun courting access to the sociopolitical structures of the British empire, which meant submitting to the dictates of the British, specifically, English education. This portion of the Muslim community's acceptance of the terms under which they would be included in the arenas under British control brought with it a corresponding move by them to emulate the new ẹlite, which had repercussions on both Muslim male identity as a self, and the poetic world, for neither fit into the new sociopolitical structure. That English literature had been advocated as the harbinger of a new, moral, colonized self, overdetermined the connections made between poetry and refinement and personhood. Culture, as urbanity and refinement (*tamaddun o tahżīb*), produced and understood as something sedimented into literature and as promoting a national character, was promulgated actively during this period. The *ashrāf* had to adjust their "cultural" self-definition to new expectations.[79] Poets, too, had to pay obeisance to new economic arbiters as the old patronage systems in Muslim courts were disbanded; this meant that they responded to what they considered to be British standards of poetic criticism.[80] The expressions of urban, urbane, cultivated, and civilized Islamic India, embodied in the various genres of poetry like the ghazal and *qaṣīdah*, spoken in Persian, Arabic, and Urdu, were under attack while there was a shift in what it meant to be a *sharīf ādmī*.[81]

The resulting adjustments were far-reaching. Lelyveld describes the implications of urban self-definition, which could be extended to include the poetic universe:

> As long as the requisite literary training for public office was a matter of private domestic arrangement, and success in one's official career depended on personal, kinsfolk alliance, the dominance of sharīf cultural styles and the hereditary advantage of sharīf families were assured. But even if alternative means for training and recruiting public servants did not necessarily shift or extend the access of social groups to positions of power, the change reached into areas of cultural self-definition communicated to individuals in the experience of growing up. For what was being suggested to any potential participant in the

> political process was not merely the substitution of one set of intellectual competencies for another. Childhood and family life, language, ideology, and religion all come into question, were threatened with a fundamental revision and an altered place in the total context of a person's life. Many sponsors of change, Indian as well as British, were quite explicit in making this connection: they did not approve of Indian family life or of the beliefs and practices that it tended to promote.[82]

Reeducation resulted in a reassessment of the community, including the forms through which Muslim civilization in India expressed its *tahżīb*; indeed, the main focus of criticism was poetry as exemplified by various genres, but falling heavily on one particular genre—the ghazal. This critique of community and poetry was primarily conducted by Sir Sayyid Ahmad Khan, one of the most influential propagators of British-style education, and by Muhammad Husain Azad and Altaf Husain Hali, the exemplary literary spokesmen of that troubled period.

The agenda they proposed in their respective spheres was not a uniform one. They did not unequivocally reject established conventions, but vacillated between a criticism of some features of the Islamic world and an attempt to bolster others; all three attempted to find legitimacy for their ideas in their own renditions of a European worldview and canon, while sometimes refusing their allegiances to Europe.[83] Although Sir Sayyid's agenda relied on social transformation through acquisition of different kinds of knowledge, including science, which he felt had helped the English secure and maintain economic superiority, he did not believe that access to these types of knowledge and the power that came with them should be universal; rather, he focused his reformist zeal on the *ashrāf*, whom he believed were best suited to positions of power.[84] Indeed, the major patrons of poetry were urban rulers; in addition to having court poets, many rulers were poets themselves, for composing and reciting good poetry (namely *sharīf*, a form that epitomized their moral values and refinement) was the hallmark of a cultivated gentleman.[85] While proposing that the *ashrāf* continue as the predominant social class, however, he also criticized them for neglecting "the cultivation of the virtues associated with their position in society, especially the sense of social duty and the acquisition of knowledge."[86]

## HALI

Altaf Husain Hali's most famous didactic poem, "The Ebb and Flow of Islam" (Madd o jazr-e islām), contrasts the prior glories of Islam with the current pathetic state of the Muslims in India. A didactic poem published in several different editions, first published in Sir Sayyid's newspaper *Tahżīb ul aḵhlāq*, in 1879, A.H. 1296; and the seventeenth edition in 1922, its styles, language (bareness and colloquialness), and many of its themes prefigure Hali's later work. The poem's larger framework concerns the forms of early Arabic Islamic heritage (voh dīn jisne aʿdā ko iḵhvān banāya, dushman ko insān banāyā; the religion which made enemies brothers, and foes human beings),[87] which were once glorious, and the current stage of *pastī*, downfall, abasement to which Indian Muslims had fallen, where the possibilities of rejuvenation were with the British. Within this framework Hali explores the cyclical temporality of decay and revival (using the boat, *nā'o*) of Muslim communities. Early Islam offers him a past when the prophet who practiced alchemy and religion turned copper into gold and separated (discerned) the pure from the counterfeit; made people honorable and taught them how to preserve health; and incited a desire for travel with its attendant benefits of trading. The principles of government, of governance in true Islam, the religion that once was great, incorporate the morality and civilization aligned with education and commerce that are scripted into British initiatives for the salvation of the colonized.[88] The literal archeology of this Islamic learning, teaching, and civilization (which include the sciences of measurement, surveying and astronomy, geography and navigation; history, archival research, rhetoric, philosophy, medicine; commerce, agriculture, and architecture) is sedimented into the monuments, the monumental buildings of Spain and Baghdad.[89] Hali's plain, bluntly virulent metaphors are reserved for, and most effectively served in, his descriptions of decline, especially the decline of poetry: "voh shaʿur o qaṣayad kā nāpāk daftar, ʿufūnat meñ sanḍās se haiñ badtar" (the impure archives/records/books of poetry and odes, in their putrid rottenness are worse than a toilet/cesspool).[90]

The most important statement that Hali made on poetry, however, is in the preface to his collected works, or *dīvān*, called the *Muqaddamah-e shiʿr o shāʿirī*, in which he espoused a critical position that underpins the force of Sayyid Ahmad Khan's rhetoric. Hali had been working on this text since 1882, though he first published it in 1893. The *Muqaddamah* has been described as "an attempt on the part of Hali to take poetry away from the hedonist aesthetics of the previous generations of poets and to bring it in tune with the moralistic and reformist aesthetics of the Aligarh movement."[91] Hali saw poetry as a potent force capable of allying itself with either side of a moral order; he wanted its fervor, excitement, or *josh* to be useful, serving moral and political ends.[92] According to him, poetry and society are intimately connected; when society degenerates, poetry does, too, becoming "a means for spoiling national morality."[93] A "forerunner to modern social art," he believed that poetry should have a utilitarian, or instrumental, purpose—it had to be understood "as a tool of instruction and change."[94] He also believed that in order to be effective, poetry needed to be controlled and molded to certain specifications; if not overseen, it had the potential to be corrupted by frivolous subject matter and thereby rendered "false."[95] Hali called for a new kind of poetry, the characteristics of which he partially attributed to Milton's conditions for great poetry: truth, passion, simplicity (*aṣlīyat, josh, sādagī*).[96] Unlike the ghazal, which relied on mystical emotion, complex composition, and dreamlike passions, Hali's notion of effective poetry would be natural, conform to ordinary idiomatic speech, and would direct its passion to describing the ordinary occurrences of an ordinary world.[97] The nuances of the ordinary were to be elaborated in series of possible topics—seasons, morning, night, forest—that reoriented the background of love poetry, and were also consonant with the subjects to be poeticized in vernaculars, that had been proposed by Colonel Holroyd.[98] Language, too, was taken away from metaphoric manipulations, and taken to (or taken back to if one keeps in mind Hali's proposals for Arabic as the seat of civilization, speaking poetically in a certain voice) a transparent simplicity that bared "fact." Nature, in these particular incarnations as a "wild" pastoral, was amenable to transparent simplicity.

Though Hali spoke of reforming (*iṣlāḥ*) all the genres of poetry, including *maśnavī* and *qaṣīdah*, he reserved a special place for the reform of the ghazal, perhaps because the ghazal, more than any other form captured the heart, effected the subtlest and deepest change, and therefore was most in need of revision. Hali's critique also focused on this one particular form because, according to him, it was emblematic of the old poetic order.

Speaking specifically of the ghazal, Hali felt that it must be "descriptive of social and political realities,"[99] even though he did not expect literature to serve any one political position. Approximately one-fourth of *Muqaddamah* is devoted to changes Hali wished to implement in the ghazal, particularly suited to his purposes because of its popularity among both the literati and those who were not functionally literate. Like other lyric genres in Urdu, it was conventionalized and subscribed to precolonial conventions, but because it was a form antithetical to natural poetry it was a potentially moralistic tool; therefore, the ghazal was marked as most ripe for reform.[100] Hali did not want to eliminate old genres of poetry; he merely wanted them to be more consonant with the changes that were taking place in the world; he wanted to harness the passion embodied in the old to new aims.[101] Harnessing passion meant diverting the *mauẓūaʿ* of the ghazal, the subjects of desire, and stretching the affective basis for it: who loved, to whom this ardor was given, the subtle shadings of passion, of *ishq*, *muḥabbat*. Passion could be a devotee's for god, children's for parents, siblings' for one another, couples' for one another, among friends, subjects' for a ruler, between humans and animals, for country, nation, community, family (*vatan*, *mulk*, *qaum*, *ḳhāndān*).[102] In wanting to reform and redirect rather than reject the ghazal, and in his heartfelt cry for rejuvenation of his community in the *Musaddas*, Hali echoed Sir Sayyid's program for the Muslim community; both called for change that would occur within the parameters of "traditional" forms.[103] Hali wanted formal as well as linguistic changes in the ghazal, but the kind of change he wanted meant that the language and topoi of poetry, as well as the language of criticism, would have to be transformed.

Hali supported Sir Sayyid in his endeavor to start a college at Aligarh, and both were involved in developing an educational institution that would prepare Muslim men to participate in a new social and political order. By doing this they attempted to reconstitute the social identifications of certain categories of Indo-Muslim men. For both, the current political realities demanded a new kind of man—one who had evolved through education to possess a certain version of morality (honesty, uprightness as allegiance to a *qaum*, or community); a rapturous pleasure in "modern" knowledge; a planed-down sense of aesthetics—one who was to be socially and politically cognizant and was to have a social conscience but who still operated within the newly scripted norms of Islam.[104] The kinds of transformations they anticipated in the construction of male identity assumed a particular understanding of male persons.[105] This was the kind of person who might have given his life to others when the *Titanic* went down. For both, the concept of a person was someone who operated in, and therefore could be defined through, a sociocultural context—his *vatan*, *mulk*, *qaum*, and *ḳhāndān*. A person was a social entity, but one who had a different relationship to the *socius*, a different kind of self produced by an education in new terms.

Hali defined the "new individualistic poet" as someone who had to try to extricate himself from the network of cultural relationships that tied him to a particular tradition, rather than as someone who merely created innovative poetic forms. Although Hali proposed changing the cultural identifications of a poet writing in Urdu, he rarely (except in the *Musaddas*) conceived of this kind of change as a universal phenomenon that applied to all Indo-Muslim men, nor did he speak of this change as effecting a poet's conscious identity. Thus a poet's individuality was tied both to his separation from a lineage of teachers, *ustād*, and to his ability to write "new" poetry. Indeed, following a particular British romantic trajectory, Hali wanted a poet to sever himself from the network of poetic lineage. He said, "There is no need of having an appointed teacher. . . . The poet's own nature is his teacher. Besides an innate capacity for composing poetry, the second characteristic a poet must have is a need to contemplate nature."[106] By saying this, Hali set himself in opposition to certain older ways where the teacher-pupil relationship and an association with a particular lineage of teachers is an essential part of the definition of a poet's persona. Also, since a poet is customarily given his tools by a teacher, in proposing that a poet turn to nature rather than to a teacher to learn his craft, Hali wanted to break with the ritualized continuity of tradition, even as he struggled with his grief at losing this tradition, and even as he returned to his own teachers for his poetic alliances, and to moments in the past of a Muslim heritage he wanted to hold on to. Breaking tradition, and moving away from the conventions of urban Muslim literati, was aligned with the work ofa particular kind of viewing, romantic, British poet. But it also resonated with the unorthodox (and therefore thoroughly precedent-bound) behavior of the lover within a ghazal.

This new man, a poet who moved away from prior practice, was a moral man, a *sharīf ādmi* who had to take cognizance of a new legal code that had rendered the desires of the past, that once had nothing to do with the law, illegal.[107] He could read poetry historically, understand the claims of particular ages, as a claim. This man would move with the "caravans of the times."[108]

Hali's attempts to change the linguistic and social universe associated with poetry had certain ramifications he took into account, and which are tentatively addressed by Laurel Steele. Although she asserts, "It is doubtful if he realized a rejection of tradition might also mean a break with it, and a subsequent loss of audience and respect," it seems clear to Steele that this is precisely what he *did* want.[109] While emerging forms of society might have less rigid poetic expectations, this very fact would mean that they lead to less of a sense of the "rightness" and "correctness" of poetic expression. In addition, I would take issue with two comments made by Steele, the first of which is her statement following Hali's repudiation of the teacher-student relationship. Even though she cites him from the *Muqaddamah* with, "The poet should read the work of older generations and rely on them insofar as they are correct,"[110] her synopsis indicates that he did *not* view his position as advocating a break with tradition. Second, I would push Steele's comment on Hali's audience a little further than she is perhaps willing to go. In moving away from a traditional, conventionalized language for poetry, Hali is leaving behind an audience with an entrenched critical apparatus. It is not just that the audience would "have less of a sense of rightness and correctness," for if the reforms Hali wanted came to pass, his audience would no longer be able to interpret his poetry with the critical tools at their disposal unless they also had access to his critical materials. So, rather than increasing his potential audience and accessibility, the new poetry might actually decrease it. Hali specifically addressed the questions of audience and the implications of his own ambivalent relationship to tradition, an issue also explored by Miraji in "Traveler," where a poet is positioned with respect to tradition and an audience at a time when his language can no longer be accommodated by an estabished interpretive community. In fact, as Pritchett's work makes clear, Hali's relationship with his past, both with prevailing poetic norms and his connections to an *ustād* (teacher) were complicated. He wanted to hold onto them, but also to transform them; he wanted to keep intact his allegiance to them, but in some radical ways to leave them behind.[111] Even as he struggled to reconstitute the poet, the forms and topics of poetry, and the desires that curved into lyric, Hali mourned the death of an era that held great poets like his own *ustād*, Ghalib.

Hali is ambiguous about many of his statements about poetry as well. For instance, for him realism is not just what is socially mandated as out there (outside the self); rather, realist (*aṣl*) subjects for poetry include events that are "real in the beliefs or thoughts of people, or real in the mind of the poet, or at least it should be something the poet believes, as witnessed by his poetry."[112] If topics for poetry are brought to "realism" through belief or thought, or through the mind, then what distinguishes these beliefs, witnessed by poetry, from the conventions that were shared as belief by older poets? What is this realism that is evoked in such a way that it *escapes* the measures deployed to ascertain, to assess, or to give viable form to the object out there; making its *hijr*, its break, its breach, its forsaking, through belief, through the mind or through witnessing? Hali's *aṣliyāt*, realism, seems to lengthen the realism advocated by colonial commentators (who want a measure of the evidentiary ensconced in their invocations of the out there) toward the more difficult sense of *aṣl*, as somewhere between radical or real (as not amenable to the immediacy of the easily "visible"), original, essential, true.[113]

## RETURN TO THE "PROGRESSIVES"

Hali's position on poetry as an agent of social change is an obvious precursor to the Progressive movement that began in the 1930s and dominated the intellectual environment during Miraji's lifetime;[114] the Progressives felt that literature should be subordinated to a political and social agenda. Between Hali and the Progressives were poets like Brij Narayan Chakbast and Zafar Ali Khan, who wrote Urdu poetry that spoke a fervent nationalism as well as anger at colonialism, and addressed some lyric to particular nationalist leaders; they could be thought of as inciting political change through poetry. Carlo Coppola, who has written the definitive work in English on the Progressives, speaks of the similarities and differences between Hali and the Progressives:

> Whereas Hali saw Islam and the uplift of Indian Muslims as the ultimate goal for literature, the progressives . . . envisioned Marxism and the rise of the proletariat class as the ultimate end for literature. Essential to achieving these ends was an acute social and political awareness among those people to whom this literature was to be a benefit. Hence, this awareness was to be inculcated by literary means. In addition, both Hali and the progressives sought to wrest literature and the production of literature from the rarefied atmosphere of the upper classes and bring it down to a broader, more general audience. In this context both Hali and the progressives were quick to set up standards for "good" and "bad" literature based on their particular esthetic orientation. Both Hali and the progressives were, as a result, very concerned with questions not only of content, but with specific problems of a formal sort: language, diction, the nature of embellishment, etc.[115]

According to Coppola, "specific problems of a formal sort" emerged from the Progressives' engagement with the ghazal at the inception of the movement:

> The ghazal came under fire from a number of critics. . . . However as the movement developed, writers and critics were forced to re-evaluate the literary traditions of the past and to rework literary imagery and forms in such a way as to integrate them with the exigencies of progressive art. As a result, old symbols such as the beloved, the lover and the rival—to use only one set of examples—were reinterpreted and expanded beyond the limits set on them by the earlier literature. The motivation for such an action was a practical one: certainly it would be easier to remodel these images and symbols which had existed and were readily recognizable to literate and illiterate alike, rather than throw them away and start from nothing.[116]

Thus the Progressives continued along the path Hali had traveled. Their agenda for writing poetry included a critical stance on the vocabulary, purpose, and worldview of such forms of Urdu poetry as the *maṡnavī* and the ghazal, which were still emblematic of what was felt to be a prior canon. But the various poets, like Faiz, who wrote consistently as Progressives, either continued using love's themes, the ground or *maẓmūn* of desire, the people and scenes like the beloved, garden, *kūcā*, or lane, *koṭhī*, that derived from the ghazal or began to sift through those metaphors for *maẓmūn* that echoed those Hali might have called for, versifying love for the land, the nation, the community.[117] By the 1940s the Progressives had constructed for themselves, through aggressive proselytizing and constant vigilance, a consistent framework of interpretation. For Miraji, too, a writer who shared the Progressives' world as well as the tenor of their historical analyses, the "traditional canon" was personified by the ghazal. In "Traveler," he too took recourse to the ghazal, pulling and diverting the language and topoi of a genre whose main themes were and are mystical and mundane love.

## THE GHAZAL: EMBLEMATIC OF TRADITION

Before one can explore the terms under which Miraji's poetry was written and the directions that it took, it is first necessary to outline the dimensions of what he produced as the tradition that he set himself against. As has been stated earlier, the understanding of the lyric in the Urdu tradition by the end of the nineteenth century is filtered through the language of one particular "canonical" genre of the tradition—the ghazal. The ghazal consists of a series of couplets (*shiʿr*) that are seldom linked, except in a very loose thematic sense, but which are much more explicitly tied together by stringent formal metrical and rhyme-scheme requirements. Its linguistic world is circumscribed in that both the poet and the recipient of the poem use and refer to a common pool of specialized "poeticized" signifiers.[118]

The ghazal describes the relationship between a lover and a beloved (unrequited/unattainable love) by using scenarios and stories set in, for example, the garden, the desert, a festive gathering, or the story of Laila and Majnun. Although the topoi are established and unchanging, holding the framework still, the *maẓmūn āfrīnī* available to an audience, the play of images and metaphors used by poets to delineate them grow or modulate to a greater refinement over the years they have been deployed. But even when the pool of metaphors used by poets spreads, it does not open up the mechanisms of signification to change, for the interpretative frameworks remain constant; only the internal limits of the worlds of signification move or become denser. What changes is the subtlety with which meaning is elaborated and read (*mā'nī afrīnī*).[119]

Another level of signification—allegorization, where one system of signification is the signifier within another system—is also available to the poet and the recipient. For example, the lover/beloved relationship can be used as an allegory for an individual soul's relationship to God. The pleasure provoked by this allegory relies on the concurrent use of both systems of signification: the ironic or playful juxtaposition of the allegorization when it is placed upon the preallegoric signification.[120]

A ghazal's reception occurs in two ways: it can be read—in a poet's complete collection (*kulliyāt*), commentary, or selection of verses collected idiosyncratically by a critic—or it can be recited or sung by a poet or a professional singer at a mushaira (poetic symposium), which is often its first mode of public presentation. Frequently, presenters at a mushaira are asked to compose ghazals using the same *zamīn*, meter and rhyme scheme, of a couplet, a line, or a theme they are given in advance. Since the couplets are seldom thematically connected, it is up to the discretion of the person who presents the ghazal to compose a selection of couplets, which are then recited or sung, words and phrases repeated, pauses carefully parsed to show off the subtle nuances and enhance the delicate pleasures of meaning-making. Each *shi'r* is recited separately, and the reciter or singer—who may be the poet—exploits emotional effects in the narration to create a particular reading or set of readings for that couplet.

The readings that emerge from the *shi'r* are understood intertextually. In a self-consciously formal way, it intersects other couplets of the ghazal with which it is being recited.[121] However, it also intersects with the "tradition-at-large," which can be described as all the couplets written and recited on the same theme in Urdu, Persian, and sometimes Arabic. To Kenneth Bryant, who examines intertextuality in the ghazal, the tradition itself is

> a kind of text . . . [that] is not the product of a single recitation, nor of a single poet; rather, it is an on-going collaborative endeavor. But

> like the ghazal, this second text is also a serial or at least a cumulative, recitation: a poet composes a *shiʿr* on a particular theme—let us say on the theme of rose and nightingale—as part of his ghazal: minutes, weeks or decades later, another poet contributes a variation of the same theme, in the form of one *shiʿr* contained within his ghazal; and so on until we reach "our" couplet, which is now the latest installment.[122]

The "tradition" can also be understood less specifically as the various worlds of signification within which the poet writes. A heightened intertextual sympathy brings the recitation of the *shiʿr* to life and points the reciter toward certain dramatic choices, which then suggest the expanse of readings for it.

A critic writing a commentary, like a reciter, has the option to write on either the whole ghazal or on selected *shiʿr*. A reading of a ghazal in this context always considers each *shiʿr* as a separate entity. The interpretative directions that are established in the oral realm are mirrored in the commentarial literature. The rhetorical strategies used for reinforcing certain readings are self-consciously intertextual and weave a corresponding analysis of earlier *shiʿr* on the same topic threading back to common reserves in worlds of signification.[123] This was the poetic palace of the *sundarī*, the woman as ghazal, resplendent in a courtyard, in Miraji's essay "Nayī shāʿirī." Miraji evoked this world, just as Hali did before him. Miraji's allegiances to it, his desires for it, his revisions of it, were in some ways more complex than those Hali voiced. As Miraji pointed out, he wrote in a time thrown forward from Hali's mourning, a time when a poet "did not know the roads taken, even as they were traveled." Blending Sufi poetics of journeys, Braj and Awadhi metaphors of desire for the divine, and his own distinctive lyric idioms with a hyperawareness that he had to traverse a journey back that had been closed to him, Miraji tried to move forward in "Traveler."

## IQBAL

Muhammad Iqbal (1877–1938) was the first poet in the Urdu literary canon of the late nineteenth and early twentieth centuries to focus on a metaphysical conception of personhood and the ways in which it folded into a *qaumī* construction (bringing religion together with the *socius*) of Indo-Muslim identity (in contrast to Sayyid and Hali, who viewed a person simply as a religious and social entity). Since Miraji moves into the provenance of metaphysics in "Traveler," I will discuss Iqbal's rather confusing idea of "person" as a precursor to Miraji, and thus as a way of situating Miraji's elaborations on person in the poem. Iqbal's notion of personhood—an entity he called *ḳhudī*—was the locus of his philosophical system. "The fundamental fact of the universe," *ḳhudī* is derived from *ḳhud* and can be translated as "self" or "identity," but its primary meaning is "self," standing for myself, yourself, and so on, as well as one's own or private or personal.[124] Iqbal's main discussion on the *ḳhudī* is found in the *masnavī Secrets of the Self* (Asrār-e ḳhudī),[125] and in his prose pieces on philosophy, compiled as *The Reconstruction of Religious Thought in Islam*.[126]

For Iqbal, all live beings are intrinsically identical finite individuals—each a *ḳhudī*. But *ḳhudī* does not have an ambient physicality and so cannot be conflated with the body, *jism*, or be "described in terms of a material morphology."[127] It is neither a unified entity nor a series of unconnected psychic or psychological states. *Ḳhudī* has no exact correlates with Islamic concepts like *nafs* or *ruḥ*, both different parts of a soul, both essential constituents of a person's being that are distinct from *jism* (body), and both in different ways connoting the "self." Here *nafs* can be said to be a negative entity, a "lower" soul, one capable of carnal desires, while *ruḥ* is a positive entity, a spirit engaged in mystical contemplation.[128] The closest Iqbal came to an exact definition of *ḳhudī* is in *Secrets of the Self*, where it is called "the inexplicable finite center of experience."[129]

Iqbal opens his discussion on the self in *The Reconstruction of Religious Thought in Islam* by reviewing the ways in which nature has been cannibalized by various sciences in Europe.[130] He locates his exploration of metaphysics by traveling to those shifts in physics, from the classical mechanics of Newton to the fractures of space-time made by Einstein, that transform notions of nature. Iqbal is attempting to work out the text of substance, of the corporeality and insubstantiality of an object or a thing, and the density or thinness of time or more properly of temporality, and how they come together in ways that do not produce the sense of an object located in a self-present material way simply at one moment. Science is the texture through which Iqbal conducts his search, but it is neither infallible nor something that must be garnered to gather the idealized perfection of modernity for a colonial subject. Science always fails itself, even as it attempts to proceed as though it were beyond failure, and it is to this paradox that Iqbal turns to sense his way to an elaboration of *ḳhudī.*

The *ḳhudī*'s essential nature includes ceaseless temporal, teleological activity. This activity is both inner experience and externally manifested creativity. About inner experience and its connection to self-cognition, as well as to the *ḳhudī*'s projection into the world, Iqbal says:

> Inner experience is the ego at work. We appreciate the ego itself in the act of perceiving, judging, willing. The life of the ego is a kind of tension caused by the ego invading the environment and the environment invading the ego. The ego does not stand outside this arena of mutual invasion. It is present in it as a directive energy and is formed and disciplined by its own experience.[131]

Iqbal took Bergson's turn to movement through temporality (that it was the underlying principle of "Reality") to the *ḳhudī.*[132] The question Iqbal asked, a question of ontology, was sited between the physical and metaphysical: What is being? Is the passage to "Reality" traversed through sense perception? Iqbal answered it with both a yes and a no. Science, that is the passages to the nature of nature taken through sense, was inadequate. Science showed as much as it concealed of its own literally physical mechanics, and of the workings of "Reality." "Reality" was metaphysical, it incorporated the physical but was also immanent in the physical. "Reality" could not be derived causally and had no allegiances to causality, because causality in its material sense required observation. Iqbal proposed a kind of movement for *ḳhudī*: with a purpose toward an end, but without causality. He turned to Alfred North Whitehead to support some of his propositions, suggesting that Whitehead had proposed a sort of organization of events which consisted of a continual flow.[133] "Reality" (here Nature) was composed of passages, passings in time (presaging Miraji's tropes in "Traveler").[134] What then, Iqbal asked, moving to a discussion on suras from the Koran, was God, and the relationship of divinity to the passing of time, to the circling of night and day? Clearly time was where one had to go, to move beyond the immediate, incomplete transactions of the physical. Bergson's "duration in time," passing from state to state so that the self was merely an accretion of specific states, was insufficient because it posed time on the same lines as space, and because Bergson also suggested that pure time was prior to self. One had to proceed to a persistence in time, a life of time, of a self, *ḳhudī*, that was intimate, internal, and profound, where change could not be sifted out from movement, and where a "now" snuck into itself pure duration.[135]

Underlying the *ḳhudī* is the "Absolute Self," or God, a transcendental entity that is omniscient, omnipresent, infinite.[136] This entity in constant motion was that self of pure duration whose properties Iqbal proposed, in a direct response to Islamic thinkers whose constructions of noumenal reality, he felt, were static and immobile.[137] Iqbal does not subsume the individual into the Absolute; rather, the individual is an independent entity that exerts itself in contradistinction to the Absolute. The relationship between the two is the subject of constant debate; it can neverbe settled.[138] For example, in "A Dispute Between God and Man," Man asserts his rights over the products of his own creativity:

> You made the night and I the lamp,
> And you the clay and I the cup; . . .
> I who grind a mirror out of stone,
> Who brew from poison honey-drink.[139]

Iqbal conceived of the *ḳhudī* as a socially responsive entity, an individual existing in conjunction with other individuals in a dynamic relationship with their collective past. For him, individuals exist in a continual oppositional cyclical movement of withdrawal into the *ḳhudī*, through which knowledge about the self is obtained, and immersion (*beḳhudī*) into a community (*millat*) is achieved.[140] *Ḳhud/beḳhud* in one's *millat* reflects the past and future (as in a mirror), and so transcends mortality. It enters the timelessness of Islam.[141] An individual and the society to which he belongs are mutually reinforcing—the community derives its force and power from individual effort, and the individual discovers his being through absorption into "traditional norms" and values.

Iqbal maintained a particular understanding of his own historical past; his valuation of it formed the basis of his ideological stance as a Muslim thinker. He conformed to the notion of the historical degeneracy preceded by early supremacy that characterizes the historiography of a particular type of neocolonial ideologue in the subcontinent, including Hali, and Brahmo Samaj and Arya Samaj thinkers, who perceive themselves as self-consciously opposed to the constructs of colonial ideology and advocate a return to "traditional" social and religious values. His past was the whole panoply of pan-Islam, unconstrained by national, racial, or linguistic borders.[142] He endorsed a return from a current state of powerlessness, through *taqdār*, or purpose, to the time when Islamic hegemony was at its height.[143] This was a response to British colonial imperial territorialism based on racialization—to the realization that he was a member of a disenfranchised social and cultural group, and to implicit and explicit critiques by the British about Muslim society:[144]

Pāk hai gard-e vatan se dāmāñ terā
tū voh yusuf hai ki har miṣr hai kanʿāñ terā
qāfilah ho nah sakegā kabhī vīrāñ terā
Ghair yak bāñg-e darā kuch nahīñ sāmāñ terā
nakhal shamʿā astī o dar shʿolah davada rishāʾe tū
ʿākabat soz bavada sāye-e añdeshshah-e tū.

Your garments are not soiled by the dust of any single native land,
You are the Joseph who sees his Canaan in every Egyptian sand.
Never will your caravan be plundered or laid waste,
You have no baggage save the starting bell. Make haste!
A tree of candles are you, your wick-like roots pierce the light;
Your thoughts are flames that dispel tomorrow's shades and make
them bright.[145]

Har kadam dūrī'e manzil hai numāyāñ mujh se
merī raftār se bhāge haiñ bayābāñ mujh se.

Every step shows me how far my destination is from me
My own speed chases the desert from me.[1]

# 5. IN ILLUMINED SHADOWS: READING "TRAVELER"

## QUESTIONS OF SELF, QUESTIONS OF LANGUAGE

For Iqbal and other pan-Islamic poets, the self was made in an uneasy relationship between the metaphysical and sociopolitical (including religion), while poets associated with the Progressive movement (and Hali before them) deliberately produced the self they evoked in their work in an exclusively sociopolitical context. Underlying both Iqbal's and the Progressives' making of selves, however, was the selves' dualistic structure—one piece of them able to apprehend in a certain register and another unable to do so—convened in the disjunctive tropes that came with Sufi poetry and the mystical correspondences of the ghazal. So the language that scripted the lover-poet self in the ghazal could still be drawn on as a reference when the self was spoken to, spoken about, spoken, or assumed in the verse composed in the late nineteenth and twentieth centuries.

Two major issues have never quite been addressed in the transformation of the parameters of poetry and self-identity that began with Hali: What form would the self take if everything around it, and therefore what it was made of, were renegotiated? And, given Hali's call for new languages in which to constitute self and to compose poetry, how were poets placed and read in the context of prior conditions for signification, judgment, reading; indeed, how would they be read if they deliberately disfigured both self and poetry for the world of a particular poem? Of course, these questions assume a break, or a hiatus in time, between the process of composition and the publicly produced and accepted details of what one read for and how one read.

Iqbal resorted to vocabulary familiar from the Perso-Arabic philosophical "tradition" (blended with twentieth-century European philosophy and physics), which conformed with his return to a pan-Islamic past in his poetry and philosophical writings. So, although his poetry was often didactic, polemical, and, because of his frequent use of archaic semantics, not easily accessible, he didn't have to face the issue of being incomprehensible to a general reader; rather, he molded himself to the expectations of a tradition that any "educated" Urdu reader ought to have access to if they were cognizant of a pre-Anglicized past—the Perso-Arabic one.

Despite the conditions of political turmoil and social upheaval that provided the impetus for reassessing the language of poetry, Iqbal and the Progressives made no attempt to incorporate any of that uncertainty into the self that inhabited a poem. Indeed, the Progressives constructed/presumed a stable identity for a poetic persona as did Iqbal with his subjective *ḳhudī*, whose basic parameters remained constant and consistent from poem to poem; this, in spite of its defining characteristic, which was unceasing motion. Many of these writers were men who belonged to the upper echelons of Urdu hierarchy, and they turned to the possible stability invoked by male subject positions, notwithstanding the destabilization (through problematic forms of stabilization and ruptures prompted by/in trauma) that faced colonized male subjects. Given this history of lyric, it is all the more remarkable that Miraji *did* write a destabilized subject into his poetry. Indeed, it was up to him to voice—in poems like "Traveler"—the ambivalence of a poet writing in a situation where the uncertainty of a lyrical subject and the language that inscribed it were confronted by established traditions of interpretation.

Miraji's voices in poetry, when they speak as the male "I," trace the winding paths of memory and forgetting. Miraji takes these byways, like Hali and the Progressives, from 1857. Walking them, he is haunted by the kinds of narratives that told the *Titanic*'s death in South Asia, and the twentieth-century renditions of Hali's lyrical mourning, which poeticized the pain attending dying stretched out toward the dubious pleasure of coming alive.

Hali segmented his past into sections that could be evoked to produce knowledge in his present, and sections that had to be laid aside to facilitate a move to that knowledge. Forms of pasts had to be brought forward, while others moved back, in a dance of forgetting and remembering that composed a present thrown into possible futures. Hali's relationship to affect and to feeling, reminiscent of the feelings that brought the *Titanic* to life, threaded through the ways that he constituted possibility. A grieving heart, the sine qua non of Urdu ghazal and *marśiyah*, haunted Hali's writing, perhaps leading him to affect, and to its ally imagination as the powers which would imbue any new lyric with *josh*. Hali's struggles toward colonial subjectivities and epistemes as symbolic (iterated specifically as law like the play of the symbolic in the *Titanic* tales) always led him backward to the erratic uncontrollable affect, sometimes leaking, sometimes exploding, through trauma. Grief and pleasure: Hali wanted so much to place them carefully in spots assigned to them, to harness their seductions to the work that had to be done in the present. But their excess eluded him constantly.

The kind of self revealed in Hali's poetry, and which he proposed for poets who were to bend *josh* to serve their reasons for writing, was an inborn genius who went to a kind of organic power to create, untouched by colonialism, but touched by his reconciliations with loss. This self created by seeing, by using discerning as a form of aesthetic measurement and observation which was akin to Jones's measuring scientific sight, and to Wordsworth's. Spatial and temporal perspectives were some of its guiding principles. Seeing, for Hali, was a transparent ability, its powers were rendered transparently and it rendered the things it saw transparently. Poetic language and prose, the modes in which seeing spoke, had to be stripped away from it; it had to produce meaning straightforwardly and was barred from metaphor (*mā'nī* and *maẓmūn āfrīnī*). The distancing operations of perspectivalism, stretching a line out into a point, were turned to temporality. Seeing in time, seeing as history, laying events and texts along a time line so one could assess them in relation to a present. Though Hali supposed his distance from historical moments, that distance had to be presented through historical narratives that drew force from Orientalist (early and late versions) and early (and cultural) nationalist evocations of returns to pasts to consolidate changes in the present.[2]

In the production of *sharāfat*, Hali returned to religion, the place that had been cited as the failure of Muslims to accommodate themselves to the British initiatives after 1857. Religion was the place of depredation, of violence, as well as the place of a refusal to conform, in British accounts of the time. Iqbal, too, faced the insurmountable issue of religion as he struggled with how to narrate selfhood in a way that would not slip easily into colonial givens. The political possibilities of a thrownness into a future had to be explored by Iqbal through metaphysics, through the metaphysical inclinations in epistemology or the sciences, the ground and forms of knowing. Iqbal had to reiterate metaphysics and science as authorizing epistemes with their uneasy alliances to religion if he were to speak to colonized subjectivities. In this he produced some of the conditions for some of Miraji's writing.

As Miraji did after him, Iqbal went to the "now," elaborating the semiotics of the fullness of the moment: *pal bhar*. The present was where the problem lay. It lay there because the present was the time when colonized communities were given a place that located them in a past which had never arrived to the moment of the "now." It lay there because the present was the moment in a historical time line of modernity that permitted this kind of evaluation of epistemes. It lay there because to reach the now as a moment in the future, a colonized subject had to leave behind his past and not bring it with him, even though that very past defined him in the present. The now stood in history, in time pulled backward and then forward.[3] Turning to phenomenology and contemporary questions in physics (probably from Bohr's/Heisenberg's wave-particle discussion), Iqbal proposed two faces for selfhood. The first, the appreciative self, was rendered in motion. Its temporality was phenomenological. Temporality was within it, and did not provide the external circumstances or formations in which it took shape. Time stretched out inside this self.

The second, Iqbal's affective self, was the form of the appreciative self that had been projected into the time of the world, the time that was constituted as space. This self lived in a temporality that had been spatialized in certain ways. Its temporality was counted up as a series of stops, each its present, which, because they were stops, were organized in space and as space. This self was also settled on a time line—time given as a certain version of history that had been visualized in space.

By his own account, Hali and Iqbal were Miraji's precursors. Both staked the ground on which he wrote. Memory as traumatic forgetting, traumatic pain, Miraji got from Hali. Bût he did not carry over the exact historical teleology that Hali had offered. Miraji held onto the subject in radical loss, whose memory flickered between darkness and light.

Miraji got from Iqbal the tendency to tussle with the political through the metaphysical. From Iqbal, too, came the poetics of telling the self through time, and through the moment, the *pal*, most explicitly in poems like "Yagānagat" (Oneness/solitude/isolation); in others, like "Traveler," Miraji told the self as event, as movement in time. Things, events, movements, stillness, death, the temporality of history, the timings of religions—all surfaced again and again in Miraji's writing. The mirror in "Samundar kā bulāvā" that animates scenes to life, coming into itself through sound, recalled Iqbal's *Rumūz-e beḳhudī.* Politics as mysticism: lines drawn backward to cull allegiances that pulled these two together went to Iqbal, to the Sufis, to Braj and bhakti.

Miraji's alliances sift through translation, sometimes doubling, folding back, sometimes curving outward on themselves. English translations of Braj, Awadhi, Maithili, Persian, Sanskrit, Bengali. His lineage is not quite Hali's, whose twists through translation were plotted around administrative demands. And his lineage was Hali's, because it was precisely those translations, fostered by administrations, that give him the allegiances that enabled his writing.

## TRAVELING INTO SELF AND LANGUAGE

Here is the text of "Jātrī" (Traveler):[4]

One came. Left.
Another will come. I've been standing here
a long time. This night, too, will pass.

I don't remember why
I'm here, what I must do.

My memory, too, has turned into an oil lamp
whose every halting, hesitant ray
laughs at me, soundlessly.
But how did I hear that laugh?

A dust storm whirls up,
rises and falls.
I can still hear its whistling,
whistling that pouts and bubbles up,
spreads, spreads . . .
I've been here a long time.
One came.

Left. Another will come.
This night, too, will pass. I hear a commotion.
Wherever I turn, there are people. Coming,
walking,
sauntering, stopping. Moving on again.
Darting forward.

They come and go, from here to there,
from there to here.
I look on, caught,
as though by a gust that rises up
from a wave of thought in my heart.

I see a ray
from an oil lamp
slithering and slipping
that lays bare the shape of my life.

I realize
the dark has turned into a lamp.
It seeps
drops of nectar
I nurse in my palm
but my palm turns into a flickering oil lamp.
Darting, it leaps up
the flame falls

the dark sits, sits,
then darts forward
like a shutter that snaps open and closes
with the sharp slaps from a storm
like a wounded, fluttering bird.

I look on. One came. Left.
I realize that another might come.
But my feet are transfixed.
I just stand there.

A drop of blood from my heart says,
This night, too, will pass.
I take a drop from my heart to my eyes and look on.
When the shutters meet
I begin to feel that the bird will flutter no longer
but will make my heart flutter.
On my palm I will nurse drops of nectar
that seep
from my eyes.

But—my life has turned into a flickering oil lamp
whose every halting, hesitant ray
is soundless laughter.
This darkness is new. It contains nothing
from the old dark.
My journey through light and darkness will continue
as before; it always has.

This is the pattern of the road:
One comes, leaves. Another
will come.
The night passes.

The glittering stars tell travelers
the road-river always flows.
Flow with it;
leave your confusion behind.

Some caravans that travel the road
go directly to their destination;
some lose the secrets of the intricate circling
dance of the stars.
But even those caravans see
the door to their destination swing open
before it shuts at nightfall.
But why am I here?
The shut door doesn't open for me.

Each sleeping grain of the desert says to me,
in this desolation,
if your dry palm were a foot,
a thorn that pierced it couldn't ask
for even a drop of blood.

Why am I standing here? I have nothing to do.
Why shouldn't I lose myself when I go for a stroll,
drown
in one, two, three, a hundred thousand whirlwinds
that come and go
just as a boat floating in a flowing wave-whirl
holds each wave flowing [out] from it
like the open midnight lotus—my palm.

I don't believe
that every traveler on the road has a destination.

Shall I join them, shall I go?

"Come with us, come on."
"Why are you standing here, so quiet, so alone?"
"We'll bring you two rare flowers
if you want . . ."

"Stop, stop, I don't need . . .
I'm waiting here for a friend."

But he's gone.

I'm still not comforted.
I've been thinking of myself as a desert-dweller.
I'd like to see a shut door open.

But it's not possible.

I long for a storm that will conceal me
completely in its drapery.
I've come to realize that every beautiful thing I owned
has turned into a flowing gust
that my hand cannot contain.
There are no drops of nectar left on my palm.
I'm just a parched, leafless, colorless desert
in which it is not possible for me to say:

One came, left. Another will come.
My night will pass.

*Another Will Come: Introduction to the Poem*

"Traveler" recalls the journey with which I opened this book. Its straightforward street language left me slipping on its slick surface, its images casting elusive shadows at the corner of my sight. I felt the quiet, ghostly laughter of the poem edging me toward a reading, taunting my inability to reach it. Its exquisiteness, recalling "A Night on the Far Side of a Wine Glass," kept pulling me back. As I traversed it again and again, the poem opened in myriad ways; like the shy hesitation of laughter that animates it, "Traveler" provokes the reader unable to attain its depths and empathizes with those who do. It lays bare the shape of the struggle between that which is obvious, ordinary, and that which eludes, demands attention, and calls forth difference. Caught in it, one has epiphanies of the battles with incomprehension and with understanding. Within the mystical traditions in which it plays, "Traveler" reaches into the heart of what a subject/person is and does, and how a subject sees himself in relation to others. It is a poem that fuses emotion with intellect, heart with mind, feeling with thinking. "Traveler" brings the longing of hope to great despair—"I long for a storm that will conceal me. . . . I'm just a parched, leafless, colorless desert"—and explores how subjectivity is encoded or constituted.

In this poem, there are no pure sensory processes; the subject is first presented in terms of an evolving series of cognitive activities from listening to thinking to conceptualizing: "I hear," "I see," "I realize."[5] All biophysiological processes are placed in the context of language; all give information as language. A subject (here a male "I") exists as a self coming to be through language, through event, or through time, through the repetitive tempo of "one came, went, another will come." He is always situated in a *socius* organized semiotically; he emerges by learning how to speak, to see in the imaginary ("lay bare my life"), to use signs as systems, negotiate in/with the symbolic. While acquiring these, the subject begins to be folded into the social. As people begin to think, conceptualize, and become self-reflexive, they accrue identifications which are profoundly social and which define them. Because languages, the rhythms of semiosis, are passed down and renewed by remembering, historically congruent connections are made with a past of an enveloping tradition insistently committed to memory. The familiarity of patterns of being is established through repetition and habit given only via unselfconscious recollection. Anyone who "forgets," forgets the past, forgets language, loses the ability to situate himself/herself and begins to struggle with being self-conscious.

"Traveler" falls into two parts, the break coinciding with the center of the poem. In the first part the subject "forgets" what he has to do and why he is where he is. With the loss of memory, he lays down his language. The poem pivots and reorients itself when the subject can describe his life—"my life has turned into a flickering oil lamp"—as something he possesses (my). The direct subject "I" has been redirected to the indirect subject "my" whose possession, life, can be seen as a object that lights itself up, facilitates its own visuality. With that event, at that moment he understands he is outside looking in, and thereby conceives of himself as social. The second part of the poem poeticizes the memory's return and with it the ability to speak, think, feel, and create in tandem with the social. Here the subject is permeated by the hegemonic, constitutive of his subjectivity or framed by the dominant. He finds himself excluded from the inexorable march of those who conform to the dictates of dominant discourse, that is, the reading on the poem's surface, which is devised for those who travel the road, follow the stars, follow the promises given by the world in payment/gift for obedience, in payment for a life without confusion. The ensuing exchange between the lyrical subject of the poem, who is struggling to subjectivity, and those who are live within the simple, straightforward rendition of the order of language is couched as a seductive call and its corresponding response. The subject's ironic response positions him beyond the borders of the hegemonic, leaving him without an ability to speak in that language (the poem plays with hegemony and dominance, folding them into one another as their relationship is repeated and re-elaborated).

### *Self and Journey*

With its title, "Traveler" calls up the interpretive frameworks of forms of Hinduism carrying with them certain assumptions, yet the poem itself is simultaneously in collusion and collision with those assumptions.[6] A *jātrī* is a *bhaktā*, or devotee who goes on a *yātrā/jātrā*, a ritualized, sometimes circular journey undertaken by devotees of a particular deity to visit the sacred sites that tell the deity's biography.[7] The pilgrims journey a sacred landscape, drawing into themselves mythographic narratives sedimented into places, learning about their *dev* or *devī* as they partake of its life. *Jātrī* change as they travel—they see, and become, through the deity. A *jātrā* can be mystical (transubstantiate), but this version, that is one which travels a geography, is made through the substance of the body. As this poem is read, however, a variant on the *yātrā*, or journey, emerges that also engages the world of the poem with another signifying—Muslim—framework: the Sufi path, or *ṭarīqh*. Here, the journey is mystical and into the self. Although the contours of journey are internal, they are described through an externalized (embodied, substantial) set of images. Farīd-ud-dīn ʿaṭṭar, for example, in the *Parliament of the Birds*, sites the mystic's journey into oneself within the peaks and valleys of mountain and desert geography. The traveler negotiates various stages, the spaces and the places of rest, or *maqāmāt*, of the landscape while striving for self-cognition to arrive finally at *m'ārifat*, or gnosis, of the divine.[8] This type of journey is, unlike a *yātrā*, linear. One goes on it with a clear goal in mind: a merging with the divine. Nicholson writes about the path in *The Mystics of Islam*:

> The sufi who sets out to seek god calls himself a "traveler" (*salik*); he advances by slow stages (*maqāmāt*) along a path (*tariqat*) to the goal of union with reality (*fanā fi 'l-ḥaq*). Should he venture to make a map of this interior ascent, it will not correspond exactly with any of those

> made by previous explorers. Such maps or scales of perfection were elaborated by sufi teachers at an early period.[9]

In juxtaposing geographical against cogitative landscapes—the symbologies of journey from two different religious traditions—Miraji alludes to the tropic shifts he will perform within the contours of the poem that will constantly throw off-kilter the expectations of a reader fluent in either tradition.

A poet who identifies the subject of his poem as a "traveler" is someone whose poetic purpose is the self.[10] Thus, the journey promised and undertaken in the poem is a journey into self, a journey in which the object of transformation *is* the self. Much of the poetry that conforms to the parameters of the Sufi journey shares assumptions about the "self" on the journey, that it has a body distinct from the soul and its soul is further divided into two parts, lower and upper.[11] Speaking to the hierarchy between body and soul, which is unfurled through concealment and the rights of/to visibility, the thirteenth-century mystic poet Rumi said, "The body is not hidden from the soul, nor the soul from the body, but nobody has the right to see the soul."[12]

Both the self and the images that are or that accompany the journey undertaken by the self move in certain ways, rebuffing or traveling away from one cluster of tropes while simultaneously clinging to or moving toward another. Images that give the carnal soul (*nafs*) substance, like darkness, are repudiated, while those that describe the "higher" soul (*ruḥ*, *jān*, or *sirr*, each having a slightly different resonance), like light, are endorsed.[13] Sanā'ī, an eleventh-century Sufi mystic and poet, wrote:

> The earth soul dies, the angel soul is born,
> Be thou a lowly foot to follow me,
> So wilt thou gain the headship spiritual.[14]

The tugs and tussles between the two characterize Persian and Urdu Sufi poetry.[15] They appear as antonyms that hug each other close, reason (*'aql*) and carnal desire (*nafs*); rational thought (*'ilm*) and gnosis (*m'ārifat*). The tropic figurations of the self and its journey play these dichotomies. Sanā'ī's mystical journey, flowing through poverty and wealth, hunger and sustenance, is written as:

> What is the provision for such a journey? . . . By looking on the Truth (God) to cut oneself off from the false (i.e., the things of the world); . . . then when thou art become a friend of poverty, thy Soul destroys thy impure Self (lower nature); thy Self becomes Soul (higher nature) inside thee; . . . then God takes away its poverty from it—when poverty is no more, God remains.[16]

In "Traveler," Miraji not only reconfigures the self—as body and soul, as upper and lower soul, caught in moral substance—he also revises the language used for the journey in the Sufi mystical tradition. In the *ṭarīqh* one must lose one's memory in order to remember the soul, whereas in this poem, losing one's memory is losing one's soul. *Jātrī* also takes journeys elsewhere—to the mythos sunk into geographies, and to the sense of journey rendered through colonialism, as displaced, homeless wandering *āvāragī*. Miraji's *jātrā* in "Jātrī" hitches onto the discourse of homelessness, of poverty that identifies types, like pirs and *qalandar*, in colonial taxonomies.[17]

For Miraji, the self, the "I," is not an entity settled into a preordained structure. The self spoken in lyric is a site whose positioning and production are constantly reconsidered. This is not to say that the lyrical voice becomes something whose subjectivity is completely fixed at the end of the poem; it courses between stasis and movement, but its ambivalence is not contiguous with the kind of subjectivity that Iqbal posits in *Secrets of the Ego*.[18] Iqbal was not concerned with exploring the shape each individual *ḳhudī* might take in a specific context; indeed, his assertions indicate that he assumed all *ḳhudī*, like monads, shared the same essential characteristics. He was more interested in proposing a universal theory of self, whereas Miraji was not involved with elaborating a theory of selfhood but rather in describing the contours of very specific instances within which individual subjects were constructed, and through which selves emerged.[19]

For both Iqbal and Miraji, the self is in motion, like the soul in Sufi poetry. Iqbal's *ḳhudī*, however, moves on a particular trajectory, with a purpose, *taqdīr*, which sends the self on a certain kind of search for stability—unlike the subject of Miraji's poem, who repudiates travel toward an end: "I don't believe that every traveler on the road has a destination." And while the identity of Iqbal's *ḳhudī* is fixed through teleological movement characterized by its unceasing movement toward self-improvement, Miraji's subject has no settled identifications when it is first interjected into the discursive space of the poem: "I don't know why I'm here, what I have to do." In fact, the certitudes of journeys that have direction are not ones that "I" wants to follow. Further, the lyrical subject in Miraji's poem is not transcendental like Iqbal's *ḳhudī*; he is specific to the textual and performative context in which he is inscribed. Miraji in "Traveler," like Iqbal, genders his subject male. This characteristic does not necessarily apply to all of Miraji's poems, where the gender identification of the lyrical subject is either ambiguous or quite clearly female (and its desire is quite complex); in "Rare Waves of Passion" (Ras kī anokhī lahreñ), for example, the narrator is female. But a male subject coming into being is a particular feature of Miraji's metacritical poetry, of which "Traveler" is exemplary.

*Journey into the "Self"*

"Traveler" opens with a movement of two entities designated merely by *ek* and *dūsarā*, which can be translated as either "one" and "the other" or "one" and "another."[20] As either, their coming and going movement provides a continuum of motion that stretches from the past ("came" and "left") into the future ("will come"). The temporally ordered movement is a leitmotif against and through which the subject performs and speaks its identifications. *Maiñ khaḍā hūñ yahāñ*: Here the *maiñ*, or the self, appears to be in the present. But he actually stands between *ek āyā* . . . , a movement in the narrative past, and *āyegā*, which projects the movement into the future. *Kis liye*, the question that follows the "I," and posed by it, sets the "I" in its place.

*Ek* and *dūsarā* allow for multiple simultaneous readings (creating a verse that would elicit two or more meanings, *kināyah, mā'nī āfrīnī*) because the two terms are nonspecific; they can be understood both as numbers and as third-person pronouns. Each can be read as events, as moments, as people, as states of being or emotion, as things. As the framing movement in which the subject-voice of the poem is situated, they allow the poem to open into overlapping sequences, one describing a series of interiorized states and the other a succession of exterior events (*bāṭin* and *ẓāhir*). The doubled frame that begins, contains, and tells the process of subject formation creates a space between inside and outside in which the poem is constantly scrambled. The tropic inversions and subversions carried into a reading framed by a familiarity settled into the tropes force a negotiation with the assumptions offered by the forms of signification into which the poem is placed.

The struggle the subject (self and I) undergoes is described through darkness and light, the two extremes through which he assumes cogency. From the query posed by him, "how did I hear," to the verbs of sensation which move the subject outward through the force of perception, "hear" and "look" to "begin feeling," and then carry him back into himself via affect or feeling, the subject travels through cogitative activities that evolve to the declaration as the poem progresses: "it is not possible for me to say." The space within which this progression occurs is neither the unconscious nor the prelinguistic; rather, it is an experiential one situated within the domain of the linguistically articulable. This becomes clear if one looks at a second possible reading of the framing movement in the poem, an omnipresent tradition whose texts and voices flow in through the nonspecific/nonoriginary series, "one came," which then becomes the nonfaceted, continually moving ground against which all linguistic/dramatic transitions of the first half of the poem take place.

Although the subject's internal activities all respond to an external set of parameters, he is located in terms of event, moments, and actions that occur both inside and outside him. Within, the subject "can still hear its whistling." Outside, the subject negotiates a linguistic, poetic tradition. The connection of the leitmotif to a tradition is established later in the poem, at the delineation/description of the road that begins with the identification "This is the pattern of the road: One arrives, leaves. Another will come. The night passes." Here the subject is doubly conceived. He stands in the discursive space between language, time, the symbolic, and the flow of his states of being, but he is not separable from any of them; he is constituted by all.

The tropes that form him with greater and greater explicitness over the course of the poem also work in two directions, as both his internalized process of cogitation and as externalized formulations of power: "I look on, caught, as though by a gust that rises up from a wave of thought in my heart." A certain type of seeing is about a momentary arrest. Seeing, as looking, is being caught. A description of what catches one's sight, holds one in the act of looking is a form of "as though": a simile/metaphor, a sudden force of wind or rain that bleeds the heart into the mind and brings feeling to thinking.

The "night," the time that signals the opening of the poem ("I've been standing here a long time. This night, too, will pass"), is the time of the poet/lover/mystic in Urdu poetry, for the night is the time when the lover embarks on the activity that makes him what he does—waiting for his beloved. It is the time when madness is rampant, when the normative, rule-bound, symbolic, ordinary, the stuff of the passing of hours, yields to excursions into worlds where rules are breached, the expected is dissolved, and the lover returns to the trauma of giving up the imaginary. At night infractions of the law are ordinary; they set the standards for the behavior of madmen and lovers. "Hai dūr jām-e avval-e shab maiñ khudī se dūr / hotī hai āj dekhiʾe ham ko saḥar kahāñ"—"The opening round of the cup at night is now far from me, and I have left myself behind / Let's see what might happen, today, when day comes to us."[21] Many of Miraji's poems begin at nightfall, are permeated by darkness, or come alive at night. In "A Night on the Far Side of the Wine Glass," the action of the poem takes place at night and closes with daybreak. In his night poems, Miraji continues to use the nightscape of the ghazal as a time when paradoxes and reversals rule. But the conventions he violates are not the socially ordinary ones usually abrogated by the lover in the ghazal. Rather, he breaks some that he believes have become conventional—violations of contemporary poetry in which he writes.

It is precisely at night that the lover comes into his own. He knows what he has to do—fit into the contours of his identification as a lover. He must become a lover by living and lamenting as a lover. He speaks as someone whom listeners recognize as a lover. His movement toward pain and figurative self-immolation affirms one of the subject's and/or Miraji's self-definitions as someone who longs for love: they must never get it, and must never have it, and, therefore, they must be someone who suffers. But Miraji slips off the night-patterned dress of images that clothe the figure of this lover, throwing it off (perhaps as he mourns his lost memory) with the subject's refusal to fulfill the teleological movement into which he has been deposited: "I don't remember why I'm here, what I have to do." This refusal continues to inform the subject's being and place throughout the poem and marks him off from travelers who promise him a gift to entice him to join them: "We'll bring you two rare flowers if you want. . . ." These are the travelers who move inexorably toward a door that opens for them at nightfall and closes behind them to give them sanctuary. The subject's response sets him apart from them: "I don't believe that every traveler on the road has a destination." And "If you want . . ." speaks the pull of desire. This is a call to the subject to lay his certainty out without committing himself to it. The "if" leaves the subject open to the offer that will be fulfilled by the other travelers, but only "if" he wants.

*Mujhe yād nahīñ* is the abnegation of memory coded as an oblique form of possession, "to me memory is not" ("I don't remember")—that is, the memory of convention, memory per se versus remembering why one is here—followed by the paradoxical play of the elusiveness associated with it (memory turns into a flickering oil lamp, whose every slithering, slippery ray is *silent laughter* [italics mine]) and hearing something that is silent sets up a poetics of recollection that rebounds into the repetitions that structure the poem. The trope into which memory fades—a flickering oil lamp—is an image of an internal process projected outward that trails into the sounds left by the storm and is contained within the unspecified movement that opens the poem. All three—the flame, the storm, and the framing movement of "one came"—elaborate in different ways the complexities of memory and its play in the structuring of subjectivity. Memory is what is elided from the subject's opening self-identification; it is indirectly recuperated over the first half of the poem through the tropes that speak its recovery. The associations established in conjunction with a linear temporality, through memory, are severed at the onset of the poem and recovered later. Memory is the lamp that lights up, lays bare flickering outlines, and allows the subject to see, to perceive shape and form and, finally, to identify and act within his own life-history.

The subject is introduced as someone who does not remember. What he does not remember is the cause ("why") and effect ("what I have to do") of his particular place, *yahāñ*, in the poem. This leads one to look toward the narrative frame that opens the poem, which is repeated after the "dust storm." But this place in the poem, too, is opaque, offering only one clue—that the subject is contained, is given to itself within a repetitive, unspecific movement. The first tangible image in the poem is a lamp, which is memory. But again, this paradox/absurdity gives the speaker just a vestige of information. The speaker's relationship to the lamp is passive; memory is something he knows he catches merely because he is aware of a trace possibly leaking or emanating from it. But it is a trace of which he is still unsure: "how did I hear that laugh?" For a reader or listener the same image is much clearer; memory is an oil lamp that lays bare the shape of life. Juxtaposed against this image which concretizes memory and with which the speaker interacts, however incompletely, is another stirring, that of a storm, the overwhelming emotional rush of creativity. The speaker's intersection is stronger and more active with this storm than with the lamp; he advances from questioning his reception of memory to "I can still hear its whistling." What, then, does memory do in this poem? The associations that accrue around memory become explicit as the image that solidifies it—the oil lamp—voyages the space and time of the poem.

Following the opening of the poem is a piece that traverses the passivity of "I don't remember" to travel to a different kind of involvement with the events that occur around and in the subject, one in which the subject is actually engaged as a perceiving, sensing, thinking, feeling self: "I hear," "I look," "I see," "I realize." This section starts with "I hear a commotion," the commotion of people who move about in various ways, but without any teleological intentions, without purpose, just "from here to there, from there to here." In the context of the kind of movement that precedes it and the other movements with similar shapes that follow, this constant to and fro in which the subject does not participate, is where the very texture of movement and of "coming" and "leaving" is brought into sharper focus—("coming" is missing), walking (*calte*), sauntering (*ṭahalte*), stopping (*rukte*), moving on again (*baṛhte*), darting forward (*lapakte*)—and named. It is called a *hañgāmah*, a commotion, or an uproar. This is the pattern of the road ("One comes, leaves") made ambiguous or more explicit. Its greater explicitness is augmented by the activity that surrounds the subject: "I hear a commotion. Wherever I turn, there are people." Yet the subject does not move; he remains a spectator. What are the implications of the nonmovement/involvement of the subject? I think the connection, however faint, is to be drawn through memory, for in memory lies the acceptance of the subject's interpolation into the flow of the linguistic/discursive: of speaking as, of speaking for, of speaking something. Once the subject remembers language as profoundly social, public, symbolic, both the language that contains him and his own slips into it become clearer. Given the threading of memory and forgetting into the pattern that weaves the road in this poem, Miraji attempts to lay down or lay aside his connections with what comes before and with the language through which he must speak (both are established through repetition and memory). The laying down that the subject performs is through forgetting; if the subject forgets his language, he cannot perform, for any action that can be spoken about occurs only within language shared with others in a world. When he picks up memory, the I picks up the language within which he was and with it picks up his ability to hear, see, think, feel, and move inside that language.

It is in the context of this re-entanglement with language that he can think and desire. "I look on, caught, as though by a gust that rises up from a wave of thought in my heart." The words Miraji chose for storm and gust, *āñdhī* and *ṭūfān*, can be used in similar ways; both can mean a tempest or typhoon. The first, however, is also used for dry storms like dust storms, and the second for wet rain storms like floods and deluges. "A wave of thought," a confluence of passion and thinking that permits understanding and creativity, is used in several poems, most notably in "How Songs Are Made" (Gīt kaise bante haiñ). Miraji uses storm and waves to signify the wetness of passion, the emotion that drenches us in a monsoon and pushes and pulls us to simultaneously perceive, understand, and feel, to look into the heart, and finally to create poetry.

Thought, the process of intellection, is not divorced from emotion. Here, there is no notion of raw, preverbal, adamitic desire separated from an organized rational principle like thought. Desire and thought flow together in "wave of thought in my heart," the seat of emotion out of which thought rises. Culmination of language, desire, and thought permit the subject to visualize his life in the context of an abstract, historicized form, to reflect on the whole. But it is only the ray from the lamp—memory—that can lay bare the outlines of the subject's life.

The two scenarios involving the illumination of shape of the subject's life and the moment when his life turns into an oil lamp—the apogee of the transformed and transforming oil-lamp images—contain the subject's life as a journey through light and darkness. Darkness, *tīragī*, also means obscurity. This section of the poem opens with darkness—the image of it turning into a lamp connotes in two ways. The first is historical (Hali breaking [*shikast*] lineage and memory so that the past and present take shape only as movements that are open ended); it turns back to an image that precedes it. The shape of the subject's life becomes clear—he hadn't understood that he had been in the dark—but the moment he does, he attains light/enlightenment, and the obscurity that had preceded this revelatory movement then also becomes light. In this first allusion the time of darkness harks back to the past and pulls it forward into the now. Out of this transformation come drops of revelation: "it [the dark] seeps drops of nectar I nurse in my palm." Miraji calls this nectar *amrit*, the drink of the gods that gives the power to see, understand, comprehend, and finally, to create. When he takes the drops that ooze from his eyes into his palm, he holds/cups his linguistic world in his hands. Only at that moment can his life turn into an oil lamp that recovers memory, the loss of which he had not even known when the poem began.

The second reading for the transformation of darkness into a lamp relies on the fusion of darkness and light. In this reading, darkness represents the subject's subjugation to shifting emotional states. The impetus of his desires, however, has two potential impacts upon him. Desire/Darkness can be salutary; it revives memory and allows him to see and create. Darkness and light also bespeak the oppositions from Sufi poetry, which this poem deliberately intersects in several places. These references are called up both with the play of darkness and light and the wounded, fluttering bird (*ṭā'ir*).[22] The subject is like a bird caught in a storm, wounded, fluttering, incapable of controlling its universe; only when the storm abates will the bird calm and the subject begin to see. "When the shutters meet I begin to feel that the bird will flutter no longer but make my heart flutter."[23]

## "SELF" AND TRADITION

"Traveler" pivots at the center around a transmutation ("But—my life has turned into a flickering oil lamp") when the self is no longer the direct subject of every action: "I look," "I see," "I take." The "I" is displaced by abstractions and concepts—like "life" and, later, "journey"—that seem to garner the symbolic. Then the "I" takes on a different form, sliding over from the direct pronoun, *maiñ*, and assumes its oblique possessive form, "my," or *merā*. The subject has now been interpolated into a linguistic tradition; his position is aligned on the basis of active confrontation rather than implicit interaction with the voices and systems of those observances, and he is forced to elucidate his own complicity with the language he speaks. He is no longer identified through the immediacy of perception, thought, feeling which render him concrete. Instead he is someone who possesses, gaining efficacy and specificity through the "my," through feeling as a thing, or an attribute that belongs to him. This produces the "I" as the powerful possessive individual, while at the same time disenfranchising him, overturning him into the oblique form. In his place, in the place of the direct subject, are the abstractions he possesses, through which he takes shape.

In the mystical poetry of Attar and Khayyam, which Miraji probably read in translation, life and journey are the signifiers of each other. By juxtaposing the two, Miraji asserts that when he has the potential to see he blends into and is complicit with the language with which he sees and speaks. The moment of compliance is a moment at which the abstract/historicized construct "my life" becomes illumined memory. Unless he picks up the memory he has laid down at the beginning of the poem—the memory of the language, the memory of why he is *there*, the memory of the world within which he lives and, thus, the language with which to give shape to his own history—he cannot conceptualize his life. He undermines his collusion with this hegemonic language, however, with the statement that this/his darkness is new; it carries nothing with it from the old dark. He seems to turn to the kind of romantic poetic subject proposed by Hali, twisting back to newness to facilitate what he does. Asserting "My journey . . . will continue," he carries on the confrontation implicit in his refusal to accept collusion. Although the tropes that color his journey—light and darkness—are the same as those that compose the journeys in some Sufi poetry, their use in Miraji's poem is unique: "nagarī nagarī phirā musāfir ghar kā rastā bhūl gayā / kyā hai mera, kyā hai terā apnā parāyā bhūl gayā." This journey is somewhere between Hali's invocation of caravans, Iqbal's appeal to caravans, and ghazal. The paradox of simultaneous inclusion in and exclusion from the prior metaphorics for the subject's journey animates the poem.

The metaphorics of something designated tradition can now be denoted: "This is the pattern of the road." Having arrived here, the subject has traveled a great distance from the start of the poem. At the beginning he does not remember why he is placed where he is, what he has to do. The place he occupies is not specified, it has no name, no coordinates in space; he stands at a juncture of an unspecific series. By this point, however, the series has been designated a "pattern," and the subject can speak of "my journey." Although he still has not quite answered the questions with which he opened the poem, "why am I here?" he, like the series, is framed within an assertion that casts him through its contours: "My journey through light and darkness will continue as before; it always has." The "I" is on a journey formed in light and darkness and projected from the past through its present into the future—"it will continue as before."

The second part of "Traveler" is the subject's journey within the domain of the pattern of the road. It is a doubled, direct negotiation with the parameters for a journey first described in the context of the "caravans that travel the road" and later spoken as a seductive call to the subject by voices that speak from within the pattern of the road. The caravans and journey circulate a hegemonic praxis followed without question, and which could be construed as "tradition," or as "habit." When the subject emerges from painting himself in the colors of light and dark into a conceptualization of himself as an entity, he enters an arena in which he can be read by others who perceive him as conforming to the same space they occupy. They can then call out to him because they believe that he, like them, follows the pattern of the road.

The norms for the journey as tradition are outlined after the pattern of the road is instituted. The first routine granted to travelers on the road is sent from above, the call of the stars that offers the abrogation of confusion by being absorbed into a flowing force, intensified by its inevitability: "the road-river always flows. Flow with it." The force is that of the interpretive community with a self-contained power whose hegemony is absolute. The information offered about this journey is posed as esoteric, accessible only to practitioners who listen and follow "The secrets of the intricate circling dance of the stars,"[24] a dance evoking the repeated gestures that announce/enclose the poem. To lose oneself in this version of a journey demands submersion and subjugation—flow with it, it always flows. Receiving the rules of the road promises resolution, no discord, no quandaries, for those who travel like this.

Another lure thrown to entice travelers who travel this road of compliance is that they will go straight to their destination. Their *taqdīr*, purpose, will take them directly to an end, *maqāmāt*. Their journey will not perplex; it will be teleological and linear. As long as they travel the road and accede to its demands, even those who cannot recall the precepts for the journey will arrive safely at their destination and be sheltered as night breaks. Harmony, flowing with the road-river, guards its practitioners from the night, the time when, if one is shut outside the doors of the tradition, one begins to forget and lose one's head, drop one's standard "street" language, and thus, the ability to speak coherently. These rules are hermetic, bringing into their fold only those who follow the road to their destination. The doors that swing open for travelers to access their mission close believers in and heretics out. They regulate the limits and the borders of the ordinary. They permit no leaks. The subject sees himself on the borders, outside the shut door that does not open for him. If the subject, who initiated his journey from the locale of indeterminacy occasioned by his inability to define himself, were a "status quo" traveler, then the possibility of certainty and the denouement of the contention woven into identity could have been very seductive. He could have been enticed to pursue the secrets of the circling stars.

For the subject, the rhetorical question "why am I here?" is coupled with the awareness that the shut door will not open for him. He does not even really quite comprehend one of the cardinal rules of belonging to the world inside the gates: "every traveler on the road has a destination." Indeed, every traveler can enter the door because they have accepted destination as a condition for their journey. By not grasping/accepting this teleological inevitability of the journey he notices himself outside the doors. Outside the door he is closed off from entrée to the customary language of the status quo and is in a kind of desolation from which one cannot respond, have emotion, voice, or tools with which to speak: "if your dry palm were a foot, a thorn that pierced it couldn't ask for even a drop of blood." The metonymic flow of lament and longing remembers the language of unrequited love from the ghazal. Bringing desert to thorn, and from there to blood that drips as a lover walks heedlessly through the barrenness of his grief, to search out his lost desire, Miraji pushes readers toward Ghalib's verse. But here the blood is not from the lover's foot; it is from his heart, which lends passion to his eyes. Blood, drunk drop by drop by his eyes, ignites his sight, allowing him to see. Without this heart blood seeping from his eyes, this blood that alchemizes into *amrit* nursed in his hands, the lover is blind, he is bereft of insight, he can never drown in waves of thought.

With desertlike tropes affiliated with silence, Miraji elides/eludes the signification they have in mystical, allegorical ghazal, where the desert, like the night, is a place the lover as mystic goes to succumb to the wet wash of passion that drowns the self enabling him to see, and to have *m'ārifat.* By not placing himself on a teleological path he has no orchestrated space within which to be, he has no secure outcome for his journey. Under the circumstances, why shouldn't he wander off and try different ways to fashion himself, try on diverse voices, lose himself in images that gift him life? But, despite his play with the inspiration of dissemination ("Why shouldn't I lose myself when I go for a stroll, drown in one, two, three, and hundred thousand whirlwinds"), he is not willing to give himself completely over to the tacit allures of mystical flight—dissolution in the divine.[25] Indeed, the subject proposes a dissolution that will allow him a continued sense of himself as an aggregate, a thing, a point from which the possibility of dissolving radiates—a boat in a wave-whirl. The node in his palm is where he holds the reserve of his forays into origination, his poetry. Without the midnight lotus—the mind—he would not have a single voice that thickens; he would dissolve into the wave washing back and forth from his mind.

Because he has been placed outside, the subject is plagued by doubts and hesitates between occupying a voice and giving up that voice. He is not sure whether he ought to join the other travelers and become one with the road-river, thereby sliding into habits of a conventional journey. He flirts with the prospect of marrying into the community: "Shall I join them, shall I go?" This is ushered by a call from the community, from the symbolic, to him ("Come with us, come on") coupled with an offer ("We'll bring you two rare flowers"). It is a seductive call precisely because it utters the subject's barren isolation: "Why are you standing here, so quiet, so alone?" His isolation is underscored by the disparity between the two voices, that of the sojourners who ask him to join them and his own. He speaks as a solitary person articulating his desire to himself ("Shall I join them?") counter to the other travelers who call him together ("Come with us").

And what are the promised flowers? A gift that may never come? Things whose value is cloaked as wonder? Are the flowers the assurance itself, given by the two travelers who represent the symbolic? Does their rarity leave open the possibility that they will never in fact be given, that the person offered them will never receive them in exchange for joining up? Are they fetishes whose being is abstracted/wonder/magical or whose value is precisely something that two sets of people read two different ways? Are they the object whose thrownness into the future projects only loss, and never a return?

The subject answers within the limits and rules summoned by the question. The flowers in some way portend the difference between the "I" and the people who call out to him. The difference between him and his callers is a difference of singular and plural. He voices a wishful excuse, a promise to himself in the guise of a response, that obviates his oneness and aloneness. He says he is waiting for a friend, another like him. This excuse is a desire and precisely one that is held in abeyance, held in wait, stretching the time between being left and possibly accompanied. Perhaps this "I" can only turn down an offer made to him of sliding into a community, even be heard, only if he speaks with the same assumptions—that one would not want to be alone, that everyone wishes to have a companion. But the moment he turns back the offer of the other travelers, the subject grasps the simple sad truth of his response. There is no friend, the friend whom he wants to wait for has already left; he is not part of any couple. That someone who shares his values will come speaks an illusory, and imaginary, desire.

The "I's" final interpolation by an interpretive community and the symbolic falls away when he perceives himself as having a place with which he identifies and which, in turn, distinguishes him—the desert. As a desert dweller he does not make his home in the sort of desert where mystics live, where a mad, lost lover could grope his way to revelation. Those desert dwellers belong with each other in their barren aloneness; they are a *silsilah*. His desert seems stripped of even that uninhabited habitus status. But this does not obviate his desire for acceptance, nor does his awareness of his loneliness reconcile him to it. He would still like to see a shut door open.

All that is left to him (perhaps as a strange form of the romantic poet bereft of the lyric that makes him who he is) is his longing to lose himself in the kind of emotional storm that would sanction him to create. The things that come of his creative impulses, however, have dissipated, blown away as wind: "I've come to realize that every beautiful thing I owned has turned into a flowing gust that my hand cannot contain." With the realization that he stands apart as an *unheimlich* desert dweller, the subject forgoes his access to the kinds of speaking, which are the provenance of communities, and forgoes the rights granted to one who joins up in the symbolic. Here, although he says it, it seems to be impossible for him to say, "One came, left. Another will come," because to say this he must be standing alongside a pattern drawn in repeated color and thrown in time. Instead, he is in a blank place, a position painted by lack, by its effacement: "parched, leafless, colorless" (*k̲hashk, be barg, be rang*). Here he is in a state where possibility is lost to him, *mumkin nahīñ*. He is alone, isolated, bereft of the things he could nurse in his hands. The only thing left to him is his hunger, his yearning, as a watcher of a language that has form, and has time, but no substance.

What is Miraji doing with this journey poem written early in his own biohistory that struggles through an unquestionably male "I"? This self, the "I" in "Jātrī," is not a proper, civilized urban man, steeped in *tamaddun o tahżīb*. He is not a moral public-spirited man. Neither is he the honest kind of person, a *sharīf ādmī*, who might make a good administrator and might be an exemplary member of a community. He is not the man proposed by colonial educators, who was abundant in the kinds of qualifications Hali, Sir Sayyid, and Iqbal wanted their Muslim compatriots to have. He is not the kind of man who would lay his life down for others, in a surfeit of chivalry as the *Titanic* began to sink. In other words he is not the ideal, idealized male subject (in the symbolic) produced in the crucible, in the traumatic death throes that accompany or toll modernity. He is not the subject desired by colonized men. The kind of subject they wanted to be. The "I" in "Traveler" is the self who must be read as the failure of that kind of selfhood, and whose poetics can never quite be read if one returns to that selfhood as paradigm.

Within the poem this "I" traverses memory; traverses kinds of temporality; traverses the ways that the communal, the symbolic, the *silsilah* come to be; traverses the couple, the imaginary, the friend who will never come; traverses the publics, the crowds that move to create the noise of the street; travels through hegemony. Miraji's "I" is stripped to bone, to event, to moment stretched in time. Perhaps his travails in this poem are about the losses and longings of memory around trauma, but this poem does not clue a reader to see trauma. The movement of crowds in it, the movement of communities, does offer a certain sense of a historical (consonant with Benjamin's). Perhaps one can only observe, at the crossroads (assembled from generations who have forgotten), in this way, in a metaphysics of ruin. "I don't remember why I am here, what I have to do." Perhaps the reconstitution of a self living under colonialism, under the deprivations demanded by a modernity that requires one to forget and remember unevenly in life after life, can only be so. One can maybe only be *nah mumkin*, without the possible, the stuff that is thrown into the future. And that stuff, no longer possible, includes the romantic poet, whose sense of self is his possession of his lyric; and includes the Sufi, whose sense of self, however grounded in the loss of self, is bound up with communities that speak together and remember together.

This "I" is neither Hali's nor Iqbal's person, but both poets provide the conditions for his telling of himself—Hali through his poetics of trauma and Iqbal through the metaphysics to which he turned to talk a *ḳhudī* into being. But Miraji's male "I" disengages trauma and metaphysics from the salvation, the redemption premised in and promised by the communal.

Women, and with them different renditions of gender, will be addressed in the next section of the book. Gender will be highlighted through reading Miraji's name; the collapse between the "I" in a poem and the name of the poet; the production of an embodied "I" that is female; the fluid depictions of "I" in coupling with a different other; the invocation of voices that shift gender as they speak; and through the play of gender in the nouns and adjectives that give poems life.

# *Four* NAMING THE LYRICAL

# 6. WHAT'S IN A NAME?

Miraji, the pen name of Sana' ullah Ḍār, is a name with which not even many aficionados of modern Urdu poetry are familiar. In fact, unless one is privy to a certain type of knowledge about Urdu poetry available only to a cognoscente of twentieth-century Urdu lyric, one can entirely misrecognize his name.[1] When I tell people that I am working on Miraji and see their inaugural gestures of comprehension, I usually hasten to correct a possible misconception on their part and add that Mira*ji* was a twentieth-century male Urdu poet who died in 1949—not Mira*bai*, the seventeenth-century's ubiquitous female *bhakta*.[2] I then tell them the story of "how Miraji got his name" because of his love for Mira Sen.[3] The three names have begun forming a triad for me, attached to each other like limbs swirling outward from an absent center. But it is only when I use or circulate Miraji's name that the other two are called up.

I don't often, but perhaps I should, include the information that just before his death Miraji was reading and translating the poems of Mirabai, which he intended to publish. As he did for many of his books, he made his own frontispiece, which read:

*Mīrāñjalī*
Mira's Offerings

*Mīrā ke gīt*
Mira's Songs

*Hindī gujarātī mārwāṛī*
Hindi, Gujarati, and Marwari

*murattabah*
arranged by

*Mīrājī*
Miraji[4]

I found that, when the frontispiece is read aloud, the names run together. The oral repetition arrays and then collapses the distinction between them—Miranjali, Mirabai, Miraji.[5] The offerings (*añjalī*) placed at Mira's altar are Miraji's invocation: *añjalī* arrangements of Mira's songs. *Mirāñjalī*: the offering is a name, a name that weaves naming (*mīrā* and *añjalī*) into doing (*añjalī*), but leaves unthreaded the sutures between the two. Between *mīrā* and *añjalī*, two words joined together, are contained a host of prepositional possibilities that stitch them into one, and sew them into the body of Miraji's title page: of, to, for, from, equals . . . Mira is the *añjalī*, hands cupped together to pour water out in prayer. Mira is the name before whom an *añjalī* is offered. Mira is the name who offers an *añjalī*. This collection of Miraji's is an *añjalī*, hands offering in the name of Mira, poured into Mira, by Mira.[6]

So, what's in a name?—in this case, an author's name? What does it do? How and where do people say it, read it, or encounter it? What is between a name, a signature, and the "I," the pronoun that designates a kind of personhood? What are the ramifications of the name story (in the life story, a biography) that brings the "I" into a certain kind of name, and that accompanies the name? What is the difference between the two Miras? Is there a difference between the three Miras? Do listeners have different expectations when they use the three names? What happens around the utterance that is the name? What happens where names are offered in benediction? What happens when one conflates Mira's name with "her real" gender but allows another Mira's name to stand apart from "his real" gender? What happens to the Mira whose name is the nodal point of the explanatory story that accompanies Miraji? Therein lies a tale, including other stories that gather around Miraji's name.

Miraji has been, even by his friends, assembled and then reproduced as a particular sort of controversial persona. A generally known description of him, and one that lives in narrative after narrative, was clarified by Manto in "Three Balls." The production of Miraji as *āvārā*, as an isolationist, drunk, dissolute, self-centered, pathologically sexual, morally bankrupt man, unsuccessful both in love and in his work, his *pīragī* struggling with criminality, requires the elision/minimization of stories that gainsay this picture of him. These other stories are then left out as unimportant or relegated to the leftovers of Miraji's historical past.[7] One seldom hears the stories of his work habits or of his relationship to his work. For example, he worked assiduously every day from nine to five, if not on a job then on his poetry. His papers, which were his only property, were meticulously organized and exquisitely written. He published continuously in numerous journals, had five books published in the thirty-five years of his life, and had five other manuscripts among his papers when he died, two of which were issued posthumously. His generosity and capacity for friendship were well documented. He was magnanimous with his money and gave it away as it came in; he was compassionate, and his friends knew that they could call on him if they needed him. And one rarely hears about his careful, searching, ferocious intelligence.

As I sifted through the various biographical narratives associated with Miraji, including my own attempts to tell his story and to explain him, I began to realize that his story was far more complex than I had envisioned. I was dealing with discursive or linguistic formations or stories in which he had been represented, presented again and again, sometimes anew. The materials available to me were the oral tellings and written narratives, including Miraji's letters, in which he had been created as a literary artifact. I had to cope with competing narratives that portrayed him in contradictory ways. But many of the accounts about Miraji that were not drawn from my own information either pathologized Miraji's complexity or ignored it. I also had to contend with the accounts of many biographers, like Aijaz Ahmad, who wrote his article "Miraji: Personality and Work" by the time theories of a self-present, self-complete unified self had been firmly entrenched, and formed the basis of judgments on intrinsic character and its flaws. Anomalies were considered trouble. And therefore an ability attributed to Miraji, that he could be read as a slippery series of distinct unconventional personalities, was evidence marshaled for a case of "multiple personality disorder," and in keeping with Miraji's general pathological tendencies. This process of pathologizing or ignoring certain facets of Miraji's personality carried over into appraisals of his work.

Narratives about Miraji constructed him as an author; indeed, he was written and spoken about *because* he was an author, and, as such, he is someone whose name is attached to or associated with work, writing, publishing, and with the oral performances of his work. And certainly, by the time that Miraji composed lyric, authors had come to have a kind of romantic solidity. The poems that they crafted amassed around them as property giving them substance. But, in Miraji's case, the shaping of him as an author was also bound up with the representation of him as a certain type of *male* personality and to the fashioning of a biography for him, a life story that lived him and lived beyond him, that conformed to that personality. Indeed, Miraji's biography superseded his work; his biographical narrative was imposed on his poetic oeuvre so that his writing came to mirror his biography. In order to make the poetry harmonize with standards that became norms for him, poems that did not "fit" were read as oddities, marginalized in his oeuvre, and thus read out. Miraji's biography and work became templates for one another to such a degree that each reinforced the other and kept it intact. Leaks were shut off as rapidly as they tended to flow.

Nevertheless, Miraji was not an entirely passive object of representation; indeed, he participated in the cottage industry to produce himself. His chosen name is just one instance of his self-reflexive attempt to reconstitute himself. As a woman's name, "Miraji" foregrounded gender and made it one of the important issues around which his recasting of himself took place. By taking a woman's name, he also established his "difference" from the properties of a tradition of Urdu poetry in which male poets often took a *taḵẖalluṣ*, a male "poetic" name. That difference called for a story, so the "author" Miraji came to be explained by and associated with a story that became integral to his name. When Miraji's work was read, it was often read in the context of the name story. Miraji was rarely returned to the *rekhtī*, a genre contiguous with the ghazal, for which poets might compose in female names.[8] This, despite his own references to it in his essays. So when the difference between Miraji and Sana' ullah was told, it was never told in the history of that name taking.

Miraji's name story is about unrequited love—Miraji's for Mira Sen—in which a male lover takes the name of a silent female beloved. In the stories, Mira Sen is an object of love who changes Miraji. A lover's "transformation by love" into someone who loses his senses (suffers from dementia) and repudiates normal life (school, home, marriage) over the inaccessibility of the beloved is a familiar theme to listeners and readers of the Urdu ghazal. The stories place Miraji's unrequited love stories, and the *naẓm* that opens his posthumous collection of poetry, firmly within the topos of the ghazal and Urdu poetry. The problem with Miraji is that because of his name, "Mira," he is intertextual with and fits the expectations of other poetic lineages, namely the bhakti one.

In the stories, too, because she is looked at but never speaks, Mira, the poet's love object, is a silenced specular object of desire.[9] He sees her, he changes, and then she disappears; what and how she feels is not a part of the narrative.[10] Both stories, repeated by male narrators, the first tentatively and the second more specifically, place Mira Sen in an enclosed feminine space, a zenana, a place forbidden to Miraji as a male. In the one version of this story given to me by a woman, Mira Sen was far from the *pardah nashīn*–, zenana-bound person she becomes in the other tales. She was a public figure, a beautiful woman whose journeys through Lahore of the 1920s left broken hearts in her wake. Though she went to a college, which was enclosed by a wall, she was someone who faithfully traversed certain sorts of public spaces, dances, restaurants, debating halls.

In the *pardah*, or sexually segregated, society of Lahore in the 1920s, men's and women's spaces were often separated from each other and many men were not permitted in some women's spaces. In the first story, the "living room" with women in it would not have been accessible to Miraji. In order to see Mira Sen as a person confined to a sanctum, Miraji had to be a voyeur who looked at her through a figurative or literal peephole.

Male sexuality was associated with voyeurism in places and times where most women were supposedly "hidden" from the male gaze. In situations in which certain women were "hidden" from men, the only way men had of establishing a sexual connection with them was through a peephole. "The encounter through the peephole" became one of the primary modes of expressing sexuality. Since most women in narratives about sexuality neither responded in kind nor reversed the peephole to look at men, they could not participate in the sexual process in the same way as men and so remained desexualized objects of male desire. Certainly the stories that construe Mira as a "hidden" body assume these historically mandated configurations of desire. The questions here are not whether or not those configurations had truth value, but what angles of desire they elicited, and what the effects of these slants might be.[11]

A way of gendering and controlling sexuality in stories was by closing women off from the "rights to the peephole." This was then a place of power given over to men that could only be maintained if it was kept unidirectional. It also required hidden women who could not look back; if they did, they could potentially displace men standing on the viewer's side of the peephole.

By pursuing Mira Sen in the second story through a space they shared and in which each could look at the other, Miraji abrogated or nullified his position of sexual power. He made himself vulnerable to her "gaze." By speaking to her just before she entered her enclosed space or house, he made her look at him before she disappeared into a space where he had no access to her at all. But since his only words to her were that he had something to say, he never actually made more than a superficial connection. And, although she turned to look at him, her response was a nonresponse, expressionless and silent. In turning away from Miraji, Mira Sen refused to participate in the game he was playing with her. So, although one story we encounter as listeners or readers is Miraji's story about *his* love for her, by turning away, Mira Sen at that moment denuded him of his power over her. Because she disappeared after their encounter, she became an empty space, a floating name that Miraji could occupy or use with impunity, and this is precisely what appeared to happen. One story remained one of Miraji's name stories and the only part Mira Sen played in it was as the other, the silent/silenced beloved whose name was taken from her and given body as Miraji's.[12]

Miraji's name stories, and the way they fit into other narratives about him, puts gender in its place. He was a man, a story goes, who needed a silenced woman in order to get a woman's name. Miraji is depicted as a marginalized or unconventional *male* character, and narrative after narrative that I read or heard corroborates Miraji's maleness—in direct repudiation of his female name. When Miraji was described by biographers, the descriptions of his life fit two different lifestyles that incorporate loss, longing, and *āvāragī*, and that may perhaps be considered masculine "modes of social dissent."[13] Both ways of being—that of a poet-lover and of a male ascetic—are repudiations of a *sharīf ādmī*, a good man, the civilized bourgeoisie urban subject replete with propriety and property, who is a married breadwinner comfortably encumbered by either an extended or nuclear family. The anomalous lifestyles thread the masculinities available to Miraji into different possibilities in different narrative lineages. One, that of the drunken, dissolute poet-lover suffering eternally from the pangs of unrequited love, and who, because of his passion ruptures the boundaries of convention, comes from the universe of Urdu literary discourse. The other, the poverty-stricken, unattached itinerant ascetic, sadhu, *sant*, commonly encountered in anecdotes ensconced in Sanskrit-Hindi stories, also surfaces as a pir, a *qalandar*, in the Perso-Arabic one. Its twentieth-century incarnation, in officially (legally) accounted taxonomies, which Aijaz Ahmad picks up on and plays with, is a vagrant whose wandering turns him criminal.[14]

The ascetic and poet-lover both slip out from under the guidelines predicated for the twentieth-century form of a secular (Hindu) urban householder embroiled in a form of colonial symbolic, *Grahasta*, by "denying the core prescriptions that create the identifications for the male—sexuality, lineage and property ownership."[15] But both positions conform to the routines of rebellion, so the descriptions of Miraji that fit these positions produce him as a customary *male* rebel. By doing so, they elide ways in which he might have been construed as an *un*conventional rebel.

As I read him and read about him, I found that I wanted to rewrite Miraji's story and reorganize his corpus to include narratives that complicated the male author/poet/lover/ascetic pictures of him that I have been describing. I wanted to rewrite him as a series of scenes, of instances that sometimes devolved into personalities called out, called forth, or produced under shifting contexts and that conformed to or played an array of positions that occasionally overlapped and every so often came into conflict with each other.[16] I have tried to do this by describing him as a man who ranged from unconventional to conventional—from insane, ascetic, drunk, and sexual to pedantic, celibate, careful, and intelligent. I also describe him as someone who sometimes indulged in bouts of self-hatred and who sometimes cared immensely about himself and his primary interest, his creative work. I do not, in the process of writing my story, want to replace other representations of Miraji with my own, but would like to put into circulation other pictures attended by "differential repetitions."[17]

I would like to return to the story of Miraji's name that started this chapter, and add that tale to the stack as well. Though I am extending the threads of Miraji's connection to Mirabai in the stories that follow, I feel that I find justification to do so in the opening sentences of Miraji's semi-autobiographical "Incomplete Self Portrait": "This [Kathiawad, the place of my childhood] is the same place where, many years before, Queen Mirabai had given birth to the magic of her songs. I did not know about her then, as I have come to know her"—which provokes correspondences between the Miraji and Mirabai that might otherwise seem tenuous.[18] I would like to propose another Mira story of "how Miraji got his name." Instead of attempting to separate Miraji and Mirabai, if I allow myself to run their names together, as Miraji does in the frontispiece of his work on her, could Miraji be thought of as a twentieth-century Mirabai? Another way of saying this is: what are the implications of allowing Miraji to sign for Mirabai, to enter the body of Mirabai through his acts of renaming?

If one allows for the slippage between their names, the name Miraji and his biography intersect with versions of Mirabai's, and his stories are intertextual with hers. As readers of a renegade poet like Miraji, this move reminds us of the necessity of reinserting gender as predominant, and rendered through other differences, into the biographical accounts of him. What if we created an alternative explanatory name story that did not regender him through Mira Sen? One of the effects of foregrounding the Mira Sen story is that it allows other stories of Miraji's desire to disappear. The "factual" evidence for the Mira Sen story is based on love letters Miraji wrote to her and his use of her name. But he also wrote love letters to a man—Bashir Chand. This too, is a statement that circulates about Miraji, but it is not a statement that calls for a story that speaks across gender, so it appears as an aside if one asks about his other love objects. If we kept the Mira Sen stories but read same sex desire into them through moments of gender transitivity, how might they read?[19] What if we don't allow Miraji to keep his "male gender" but perform on him the move his name makes—to femaleness? What if we shifted the erotic direction of the Mira Sen story? We might ask for it to be read in two different erotic registers: heteroerotic and homoerotic. We could read Miraji as a person whose changed name placed him/her in the context of a series of stories about a woman poet. The intersection of his story with Mirabai's makes him doubly unconventional; now, instead of describing him as an unconventional man, we can argue that *he* was living as an even more unconventional woman.

Both Mirabai's name and hagiography have been used to add to her oeuvre. Some of the recent work on Mirabai makes it clear that even more so than for her male mystic-poet counterparts, her name (and the hagiographies that were associated with it) was a cloak that could be assumed and, indeed, *was* assumed by both men and women who composed as Mira, adopting her name, a particular hagiography of her, and a style of composition. Poems ostensibly by Mira would fill lacunae in the hagiography, and transform or explain knotty stories associated with her. So Mira's corpus and hagiography molded each other over time. And since they were not collected in the appropriate annals of bhakti literature and biography until the eighteenth century, at least two hundred years after her supposed life, Mira's corpus and story, like those of other bhakti poets, were freely available to anyone wanting to add to them.[20]

One version of Mira's hagiography tells of a queen who, for the love of her Lord, the god Krishna, repudiated her family and husband and traveled with a group of itinerant musicians. In variants of the story she either resists her family actively and behaves like a besotted *bhakta* even while her husband is alive, or else she becomes a good wife, eliciting her cuckolded husband's devotion, and leaving the family fold after she is widowed, which was a less controversial choice for her to make. The nineteenth- and twentieth-century renditions of Mira, produced under nationalist and ostensibly nationalist auspices, domesticate her.[21] In either case, Mira is depicted as an ascetic who was also a poet-lover. Miraji's stories, then, rather than just conforming to male paradigms for the poet-lover, could be read as the twentieth-century parallel of hagiographies of the woman *bhakta*, whose name he had taken as his own. As someone who was inscribed into the bhakti tradition, it would be possible for Miraji to compose, as Mirabai, poems that could then be ascribed to her. In this case he would, as "Mira," be subsumed under the poet who might or might not have lived, perhaps in the seventeenth century, a move consistent with conventions folded into certain kinds of compositions. But what did it mean for Miraji to compose as Mirabai?

In the kind of Krishna-bhakti which Miraji turned to in his *naẓm*, in poems he wrote up for *Is naẓm men*, and in the essays on poets like Vidyapati and Chandidas, one predominant narrative position for both male and female poetic personas was that of the female herder (*gopī*), Radha, whose relationship with Krishna was the exemplar for any human-divine one. Singing as Mira, unlike singing as Surdas, allowed composers/singers to collapse the distance between the gender of the lover lamenting in the poem and that of the poet. These voices, given to Mira, recorded the cadences of an anguished, angry relationship on a scale between consummation with and separation from a notoriously unfaithful lover, a set of stances common to a great deal of mystical poetry. They also spoke a language of transgressive though redemptive, unidirectional sexuality, of the repudiation of conventional social bonds—husband and home—and of their turn toward an extramarital desire for Krishna.[22] This lineage of Mira's might offer narrators of Miraji's biography and readers of his poetry an alternative, nonmasculinized model for a transgressive stance on desire and convention.

In Miraji's case, however, he didn't quite compose as Mirabai: he translated her work into Urdu. His translations of Mirabai's poems into this language, different from Hindi, Gujarati, and Marwari, turn to another poetics, and his move to write as Mirabai takes issue of authorship and signature in a direction other than the ways they might have been articulated to that point. It transfers her work into his name, which is her name.[23]

One important distinction between other uses of Mira's name to expand her corpus and Miraji's use of it is that, unlike other composers whose individuality and gender identity collapsed into hers, Miraji did not entirely become a female Mira. Under the rubric of the name he still retained an identity that kept, among other things, his gender. His name stood at the nexus of two tales. He had another Mira to add to his name—a Mira who, unlike the two poets, only existed as a character in another person's story.[24]

In the love story, Mira disappears into Sana' ullah, who becomes Mira; in the translations, Miraji, who has become Mira, transforms Mira's work into his own. Anyone who has read any of the poets about whom Miraji writes and translates, including Sappho, Baudelaire and Mallarmé, will immediately realize that translation as transformation and as deformation, that opening up the spaces of the original to somewhere else that might have been between the lines as he signed for them, are particularly pertinent to Miraji. The illusion that signing for another poet is a mimetic activity, a transparent representation of them, is quickly dispelled when Miraji's reading of a poet collides with another's. So Miraji's translation of Mira, or Miraji's incorporation into Mira's lineage (i.e., Miraji's slide into Mirabai) is certainly not an easy slide, and is akin to one proposed by Benjamin.[25]

What are the implications of leaving aside the complications of translation as exemplary reading practice for a moment and focusing on the act of placing Miraji in a lineage of poets associated with Mirabai? Although both men and women composed under the names of the male and female bhakti poets, Mira's is a special case. One song line commonly associated with her was predominantly sung by rural women who sang ostensibly "women's" songs, another song line was sung by rural men.[26] For male poets like Surdas, only a small portion of their work was likely to be considered modeled after women's songs. But much of Mira's work was considered a part of this women's "tradition."[27] For Miraji, too, if a part of his oeuvre were to be assigned to Mira's lineage, it would be given the nomenclature of rural women's song "traditions."

With Mira, even more than with a poet like Surdas, the transcriptions of oral performance traditions attributed to her are less likely to be inscribed into a manuscript.[28] Therefore, the scripting of songs assigned to Mira is considered more unstable and unreliable than those of other poets. One of the implications of scripting in the bhakti tradition is to authorize the work; that is, to assimilate it into a particular religious lineage (*Vallabh sampraday* for Mira). Along with moving the work of a poet into an authoritative, authorizing manuscript tradition, the process of authorizing includes the shaping of an appropriate hagiography for the poet.[29]

Therefore, by translating Mira's songs into a written form, Miraji performs one of the authorizing moves for her songs. But in bhakti, and specially in bhakti circles local to parts of rural Gujarat and parts of rural Rajasthan, the relationship between the written, scripted form and the oral performance genre (between writing and voice) is often fluid and flexible, the oral and written recycled back into one another. The temporalities that recognize song and script do not assign either of them a simple status of prior. Although by translating Mira into a script Miraji formalizes her poetry and stops it in time, for him the scripts are just that—scripts that will be moved or translated back into an oral performance genre.[30] In his case, the assumptions about the song he writes into his *gīt* were performed on the radio:[31] songs are ephemeral, they die as they are sung, and it is precisely their death that is voiced in a script. Radio performances in the 1940s, which were often "live" sessions, paradoxically enhanced the disembodied voicedness of songs—they flowed from an instrument (the radio) and the bodies composing/singing them were presumed by listeners in an act of faith. In Mirabai's case, songs sung in *kīrtan* or *bhajan* (chants) (not on the radio, and not in the movies) were given body literally through their capacity to possess the singer, and given body as they were shared, *bhaj*, by the other bodies in a communal gathering.

Are *gīt*, then, the songs that Miraji translated in the slip between names, the bodied voice given to writing? Are they the exemplar of voice, as Miraji seems to imply in *gīt kaise bante haiṅ*? Is Mira the name whose script renders voice into life? What is the relationship between writing as translation and voice, when voice, too, is translation of voice and of writing? Where is voice in acts of mirroring? Is the mirror the imaginary that brings into the visual the voice that appears to tear the mirror image open? Is voice the echo that rebounds from the past, through women, through Mira and Sappho: Is the echo stalled to hold death at bay in a house of mirrors, the house of repeated writing? Where is death? Where its arrest? Where the life beyond death, the life after death, the life to death?

*Prophecy from Another Time*

After my life has come and gone, after my death perhaps
in a spring season

when a call returned drifts in
my songs will be heard, once more, the world over!

Is lyric the song of love, that song of longing which lingers and never consummates itself?

Far off
In the tall indigo jungle
black, blue-black clouds crowded.
In the forest, a black koel called
black shadows on the ground
black, wet eyes
black, blue-black hair.

Close by
In the center of my heart. Slowly
slowly sighs rose
sorrow poisoned the nectar
sorrow's fierce, fiery glances
sorrow's yellow-black eyes
sorrow's soft, whisper step.

Is lyric the voicing of translation, of reading as deformation; here and in Miraji's work on *gīt* produced as a possible passage of the space between women? What of the hiatus nestled into writing as a woman, writing here in this poem without ever speaking gender? What of the hiatus, the space between, between one voice and its repetition, one voice and its scripting, one voice singing itself in time? Is this the "now" that affords life infinity?

What of the ways in which Miraji's work was read? If, as I say, his work is "literally" or "mimetically" imaged through his biography, the questions then are: In reading his work, were particular parts of his biography more frequently highlighted than others? Are they used separately, or in conjunction? How are they brought together if they are? Are there forms of pathologization peculiar to questions of self and authorship in the twentieth century and unconnected to his biography that are highlighted when readers read Miraji's poetry versus when they tell stories about his life, or are life and poetry woven into one seemingly seamless web? What connections, if any, can be drawn between biography, gendering, and reading? What happens to the incitements into epistemology, the trouble offered to ontologies, the lingering of temporalities when one sustains as truth the concerns that appear to bridge biography and pathology as biology?[32]

In order to address the above questions it is necessary to go to readings of Miraji that focus exclusively on him, as well as go to places where he has been situated in a historical story of modern Urdu literature. Most readers who sign for Miraji, like Aijaz Ahmad or Muhammad Sadiq, pose their readings as continuous and ahistorical, always present and, thus, curiously stable. But it is evident that different readings are fissured by ambiguities and even readings by one person changed over time. What happens, when Miraji is spoken of, to writing as a woman *bhakta* in Urdu? This lineage draws on desiring language whose scapes ply *Krishnā līlā* and its history is given voice through Amir Khusrau, Braj, Deccani, perhaps Chakbast? Each reading of Miraji that I have encountered produces a slightly askew version of him which bends him into various alignments.[33] As I travel through readings in the closing pieces of the book, I will detour back to gender, voice, mirroring, temporality, death, life beyond death, and finally, life after death.

*Prophecy from Another Time*

After my life has come and gone, after my death perhaps
in a spring season
when a call returned drifts in
my songs will be heard, once more, the world over!

Naqsh-e faryadī hai kisī shokhī'e taḥrīr kā
kāghazī hai pairahan har paikare taṣvīr kā.[1]

Whose willful writing, in a semblance of complaint (is)
a garment papered over, each featured guise.

Muqaddar par hī gar sūd o ziyāñ hai
to ham ne yāñ nah kuch khoyā nah pāyā.[2]

If fate's whim turns probable loss, possible profit
I have neither misplaced nor uncovered
I have, here, neither failure nor gain.

## 7. READING GENDER, CHARTING THE OBSCURE

Muhammad Sadiq, an eccentric critic, is someone whose readings of Miraji changed over time.[3] Sadiq published two short pieces on Miraji in the two editions (1947 and 1983) of *Twentieth-Century Urdu Literature*. Both narratives sit firmly within Sadiq's historical arraying/arsenal of Urdu literature. Both are narratives about an unconventional authorial presence, but each mediates the issue of unconventionality in a different key. Although the two have a great deal in common, their discrepancies explore the rifts that slide open in the seemingly translucent telling of history to expose displacements in Sadiq's position over time—displacements that provide insights into changes in the modes of reading Miraji.

In order to see the technologies at work in both, it is necessary to focus on the areas where the picture is so transparent that it seems "natural" and the apparatus for description and depiction disappear. It is essential to look sharply at what the picture produces, at how a reader is trained to look. To do this one needs to darken the singularities in the transparent and obvious sites. At the same time one must magnify the places where the picture blurs, the visual details lost in an unclarified word or phrase. This perspective helps to foreground some of the operations of gendering and assigning sexuality.

Sadiq's portraits of Miraji appear detailed, but at the same time they are curiously denuded of biographical details. One of the stories in wide circulation is completely absent from Sadiq's accounts—the name story. By reading sections from the two pieces against each other, the congruencies and discrepancies between them, which each offers as evidentiary substance, can be seen in greater depth:

> [*Some six years ago,*][4] [A little over forty years ago,] an unkempt and out-at-elbowed young man, with drooping mustaches, and a mop of brown hair, surmounted by a black sweaty capsharp nose, thin sensuous lips, sunken cheeks, and eyes whose glint conquered no less than charmed, was seen promenading the streets, squatting on the bridges, or visiting the literary coteries, of Lahore. He was looked at sideways at first, what for his free-and-easy ways and his seedy attire. But he aroused some curiosity by his ready wit and ideas among the young—the only people in India who have some curiosity—and in a short time he was installed assistant editor of a go-ahead journal. Such was the beginning of Miraji's literary career.[5]
>
> Miraji is the genius of Bohemia. He is at home in it. Others may declaim against conventional codes. Not so Miraji. For does not declaiming against morals show that you inwardly feel their force, and shout merely to drown out the voice of your conscience. [*Miraji is as innocent of conventional morality as a new-born babe.*]
>
> [Miraji's life, as we know it, provides little evidence of an inner struggle; and yet one must be a perfervid devotee not to have noticed occasional signs of swagger and pose about him. Like most young men he was eager to live up to the reputation for unconventionality he had come to enjoy.]
>
> Miraji's moral and literary nonconformity has strongly reacted on the literary life in Lahore. He is, to-day [*sic*], the object of a strong cult, and has done much to free the imagination of the rising generation of writers from the cramping sway of conventional opinion.
>
> Miraji is a vers libriste. His themes are mostly sexual. His attitude is cynical. Poetry in the ordinary sense of the word, there is none in him; for his themes being what they are, he uses a poetic diction as close to the spoken language as possible. It has polish, sparkle; wit and flow,

with occasional incursions into downright slang. [*It is a style which he has evolved himself, and which suits his moods like a glove.*]

[He is the first poet, to my knowledge, to break away from the poetic diction of an earlier generation.]

[*Miraji's poetry is wrapped in impenetrable darkness. It is the most baffling poetry that I have ever read. His symbols are vague and arbitrary. And then his flashing wit, his abrupt transitions from symbol to symbol, and from the symbolical to the matter-of-fact, and back again to the symbolical—it is not at all the poetry for a plodding reader. And yet there is method in his madness. You have only to penetrate his reserve, and know his symbols, and then it is all plain-sailing. But can you really do so? This way madness lies.*]

[The greater part of Miraji's poetry is exceedingly obscure. This is largely due to the use of private symbols and abrupt transitions. Of him it may be said what Ben Jonson said of Donne: His verse will perish for lack of being understood. There are some of his admirers who claim to understand him; but it has been observed that this is for the most part in regard to poems which Miraji himself provided the key. Defending his obscurity Miraji wrote:

> My poems are different from those of other poets; and since it is the law of life that everything in the world is not meant for all, I would like to say that my poems are for those who have the ability to understand them. To try to understand them. . . . Many persons are under the impression that I am willfully obscure. Now a little thought would convince anyone that life, too, is a smokescreen, a labyrinth, a mystery. If we fail to understand it we are not alive; we are dead. There are degrees of insight in different persons, and the different ways to use it are another name for life. *Mīrājī kī nazmeñ*, Foreword.

The argument is somewhat confused and trips quite a bit, especially with regard to life being a mystery which it is our business to resolve. Here all one need ask is: Is Miraji obscure because he is trying to grapple with experiences or states of mind too deep for words; experiences and states of mind which transcend the categories of everyday speech? A study of his poetry does not lend support to this view. Miraji is obscure because he uses private symbols. Once they are explained, we find that his poems are related to common everyday experiences. They are mostly sexual and have little or no depth.

Nor is he difficult because of thick coming fancies; ideas coming pell-mell, so that the reader cannot keep pace with them and feels lost.

Finally, in regard to the mystery of life, what has Miraji done to resolve it? Some of the great poets of the world have tried to resolve it, or at least to present it vividly. But to make what is intelligible obscure, as Miraji does, by playing hide and seek with the reader by an arbitrary use of language, is not the way of poetry which strives to make things intelligible, instead of draping them in darkness. . . .

Viewed thus Miraji has nothing in common with the Symbolists: he is obscure because he uses arbitrary symbols.

In another respect, Miraji's poetry is a reversion to the old tradition of Urdu poetry which was saturated with references to Indian life and Hindu mythology, and which the reformers, Khan-e-arzu, Mazhar and others studiously discarded, bringing it in line with Persian traditions. Miraji is powerfully inclined towards Hinduism and its mythology, and makes free use of it. His preoccupation with it is not a defiant gesture against current middle-class morality; it is the direct result of the high place accorded to it by Hindu thinkers.

"Chal-chalao," which prefaces *Mīrājī kī naẓmeñ*, the first volume of his verse, may be taken as summing up his attitude towards life at the purely sensuous level. Mutability, he tells us, is the law of life. There is nothing stable here, and all we need to do to make life significant, rich both in possibilities and achievement, is to make the most of each fleeting gleam of beauty. Intensity of perception and immediate responsiveness to each item of this enthralling and variegated show—this is all that is possible in a world the essence of which is eternal flux.

Miraji is justifying his free and easy habits in the poem; he is the "Constant Lover," in the sense that he is true to an ideal and not to any one person. . . .

Miraji has tried his hand at themes other than sex. These poems are straightforward and comprise gits, gazals, and poems in conventional forms. His gits are so overcharged with Hindi that except for the Urdu script they are Hindi in sentiment, diction, and imagery. The best of them, quoted below, is in Urdu. In its languorous flow it aptly portrays the poet's unrealized hopes and yearnings.

The heart yearned for unknown cities;
The yearned for cities remained unknown.
Absorbed in these fancies
We continued to hear in the heart's city
The songs the heart loved to hear—
The songs that beguiled us into happiness.

Nights pass and days
and then new nights and new days.
But the foolish heart is so obstinate
It still sighed for the old beautiful dreams.

One who dallies with thoughts of the unattainable,
Said to him the actual quietly:
Gone are those times and things,
And what remains of them is mere stories.

And now I pour nectar into my songs,
And thus extinguish my heart's fire.
And now the heart takes only those to be fools
Who stayed wise
In days past.

And here are lines from one of his finest gazals with a theme similar to that of the git. It is the picture of a desultory, aimless life divorced from high ideals, of vague memories of the all too few happy days that shed a momentary light and then left him in the dark:

From city to city roamed the traveler and forgot the way home;
What is thine and what is mine, he forgot his kith and not kith. . . .

Miraji's poetry is of value for its style. He uses vers libre with deftness. His importance, therefore, lies in his influence which has been both wide and deep. He was the presiding genius of the *Ḥalqa-e-arbab-e-ẓauq*, Lahore, a society that did more than any other organization to popularize modern trends in Urdu poetry. He had the gift of arousing enthusiasm in his friends and fellow workers. It is significant that it was his personality that held the Halqa together; and if it is still something like an influence in literature, it is because of the momentum he gave it. But while giving him credit for all this, we cannot forget that he set the fashion for obscurity which marks or mars quite a large part of contemporary poetry. Under his influence sex usurped the field and for some time drove out other motives. He, too, was responsible for the indiscriminate use of Hindi words, and this especially in gits.

What was Miraji's total contribution as a poet? . . .

. . . In what respect is he a great poet then? It appears that Dr. Abdullah had his potential poetic gift in mind; and here, no doubt, he is right. Miraji made his presence felt. In his varied gift he was second to none; only he could not turn them into account.]

Sadiq begins both his pieces on Miraji neither with his literal birth nor with the birth story of his name, but rather with his literary birth, whole and named as a poet in Lahore: "such was the beginning of Miraji's literary career." The opening moments of Sadiq's narrative create, through flashes of a body, Miraji's visual presence when he made his appearance on the literary scene; he is embodied as an unconventional presence, with touches of the unkemptness of a sadhu. As the paragraph progresses, the picture of Miraji turns transient, moving him from location to location and, in the process, depicting someone transitional and nomadic, situated between urban spaces. It continues the portrayal of him as an itinerant city sadhu, as someone who does not hark the conventions of social order. By the end of the opening paragraph, however, Miraji is stilled: stabilized and "installed" as a member of a literary universe as "an assistant editor of a go-ahead [unnamed] journal."

This paragraph locates Miraji in several ways. First, it constitutes him as a visual male object. He is circulated in the paragraph as a male within a masculinized public domain. The description situates him by *not* placing him within a household, thus implying that his identification is elsewhere. Then, at its close, it finally places him in a literary scene.

Both the 1947 and 1983 readings frame the visual from within the glance of their time, angling the glance and marrying it to a feeling that tells you how you saw what you saw: "looked at sideways at first . . . but he aroused some curiosity . . ." The askance look of a potential reader is never swapped for a "straight on" one; Miraji never becomes completely orderly in Sadiq's readings, for Sadiq continues to gaze at him "sideways." This indirection discloses that those who wanted to might and could read Miraji. Readers who were likely to be amenable to him are those curious about the unorthodoxy—those who look across rather than look for.

The first clues of a deviation between Sadiq's two presentations of Miraji reveal themselves at the end of the second paragraph, where Miraji is represented as the unconventional "genius of Bohemia"; yet at the same time, he is not visualized as someone who noisily advocates against conventionality. Miraji is at home in unconventionality, his *gharānā* is there, and being eccentric is flawlessly, without remark, natural for him. In the 1947 version, with the metaphoric equation "as innocent of conventional morality as a new-born babe," Sadiq completes the process of naturalizing Miraji's unconventionality by making it originary, turning it into a characteristic that existed prior to socialization, almost prior to language. Miraji is the innocent, a *nādān* baby, unclothed even as he is thrust into the world.

The metaphoric move that completes this 1947 paragraph is replaced in the later version, in which Miraji's unconventionality is explained or translated somewhat differently. It is no longer an intrinsic quality, prior to socialization, predating language, but an extrinsic sign, mired in language, told through it, and a self-consciously chosen signifier. It becomes a pose, a costume, a behavioral "swagger" on a par with his "unkemptness," or something he dresses himself in because he has to "live up to the reputation for unconventionality he had come to enjoy." The "little evidence of an inner struggle" that Miraji's life gives, which surely ought to follow *tout de suite* from Sadiq's opening description of Miraji's being at home in Bohemia, appears to be the site of exertion for Sadiq. In the 1983 version of his essay, Sadiq pushed hard to move Miraji over from the form that Sadiq himself had given the poet, as someone with an ingrained, natural, presocialized ease with unconventionality to someone whose unconventionality is the end result of much labor, someone who is worldly-wise. Rather than an unconventionality that is explained as natural because it does not respond to a public conventionality, Miraji's unconventionality becomes unnatural because it responds to public perception of him as unconventional. Sadiq tries to move Miraji from an "authentic" unconventionality to an "inauthentic" one. This revision that Sadiq makes in the 1983 version reveals his own discomfort with his depiction of Miraji. This discomfort fissures the rest of his discussion on Miraji. And nowhere is Miraji moved into the idioms of a modernist secular twentieth century, as was the case with Ahmad's portrayal of the poet. And nowhere in Sadiq's portrayals is Miraji a poetic lover.

In both versions Sadiq goes on to talk about the influence of Miraji's "unconventionality" on "the literary life in Lahore." In the first version, instead of Miraji responding to others' expectations and cramping himself by his conventionally motivated unconventionality (as he does in the later reading), Miraji reproduces/reiterates his unconventionality in the "imagination" of a "rising generation of writers." He enables them to free themselves imaginatively from the "cramping sway of conventional opinion."

Sadiq then travels in both versions from the social Miraji to his poetry. He says that, "Miraji *is* a *vers libriste*" [emphasis mine]. Here Sadiq is not just alluding to Miraji's facility with free verse but is also implying that his verse is free of certain lyric conventions. "*In him*," says Sadiq, "*there is no poetry in the 'ordinary' sense of the word*" [italics mine]. But what is the "ordinary" sense of poetry? Sadiq moves seamlessly, not into what the poetry *in* Miraji is or how it differs from the ordinary sense of poetry, but into themes, diction, style, and the formal characteristics of Miraji's poetry, where the "unordinary" sense of poetry appears to be located. His themes "being what they are," that is, "sexual"; his "poetic diction as close to the spoken language as possible . . . with occasional incursions into downright slang"; and a style "he has evolved himself," and "which suits his moods like a glove" are markers of poetic unconventionality or differences from conventional poetic modes. The slip Sadiq enacts between what Miraji is, or Miraji's identity, and the effects that produce this identity, allows Miraji's identity to be read as catechresis because it collapses identity and effect.

It is apparent that as a reader of Miraji's poetry Sadiq is grappling with something unusual, and that he does not have the requisite tools. The unfamiliarity Sadiq faces would be easier to contend with if Miraji's poetry, using a "poetic diction that is as close to the spoken language as possible," did not give the illusion of accessibility.

In the 1947 version of Sadiq's tale, the statement "it is a style which he has evolved himself, and which suits his moods like a glove," mediates between a language and themes that seem familiar and obscure: "Miraji's poetry is wrapped in impenetrable darkness." As a reader, Sadiq is confounded by Miraji's poetry, and he is willing, at the conclusion of his early discussion, to expose his failure to read it: "it is the most baffling poetry I have ever read." But by this point in Sadiq's first piece, his own engagement with Miraji's poetry had become less and less clear. Though the 1947 piece opened with a graphic visual portrait, it eventually blurred into the vagueness of reiterated adjectives that seem to promise the surety of collective agreement (after all, we all know what they mean) but only come into certainty when they have been amended by the specific that can be pointed out (*this* is what unconventionality is)—conventional and unconventional. Reiteration provides the illusion of clarity, but when one begins to ask Sadiq (the writer who speaks through his piece) for corroborating details the piece becomes baffling. Sadiq was not the only mystified reader of Miraji; Miraji's poetry was considered difficult to read then, and it still presents problems for readers of modern Urdu poetry, because Miraji disturbed the alignments of possible readings in ways that were incomprehensible to "conventional" readers. Faced by some of Miraji's poetry, readers seemed unable to marshal legacies of acceptable incommensurability, like the lines from Ghalib with which I opened this chapter.

For Sadiq, in the 1947 piece, Miraji's crypticness resides both in one site (symbol) and in the passages between poetry that seemed straightforward and poetry that seemed obscure. So, Sadiq calls Miraji's poetry incomprehensible because he feels that the poet uses "arbitrary," or unusual, and hence seemingly random, symbols and "abrupt" transitions between different modes of writing, "matter of fact," and "symbolical." So, Sadiq turns to haphazardness (as aimlessness) and a shrunk spatiality/temporality to bare Miraji's obscurity. But, says Sadiq, there is method in his madness—even as it is a method that leads to madness.

Where, then, does Miraji's poetry lie for Sadiq, writing in the 1940s? What does "madness" mean? How does one recognize it? Sadiq responds in his later piece to this question—which he poses but does not answer in his earlier one. Sadiq's solution goes to what Miraji is, and therefore is seen as, rather than what the reader cannot see. He responds to his own earlier question in the later, rewritten, more extensive piece on Miraji, but in a way that deflects the onus onto Miraji, rather than onto a reader facing "baffling codes" that challenge him to a point where his strategies for reading them falter, flounder, or misfire time and again.

In the later piece, in which Sadiq conducts an exposé of Miraji, Miraji is unveiled as both pathological and banal.[6] Thus he is denied the incomprehensible complexity that Sadiq meets when he sees himself reading Miraji.

I would like to digress for a while and turn to a chart that I found among Miraji's papers while I was in Bombay speaking to Akhtarul Iman. This chart opens a space in which the body of categories is hollowed out and eviscerated by providing an option to read them against and through "obscurity," or incomprehensible complexity. The chart may offer resolutions to Sadiq's difficulties.

## THE CHART

In the summer of 1989 I was in Bombay interviewing writers who had known Miraji. Miraji lived on and off with Akhtarul Iman while he was in Bombay in the 1940s, and when he died his papers remained with Akhtarul Iman, who kept some papers from public circulation but sent two manuscripts of poems, which he said Miraji had prepared for publication, to Mukhtar Siddiqi in the 1960s. These were published in 1968 as *Pābañd naẓmeñ* (Foot-bound verse) and *Tīn rañg* (Three tones), along with an edited book on Miraji: *Mīrajī: Shaḳhṣiyat aur fann*, a series of essays on Miraji accompanied by poems and prose pieces by him. *Sah ātishah* (With fire) was sent by Akhtarul Iman to Pakistan a short time before his death and was published in 1992. Since the books of poetry published during Miraji's lifetime were no longer easily available, by the time I met Akhtarul Iman I had read only these posthumous volumes.

Akhtarul Iman and I were in his house poring over manuscripts Miraji had prepared. All the poems in them had a notation or signature, which we agreed must be Miraji's, on the top of the page. A majority of the poems were dated, some as early as 1929. Among the papers that were "unsigned" were lists of poems, annotated with their prior publication record in journals, and *gīt* in *nāgarī*. The chart was among the unsigned papers. The papers I took away with me to photocopy were being eaten by worms, so the photocopies looked like film strips that had been seared at the edges. I knew then that by the time I returned to India these pages would have been consumed.

So the chart I have is a photocopy of a sheet of notebook paper fractured into columns ruled in by dark, pressed-down pencil. Photocopied on paper longer and wider than the original, the chart's edges are stippled with gray-shaded dots and its corners blur into the photocopy paper. Along one axis the chart transmutes into the photocopy; along others, where limits of the paper have been photocopied in, the chart stands apart.

Photocopying in India at that time was not the facile process it has become in the urban United States. Photocopy machines were not easily found, so the machine was a kind of Grail; it required a bodily commitment to the mechanics of reproduction. It was a fairly recent alternative to the circulation of books (and pushed sometimes along the same circles), which have a short life span on store shelves.

Books have to be followed, like private papers, into personal libraries; they are often distributed not by sale but by borrowing. The issues of the closure and openness of circulatory mechanisms associated with ownership, authorship, copyright, and the distinction of public and private cannot and do not operate in the same way as they would if the transfer of "texts" occurred in a so-called free market. This situation has ramifications for the publishing system. Texts are available on the Indian market in pirated versions, like pirated videos or tapes, and their appropriation is not contested legally. When texts are transferred to the United States, they are often photocopies.

What, then, does this say for my photocopy of the chart I found in Miraji's papers? Akhtarul Iman made it clear to me that he was not interested in giving the chart to anyone else, so I am in the process of circulating a facsimile of the chart through a piece of writing that is in a language and to an audience unfamiliar to/with him.

This chart, or table, has two axes—a horizontal axis that enumerates/

| *naẓm* (poem) | *āzād* (free verse) | *jinsī* (sexual) | *dīgar mauẓūʿ* (other) | *mub-ham* (obscure?) | *romānī* (romantic) | *żātī* (personal) | *pāband* (foot-bound) | *mauẓūʿ* (topics) | *mub-ham ijtamāʾī* (obscurely social) |
|---|---|---|---|---|---|---|---|---|---|
| 1. (Going, going . . .) "Chal Chalāʾo" | | | | | | | | | |
| 2. (Devadasi and pujari) "Deva dāsī aur pujārī | | | | | | | | | |
| 3. (Without access/reach) "Nārasāʾī pā" | | | | | *X* | | | | |
| 4. (Sorrow is the heart's intoxication) "Dukh" "Dil kā dārū" | | *ji* | | | | | | | |
| 5. (Later flight) "Bʿād kī uḍāv" | | *ji* | | *mub* | | | | | |

itemizes interpretive groupings and a vertical one that lists some early poems written between 1932 and 1943 (mainly in Lahore) and collected in *Mīrājī kī nazmeñ* (1943). Each poem in the list has checks under the category column it fit into, and several fit more than one classification. For example, "B'ād kā uḍāv," which is in Appendix A of this book, is both *jinsī* and *mub-ham*. A few poems were not categorized at all. The categories on the horizontal axis range from formal features of poetry like free verse or "foot-bound"/metrical verse, to thematic ones like sexual, romantic, and social.[7]

Two categories—*dīgar* and *mauẓūa'* (other, again, further, next, besides, as in *dūsarā*, topic or theme) and *mub-ham* (obscure, uncertain, ambiguous, murky)[8]—are curious precisely because they attempt to name areas that cannot be classified within the available group. Because they allow for nonclassifiable, disorderly places in the chart, they disrupt the possibility of completeness or closure for it. So with them in it, the chart could never form a bounded, sealed system. The hole or place of elision, or the elsewhere, *dı¯gar, du¯sara¯*, which gestures outward, is written into the categories. The gaps or openings offered by typologies that elude the process that produces them prevent the seamless engendering of any all-encompassing system. Even if readers want to use the classifications available in the chart, their eyes have to walk by the spaces in Miraji's chart, the gestures that prefigure incompleteness. They are always confronted with the potential lack of closure for a reading.[9]

The first such category, "another topic or theme," adds another, an all-purpose alternative possibility onto the classes assembled, where anything that does not fit into the cluster of classifications can be put. It has a curious assignment in the spacing of the chart. It sits between "sexual" and *mub-ham*. It is not merely appended to the list, but like *mub-ham*, breaks open the middle. Because this is a "category," which deals with poems whose "theme" is other, another, possibly outside, it does not necessarily mean that the poems that might fit into it are universally "elsewhere" or "without a theme"—just that there is no category within those collected in the chart into which they can be fit. Through *dīgar*, poems are offered another (besides) or perhaps a double option. It is possible to find, perhaps, a world where this not-quite-classifiable poem gathered under *dīgar* may be orderly. This category of "another/other theme" also places limits, the outer limits of a set quite squarely at the heart of this body of ordering.

But because this category appears open, it does not mean that if it is viewed from a certain angle, from another dimension, it could not also be seen as shut. Since it is named, it could be understood as a fixed or immobile space. Inserted into a ready-made system of representation, it is a prerogative that can be exercised by readers to slide out of that system and perhaps into another one or to slide between several others. But because it is placed within something as an ellipsis, a gap, a possible, an elsewhere, it is also part of that system. It encapsulates the limits within. If a category from another system were to replace it, then that space would become not just a "named" yet mobile space available for fleeting passages through, and available for invariably fluid use, but a closed space, coupled to or intertwined with another system of representation. This category, traversed through *mauẓūaʿ*, still allows for the possibility of inserting another name, another order, even though one may need to shift frames, traverse space-times, to do so. It sustains the illusion that it is possible to read these poems through typologies tallied up.

I am considered a somewhat renegade reader, intervening by reading poems that have rarely been spoken of, and in this way changing the shape of Miraji's oeuvre. For me, this space of the other *mauẓūaʿ* makes it possible to perform readings on poems like "Solitude"[10] (Yagānagat) or "Call of the Sea" (Samundar kā bulāvā) that might be followed by empty spaces if they were put on the chart. One question that surfaces as I read raises the issue of knowledge/power: where do my readings fit in a history of reading Miraji? In a situation in which poems are readily and frequently categorized, understanding who is assigned controls of the categories that produce the proper forms of knowing, and who controls the forms of knowing through which categories are assembled, and understanding where that places certain kinds of readers is essential. If one examines the categories that have been made available, as such, from a different perspective and performs readings that interrupt them, then what happens to those categories?

Reading was a categorical imperative for Miraji. He wrote at a time when formal and thematic transformations of poetry were taking place and reading strategies for twentieth-century Urdu poetry were being worked out. Pasts were being produced in the present. Miraji was involved in the drawing up of blueprints within which to read. The major, and obvious, contribution he made in this direction is compiled in a volume of readings of contemporary poems, *Is naẓm meñ* (In this poem), which includes his own reading of a poem composed with a friend, Qayyum Nazar.

In the 1920s, 1930s, and 1940s, as the canon of "modern" Urdu poetry was being molded, new communities of readers were being formed through the radio, film, and journals. In the criticism he wrote, Miraji appealed to, enticed with, and confronted the modes and methods through which he was read. As a "subject" living and working in a colonial framework, his literary stance is self-reflexively determined by his sociopolitical circumstances; his language, both poetic and critical, often inadvertently responds to colonial categories for his universe.[11]

The construction of categories that would include a gap (a space, an opening) or ellipsis is an issue pertinent to Miraji because, as I have made clear, over time he became both marginal and privileged.[12] He was read as a figure around whom Urdu literature of the time was constituted, but also as one on whom the tactics of marginalization were practiced. These, like pathologization, abridged his oeuvre to harmonize with the ways in which twentieth-century taxonomies of pathology (sexuality) were understood. He was one of the limits at the heart of the poetic universe in which he lived. Therefore, the kinds of readers who presumably read him came from and occupied both pivotal (Progressive) and alternative locations. The chart hails the stances his readers might have been likely to take on him.[13]

Some of the categories in the chart, such as social and political ("The Clerk's Love Song"), are those that the Progressives appropriated (as their provenance) to describe poetry they valorized. Another—romantic—could certainly be used to read Miraji's poetry, but was seldom used by Progressive critics at this time to inform their own poetry. One is a category—sexual—into which Miraji's entire oeuvre is often fit. Because this list of seemingly conventional *mauẓūa*ʿ includes *dīgar mauẓūa*ʿ, it transgresses its own boundaries and gives readers spaces in which to deposit those poems or pieces of poems not often associated with Miraji's poetry. A *dīgar mauẓūa*ʿ space seduces readers who want to read poems "outside a theme." This space for fluidity discharges a special service in a poetic world where conformity and inflexibility were slowly being deployed in the arsenal of arguments. It supplies the breathing space of the margins. These were the outer limits of Miraji's absorption to a centralized position.

The other incommensurable category in this chart is *mub-ham*, a word that appears in poetic criticism written by Miraji on other poets' works or appears when Miraji talks about the practices of reading. Miraji begins his elaboration of the process of reading as a form of unpacking with his discussion of Mallarmé and with his translations. According to Miraji, Roger Fry's and Charles Mauron's translations of Mallarmé leave their seductive traces on his memory, which he pursues a few years later when he begins to read the poetry of his contemporaries. Reading lives somewhere between translation and exegesis, somewhere between transformation/writing and literal unpacking. Mallarmé becomes for Miraji the exemplary poet, whose *mub-ham* practice, like Ghalib's, offers the votary the truth of reading—a truth that marries translation to transformation, the essay to exegesis—"illumination in a serious way."

Derived from *b-h-m*, like *ib-ham* (murky, cloudy, misty, messy, or unclear) *mub-ham* (ambiguity, double meaning) is an adjective that Miraji uses in his essays on other poets' works, when a poem is hard to read, when a poem is not transparently self-evident, or when a poem is "difficult." *Mub-ham* suggests the above meanings, but it also has a positive valence that allies it with another word in Miraji's oeuvre—*anokhā*, or rare, uncanny, wondrous, strange, magnificent.

*Anokhā* appears in "Traveler," which has been allocated *mub-ham*-ness in this chart. *Anokhā* flowers in the body of "Traveler." It describes the two flowers that are offered to the protagonist, the "I" in the poem. Rare and uncanny, the *anokhā* thing is a fantastic seductive object, like the Grail or a prize that hovers somewhere beyond the edges of perception, and that might be awarded at the end of a journey.

> I don't believe
> that every traveler on the road has a destination.
> Shall I join them, shall I go?
>
> "Come with us, come on."
> "Why are you standing here, so quiet, so alone?"
> "We'll bring you two rare [*anokhā*] flowers
> if you want . . ."
>
> "Stop, stop, I don't need . . .
> I'm waiting here for a friend."[14]

*Anokhā* here carries the future in it as the promised overture. The promise forwarded at the end of the clause of possibility, "if you want," *anokhā* takes the present into the future, which will then reach back toward the present to turn its course, "if you want." And what are the promised flowers? A gift that may never come? Things whose value is cloaked as wonder? Are the flowers the assurance itself, given by travelers who represent the symbolic? Does their rarity leave open the possibility that they will never in fact be given, that the person offered them will never receive them in exchange for joining up? Are they fetishes whose being is abstracted/wonder/magical or whose value is precisely something that two sets of people read two different ways? Are they the object whose thrownness into the future projects only loss and never a return, whose value only persists as wonder? Are they "the thing," or "*objet petit 'a'*"?[15]

As the holdout, promise, thing, ensconced in a teleological journey, cupped within a Sufi's movement toward mystic revelation, *anokhā* can suggest/allegorize a changed state. In the title of the poem "Rare [*anokhā*] Waves of Passion" [*ras rang*], the words for passion or "color/aesthetic emotion/desire/juice/sap," come together with *anokhā* so that the word *anokhā* makes something rare or mysterious tangible. This is a charged state or a state of desire, a woman's desire, spoken by the woman whose voice is in the poem.

Both *mub-ham* and *anokhā* are used for the subtle, the mysterious, the fantastic, or to describe something that cannot be elucidated, cleared up, turned dense in the language available to Miraji, perhaps even within "language" (as symbolic) understood as something that defines or circumscribes the dimensions of human experience.[16] They are perhaps the words that bring back the imaginary or the real as the possibility of flowering into wonder brought back in the symbolic and pointed to as impossible.

Miraji also uses *mub-ham* in *naẓm* that form around the parameters of *gīt*, which are, for him, poems that speak about and in the language used to translate mystical experience. In his chart, *mub-ham* carries those registers of use to describe or open a space for the inexplicable, or to provide a space where "ordinary" categories of language do not quite work, or perhaps only do their work through difference that is never entirely said in writing. But *mub-ham*, unlike *anokhā*, is a word that is used for uncertainty, so it represents not just the possible, the mysterious, but also something that cannot just assume shape. *Anokhā*, unlike *mub-ham* (which seems to be in the present), is not the enigmatic in the now of the poem, but the enigmatic that might be brought back to the time and space of the poem from somewhere else.

When it is used in Miraji's chart for his own poems, *mub-ham* is coupled with one or more *other* categories. According to his chart, *mub-ham* poems also simultaneously fit into or can be read in other categories—sexual, for example. One instance of a poem that falls into *mub-ham* as well as another category is "Later Flight" (Bʿād kā uḍāv),[17] which is classified in the chart as both *mub-ham* and *jinsī* (sexual).

*Mub-ham* is both excess and ellipsis; it witnesses a quality that a poem possesses in addition to another more accessible qualification. Using *mub-ham* is a way of pointing to the "excess," the part that leaks over after the poem has already been classified or placed in a category through which it can be interpreted. *Mub-ham* also stretches out a system of classification from within itself. When used alongside *jinsī*, it attests to the fact that analyzing a poem as *jinsī* will not render a complete reading. As the ellipsis written into the deployment of any category, it shows that one category may not be sufficient for reading certain poems.

Because *mub-ham* plays with shifts, uncertainty, even ambivalence, it demarcates a nonspecific spacing within which to place any differences. When used on a poem, it allows for *any* alternative reading as a second or double reading (*kināyah* in *māʿnī āfrīnī*). But the double does not necessarily repeat over two poems. So for two poems that are both *mub-ham*, their *mub-ham*-nesses cannot necessarily be mapped onto one another.

Opening a poem up to a *mub-ham* reading destabilizes an analysis which would place the poem in a particular category. Providing *mub-ham* as a classification allows poems to be simultaneously easy to read—if they are read within one of the thematic options—and "difficult" to read, because they also cannot be "completely" read within the thematic options available. The two "alternatives" I think point to the fact that some poems of Miraji's can be read in ways that are not easily accessed, and thus maybe metaphysical, *anokhā*, rare, wondrous, seductive, strange.

Where then would a poem like "Call of the Sea," which speaks itself into life at the province shared by *dīgar mauẓūʿ* and *mub-ham*, belong? Its topos cannot be classified, and it is *mub-ham*. How can it be read, and who would read it? In order to understand this poem I would need a different angle. Is gender one such possible perspective? But here, in this poem, gender is not about bodies, not about sex, but about the miniscule movements danced by words that read across gender? I'd like to return to Sadiq's dilemma as a reader of Miraji, which I had been addressing before I digressed to the chart. I would like to see if the chart, viewed as a series of reading arrangements, or as arrangements that perform the failures of reading, is useful for Sadiq's readings.

## SADIQ AND THE CHART

As he was described by Sadiq in the 1947 article, Miraji was a "naturally" unconventional social animal. His poetry proves not so easy to categorize. It appears to sit in an unstable relation between the at-hand (matter-of-fact, mainly sexual themes, diction close to the spoken language), and the inaccessible (baffling poetry, symbols vague and arbitrary, random shifts between ordinary language and symbols). Sadiq's challenge to a reader of Miraji is: "You have only to penetrate his reserve, and know his symbols, and then it is all plain-sailing. But can you really do so? This way madness lies." Even Sadiq's challenge is ambushed, tied down somewhere between plain sailing and madness, mediated by "can you really do so?" Is this challenge, the *dhamkī*, one meets in "Jātrī" (Traveler) and "Ābgīne ke us pār kī ek shām" (A night on the far side of a wine glass) of leaving the symbolic and facing down what remains after it? What leads lead to madness? Perhaps that is something you can penetrate, know, and plain sail. The three imply the capability of a reader to go into, grasp, and be comfortable within a particular episteme. For a reader like Sadiq the epistemic experience of Miraji's poetry is one in which his comfort is hazarded immediately by the impossibility of that very comfort. The moment you think you can read it and know it, you face the likelihood of not knowing it. Whose, then, is the madness? Sadiq leaves this open: it could be Miraji's, the reader's, something belonging in the poetic world, or all three.

The chart helps us to grasp Sadiq's conundrum. The destabilizing effects of *mub-ham* at the heart of a group of categories create precisely the kind of uneasiness that Sadiq feels when he is dislocated by Miraji's symbols. *Mub-ham* pushes beyond limits, but is also the ellipsis within limits. *Mub-ham* allows for the possibility of madness if readers try to cloak themselves in epistemic comfort even as they face their inability to know. *Mub-ham* also permits readings that transgress a system of reading, and in such a way that what happens are "mad" readings. Certain poems that are *dīgar mauẓūʿ* and *mub-ham*, that cannot be pulled into a system, push a particular kind of reader toward a transgressive reading perspective that is "mad," that exceeds the boundaries of what one ought to know if one were anchored in the group of people who traveled the road in "Jātrī." Perhaps the metaphysics of the self that Miraji elaborates in that poem, where desire and the undoing of language come together, cannot be looked at from a settled gaze angled through propriety, but can perhaps be seen through where a reader looks at what gazing is and how they do it.

It is precisely this perspectival shift, the ability to look at a seemingly familiar world askew, to create something so that the supposedly familiar turns uncanny, that Sadiq elides in his reconstituted 1983 reading of Miraji. How does he do it? The baffled "I" (the baffled reader, a confused Sadiq) is replaced by a "one," a "we," or the impersonal, objective narrative. In this second version, Sadiq does not bare himself as a reader and make his act of reading a naked one visible to another reader; rather, he disappears behind his readings. He obscures his perspective while rendering his positions transparent.

In this second reading, Sadiq continues to call Miraji's poetry "exceedingly obscure," but displaces the onus of the obscurity of Miraji's poetry onto poetry: mere meaningless linguistic manipulation. For Sadiq, Miraji's "private symbols" become new signifiers for indicating old material that are unclear only because they are "private" and hence inaccessible to someone else.[18]

The word "obscurity" that Sadiq uses in his essay on Miraji is glossed by a translated passage from Miraji: "defending his obscurity, Miraji wrote . . ." Obscurity, in one of the two passages that Sadiq cites as Miraji's defense of his own obscurity, is *mub-ham*. The passage to which Sadiq refers is taken from Miraji's preface to one of his early collections of poems, *Mīrājī kī naẓmeñ* (Miraji's verse), the collection Miraji tallied up under his chart. This passage opens in the Urdu with *bahut log samajhte haiñ kih maiñ ṣirf mub-ham bāteñ kahtā hūñ.* ("Many people believe/feel that I say merely *mub-ham* things"; Sadiq's translation is: "Many persons are under the impression that I am willfully obscure.")

*Mub-ham* itself is obscure, though hardly willful; difficult to image, it eludes signification. "Obscurity, too" says Miraji, in Sadiq's translation, "is a relative term" (*ib-ham bhī ek iẓāfī taṣavvur hai*). (Instead of the translation Sadiq offers, I would translate this as *ib-ham*, which is also an excessive, extra, relative idea/concept. Sadiq's translation of *taṣavvur* as a "term" rather than as the more complex "idea/concept" follows upon his simplification of *mub-ham* or *ib-ham* from the allusive/illusive, additive, meanings that both call up [through the work done by *iẓāfī*] to "obscurity.") But both *mub-ham* and *ib-ham*, in their *iẓāfiyat*, or possibility of accrual, are less available than "obscurity." They slide and shift between occult, dumb, uncertain, obscure, murky, and their slipperiness is integral to understanding them. In the paragraph cited by Sadiq, Miraji appears to leave *mub-ham* open, whereas Sadiq closes it off, shuts the translation down by shuttling meaning (as reading) in a particular direction, before he cites the passage.

The implication behind the moves that Sadiq performs is that this kind of obscurity, this kind of *mub-ham*, is arbitrary, and therefore inappropriate. Sadiq seems to insinuate that there is a proper kind of obscurity, that obscurity has its own ethos, its own proprieties, and its own etiquette. Its etiquette, if formed, is one form of the transcendental. Because Miraji does not appear to grapple with "states of mind" or "experiences" that transcend the categories of ordinary speech, and his poems are "related to common everyday experiences," Sadiq suggests that Miraji is an obscurantist. Miraji's poems are deliberately and *uselessly* obscure. According to Sadiq, once the private symbols that create *mub-ham* are explained, we find that they are "mostly sexual and have little or no depth." Miraji's poems vanish into sexual ephemera. What this move allows Sadiq to do is to make obscurity disappear by reading Miraji's poetry as useless detritus, debris, and therefore uninteresting allegory.

For Sadiq, if one is to talk about the everyday, the only reasonable way to do it is to go to the language of the everyday, ordinary language. Curled up in Sadiq's call is a charge for linguistic transparency and a one-to-one mapping of subject and language. This is an odd, troubling turn on Sadiq's part, because the period in which Miraji wrote was one in which many poets, like Faiz, were exploring a new allegorical use of earlier poetic (rather than "ordinary") language. So would one toss out all those experiments on political poetry along with Miraji's if one were to follow Sadiq's lines of reasoning? One would also toss out Miraji's straightforward use of language, that in his metaphysical poems like "Jātṛī," "Yagānagat," or "Samundar kā bulāvā," is both straight on quotidian Hindustani and askew, and needs to be read obviously and through *kināyah*.

Sadiq also implies that one is given permission to speak *mub-ham*-ly only if one speaks of the *mub-ham*. But what he can't see is that Miraji does exactly this. A poet is only permitted to create new linguistic forms if he or she speaks of something outside the province of the everyday. There is no allowance in this reading for perspectival shifts within the normal—what Miraji terms, in Sadiq's quote from *Mīrājī kī naẓmeñ*, "degrees of insight."

Sadiq does not even permit the sexual thematics of Miraji's poetry to stand as appropriate indicators of poetic unconventionality. In a quick, facile move Sadiq disposes of instances of unconventionality in Miraji's poetry with the statement, "His preoccupation with it [sexuality] is not a defiant gesture against middle-class morality; it is the direct result of the high place accorded to it by Hindu thinkers." Sexuality or sexualized images, which could be considered unconventional, are in fact relegated to the supraconventional, a reversion to the old, but the old configured through Hinduism rather than Islam. Sadiq closes his 1983 reading of Miraji by saying that the only unconventional poetic acts that Miraji performs are stylistic.

The shift made between the two readings of Miraji by Sadiq is one that is performed on Miraji in many other venues. For example, the two different editions of Miraji's early collection of *naẓm*, *Mīrājī kī naẓmeñ*, have two different prefaces. Although this act of changing the preface could be considered a harmless one, neutral, and on par with a small scribal error, a mere accident of scribal vision, it has serious implications for the readings of the poems that follow. Since the first edition has virtually disappeared from popular circulation (except as archival material relegated to libraries where one needs a letter of authorization to enter, or except in a photocopy form), the new edition and new preface will stand in for it. The replacement reveals a great deal about the direction in which readings of Miraji have headed. The preface in the first edition is about poetry, time, temporality, and reading. Three paragraphs around which the preface circles deal with the issue of reading. One of these is the one Sadiq cites in his 1983 essay on Miraji. Each begins with "Some people say/believe/feel . . ." Each turns to one of three issues with which Miraji then deals: sex, *mub-ham*, and his predilection for writing free verse. (These are also three concerns brought up by Sadiq.)

The newer edition of the poems begins with a piece by Miraji that is possibly the most circulated piece he has ever written—"*Nāmukammal sailf-porṭraiṭ*" (Incomplete self-portrait)—biographical fragments of Miraji's childhood (included in Chapter 1) that speak about Miraji's relationship to his sexuality, sexual awakening, women, the articulation of his sexuality in the act of looking—sexuality as voyeurism. The version of it that introduces Miraji's book has been renamed—from "Incomplete Self-Portrait" to "Miraji." As one reads it with the new title, one forgets its necessary incompleteness and fragmentariness (its piecemeal rendition of autobiography that is necessarily never completed) and it turns from some stories about Miraji to *the* disturbing story of Miraji's gendered relationship to desire, which in turn becomes the metonymy for Miraji's entire oeuvre.

In the change in the preface between the first and second editions of this book of poems, the onus of responsibility for reading is thrown from the readers back onto Miraji. In the first preface Miraji confronts readers with where they might go as readers versed in popular understandings of his work, without giving them a set of tactics with which to read, so he leaves the burden of and the responsibility for reading on his readers. In the second preface, given where it is situated, it is almost as though Miraji (the voice from the grave, the originary voice) were providing a convenient frame (that fits at least some of the readings he says in the earlier preface, readers perform) within which to read the poetry.

Like these other shifts that convert Miraji's work over time, Sadiq's too is a shift that erases the difficulties in Miraji's poetry. One disappearance enacted by Sadiq is that of the question of gender and the attendant questions about sexuality that do not merely restate the obvious. It is quite clear that in both of Sadiq's representations of Miraji there is no possibility of

Miraji speaking either as a woman *bhakta* or, specifically, as Mira. Nor does Sadiq go to Miraji's elaborate evocations of gender when he, Sadiq, talks about Miraji's contemporaries or when he cites Miraji's comments on the poetry of his contemporaries. Rashid is one such instance. In Rashid's work, as Miraji sees it in *Is naẓm meñ* (In this poem), colonialism and gender/desire dance out a complex relation to power. Colonial desire becomes the desire of a European white woman who tries to escape the tribulations of war, *jañg*, that are tearing her worlds apart by traveling across the sea in pursuit of satisfaction. Her quest opens up the desire in colonialism to a desire for resolution, premised on a break in the center that cannot be healed there. Her search demasculinizes Europe, the colonial local is transacted through a feminine imaginary. She offers herself the alleviation of the *pardah*, the enclosure of the feminine, but cannot find herself mirrored there. A masculine symbolic is rendered inadequate to the task of colonization in this poem. Rashid's movements here refuse to concur with the kind of masculinity seen in the narratives of the *Titanic*.

What she, the colonizer, sees and hears instead is the mourning over plunder, lament repeated so that it sediments into foundations, hordes of angry young crowds of raging workers. In Miraji's words:

> The romance of this strange woman's dream, which, at the beginning of this poem, was personal [individual thing], is by the end, an authorization, it authorizes the capacity of, the condition of a social collective. Where, at the inception [of the poem] her "nature" [tribe] wants only to search for a place of rest, by the time it closes, the romance of her dreams becomes a new thing. Hope/desire, which Westerners had (and have had) from the East, but in realizing it, the East seems to hesitate (looks like it is hesitating). The form of that hesitation (the face of that hesitation) carries through (is described) from the beginning of the poem to its middle. Because of this reverence for their own longings, Westerners are facing down their enemies, how can its reflection land in the East (be found in the East). Between East and West is the obstruction/hindrance of a wall of oppression. A wall of color obstructs, impedes, disturbs—knowing its reality this woman appears to the poet as though she were trembling with a murky [*mub-ham*] terror. What sort of terror it is, you ought to consider for yourself.[19]

## RETURN TO AND CONVERGENCE UPON GENDER: POETIC VALENCES

Gendering is not a benign phenomenon.[20] It is tightly woven into the power/knowledge nexus.[21] When Miraji's poetry is read, gendering becomes very complex. When I speak of "gendering" I speak of several layers of assigning gender to particular sites. Into it I place nominal gendering—giving or ascribing generic names (man and woman) and specific names (those given to men and to women). Into it I place what I call cursive positions (pronouns): I, she, and he.[22] Into it I also place those practices of gendering that are not marked as such; for example, certain words for voice, which are gendered in Urdu and whose use in Miraji's poetry play out dynamics of gendering. Into it I place poetic voicings that translate through gender to recall lineages of desiring subjects through whom desire is then angled. Into it I place multiple renderings of gender through time, through other ways in which subjects come to be; in Miraji's case religion, class.[23]

The grammar of gender in Urdu has peculiarities exploited by Miraji in his poetry. The gender of a pronoun is confirmed by another gender marker, something outside it; pronouns need verbs, names, or adjectives to give them gender. When a phrase contains a verb or noun that gives you the direct first person, the verb tells you the gender of the person "doing." If the protagonist of the sentence stays in the third person or in the indirect first person (in an instance when a pronoun is transformed by a postposition *us kā*),[24] it is possible with certain verb forms to fall into what I call "default gendering." Here the gendering impetus does not sit with the pronoun but falls on another grammatical form in the sentence. If there is another available direct noun or pronoun in the sentence or phrase, it couples with the verb to offer a possible gender for it, but if there is no free substantive form, the verb usually takes on the masculine singular form—the default gender position, criticized by feminists who want to offer the feminized singular as a "default." This then becomes the "neutral" position for that pronoun. In the case of a sentence in which the verb falls into a default position, the pronoun (protagonist) does not escape gendering; rather, its gender is assigned contextually, in agreement with what is written or spoken before or after the default verbal position used. This requires the cooperation of a reader or listener who reads or hears a gender in the pronoun. So he, she, or I appears with a gender confirmation that is deferred to other places—to a verb, to another sentence and a reader/listener who allows the pronoun to be read as gendered. Unlike English, gender is always assigned to the cursive pronomial positions through something else; it is always conferred by a relationship instituted through another grammatical form or term, and a reader. So although a place, a thing, a being, is often spoken of as though it were gendered substantively a priori of and irrespective of the grammatical negotiation that confers gender, the grammatical transactions that take place while giving something a gender belie, yet also produce, this substantive assumption.

Miraji exploits these movements in his poetry. In "Taḥrīk" (Movement), for example, the "I" makes its appearance once, as the possessive form *merā*, or mine. *Merā* is written in when the poem changes direction immediately following the oblique possessive pronoun for the beloved, *uskī*. This poem, which brings *ārzū*, longing, into embodiment through landscapes, occludes the gender of the subject feeling. Longing here is not slanted through a particular gendered body, so it floats to lodge where even a reader might bring it. Longing assumes semantic density through embodiment, thickening as emotion condenses, and flows down a body—eyes, hair; glance, eyes, step.

Dūr, ūñche nīle jañgal meñ
kāle, kāle bādal ā'e
ban meñ kālī koy'il bolī
dhartī par haiñ kāle sā'e
us kī kālī rasīlī āñkheñ
us ke kāle, kāle bāl

pās—mere dilke manḍal meñ
dhīre, dhīre uṭṭhīñ āheñ
dukh ke amrut meñ bis gholī
dukh kī tīkhī tez nigāheñ . . .

Far off
In the tall indigo jungle
black, blue-black clouds crowded.

In the forest, a black koel called
black shadows on the ground
black, wet eyes
black, blue-black hair.

Close by
In the center of *my* heart. Slowly
slowly sighs rose
sorrow poisoned the nectar
sorrow's fierce, fiery glances . . .[25]

Gender emerges in eyes and in the gaze; these are weighted through gender.

The opening stanza of the poem could have come from Mira, it could perhaps be Miraji writing as Mira, writing in the patterned lights and shadows of bhakti spaces. Signed by a woman, Miraji, the poem reads through her body. It looks through the feminine gaze, but one that must be read through a deliberate suturing that covers, or skips over the lag, the gap, between poem and signature. So the poem comes to be read as one composed by a woman. Whomever the "I," the "I" who resolves to obliqueness, the eye is feminized. If, however, one rounds the poem's resonant repetitions out through the body of Miraji's biography, as it has been told in most versions, this poem is one whose protagonist might have been masculine. But the protagonist is one whose scenes of yearning and loss and anguish are probably pulled from songs sung in women's voices, and perhaps culled from voices singing through the signature of a woman *bhakta* poet, Mira. These scenes travel lineages of desire, longing for desire, revealing these lineages, without exposing the "I" in any self-evident fashion.

Gendering is not a benign phenomenon. Discussions on it in the past ten years have made this statement almost an inevitable one. These discussions focus on the alignments of power/knowledge, the play and deployment of gender, and the transfer and exchange of gendered bodies in circulation that establish and solidify certain gendered spaces. It is also clear that the operations of gendering are not transparently evident, although the ease with which gender is assigned or assumed makes them seem necessarily so.

In Miraji's case, gendering is a *mub-ham* phenomenon or a *mub-ham* series of phenomena. In order to understand all the movements that call gender out or forth, it is important to make distinctions between different positions where Miraji is implicated—Miraji as the subject of biographical stories; Miraji as the generic author of all his work; the gender of the signature on each poem (if it is not collapsed into the subject of the biography of Miraji); gender of the signatory of each poem (if it is considered the same as the Miraji of biographical narratives); and the gender of the protagonist in a poem, if it has been noted or pointed out.

As I have shown earlier in this section, Miraji is constructed as a male through certain tales—and named a man. It is important to remember what disappears in the telling of the tales: they are narratives in which an author of the biographical tales creates a male author—Miraji. Gendering Miraji is a process that occurs between. It appears to need an apparently unhampered cooperation between the readers of the stories and the narrators of the stories to read the gender of the protagonist as masculinized. Miraji's agreement with the gendering process is also seemingly elicited by the authors of those stories when they tie fragments together, in referring back to stories, poetry, biographical fragments, and letters ascribed to him. Then Miraji is called up as the true "reference" through a series of corroborations. Although the verifying narratives ascribed to Miraji are used as proof, they work as proof only because they are cited as causal, and not merely as causal but as the single point of origin for the series of matrices that gender Miraji. These narratives, like the Mira Sen story, work because they are acceptable gendering stories—that is, they are about unrequited love as encounters between a "man" and a "woman." Citing them as exemplary tales erases competing ones, like letters written by Miraji to Bashir Chard, which lay out other scenarios of unrequited love.[26]

The stories, including those by Sadiq, can only continue to be circulated and read in a certain way if readers collectively continue to read them that way, under pressure from desires that produce nationalist subjects, citizens-to-be, desires that turn to specific valences of ordinariness to make their claims. The reading and construction of Miraji as "male" opens a gap between him and Mira, then, and almost without a pause closes the gap between the female name and the male nominalization of Miraji. The interval between name and author has to be closed so rapidly that the transformation is microscopic; in its immediately visible form it seems not to have even taken place. Reading these stories as I do, at the nexus of collective queries and concerns about marrying gender to sexuality in particular ways, I will ask readers to hold open the pause between name and gender and offer other readings. I may well curdle Miraji's gender around his/her name, despite almost all the stories about him/her.[27]

In the poetry attributed to Miraji, a complex of scenes concerning gender are laid out. Some poems, like "Traveler," have a masculinized "I"; some, like "Rare Waves of Passion," have a feminized "I"; in some, like "Movement," where the subject always appears in an indirect form, the gender of the "I"/protagonist, that "one/respondent" (because they never appear as an "I" or a "he" or a "she") is never made explicit, and gendering in different lines relies on other nouns in the line. If one reads Miraji as masculine in different poems he wrote, the readings sometimes call for a shift, a break, or a gap between the gender of the person to whom the poem is assigned (the gender of the ostensible author) and the gender of the protagonist in the poem. This gender break opens up the process of conflating the author situated in the frame around the poem with the "I"/protagonist of the poem. This is a *mub-ham* situation. If one reads the authorial positions as open and stabilizes the frame, one allows for possibilities of reading that can be very discomfiting. As with Sadiq's second-reading closure of the *mub-ham* space he had opened in his first reading, various strategies are used to close down the gap between the author and "I." One such maneuver is to say that in the case of "Rare Waves of Passion," Miraji the man is writing as a woman, but just for the duration (space-time) of the poem.[28] These strategies bring to the fore the double play of reading in creating both the author of the poem (folding gender into name), and in inserting the author into the poem as the "I" (folding name and gender into the "I").

What are the ramifications of the disjunction created between the author outside the poem and the "I" inside? What if one did leave undecided the gender position of the person outside, and read Miraji into the feminized protagonist's position as a "female" writer? What about those poems in which the "I" is "male" but only with respect to another place that is female or feminized and the relationship between the two is played out in the piece? Would one automatically interpolate a male Miraji into the "I" of the poem or would one make a different kind of closure and leave open the gender of the author, assigning Miraji both positions? What if one left those undecided? What happens in those sorts of undecidabilities? What would the implications be if poems were read with Miraji gendered in both positions? What dynamic does that play out?

Aijaz Ahmad is one reader who assigns Miraji both positions simultaneously.[29] It would take too long to explore Ahmad's strategies and their symptomatic failures in detail here. But it is useful to skim the tenets of his arguments to see where they might lead. His explanations resort to biological and biographical frames outside the poems. He reads Miraji's (the author's) gender as (primary and) masculine and reads into poems with two gendered positions, a doubling, with Miraji the poet dramatizing both genders (as in the poem "There Was a Woman" [Ek thī aurat]). Ahmad sees this doubling as the actualization (embodiment) of a pathological disorder—masturbation/narcissism. This move unveils Ahmad's reading position. Simply stated, his tautological/circular argument goes as follows: "Miraji is crazy; he is crazy because he cannot have a relationship with a woman, and his craziness is externalized in the failure to describe completed relationships with women. So women in Miraji's poems are actually Miraji himself, and poems that depict desire between men and women are only describing Miraji's acts of masturbation." Something that Ahmad never explains is what he believes constitutes a completed or successful relationship between a male position and a female position in a poem. In his short discussion of "There Was a Woman," Ahmad seems to be also saying that the poetic representations of women with whom the "I" conducts relationships that are not incompletely sexual, that is, that are maternal, and with whom the "I" could reverse its positions, are symptomatic of degeneracy. According to Ahmad, the result of Miraji's degenerate poetic explorations is a loss of poetic authority. Ahmad's argument is interesting because it poses Miraji in certain ways—as nonauthoritative, that is as someone who can take either gendered place in his poems. Ahmad's argument is also interesting because it performs or displays Ahmad's anxiety. Ahmad's anxiety about his own desire reveals the possibilities that other readers might encounter within themselves.

Ahmad's opening critique of Miraji—as someone who acts, is theatrical and as someone whom Ahmad sees quite literally slipping between a series of placements—exposes the lineaments of Ahmad's anxieties. According to Ahmad, the characters Miraji becomes in his life perform a mutually transformatory dance with his art. These characters are predominantly male ones. They take on positions and identifications ascribed to certain kinds of male figures. However, when Ahmad begins to read Miraji's poetry, he reads the poet's genders quite differently in the context of his work. Ahmad places Miraji in both the gendered positions available in poems like "There Was a Woman." Ahmad seems to speak of these positions as naturalized appearances of gender rather than as those that appear to play out a drama in the guise of poetic personae like lover and beloved.

In the process of reading Miraji's poetry, Ahmad seems to be negotiating his own identifications with and disidentifications from the poet. These prove to be sites of trouble for Ahmad, perhaps because they are detoured through poetry that is thick with desire and therefore mires Ahmad in unwarranted states of longing. As a straight, homosocial reader, when Ahmad scripts Miraji into both genders in certain poems, and tries to read through that scripting, he finds himself negotiating the fraught terrain of identification through Miraji. Ahmad, like Miraji, ends up discomfitingly balanced between the poet as male who desires, and the poet incarnated as the woman being desired in the poem. If Ahmad reads himself into the place he assigns Miraji as the desiring male, he traps himself in the same masturbatory dilemmas into which he has placed Miraji. Since Miraji is both the "I" who desires and the object of the "I's" desire, when Ahmad desires the woman in poems like "There Was a Woman," he finds himself desiring Miraji. Reading the mess of gender in Miraji's work is not a benign phenomenon for Ahmad. Reading Miraji's work guides Ahmad straight down the path of difficult desire, desire that Ahmad enacts, but needs to repudiate even as he acts it out.

What are the configurations in which the woman and/or "I" appears? Does it only make sense to look at the dynamics of Miraji's poetry from the places engaged by masculine desire or a male gaze? What if one angled the self/other in multiple directions (masculinized, feminized, neutral, unspoken) in such a way that one took the self as feminized in a strong sense into account? What then might one read into Miraji's explorations of gender?

How might one introject colonial subjectivity (the good male subject) into these readings, and into the subjectivities through which Miraji writes (as a not quite man, not quite woman)?

## ENDS OF DESIRE

I would like to look at a series of poems written by Miraji at different times, beginning with "Devadāsī aur pujārī" (Devadasi and pujari). This was one of Miraji's early poems, probably written in Lahore, and published in *Mīrājī kī naẕmeñ*.[30] It is the second in the collection, and was probably composed between 1932 and 1934. It is one of very few poems that Miraji does not fold into categories in his chart.

The poem measures out a dance between a masculinized "I" and a female figure, a *devadāsī*, a courtesan employed as a dancer in a temple. Taken literally, the name *devadāsī* is a compound word that couples *deva*, or God, with *dāsī*, or female slave (the coupling is familiar from bhakti). The poem reads as follows:

> Look, come see a dance, the dance, the undefiled dance of a devadasi
> slowly, slowly sorrow's shadow slipped off my heart
> she measures out her feet, softly, softly, my mind wants
> to become moonlight, extinguished on the floor
> hidden behind a stone pillar I should look at her
> silently, silently realize in wonder that
> like a goddess-statue come to life you are dancing, dancing
> like a forgetful queen of an army of water-sprites descended to earth
> and ripples on water stir so, flicker
> or a restless jungle deer who slithers on leaves
> a cobra/female in a darkened jungle hiss and sway
> like my lusting eyes sliding over her body
> the devadasi stroking the earth, exposes colors
> black, black glittering eyes like lightening dance
> and pearl-diamond jewelry glitter in light like this
> in a high, blue-black sky-canopy, like stars and moon glimmering
>
> when I see
> the fold of her slip taut under her arms
> then should the ordinary thud of my heart
> and my breath sharpen fast
> when ripples flow through the long, loose, limber skirt
> and its swirl subsides

every vein in my mind shudders
a melody of signs pours
coming forward, retreating, arrested, still shuddering carefully
carefully she falls, falling with care
fearful, hesitant, then with pleasure, fearlessly coming forward
let the hesitant boat of dharma roll, my dharma drop

dancing, dancing when [she] tires, tiring when there's confusion
it should take my composure, my peace, my wisdom

then this sweet scene should dissolve
the shadows of the long stone pillar fold themselves around her
like crowding clouds gather lightning into their skirts.

The names in the title that frames the poem are of the two players, a devadasi and a pujari; naming them situates the poem in the space where they might be—the temple. So the title transfers the poem into and unfolds it in a semantic or poetic lineage/space, the "Hindu tradition." The two names/roles are clearly gendered; the pujari, or priest, is male, and the devadasi, or temple dancer, is female. The title folds a reading of this poem into the historical relationship between two ritual performers, both dedicated to a deity that they service, whose *darshan* (vision, or revelation) both seek. The title leads us to the implicit raison d'être of a temple, a divine entity or icon. In idealized interactions between a devadasi and a pujari in a temple, their connections would not be made directly, but through the intermediary, the deity, for whom both performed. But this divine third is never a solvent player, never comes into being as a player in this poem; it remains an empty space, unnamed and not visualized. We never find out whether the divinity is male or female. The poem circles, magnetized, around this empty site.[31]

It opens with a call that is sent outward, not directed by and not located in a caller or a specified someone or something that calls. The call is a general invitation to look, an invitation to enter the body of the poem and gaze upon the dance of the devadasi—"Look, come see a dance, the dance, the undefiled dance of the devadasi."[32]

The temple as a sacred site is one in which looking, *darshan*, is an important part of the exchange between worshipper/devotee and divinity.

*Darshan*, from the verb *drsh*—which connotes to see, to visit, to discern, to perceive, to learn or know, to discover or examine—is the fulcrum of a mutual (two-directional) exchange between devotee and divinity.[33] A devotee does *devadarshan*; enters the space of a temple with appropriate offerings to pay a visit to the presiding deity. A deity responds; giving *darshan*, or an audience, to the devotee. *Dekhnā*, the infinitive form of the first verb in the poem and etymologically related to *darshan*, pulls the poem toward these resonances.

What a viewer, someone who is called to do *darshan* in this poem's space, is invited to peruse as they are enticed toward a scene is not a statue of a deity (the still moment at the heart of a temple) but a dance, a *nāc*, or movement.[34] Only as the rhythms of the first line come to an end does a reader/viewer know the "who" that dances. Until that point, the tug of desire is for a dance, not a person. So what a reader is asked to look at are the variations, aftermaths, transits, or the subtle lyrical steps of danced patterns.

This poem is one in which an arousal is being performed through the secularization of the ritual business of and around *darshan*. *Dekhnā*, the Hindustani verb "to look," is a sort of flattened version of the Sanskrit *dṛsh*; *dṛsh*'s frisson on the tongue is lost as it turns into *dekh*. *Dekh* holds ordinariness in its purview, close by, whereas *dṛsh*, taken into Hindi, or in this case Urdu, might edge semantically into the religious. In this poem, *dekh* looks over the desires that bring the secular to the religious, and vice versa, resignifying the business commonly transacted in temple spaces. The conduits for this resignification are the two figures pointing to the secular precisely because they never come fully into named being in the body of the poem—the temple and the deity. The first, the temple, is alluded to as the tacit site where the looking takes place; the second, the deity, is collapsed through the play of metaphor/simile/likeness into the figure of the devadasi—"like a goddess-statue come to life."

So, *dekhnā* performs here as something that is not quite *dekhnā* and not quite *darshan*, although it calls up some of the registers of both. What does *dekhnā* do? What resonances from its implicit siting/citing in the disappeared body of the temple does it carry with it? What does the verb "seeing" carry with it when what is to be looked at is movement or a dance, and not a thing or a body in stasis? Where or how would gender work in this recital of the activity of looking?

My contention is that the verb *dekhnā*, and the noun, *nāc*—the movement that is to be looked at—are not references to "reality" (though they circle around absent/present divinity appearing here perhaps as an incarnation of the Lacanian Real). Neither refers to a performance in a literal temple or to a "real-life" performance by a "genuine" devadasi who engages with the "true" desire of a watcher called to look. So what is the act of looking? In order to see what one, as a reader, is expected to look at, one must avoid the lure the title throws out—the promise of stability brought by naming—and reach toward the play of the grammar in the poem, which undermines the stability held out by those names.

The gender demarcations of the title, female for *devadāsī* and male for *pujārī*, are not maintained in the first three lines of the poem. The two opening lines have no direct subject; nor do they have a direct pronoun, an "I," "he," or "she" whose gender is disclosed. In this poem, the "I," "he," or "she" are indirect possessive pronouns and therefore concealed. The gender of the verb and the activity performed by it is given through the noun attached to/possessed by the indirect pronoun. The two nouns are the "dance" *of* the devadasi and the "shadow" of the heart *of* the "I." The devadasi—although the word itself is considered a gendered name—and the following "I" (or "my"), strictly speaking, are ungendered.

The opening moves of the poem evoke sets of correspondence between two movements that are effects of or assigned to two different pronomial positions. The dance of the devadasi is layered against the shadow/sorrow/heart of the "I." As the poem progresses and the genders of both positions (the *devadāsī* and the "I") are unveiled in the third and fifth line, correspondences are drawn between a "she" and a masculine "I." As one reads the poem, it is clear that the two positions, the "I" and the devadasi, are mobilized differently. Unlike the devadasi, who is named in the opening line, the "I" is never given, never designated as a named person in the body of the poem, its movements never ascribed to a *pujārī*. Its collapse into the name *pujārī* of the title is assumed but never made clear. The edges of the rift between the "I" and the *pujārī* may be slid together so that the pujari becomes the protagonist of the poem, but this closure does not *have* to occur.

The "I" initially invited into the lyrical by the *dekhnā* (by the call to look which unfolds the poem) slowly (*dhīre, dhīre*) gains a sort of thickness, through its looking (looking as touching) and as the poem burrows deeper into the body through its evocative emotional valences (veins shuddering). As long as it is not obvious that the "I" is male (indirect possessive pronoun), its activity (like that in "Taḥrīk") is displaced onto the subtle play of a shadow on its heart, but the tense is clear—it has the translucent crispness of the narrative past. When the "I's" gender comes into focus as male, through a direct pronoun, its limbs begin to move as though of their own accord, rather than urged on by something else, a shadow that belongs to the "I." However, the moment this happens and the "I" begins to feel, to conduct itself without something like a shadow mediating its movements, everything the "I" does, longing, going, looking, is guided through the subjunctive—*cāhe, jā'e, dekhūñ*. So its activities never come clear when they might, and the "I" travels the murky realm of the subjunctive, the potential, the possible, or the if-then. Though it is not a tense that can be comfortably and fluently translated into English grammar, the subjunctive in Urdu/Hindi offers a clearly demarcated temporal space.

Once it is gendered male, the "I" circulates in a precisely outlined temporal space, but is not situated on a time line stretching out between past, present, or future. The "I" operates outside these particular lineaments of linear temporal fixing/fixity. So the fixity/fixing of gender here is undone by the fluidity sanctioned by the subjunctive. The poem plays with this tautness between fluidity and fixity. Being in the subjunctive, desire comes to be as possibility. Tight up against this versification of desire is the allure embodied in the gaze, given substance through looking. Looking fixes, sticks down the place from whence it comes. So the places of the "I" shuttle between the possible and the sort of certainty that is constantly deferred (though fixed).

Returning to the dance, the place where the poem begins, *pavitra nāc ik devadāsī kā* (the undefiled dance of devadasi), I ask: What is the dance? Why is it *pavitra*, or sacred, holy, undefiled, clean, sanctified by ceremonial acts, purifying? Is the purity of the dance an allusion to sex that is withheld? Probably not, for the dance appears to be sexualized. The few moments in the poem when the figure of the dancer is brought into focus are moments when the grain of the images turns sexual—"the fold of her slip taut under her arms." But even as the dance seen as a sexual one almost petrifies its reading, its fastenings are unloosed. The poem breaks open the process of reading it, and the dance, with the word *pavitra*.[35] The subjunctive, the if-then, swirls out the rhythms of the poem, so that they can be seen synchronously as both sexual and *mub-ham*.

What then might a *mub-ham* reading of this poem be? The lines that draw the poem to a close offer such an alternative reading. The simile which ends the poem—"like crowding clouds gather lightning into their skirts"—folds the shadows thrown by the architectural space in which the dancer dances around her. "Crowding clouds" gather the temple, the place where the dance is, into the poetic metaphoric space called out in the last line: that of the Sanskrit-Braj lyric lineage. The dancer and the dance are both formed from that lyric past and written back into it.

What role does, then, the dancer play? Where does watching the dancer lead us, as readers? The dancer becomes a kind of interface for the poetics of reading. She tells us little about the representation of women (in general). Rather than producing a reading of representation, she produces a representation of reading. Introduced with "she measures out her feet," she comes to life in a drummed invocation of similes—"like a goddess-statue, like a forgetful queen, like a restless jungle deer, like a cobra-female." Wrapped into a lyric space, she throws a textual shimmer which unveils colors under a lusting reading gaze that slides over her body. She is the text measuring out similes as she is read. Through the dancer the poem speaks a desire that unwraps the longings, and the hunger, at the heart of reading poetry (*jinsī* and *mub-ham*).

Reading the dancer as text offers insights, glimpses into Miraji's understanding of the practices of reading. Reading builds similes as it moves through textual time-space. Similes, the words connected by *jaise* in the poem, do not demand the difficult metaphoric collapse between the two elements that are compared. The "like," or *jaise*, that couples the words of a simile opens a space between the object described and the image to which it is hitched. In this poem, that interval is held between what is read (body of the dancer) and the reading (body of the text). The reading, the description of the dancer, is created in a pairing fueled by desire (however held in abeyance) for the text/woman. The text, however, is only exposed in the guise of the similes forged by reading. Another way of saying this is that the text is covered, clothed in images/similes that assume shape as one reads. But the poem tells one nothing about an "authentic/original" text that might lurk or linger under the clothes, or even whether any such entity exists, and what dimensions it/she might have. The text/body that sits behind the shifting readings is only available as the afterimage of practices. This shadowing, the blanking out of a "text," rerouting it through the nuances of the couplings danced during reading, occasions an important theoretical gesture. "Reading" in this poem gives you only a poem invoked in the similes a reader makes as they are drawn toward it. It also gives a reader the possible color, shadows occasioned by reading here, which can be seen only after space-times that came before (narrative past) and are only glimpsed in the space-times that hold the "if-then" open.

Reading in this poem is gendered movement. The places offered the reader/spectator are those of a male "I" and those given the text feminized. But both places are constantly contingent ones. The conditions for contingency, however, are different in both cases. Reading positions (those of the "I") are kept fluid through their grammar—that is, the tenses of the verbs in which they come to be—whereas read positions (those of the text) are kept fluid by mediating image shifts through similes. The desire for what you look at is thrown out through the subjunctive "if, then," and through a series of "like, as." Reading here is not an accretion of continuities that settles into past, present, and future, not an accumulation that sediments into a series of *A* or *B* or *C*. The if-then (when-then) and like-as keep the patterns of reading in motion—"if this were the case, and *A* were like *B*, then . . ." The poem does not sit in ontologies, the being of things; it is roves through sight. Its verb is not "is" but "look/gaze/see/peruse/perceive." As you read you traverse the spaces from a narrative past, or a present, into a series of iterations that hold the verb "to see" open. So the poem seduces readers to come into it through a promise of a "now" you will see, a promise of a future. As readers go into the poem's future they find themselves seeing intimately (familiarly yet dense with wonder): "when the girl is in this place like a statue come to life . . ." The "I" that looks at a "her" conjures into an "I" that looks at "you": a you that, when you are like this wonderful thing, I may see; "I" as desire will course through my entire being. What I may look upon is like an expanse which if it were thrown open, is like a slip, if it were drawn taut, tightened. How does Miraji's invocation of fetishism in his self-portrait, which gives also readers a view into his practices of reading, figure here in this particular rendition of holding open?

The question of where Miraji (author, signatory) is placed has been answered indirectly as I traveled through a reading of the poem. Miraji's work (author's corpus) is embodied here as the dancer. This binding of dancer and poetic corpus is borne out by Miraji himself in several pieces where he calls poetry the "women" in his life. The name Miraji, appended to any poem, is never brought into its world unless a reader chooses to close the gap between the poet and the "I" within the poem. My reading places me in the position of the masculinized "I," and the poem in the position of the dancer whom I am called to see. The implications of inserting me into a poem as a masculinized reader are somewhat troubling. They make me uneasy, reminding me of the ways that Ahmad was disturbed as he wrote about Miraji. But against the grain of my discomfort with this place is my awareness that a reader for whom the collapse of gender is less marked (female to male) can also be made uncomfortable if they put themselves in the position of the "I" (especially if they are a reader who demands that Miraji be read into the poem), for they too have to deal with a dilemma. They traffic in a sexual encounter with a figure situated between two genders, a trafficking which pulls into its purview all that is implied by a (homoerotic or complex heteroerotic) desire for a male/female poet.

## SEA/GENDER AND READING

"Call of the Sea" was first published in *Tīn rañg* (Three tones) in 1968, about twenty years after Miraji's death. *Tīn rañg* culled poetry from three genres—*naẓm*, ghazal, *gīt*. The published edition was based on the version that Miraji arranged as a book for which he did the *kitābat*, frontispiece, and table of contents. The published collection contained a few more poems than the one in Miraji's papers and was organized slightly differently than the manuscript.[36] In both Miraji's and the published versions, the *naẓm* were arranged alphabetically—according to the Urdu alphabet—but instead of beginning with "Ābgīne ke us pār kī ek shām" (A night on the far side of the wine glass), the published version began with a poem that was not included in Miraji's, "Ajantā ke g̱haur" (Ajanta caves). The reordering of the *naẓm* in the published versions of *Tīn rañg* has certain aesthetic and critical intonations. That the volume could be reorganized raises questions about the understanding prevalent at the time when it was published, of the status of the "book" and the relationship between a "book" and its ostensible author.

"Call of the Sea" was probably written in the 1940s, either in Poona or Bombay. Its incarnation in *Tīn rañg* was not its only published appearance; it has also been included in exemplary collections of Miraji's poems that accompany articles on him. Its most recent form is in *Kulliyāt-e mīrājī* (The complete works of Miraji) (1988). One of Miraji's few *naẓm* translated into English, it accompanies others in *An Anthology of Urdu Poetry* (translated by Bakht and Jaeger), but it was first published before Miraji's death. According to Miraji's notes on his manuscript of *Tīn rañg*, "Call of the Sea," like most of the other *naẓm* in his manuscript, had already been published in a journal (in this instance in *Shahkār* [Masterpiece], Lahore).

This poem is like many other *naẓm* in that it is visually complex. It splays across pages, using spacing to dramatize sound and breaks in meaning. Unlike "Traveler"—of which I have already spoken, which has, in the Urdu version, a very simple visual format, a continual stream of words broken only by punctuation—"Call of the Sea" is blocked off into pieces, each one marked by a period or question mark and a space. So the spaces between two images, between hunks of words, punctuated sometimes by a period after the first image, need to be read into "Call of the Sea."

Rather than being read as a stream of words modulated by meter, "Call of the Sea" can be read along clusters of images, each held apart from another by a hiatus in time, visualized as a gap in space. If the poem is scanned quickly, many of the clusters of images resolve into graphic sets of dialogue and recall or capture the spatial temporality of film. Shifting the spaces, eliding or deleting them, is like superimposing two frames in a movie. Taking the spacing out produces other visual compositions, blends voices, so that one gets another translation, something created as a density when the moments between words are respoken. The poem demands the opaqueness of translation, calls for a translator accountable to their reading as the poem's afterlife. Since the poem is about reading, transforming its terrain changes the metaphysics of which it speaks.

Every published version of "Call of the Sea," including the one in *Tīn rañg*, rewrites the spaces between images, none conforming to Miraji's manuscript. "Call of the Sea" incites questions about reproducibility and repetition in an economy of scribal / mechanical reproduction. One version of the spacing, however, is sometimes explained away as scribal error. That is, it could be explained as a *mistake* made by someone who copied the poem down without reading it. Miraji's handwritten version of the poem sprawls over two pages, and unless one assumes that a period is usually followed by a space, it is conceivable that the image on the first page which is closed off by a period could be run into the one after it on the next page. This is precisely the decision made by one "translator."

Another transformation that occurs between different versions of the poem is the conflation of two words that are lexically continuous—*ṣadā* and *nidā*.[37] Both are words used for voice, noise, or sound but the primary meanings of each are different. *Ṣadā* is used for echo (or invitation to a wedding) and *nidā* for a call (a call to prayer, an invocation, or a voice from heaven). In a poem that plays off the images of a mirror and mirroring and throws images up against the oral/aural call and its echo/response, the play of call and echo is essential to any reading. Again, a shift—this time of an innocuous mirrored word—is a rereading of the poem. Blending the two words merges the voices in a call-response sequence. Miraji's poetics lean on space, distance, intervals, and the transactions between aural and visual, so sifting them into different combinations gives a translation or a reading of this poem another cast.

If one goes back to the chart discussed earlier in this chapter, many supposedly sexual poems could have alternative, *mub-ham* readings. In the chart, some poems are "merely sexual" and others are *mub-ham*. These *mub-ham* readings are occasionally metacritical in that they review the process of reading as one reads through a poem. "Call of the Sea," like the *devadāsī* poem, is probably *mub-ham*, and could perhaps offer a sight-line into reading.

### *Reading "Call of the Sea"*

"Call of the Sea" enacts a series of relationships: between creating and reading or reading and what is read; between voices that come from another place and the place to which they come; between something that can be given a voice and something that cannot; between visual and oral representation. These various relationships, however, cannot, as I have attempted to do in the previous sentence, be pulled apart from each other and described as separate. So, in this poem the relationship between creating and reading is entangled with all the others. The process of giving a voice is spoken into reading as well as creating.

> These whispers say, "Come quickly,
> calling you again and again for years
> a deep tiredness has worn-out my heart."
>
> Echoes, ephemeral, lingering, are heard.
> But this strange voice keeps coming.
> Calling again and again has never tired anyone,
> and probably never will.
>
> "Dear child!" 8
> "I love you so!" 9
> "Look, if you do this 10
> I'll be furious!" 11
> "Oh God, oh God!" 12
>
> At times a sob, a smile, or a fleeting frown.
> But these echoes have kept on coming.
> Through them a brief life mingles with eternity.
> But this strange voice, worn-out by fatigue
> threatens to drown every echo.
>
> Now no eye flickers
> no face smiles
> nor frowns
> only ears listen.
>
> This is a rose garden—a breeze ripples,
> buds burst open,
> spread their perfume
> bloom again and again, wither
> and drop.
> They make a velvet carpet on which the fairies of my desires
> saunter with a rare elegance.
>
> The garden's like a mirror
> in which every form is reflected,
> adorns itself

and dissolves
never to reappear.

This is a mountain—silent, tranquil,
A spring bubbles, asks, "What's on the other side of this
rocky crag?"
But the mountain's skirt is enough for me.
There's a valley in the skirt,
a river flows through it.
There's a flowing boat in it
a boat that is a mirror.
Every form is reflected in the mirror,
but when it dissolves
it never reappears.

This is a desert—vast, parched, leafless.
Its whirlwinds are the embodied reflections
of violent demons.
But I'm far away.
My eyes are glued to a clump of trees.

Now there's no desert,
no mountain,
no rose garden;
now no eye flickers,
no face smiles,
nor frowns,
only a strange echo says, "Calling you again and again
a deep tiredness has worn out my heart."

Calling again and again has till now never tired anyone,
and probably never will.
So then this voice is a mirror,
and only I
am tired of calling.

No desert,
no mountain,
not even a garden,

now only the sea calls out to me
everything comes from the sea and must return to it.[38]

Like "Devadasi and Pujari," "Call of the Sea" opens into the space of a call. This voice calls directly out to an unidentified person or place. The first line offers no clues that give you the identity of the speaker, that tell you who the speaker is or where they might be. The only information about either the addresser or the addressee is extended by the adjective that modulates the texture of the voice that is calling, and the pronoun, "you," at whom the call is directed. The texture whispers, is gendered feminine, and it is to the whispers that this call is attributed—"these whispers say." The opening voicing in the poem can be framed by and read through its title, "Call of the Sea." Although the first line gives you no material about who/what is calling and who/what is being called, the title has already set up an expectation about the place from which or the thing from whom the call will come—the sea.

If the poem is read quickly, the hiatus between the title and the first line is likely to be effaced, but it is important to keep their separation in mind. The act of bringing together *samundar* and *sargoshiyāñ*, sea and whispers, is not a benign one. It is a gesture that subsumes one thing to another so that both give up the separation between them. The poem plays with this separation between voicing and mirroring, between sound and nominalization.

The space between the two is augmented by the different genders of the words for sea and for whispers. *Samundar*, or sea, is masculine, and whispers, or *sargoshiyāñ*, feminine. So when the title is read into the opening line of the poem, the femininized voice of whispers speaks for the masculine sea; alternatively, when the unidentified feminized voice that calls it is given an identity in the context of the title, its identity is a masculine one, that of the sea. The masculine sea speaks because it is read into that place, for feminine whispers; when the sea speaks, it speaks with a feminized voice and from a feminized position. This conflation between a sea that calls but does not speak and a voice that calls through the content of its words anthropomorphizes the sea and familiarizes it. Anthropomorphization is, to use Paul de Man's words, "an identification on the level of substance."[39] In "taking one entity for another," in this case an entity that is nonhuman for one that is human, anthropomorphization (through the process of identification) makes something that is other or outside, and therefore inaccessible, something familiar, similar, and accessible. In this poem, something is made familiar through gender; this comes about when something speaks that may not or should not have this power; it takes place when a texture of voice is "read" into nature—for example, whispers for sea. Reading transforms by gifting the sea with voice, feminizing its speaking. But the sea, if it is slid into voicing, is not conferred a mouth, an eye, a mask, or a face; it is not endowed with a body coming to be as it grows through an expansion of tropes, but like the Sappho who speaks for Miraji in "Prophecy from Another Time," sea becomes a voice, a call from an elsewhere.

*The Sea*

The poem is framed by the title "Call of the Sea." The pervasiveness of the frame, as hegemonic, is intensified by the light syllabic meter that lies under the poem like a base line, a flowing sequence of a short syllables succeeded by two long ones. The quick sharp short syllable chased by prolonged long ones echoes waves, rising slowly and slapping down, only to withdraw and resurface. The wave drift is thickened by the softened sibilance of words, *sa*, *shi*, which have no hard-edged retroflexes to jar the metrical flow, "*yah sargoshiyāñ kah rahī hain . . .*" The sea's pulling undertow sifts the words through it inexorably, demanding to be attended.

Miraji is a poet attuned to sound; he uses sound to occasion sensuous aural effects, by underscoring or playing against possible meanings in a poem. As with most other Urdu poetry composed in the twentieth century, his poems are meant to be heard, rolled in the mouth, and read visually off the page. The slow, wavelike wash of the poem pauses at certain moments. When this poem is read aloud, the breaks and meter both transform how it feels in the mouth. The only moments at which metrical- as well as meaning-enjambment occur are those when a scene is being assembled—the garden, the continuous stream of comments in the beginning of the poem—when the flow of sound weaves the sinuous, incessant pictures or voices into a whole. Pauses demarcate one picture from another, but they do not really disturb the wash of the metrical wave. As one listens to the poem, the sound of the sea becomes the dominant base over which all the notes of other sounds in the poem are played. The base gains volume as the poem moves on, and these possibilities are crystallized in the final lines of the poem. The images and sounds of the poem dissolve into the sea whose call introduces/frames their production—a sea in the face of which every voice and image is ephemeral, fleeting: "now only the sea calls out to me / everything comes from the sea and must return to it."

Because of the expectations spawned by the syntactic and formal organization of the poem, "Call of the Sea" is read in for each *voice* and *echo* in the poem. Identifications in this poem are made like filmic ones. The spaced movement of seemingly disconnected, perhaps even incoherent tropes and voices following one another when one reads the poem off the page, or listens to it as music in time, allows identifications through the contiguity of two movements. Though the poem never explicitly connects voice and image, when a voice is followed by a picture the aural turns visual because voice and image chase one another. Pronouns, too, are coupled not because they appear in the space of the poems, but because a specific noun or pronoun can be slid into the place of something unspecified—the You can become an I, because the "I" is never specified. Not until the end of the poem are voices or echoes attributed to anyone or anything. By this sleight of reading, the sea as the only identified element that speaks (calls) can be read into the poem whenever unidentified voices or echoes appear. In the interim, the poem has floated through voices and spaces that are read through metamorphoses of reflection: like a mirror, is a mirror, embodied reflections.

As the poem progresses, "voices" and "spaces" are gathered, collected, then sometimes scattered and reclaimed into something different than themselves. The retrieval is performed by turning a voice or a space into either an echo or a mirror. As a reflective surface or as a returned voice, the surface or voice becomes whatever presumably stands before it. In the lines "The garden's like a mirror" or "a boat which is also a mirror," when the garden or the boat mirror or reflect, the reader (whose gaze outlines the limits penciled in to draw, in each case, a particular and different object [garden/boat]), slides inward from the frame, curling into the limits to focus on the forms reflected within the edges of the mirror. These forms, those seen in the mirror but never outside of it, are precisely without special form; each emanation of them in a mirror is repeated as the same, "every form is reflected." Their identity, the quality that makes these reflections what they are, is that they disappear never to reappear.

Mirroring is a curious process in this poem because it is a process that never shows you what is outside. What you see as you look into a mirror is reflection. If you wish, you can name this an outside, but the outside is only what can be seen in the mirror. Standing before the mirror gazing in, then, gives you only what you see. To posit the mirror as an outside, then, is to perhaps see through the mirror to the other side. To ask to look for something outside may be to say that this is the after-effect of an origin that stands before. In the metaphysics of this poem, this kind of after-effect would require a certain deformation, an awkward visual twisting of time and space to produce the before as a prior, as an origin, and as a thing that is in front of the mirror. Since mirrors cannot hold the forms reflected in them, so that the forms can be stilled into stopped pictures or photographs, by the time a reader twists around to bring the origin into view, the form in the mirror has already dissolved, never to reappear. And another scene takes its place in the poem, yet another entanglement with mirroring. Is this what Miraji believes to be the play of language?[40] For there is no "I" so far in the poem; it is a *silsilah* of voices and scenes.

When does the "I" appear in the poem? Only upon several returns to the mirror, each return bringing the mirror closer in, carrying mirroring closer to the scene. The first incarnation of the mirror follows the rose garden: a garden that consummates itself in a voluptuous successive flowering of smell that drops down to the ground to make a velvet carpet on which the fairies of my desires (*merī ārzū'oñ kī pariyāñ*) stroll with a strange/unusual/rare elegance. This garden is *like* a mirror. The second coming of the mirror is at the heart of a scene, a mountain, a valley, a river, and on the river is a flowing boat. A boat that absorbs into itself the quality of the water in which it flows. *Bahanā*, flowingness, makes the boat a paronym of its scene, a partial translation of the places it traverses, of the locales through which it is supposed to move. This boat *is* a mirror. The "is like" and the "is" are the words that strap the frame's form (*gulistān*, rose garden, and *nā'o*, boat) to the mirror. As the poem takes the relation of mirroring to scene from "is like" to "is," from establishing a simile to speaking paronymic metaphor, the act of mirroring is more intimate to the scene. The poem goes from a place in which the mirror and frame are held apart from each other, the gap and interval between them sustained by "like." This frame, the garden, is one that outlines the scene that plays out in it, a scene where desire walks through time that blooms and fades away. Once the poem arrives at the boat, the frame/boat which "is" the mirror is in the scene, is so deeply sunk in to its scenario that it has filtered the substance of its components into itself. The next appearance of the mirror is not as a mirror at all. By now the frame has fallen away, and the poem seems to have reached deep into the space of the mirror to open onto a spread out *phailā hū'ā*, desert, *ṣaḥrā*, *ḳhashk*, *be barg*. This is a scene seen through its desiccation, its not having. Here the whirlwinds are embodied reflections, demonic desires, and the "I" comes into focus for the first time: "I am far away."

The final act of reflection or echoing is performed by the "I" of the lines—"Calling has never till now tired anyone, / and probably never will."[41] So this voice must be a mirror and only I am tired." These words signal a return to the call/echo with which the poem opened, and recalls their cyclical reappearance over the course of the poem:

(1) These whispers say (are saying),[42] "Come, come now,
calling you again and for years
a deep tiredness has worn-out my heart."

Echoes, ephemeral, lingering sound/ have been heard
[*sunī haiñ* (who has heard not included)]
but this strange voice keeps on (is coming) . . .
Calling again and again has never tired anyone
and probably never will.

(2) At times a sob, a smile, or a fleeting frown.
But these echoes keep on coming,
through them a two-day life meets eternity (in the future)

But this strange voice worn-out by a deep tiredness
threatens to drown every echo.

(3) Only a strange echo says (is saying),
"Calling you again and again,
a deep tiredness has worn-out my heart."

Calling has never till now tired anyone
and probably never will.

So, then this voice is a mirror
and only I
am tired.

(4) "Dear child!"
"I love you so!"
"Look, if you do this
I'll be furious!"
"Oh God, oh God!"

In the first (1) and second (2) repetition of the voices and echoes two temporal events are described. The first event enacted in the poem, the whispers speaking, is in the present progressive tense, a syntactic form used to describe an ongoing activity. Because this event—"calling you again and for years"—is in progress, it describes an unchanging call that stretches from the past into the present of the poem without duration written into it, and is not understood as transient or mutable. It is a call from a beyond. It is an anterior call whose voice, seducing through "come," is in the guise of a familiarity wanting to draw you to it. In the second event, the time-bound echoes, unlike the whispers, are described as located firmly in the past—"have been heard"—and as ephemeral, though lingering. If, however, echoes like "a sob, a smile, or a fleeting frown" perform in the present progressive tense—"keep on coming"—they help a "two-day life" meet future eternity. So, despite their transient status they are thus permitted access to an ongoing, atemporal state. What gifts them transience or time-boundness while also giving them the being of beyond death? Is this the kind of temporality that begins elsewhere, beyond the time of a line, that cannot return to a point of departure, even as voices/echoes eventually arrive into a temporality that assigns them a past? The call/echo sequence, timed as it is through differential temporalities (the continuous and the past) seems to never quite place voice in time, even though it is anterior (as prior). Echoes gain time, drift in time, as they emerge, so they appear not to carry with them a sense of something that has been lost in the transition they have made from call to echo. They live somewhere in the tones between whisper and calling.[43]

In the Urdu, a metrical sequence that carries over fuses the series of spoken moments in lines 8–12 (4) into a narrative chain. This voice or these voices are framed by sentences (sequences 1 and 2) that allow them to be read as echoes, or as "mirrored back" voices. Conflated with "a sob, smile, or fleeting frown," and the direct speech in lines 8–12, echoes become a series of events enacted in the *present* of the poem. They are presented as speech that stands on its own, even though, as echoes, they perhaps rely upon the voice sent out and returned so that they are mirrored back; that is, they are a reflection of something else. What, then, makes them echoes rather than an autonomous voice or call, and how is it that these echoes make a "two-day life meet eternity"? Finally, what is one to make of the relationship of voice to echo where the *anokhī nidā*, strange/wonderful/rare voice, a voice from the beyond, "threatens to drown every echo"? Is there a connection, a symbiosis between this *anokhī* voice and the *anokhe phūl* we saw in "Jātrī"?

Lines 8–12 can be read as a series of responses to someone's actions, and if spoken by a single voice could be a series that gets ever more pungent and angry—progressing from affectionate teasing to despairing rage. If these voices are echoes, what makes them echoes? Because none of the sentences have direct pronouns the gender of the voice/voices is not clear.[44] The sentences spoken by the voices are short, punctuated by commas (incomplete breaks, perhaps pauses), and culminate in an exclamation. They push into the present, the possibility of doings, goings on that are absent and that are told here merely as a sequence of responses. They begin by enunciating, naming a child, then speak the if-then (through emotion, rage), and finally seem to image the possibility of the fulfillment of the if-then—if you do . . . then I will be angry, Oh God . . . !

The empty space of the actions (never described) to which the voice/voices respond can be filled in by a reader, as the readerly version of an if-then. If the voice here is the voice of this character in a family drama, then this is what the drama portends. When I first read them, their content seemed to provoke me into seeing in them the voice of a mother reacting to a deliberately mischievous child. But if they are understood as maternal voices, from where might they come? Are they from the poet's past, the poet's beyond (his grandmother, mother, or his sister) or is the sequence an echo, Miraji's voice (transmuted into very special feminized one)? Are the voice/voices even female?

The voices speak a disjunction between love, a love that is full, complete, "*mujhe tum se kitnī muḥabbat hai,*" and anger that pulls the one speaking away from the child, the *pyāre*, the loved one spoken to here. At times a smile, a sob, a fleeting frown, a face takes shape in its changes—after which we return to echoes. Through the echoes that chase these voices, a brief life mingles with eternity. These voices that circle and then pull apart have no mirror near them; they assume no relationship to mirroring. If they are the voices that articulate the separations of childhood, whether from a mother or a father, the mirror that might reflect the separations comes after, broken apart from the voices by three other movements of lyric. The specular shows itself almost shyly, briefly here as a face.[45] Is this the voice, the shy face, of an other? Is this an other who must have no gender if it is to be understood as another person whose speaking comes from nowhere?

By the time the poem has ended, two separate regions—that of the "I" and that of the sea—have been mapped out, with the sea (the final arbiter) as the privileged territory. "Voice" as "echo" is left with the "I" and thus separated from the "call" of the sea, and by the close of the poem the sea that calls is voiceless. But this identification (sea with voicelessness) is new in the poem, because, until all voice was finally claimed by the "I" (the only voice that did not turn into an echo), the sea might have assumed all the voices speaking. When the sea is in a subject/object dialectic with the "I," the sea is the locus of power. The sea also has been given a temporal quality different from the "I"—the "I" is transient and the sea is not. What work is being done by this realization/process, which consists of both attributing voice and having voice taken away?

Death, dissolving into that sea that carries the bodied poem on, is not avoided here by handing out a stable temporality to any of the figures in the poem. The ironic consciousness ("I") realizes that it has not eluded death by identifying with nature/sea and borrowing its temporal continuity, or by borrowing its voice from the beyond. Instead, the "I" seems to somehow have contained the sea by giving it its temporality.[46] This awareness of the possibility of borrowing something from somewhere else creates mirrors where desire is activated, makes things over in its own image (even when the "I" has not happened), to give something a quality it did not possess. When the echo becomes the call, the call is treated to a commentary in the voice of the "I": "And I am tired of calling, I am the voice and the echo, and my voice is a mirror." Only then does the voice become a mirror and exchange the quality of its auralness with the visuality embodied in the mirror.

Just as the call of the sea frames and is thus read for unidentified voices or echoes, the sea is also read for three landscapes that appear in the poem. The poem has three consecutive visual scenarios that are introduced by the three words garden, mountain, and desert, which name landscape genres. Each scenario opens with a sentence that designates and authorizes—"*This* is a garden, *This* is a mountain," and so on. The clause "this is" carries with it an inviolable epistemological certainty.

The visual potential contained in each landscape genre word is actualized when the scenes that follow them unfold. The scenes contain oral or other sensory activities, but these activities, subsumed under the visual, are used to reinforce the pictorial content of each landscape. Each scenario ripens without undermining the confidence of the opening line. In the space created for and by each scene the activities and personae are described in the same assured timbre, as though the scene were being viewed and recorded by an objective eye/I. The texture of their elaboration allows each landscape to be read as a possible depiction of an "ontologically real place." One could call each a mirror image or mimetic representation of a "real" scene from "nature." What is the relationship of the word "sea," used in the title, and these landscapes? When "sea" as a type of landscape is reread into the poem in the context of the other landscapes, it carries the possibility that it too might be an image. So, the "sea," too, for a mere moment, can be evoked as specular. The sea becomes a mirror that can dissolve each scene. The connections between the final image of a mirror and mimesis (the act of mirroring producing language, the act of mirroring coming closer and closer to the "I" until the "I's" voice becomes a mirror) that this imaging of the sea provokes move mirroring in this culminating event from an act of representation to an act of mystical dissolution.

For readers of twentieth-century Urdu poetry familiar with the discussions on socialist realism, visually depicted landscapes and the words that evoke them carry a representative charge and function.[47] Readers of Miraji's poetry often expect these landscapes to represent the ontological object "nature." This expectation is one that haunted the readings of Miraji's poetry. "Reality" was, for Miraji, mediated by language. Miraji felt that the "reality-loving" poets did not reveal "reality"; rather, they produced a representation (perhaps an image in a mirror framed by the spaces of their poetry) that they called the "real."

Commentators on Miraji's poetry are ambivalent about whether the landscapes in it are, in fact, mimetic. Both Wazir Agha, in the article "Miraji: One Example of Earth-Worship,"[48] and N. M. Rashid, in an interview with Carlo Coppola, speak about landscape imagery in Miraji's poetry as having two sources: "real nature" and images from lyric traditions. Both commentators face the same dilemma—how to fit Miraji's poetry into the aesthetic norms of the PWA, just as the narratives about Miraji's body and voice had to conform to biography in some seamlessly naturalized way. But the landscapes in "Call of the Sea" can hardly be called a transparent representation of "nature." Whether the provenance of these images is the Urdu lyric tradition, or Miraji's other poetry, what a reader has to contend with are the implications of dissolving them into a mirror that does not reflect the "reality" but may cohabit with the Lacanian Real.

## *MUB-HAM* READINGS

I would like to return to mirroring, multiple Miras, and *mub-ham*. Both mirroring and gendering are *mub-ham* phenomena. Mirroring is linked to gendering in very complex ways, and neither are benign phenomena. Treating them as benign obscures other ways in which they might work and renders them *mub-ham*.

When he evokes mirrors/echoes in "Call of the Sea," Miraji challenges the transparency and the literal visualness of mimesis as it is used by the group of poets he calls the *ḥaqīqat parastī* (reality-loving/Progressive) poets. Blurred by the recourse to natural or true depictions of life are the acts of translation and mediation performed when "reality" is depicted. Miraji's description of the Progressives functions a little like a "straw man." The "reality-loving" poets provide reading positions against which Miraji writes, and his portrayal of them is more an articulation of general polemical positions held by the PWA, rather than a reference to the specific practices of any one poet (whose work often belied the injunctions attributed to the PWA). Miraji needs a simplistic representation of "reality-loving" because as an interpretive (rather than creative) practice it becomes the criterion by which Miraji's poetry is judged. In poems like "Call" Miraji asks readers to thematize mirrors as frames that reflect interpretive tenets and synchronous reading practices rather than to understand them as conventional (mimetic) representations of "nature." In this context, where mirroring seems transparent, and its meaning taken for granted, Miraji's uses of mirrors as playful *metaphors* for acts of representation and allegories for the processes of reading would make his poetry *mub-ham*, or difficult to read.

Mirroring is gendered praxis. When mirroring or mimesis occurs without question, the person who makes the mirror, stands in front of the mirror, assumes shape in the mirror, and creates the conditions under which the operation of mirroring takes place is often rendered invisible. The moment this person or position comes into focus, they are assigned a gender, if only inadvertently.[49]

In both the poems I discuss in this chapter, the dynamics between the "I" who looks and the figure looked at, or between the voices/echoes calling and those heard, are gendered dynamics. The poems' negotiations between "I" and what is seen, perceived, and narrated become scripts for the scenes of reading or the spaces in which readings take place.

The first poem, "Devadasi and Pujari," is trapped in the visual. Visualization is an enticing act and an act that offers the promise of seduction. The voice that opens the poem slips immediately into relationships that are explored visually. Here the woman, the dancer, the seductress, is the text. The reading "I"/eye reads through a desire actualized in a gaze that creates. Seduction is integral here to the process of reading. But in order to allow for seduction, the woman/text looked at has to be separate from the "I"/male who does the looking. Woman becomes mirror, but what is seen in the mirror is still the image of the woman. Woman is both the mode of representation as well as the object that is represented.

"Call of the Sea" does not visualize gender and reading in the same way. Texts take forms that are both oral/voice and visual. But oral renditions do not have to assume visual shape. The voices/echoes are feminized but do not become female bodies. Mirroring or the process of reading depicted in images is eventually gendered. The moment that the position of the reader is articulated and brought into the scene of reading, the responsibility for what is seen/heard is thrown on that position. But since this poem (unlike "Devadasi and Pujari") did not open with a woman's body as text, the poem is not trapped/seduced by the separation between an "I" who reads and the text. It (the poem) allows the "I" to collapse into mirror/echo. If one uses seduction as a metaphor for reading in "Call of the Sea," reading would turn into a process of autoeroticism because what one sees in the text/mirror and hears in the call/echo is oneself. The "oneself" calls for a gender collapse, and the feminized call/echo is absorbed back into a masculinized "I." The voice that calls from the elsewhere, that dissolves back, as feminized echo, into masculinized "I" in "Call of the Sea" never completely resolves at the "I." "Call of the Sea" closes with a final dissolution, one where every scene in which a mirror comes forth is taken away, by a litany of repeated *nos*: no desert, no mountain, not even a rose garden. In the final lines of the poem, it is as though the poem winds backwards, tightening with every turn, to arrive again at the title: "Call of the Sea." Here the "I" is again given an oblique form, *mujhko*, one that never needs to reveal its gender, so gender too winds backwards, taking voice and echo away. All that is left is the sea. The sea (*samundar*) here is masculinized, and into it is absorbed every *sh'e*, each thing. The word for each thing is feminized. At the poem's conclusion, (each voice) rises out of the sea as feminine, and lapses, *jākar milegī*, back into it.

"Call of the Sea" attempts to articulate the limits of doubling, of repetition, language that multiplies itself, repetitions that unfold only to revert. Perhaps it is about names offered at the limits of what one can say to see, or see to say: mirrors wedged into the thickness of discourse that open the spaces of images, only to erase them. The poem's wave like succession of sounds to infinity, perhaps approaches closer to the moment when language might give birth to terror, to violent demons that whirl out as an image in it. "Call of the Sea" (like "Yagānagat" [Solitude]), seems to push at the temporal spaces between infinities between *fanā* and *baqā*, between end and beginning, pushing them out into the echo house, the mirror worlds of language. But the poem does all it does through gender, giving it and taking it, but never refusing the work done through it. Is the sea the masculine other, the beyond, that when it takes shape takes shape in the feminine, that through which the "I" must eventually come to being and through which the "I" then must disarticulate?

I would like to circle back to Miraji/Mirabai/Mira Sen to review mirroring/voicing in another key. In the love story, Mira disappears into Sana' ullah, who becomes Mira. In Miraji's translations of Mirabai's work, Miraji transforms Mira's work into *his* own. Anyone who has read any of the other poets Miraji translates, including Baudelaire and Mallarmé, engages with similar issues around reading/translation. The illusion that signing for a poet (reading) or signing for another poet (translation) are mimetic activities or transparent representations of them, is quickly dispelled when it is clear that Miraji's readings do not even venture toward anything that could be construed as an original. His readings are always deformations that arise at moments of danger.[50] So Miraji's translations of Mirabai's work as well as the translations/readings practiced on Miraji poetry should incite discussions about mirroring/echoing and their relationship to the "I." They should tempt deliberations that occur at the cusp between the end and the beginning. They should be cupped between life and death, holding deliberately to longing and loss. As long as these couplings between life and death go unrecognized and unaccounted for, both gendering and mirroring and in particular the question of who takes responsibility for them, so aptly illustrated by "Call of the Sea," will remain *mub-ham*.

*

To death we are not accustomed; [or: Death being that to which we are not accustomed,] we approach it either as the unaccustomed that astonishes or as the unfamiliar that horrifies. The thought of death does not help us to think death, does not give us death as something to think. Death, thought, close to one another to the extent that thinking, we die, if, dying we excuse ourselves from thinking: every thought would be mortal; each thought, the last thought.[1]

I must live. I will seize this moment, crush it with a snap of my fingers, and make it a witness and confidante of endless time [Mujhe jīnā hai. Is lamḥe ko cuṭkī meñ misal kar maiñ zamān-e be karāñ kā shāhid o damsāz kar dūñgā].[2]

The true picture of the past flits by. The past can be seized only as an image which flashes up at the instant when it can be recognized and is never seen again.[3]

He asks himself where this gift of ignorance comes to him from . . . , the play between presence that is seen, even if it is not seen. . . . It is a separation that isn't one, a split nonetheless, but one that does not let itself be perceived and that is not really denounced, since it is supposed to introduce an interval between the visible/invisible and the sayable/unsayable. . . . He senses strongly that the idea of dying has been pulled into this ignorance, and when, through a certain slippage of words, she suggests to him, as she grapples painfully with things she does not know, that she seems deprived of an end and that if she had to die, she could do so only by dying his death, this though appears to him to belong to the play of ignorance that occurs between speech and presence.[4]

When in transactions one "pays by a check" so that there will be a trace of the payment, the trace is inscribed in the very order of the world. But a real trace disturbs the order of the world. It occurs by overprinting. Its original signifyingness is sketched out in, for example, the fingerprints left by someone who wanted to wipe away his traces and carry out a perfect crime. He who left traces in wiping out his traces did not mean to say or do anything by the traces he left. He disturbed the order in an irreparable way. He has passed absolutely. To be qua *leaving a trace* is to pass, to depart, to absolve oneself. But in this sense every sign is a trace. In addition to what a sign signifies, it is the past of him who delivered the sign. . . . A sign stands in this trace.[5]

*

# EPILOGUE: ENTRANCES TO LIFE AND DEATH

It was a mild, damp monsoon afternoon. I was ensconced in a car, curled up with a map, on a search for Miraji's grave at the Marine Lines Graveyard. By the time I found the high white-washed walls, again, running tightly across the pavement, the rain had begun to fall like dense cloth, muffling, weighing down. I walked through the wrought-iron gates molded into flowing patterns and entered a place that seemed set aside from the rumble of the street outside, from the dank roar of trains, rails rattling slow dyings as they hurried to the downtown commuter station.

Silence thickened as I walked in, the wash of water echoing the small sounds of a sudden crow. Sounds so light and little they only reminded one of the way the walls held silence. In the uneven shadows of palm, mango, and neem, approximate rows of graves lay packed, packed one against another, slowly crumbling. I walked down the lines, marking names, re-marking the Gujarati incisions that told death. Along the right, pots of flowers, sharp orange, surprising pink, banked. On the left a slightly askew mausoleum, its age tolled in the brick that disinterred itself in the monsoon mold. Here, here, and there, marble three-tiered graves, deeply etched flowers incised into their smoothness. Older graves of stone, with delicate jalis. The walk cut the graveyard into pieces, clean, swept, loved. I could not find Miraji. Akhtarul Iman had warned me I might not. And I had driven by the walls each time I came back to Bombay, holding on to the possibility that I might not. But after Akhtarul Iman's death, returning to the Bombay that seemed so bereft of his presence, I wanted to see if I could find Miraji's headstone. Even a nameless one that might, just perhaps, have been his. It was to be my mourning memorial to Akhtarul Iman.

Mourning traces into life. A voice from the past, sometimes a voice from beyond, here given name. Miraji as a ghost who stands up before you asking his due, while you, the person whom he asks to trace him into life, are suffused with a strange happiness, feelings dissolving, strings of tears pouring from your eyes.

This is where I began this book, with Yusuf Zafar and a ghost. The ghost, Miraji's phantom, comes into being as supplement in Zafar's story, as though he were materializing out of Zafar's feelings and the empty space where Miraji might once have stood. Zafar's story is told over as it is written down reuniting a reader with the ways that Miraji has dematerialized out of recollection. What is this leaking of affect that seems to edge a phantom into tenuous shape? Where is the body that shits, and pees, and vomits, this body of a poet formed out of such an excessive giving of flesh that appears in so many biographies of Miraji? What does this have to do with Miraji's work, and the work on Miraji that I have laid out in this book?

In this book, I have tried to keep true to my allegiance with Miraji, witnessing, and embodying through the forms my ordering took, the difficult *mub-ham* shapes of his writing. The archives I have brought to bear on the poet have traversed the distances between Pakistan and India, struggling across the edges of a postpartition tearing or breached births of necessary nationhood. My materials have come from both places. I owe the Pakistani writers and members of the Halqa who have kept Miraji's phantom speaking, the life of this work. I have read Pakistan, as I perused the collections that ensued in Miraji's name, his afterlife, giving life to places and people I have sometimes found only through them. I have read India in the same way, seeking the afficionados of a poet tucked into libraries and bookstores. To hold to both India and Pakistan (and in moments, Bangladesh), in this way, is to demand all the places for Miraji's legacy. Miraji died in India, in a grave that only lives now through the traces of story, but he wanted his body to be buried in Pakistan. He belonged uneasily to the Progressives, and I have claimed that for him, against many who believe otherwise. I have claimed that for him precisely because he, like them, fought to keep open with both hands the intervals, the gaps, the continuities that coupled Hinduism and Islam and that have been rapidly shutting down, like faux teak doors made from pressed board swinging shut from their sticky heaviness. The memory of his painstaking, learned, artfully scripted translations from across the subcontinent offers a particularly apropos lesson in this time of the violences of politico-religious partitionings.

Miraji's incomplete biography was composed of fragments fitted together through feeling, sometimes *musalsal,* sometimes disjunct, like ghazals. These were the lines his poetry traced, and these were the lanes, *galiyāñ,* his prose walked. Through it all was an enormous amount of emotion, sentience and sentiment, cupped, seeping out like blood, thrown into the air to disperse in drops. Feeling insinuated its way into every crevice, every pore, through every *rāg.* Much of the feeling was about longing, the lingering pathos of love.[6] To cobble Miraji's writing together in a composite way along a very straight line, sweeping aside the anguish, the pleasure, and the pain that animates his work, is a violent disruption of it, of a kind that has failed with the ghazal.[7] It is the kind of violence that lays to one side, almost casually (as it must, to ensure that its invasiveness be practiced without notice), the insurmountable difference between beings brought to life under colonialism. To do so it must forgo the histories of colonization and death of flesh, must brush aside chronicles of lives and forgetting. To do so, it must abrade affect that grows through the body, detour affect elsewhere. For embodied affect works hard in Miraji's writing. As does the historical. As does the fragmentary.

Modernity in the colonies is not how Aijaz Ahmad has invoked it in his poignant and powerful essay "In the Mirror of Urdu: Recompositions of Nation and Community, 1947–65," as modernism.[8] Miraji's production of modernism cannot be positioned in an easy teleology, or not, as the case may be, with Ahmad's somewhat flat version of European modernism. Miraji, if he is at all a modernist, is one in a sort of Benjaminian vein, for whom eruption at the point of life and death, in an uneven, mobile triangulation (through translations) with colony/nation-to-be and metropole, constitutes modernity and the historical. Modernization is precisely, as Ahmad suggests, where the Progressives wrote, at the nexus of the political. And it is precisely where Ahmad might also have put it, post the partition, at the point of the exile, dislocation, memory, loss, bereavement, retrieval through the fragmentary, the debris, the ordinary, infected by affect, to become the surprising familiar and the horrifying unfamiliar.[9]

In this book I have withdrawn some of Miraji's work back into the fragment, mobilizing it through the historical, reading forward, backward, inclining the lyrical toward the historical, so both haunt each other. Each section, *musalsal* and disjunct, repeats some of the same spaces. This, in the hope that the seams that suture them into difference, and into investments that provoke the ordinary, can be seen and can be fleshed, so that the density of disciplinary apparatuses may thin and thicken to tear open. Each section iterates the material of the historical and leans over into the closeness of Miraji's texts. Each section takes as its allegory the supplementary material from the *Titanic* with which I began. Each section reaches into trauma to gesture toward the incommensurable diachronies that might raise the "ethical at the point of its collapse."[10] And each section simultaneously twists, in a plethora of ways, the impossibles and possibilities accorded by a recourse to gender.

> Gardish-e sāg̱ẖar-e ṣad jalvah'e rañgīn tujh se
> ā'inah dārī'e yak dīdah-e hairāñ mujh se.

> Yours: the showy circling splendor of spectacle cupped in wine.
> Mine: a single astounded glance of surprise, a likeness mirrored.[11]

# APPENDIX A. BEVELED GLASS: SELECTED TRANSLATIONS

*Going, Going . . .*[1]

A glance and promptly lost
beauty assaulted me
buffeted my ocean mind to storm.

Glimpsed wavering wind, she shuddered
flooded Ganga, sky-river, with milk
cloaked the moon
soothed the stars asleep
the wind effaced
old prayers lost to feeling
the effigy in my mind, temple, shattered.

Epiphanies birthed by day
this day, too, fresh
a night cleansed
new beloved, love refreshed
each thing,
cleansed

for a mere moment, she
slipped into sight, shimmered

clean beauty, and I, lost.
"Don't get to know me . . . you'll be lost."
"Don't profane yourself, how? How?"

Deeded desire, evanescent
didn't you think it an offering?
Eye dialogue, speaking heart . . . why call that passion?

Incandescence
warm your heart
wherever you find it
as long as earth is
as long as time is
these visions, pleasing
flow away.

One ephemeral spark cupped in a flickering glance, fills me.

We journey the world
our caravans skirting the directions,
each home, each jungle, each desert
each mountain's bared grace
will draw my mind to lust
will slip into sight, if only for a moment.

Each landscape, each person's kindness
the soft sorcery of women
lies in our power, transient
the moment passes, each thing dissolves.
One ephemeral spark cupped in a flickering glance
fills me. Why call that
passion?

Deeded desire, evanescent, didn't you think it an offering?

The moon scrapes the horizon
stars measured in a breath
the time given a life, if you really think it over
is just a breath long.

*Tall Building*[2]

Countless eyes painted on your face, you stand
a rare monument
a guardian of civilization
your body moonlight
like a storm rising up from man's mind
like a whirlwind in man's mind.

As the waves roll away, I hear songs, but
raging with tyranny,
the lingering shadow of mourning
keening a lingering dirge
their words are tales without dreams.
Is a lamenting soul restless in your heart?

Subdued, the ripples of your song dissolve. I begin to see
the cloudy dregs of bitter wine in a cracked cup
intoxication clouds my eyes.
Why does the spilling darkness of night frighten me
Your eyes, flickering in the spilling dark don't
scare me
I've lived in greater darkness
In my soul's dark, stars have flickered in anguish
sometimes
they'd forget and loose ecstatic darting flames
like your melody which stretches open its arms and hurls itself from
your windows
seduced by
the shawl of space.
In my desolation I remember my spilling tears
those tears, those flames of joy.
But it was just a dream, the flames darted forward as though in a dream,
the wings of my imagination were the wings of a maimed bird
fluttering till they trembled futilely
the tautness of my limbs
held me from living.

Writhing once, curiosity would release me on the wind of freedom
but
I regret that the moment my pain began to soothe me
my shackles were lifted
I forgot my soul's dark, to soothe my nerves,
I came to
I measured the height on which you stand, countless eyes flickering.

I'd been told strange stories about you, that
in your pregnant body
a bed has been laid out
on which a succulent woman rests
her loneliness
tasteless tiredness
rubbing away at her mind.
But she's restless
she waits
for the curtain to shiver
her dress to slither away like a cloud
and at the door an unknown, strange person appears
she doesn't care
whether his manners please her or not
she wants one thing from him
that he draw a rare portrait of a building
built from flowing nerves
whose body disgusts her
and quickly turns into an adversary.
The night's soulless spectator begins to see the
voluptuous woman, artless, irreproachable, without desire
as a crumbling wall.
Forgetting her tired music
in a flicker of an eye
she'd knock down
the rare portrait of a building
built from flowing nerves

like a sand castle
like a collapsing wall that crumbles.

These stories, flitting fragrances
would dance whenever they wished
through my mind.

Now, I look at your countless eyes
and see one flickering eye.
Are there any flames of joy in that flickering eye?

I want to shut the eye with my hand, now.

*Later Flight*[3]

He'll kiss her. What gives him the right?
D'you see how far he flew?
Black-faced, black-skinned, kohl-black . . .
If I weren't a man, I'd curse you.

Hair scattered over a shoulder
her bindi, a shooting star,
at rest
as though someone had paused unexpectedly while walking.
In the bathroom, I saw
a finger stained red,
that foretold the star's arrival.
It passed, but left in its wake
like a faint footprint on night's path,
a story
that would make a listener exclaim to me:
the song didn't need that trembling note.

I heard the same trembling note, once
as a trembling dress, slithered
to the floor. Caught,
dangled from the bed-post
to which the curtains were tied.

"Don't bother with it, let it be, let it stay there."
She closed her heavy-lidded eyes again
suddenly covered them with a hand
and if she opened them now, for a moment
those eyes
that had refused to look at me:
I wonder what they'd look at—
and where'd she put her hands, what would she hide?
She'd put them—
where eternity without beginning and end
was the moment.

At that moment, her bindi
looked
like
a shooting star.
It left behind
a story
on night's path
which made a listener exclaim:
the song didn't need that trembling note.

I can't see the trembling dress any longer
but my eyes don't need it any more.

It was a miracle in a night-storm, it receded.
What a storm!—A blind deluge.
As it abated
I remembered Noah
Noah, who'd said to his sons
"Open the cage, let it go—this dove
it'll find land for us."
The dove quickly returned—a failure
its fate preordained.
A crow was let go—"He'll find land."
Did you see how far he flew?
What gives him the right?
Black-faced, black-skinned, kohl-black.

*Rare Waves of Passion*[4]

I want the world's eyes to follow me
follow me
as though I were a tree's supple branch
(follows an arched supple branch).
But its leaf-load
like a dress, thrown off
with the bed-spread,
on the floor in a crumbled heap.

I want gusts of wind to wrap themselves around me
pout, tease, laughingly say something
pause shyly, collect themselves
with playful, passionate whispers.

I want to move on, walking sometimes
sometimes running forward
like wind, skimming the ripples in a stream, rustling
flows on, doesn't pause.

If a bird should sing somewhere, sweetly
its voice, warm waves, should collide with my body
and return, not pausing.

Sometimes warm rays, sometimes soft gusts
sometimes sweet, sorcerous words
sometimes one thing or another, newer,
ever newer colors bubble up
bubble, burst
in the spilling air.

Nothing should remain enclosed by the circle of my joy
the edges of the circle close in
the wide-open wheat field lies stretched out
far off the sky's tent, made up as a rare bed
entices me with passionate suggestions.

The sound of waves slapping dissolves in bird song,
slides
slips away.

I'm sitting
my veil slips off my head
I'm lost in thought,
someone will see my hair
the edges of joy's circle close in.
Enough, let nothing new enter the circle of my joy.

*Call of the Sea*[5]

These whispers say, "Come quickly,
calling you again and again for years
a deep tiredness has worn out my heart."

Echoes, ephemeral, lingering, are heard.
But this strange voice keeps coming.
Calling again and again has never tired anyone,
and probably never will.

"Dear child!
I love you so!
Look, if you do this
I'll be furious!"
"Oh God, oh God!"
At times a sob, a smile or a fleeting frown.
But these echoes have kept on coming.
Through them a brief life mingles with eternity.

But this strange voice, worn out by fatigue
threatens to drown every echo.

Now no eye flickers
no face smiles
or frowns
only ears listen.

This is a rose garden—a breeze ripples,
buds burst open,
spread their perfume
bloom again and again, wither
and drop.

They make a velvet carpet on which the fairies of my desires
saunter with a rare elegance.
The garden's like a mirror
in which every form is reflected,
adorns itself
and dissolves
never to reappear.

This is a mountain—silent, tranquil,
a spring bubbles, asks, "What's on the other side of this rocky crag?"

But the mountain's skirt is enough for me.
There's a valley in the skirt,
a river flows through it.
There's a flowing boat in it
a boat which is a mirror.
Every form is reflected in the mirror,
but when it dissolves
it never reappears.

This is a desert—vast, parched, leafless.
Its whirlwinds are the embodied reflections
of violent demons.
But I'm far away.
My eyes are glued to a clump of trees.

Now there's no desert,
no mountain,
no rose garden;
now no eye flickers,
no face smiles,
or frowns,
only a strange echo says, "Calling you again and again
a deep tiredness has worn out my heart."

Calling again and again has till now never tired anyone,
and probably never will.
So then this voice is a mirror,
and only I
am tired of calling.

No desert,
no mountain,
not even a garden,
now only the sea calls out to me
    everything comes from the sea and must return to it.

*Movement*[6]

Far off
in the tall indigo jungle
black, blue-black clouds crowded.
In the forest, a black koel called
black shadows on the ground
black, wet eyes
black, blue-black hair.

Close by
In the center of my heart. Slowly
slowly sighs rose
sorrow poisoned the nectar
sorrow's fierce, fiery glances
sorrow's yellow-black eyes
sorrow's soft, whisper step.

*Solitude*[7]

There's no evil in an age
it's only the endless swing of a river.

I'll say this:
I'm not evil.
I'm not an age,
I'm not the swing of a river.

I don't know what's in evil,
what's in an age,
and I'll add:

anything that stays alone
is destined for death.

Evil, good, an age, a river—these things
are from eternity's household
I'm not a part of any household
I'm separate,
I'm solitary,
I'm a stranger.

These houses, these jungles,
these flowing paths and rivers
these mountains,
the tall building I suddenly notice
these desolate tombs,
a mosque attendant chained to death
laughing young children
a dying traveler hit by a car
breezes, greenery, the few clouds that
float back and forth across the sky.
What are they?

These things are an age, they
are the endless swing of a river.

These houses, the jungles
roads and rivers
buildings, a mosque attendant
breezes, foliage and clouds floating across the sky
all these, each object is from my household.

I'm an age, from my every breath rises
the endless swing
of a river.
But there's no evil in me.

How can I say this—
death and
eternity mingle in me.

*Tease/Teasing*[8]

You're soft.
You're so hot.

You're so impudent/bold.
Come closer, listen to me . . .

Go . . . go away . . . why won't you listen
Do what I want . . .

Please let me be

take me.

*Jew*[9]

In chase, a hundred hunters
hounded one prey.
Wealth, manners, intellect
all empty.
Chanting, intoning Hari's name
the prey screams, "Do your worst."
The ways of the world have turned over
look at all the trades.
Those born in the world are macabre
shunned by even their mothers.
When the end comes, the victories
of one's enemies will be overturned.

Stupefied by the fog of one's mind
when life's chains are smashed open
when the web of time is ripped open
the wall encircling the earth,
can be seen in the distance,
a world of freedom.

*Traveler*[10] *(first version)*

Someone came. Left.
Someone else'll come. I've been standing here
a long time. This night, too, will pass.

I don't remember why
I'm here, what I have to do.
My memory, too, has turned into an oil lamp
whose every, halting, hesitant ray
laughs at me, soundlessly.
But, how did I hear that laugh?

A dust storm whirls up,
rises and falls
I can still hear its whistling
whistling that pouts and bubbles up
spreads, spreads
I've been here a long time.
Someone came.

Left. Someone else will come.
This night, too, will pass. I hear a commotion.
Wherever I turn, there are people. Coming,
walking
sauntering, stopping. Moving on again
darting forward.
They come and go, from here to there,
from there to here.

I look on, caught,
as though by a gust that rises up
from a wave of thought in my heart.
I see a ray
from an oil lamp
slithering and slipping
that lays bare the shape of my life.

I realize
the dark has turned into a lamp
it oozes
drops of nectar
I nurse in my palm.
But my palm turns into a flickering oil lamp
darting it leaps up,

the flame falls
the dark sits, sits
darts forward like
a shutter that snaps open and shuts
with the sharp slaps from a storm
like a wounded fluttering bird.

I look on. Someone came. Left.
I realize that someone else might come.
But my feet are transfixed.
I just stand there.

A drop of blood from my heart says
this night, too, will pass.
I take a drop from my heart to my eyes and look on.
When the shutters meet
I begin to feel that the bird will flutter no longer
but make my heart flutter.
I will nurse drops of nectar on my palm
that ooze
from my eyes.

But—my life has turned into a flickering oil lamp
whose every halting, hesitant ray
is soundless laughter.
This darkness is new. It contains nothing
from the old dark.
My journey through light and darkness will continue
as before/it always has.

This is the pattern of the road:
someone comes, leaves. Someone
else will come.
The night passes.

The glittering stars tell travelers
the road-river always flows.
Flow with it leave your confusion behind.

Some caravans that travel the road
go directly to their destination
some lose the secrets of the intricate circling
dance of the stars
But even those caravans see
the door to their destination swing open
before it shuts at nightfall.
But why am I here? The shut door doesn't open for me.

Each sleeping grain of the desert says to me
in this desolation
your dry palm is a foot
the tip of a thorn pricking it can't ask you for even a drop of blood.

Why am I standing here? I've nothing to do.
Why shouldn't I lose myself, when I go for a stroll
drown
in one, two, three, a hundred thousand whirlwinds
that come and go
just as a boat floating in a flowing wave-whirl
contains each wave flowing out
like the open midnight lotus—my palm.

I don't understand
that every traveler on the road has a destination.

Shall I join them, shall I go?

"Come with us, come on."
"Why're you standing here, so quiet, so alone."
"We'll bring you two rare flowers
if you want . . ."
"Stop, stop, I don't need . . . I'm waiting here for a friend."

But he's gone.
I'm still not comforted.
I've begun thinking of myself as a desert dweller.
I'd like to see a shut door open.
But, it's not possible.

I long for a storm that will conceal me
completely in its drapery.
I've come to realize that every beautiful thing I owned
has turned into a flowing gust
that my hand cannot contain,
there are no drops of nectar left on my palm
it's just a parched leafless colorless desert
in which it is not possible for me to say:

Someone came, left. Someone else will come.
My night will pass.

*Traveler (second version)*

One arrived. Left.
Another will arrive. I've been standing here
a long time. This night, too, will pass.

I don't remember why
I'm here, what I have to do.
My memory, too, has turned into a flickering oil lamp
whose every slithering, slipping ray
is silent mocking laughter.
How did I hear its laugh?

A dust storm swirls up,
whirls and dissolves
I can still hear its whistling
whistling that spouts and bubbles
spills over
I've been here a long time.

One arrived.
Left. Another will come.
This night, too, will pass.

I hear a commotion.
Wherever I turn, there are people. Arriving,
walking
sauntering, pausing. Moving on again

rushing forward.
They come and go, from here to there,
from there to here.

I look on, caught,
as though by a gust that swirls up
from a ripple of thought in my heart.
I see a ray
from an oil lamp
slithering and slipping
silhouette the shape of my life.

I realize
the dark has turned into a lamp
it oozes
drops of nectar
I hold gently in my palm.
But my palm turns into a flickering oil lamp,
its flame leaps up suddenly
falls
the dark sits, sits
leaps forward—like
a shutter that snaps open and shuts
with the sharp slaps from a storm
like a wounded fluttering bird.

I look on.
One arrived. Left.
I realize that another will come.
But my feet are transfixed.
I just stand there.

A drop of blood from my heart says:
this night, too, will pass.
I take a drop from my heart to my eyes and look on.
When the shutters meet
I begin to feel that the bird will flutter no longer
but make my heart flutter.

I will hold on my palm
drops of nectar, that ooze
from my eyes.

But—my life has turned into a flickering oil lamp
whose every slithering, slipping ray
is silent laughter.
This darkness is new. It contains nothing
from the old dark.
My journey through light and darkness will continue
as it always has.

This is the pattern of the road:
one arrives, leaves. Another
will come.
The night passes.

The glittering stars tell travelers:
the road-river always flows.
Flow with it
leave your confusion behind.

Some caravans that travel the road
go directly to their destination.
Some forget the secret of the intricate circling
dance of the stars.
But even those caravans see
the door to their destination swing open
before it shuts at nightfall.
But why am I here? The shut door doesn't open for me.

Each grain of the sleeping desert says to me:
In this desolation
your dry palm is a foot
pricking it, the tip of a thorn can't even ask:
Give me a drop of your blood to drink.

Why am I standing here? I've nothing to do.
Why shouldn't I lose myself, when I go for a stroll

drown
in one, two, three, a hundred thousand whirlwinds
that come and go
just as a boat floating in a flowing wave-whirl
holds each wave flowing out from it,
like the open midnight lotus—my palm.

I don't understand
that every traveler on the road has a destination.

Shall I join them, shall I go?

"Come with us, come on."
"Why're you standing here, so quietly,
so alone."
"We'll pluck you two flowers from a rare twig
if you want . . ."

"Stop . . . stop, I don't need . . .
I'm waiting here for a friend."

But he's already left.
I'm still not comforted.

I've begun thinking of myself as a desert dweller.
I'd like to see a shut door swing open.
But, it's not possible.

I long for a storm that will cover me
completely with its drapery.
I've come to realize that every beautiful thing I've owned
has turned into a flowing gust
that my hand cannot hold,
there are no drops of nectar left on my palm.

I'm in a parched leafless colorless desert
where I cannot say:
One arrived and left. Another will come.
My night will pass.

*A Night on the Far Side of the Wine Glass*[11]

"This isn't a goblet." I pick up a glass sliver
Pick it up and toss it into clear pond water
to make some ripples.
Whose hand lifted the veil of day and night
so that the dancer, pirouetting on a glittering leg
unveiled a glimpse of a signpost
seduced, drew my glance to her.

Bring it here.
Let the swan-goblet swim on.
Bring it here.
I'll drink every dreg of thirsty thought.

Why should forgetfulness clutch my gown? Isn't she the
whore whose shawl traps thousands of heaving breaths
that foolishly ripple and dissolve?

My shriveled, half-dead wrist holds
spilling space
in every vein, blood drops shiver—
sweat on the dancer's forehead.

Whose soft hennaed finger stroked the blue lotus
so that every petal shivered?
I fear my shriveled loneliness may now dissolve.

Get up, come to me . . . come to me . . . why so unsure?
What were you drinking to? Why did you boast:
I will drink the blood of my past life.
Leave me, bring the sleeping dancer, who with her cold eyes
with a single pat, puts my bounding heart
to sleep in warm sighs.

I must live. I will crush this moment
with a snap of my fingers and make it
a witness and confidant of endless time.

Bring it here.
Let the swan-goblet swim to me,

Let the scene rise up again that once stood before me
and suggested to me:
"Your every breath is death-bound."
Your bright flowering face has made my dust heap bloom
it disturbed me/swept me up,
as a gust of wind sweeps
a shriveled petal along
never stopping
flows along, flows along, sweeps along.

Have you ever seen sparks in a fireplace?
Laughingly stroking your cheek, painted red
every finger
oozes blood.

A thin sliver of delicate succulent fruit touches
my tongue, look—
the simple whiteness of a plain robe crushes dry leaves.

Stay wrapped around me.
Let me imagine that a sip of your arms
will make my heart giddy,
or shall I
in profound emptiness
black darkness
rocking and rocking again
close my wet eyes?

This morning robe betrays the secret:
Don't think, silence is better.
But a wave splattered with foam comes flooding
across my thoughts.

Bring it here.
Every twisting movement of the swan's warm throat makes
the billows in the dancer's skirt swing
who until now
sat hidden at my side.

But
why do you regard me as a foolish child?
I am not a foolish child
nor are you a foolish child—

I understand!
Whenever the swan-goblet keeps time
with the gurgling wine flask
the smooth surface of the wine bubbles
and each bubble is a foolish child—
each touches the dancer's skirt
calls out to the past night
and dissolves.

I said, I've always said
I alone will clutch the dancer's skirt.

And each bubble will cry like a foolish child
each is a secret
that I alone can unravel.

Casually forgetful
each says again and again
bring it here.
But nobody listens.
Let the glass swan swim on.

Tired, the dancer returns to my embrace
and I too feel that I might go to sleep.

Take your white dress off
don't stay wrapped up
my shriveled petal!
Plucking you like this
I will turn you into a garden, so that
every flower cluster will glitter.
Let the glass swan swim on.
Let the swan swim to me.
I am not blind. Yes
    let the swan go on swimming.

*Lip of a Full River*[12]

She sat down for a moment, intimate
a seated icon
a vision obscured
sword's honed flash vivid against earth's mud breast
quick as a spurting spring.

A wave twisting, washed over my heart
had these brambles woven
a mountain circle,
in its skirt I'd stand still
transfixed.

If something so impossible could happen, why couldn't this also

a bed spread out on a stead of dried leaves
becomes a melody, an instrument
synchronized harmony
the voice had woken up
its music stretched awake, held back
at the edge
of hearing,
veiled eyes conjured just one seated statue in my mind-enclosure.

I begin to remember—ears helpless
when the sound of writhing rose from crumpled leaves
when every wave in the skirt began to glimmer
the shadow of the sword fell
drawn swiftly in a hidden room
like lightening glittering artlessly.

But every fold in the wet skirt dissolved
the water sylph hid even as I saw her
I stood still, caught
the sword's honed flash vivid against bare mud breast, quick
like spurting spring.

I'm not in its skirt now
brambles not woven into a mountain circle

instead a veil, through which I see an unfamiliar sight
the pure unviolated form of a bride.

Yes, creating a groom in my imagination
I'll take him to a secret room behind the veil

the sword's honed flash, vivid
against bare mud breast
like a restless heart that had begun to turn
like lightening, artless
the sylph rose from her secluded corner.

Life tepid
its every drop a humid step
slithering on dried leaves
I, too, come into myself
a nameless firefly.

I saw a thickly languorous cleft
leaving an eddy
a curved bow with
lightning sharpness let fly
the arrow
coiled coquettishly
shivered and dropped, like
a rock hurled off a hill fort

nothing held it back, nothing
a bed spread out on a stead of dried leaves
on which an unfamiliar sylph stretched languid, and I
nameless firefly,
staring, watching hopeful
for the water sprite to appear
a mirage
I, flute poised, turn
into a herder.

But where will the sprite come from, I saw her
on the bed, casual,
I'm sorry to be standing here

desolate,
soiled hands, wet
eyes smoky
I didn't wipe the wet from my eyes.

*Far and Near*[13]

My heart drums a rhythm
your heart drums
a rhythm
but distantly.
Voluptuous spring will grace and depart the landscape
like this, distantly.
Stars will glimmer,

like this distantly.

Everything will stay, like this
distant.
But the taste of your desire
its savage music
will sit inside my heart,
close.

*Devadasi and Pujari*[14] *(first version)*

Look, come see a dance, the dance, the undefiled dance of a devadasi
slowly, slowly sorrow's shadow slipped off my heart
she measures out her feet, softly softly, my mind wants
to become moonlight, extinguished on the floor

hidden behind a stone pillar I should look at her
silently, silently realize in wonder that
like a goddess-statue come to life you are dancing, dancing
like a forgetful queen of an army of water-sprites descended to earth
and ripples on water stir so, flicker
or a restless jungle deer who slithers on leaves
a cobra/female in a darkened jungle hisses and sways
like my covetous/lusting eyes sliding over her body
the devadasi stroking the earth, shows/exposes colors

black, black glittering eyes like lightning dance
and pearl-diamond jewelry glitters in light like this
in a high, blue-black sky canopy, like stars and moon glimmering.

When I see
the fold of her slip taut under her arms
then should the ordinary thud of my heart
and my breath sharpen fast
when ripples flow through the long, loose, limber skirt
and its swirl subsides
every vein in my mind shudders
a melody of signs pours
coming forward, retreating, arrested/standing-still shuddering
carefully carefully she falls, falling with care
fearful, hesitant, then with pleasure, fearlessly coming forward
let the hesitant boat of dharma slide/roll, my dharma fall/drop

dancing, dancing when (she) tires, tiring when there's confusion
it should take away together my composure, my peace, my
intellect/wisdom

then this sweet scene should dissolve/vanish from my sight
the shadows of the long stone pillar fold themselves around her
like crowding clouds gathering lightning into their skirts.

*Devadasi and Pujari (second version)*

Look, come see a dance, the dance, the clean dance of a devadasi
slowly,
slowly sorrow's shadow slipped off my heart
she measures out her feet, softly
softly, my mind wants
to become moonlight, extinguished on the floor

hidden behind a stone pillar I look at her
silently,
silently realize in wonder that
like a goddess-statue come to life you are dancing,
dancing like a forgetful queen of an army of water sprites stepping
onto earth

and ripples on water stir so, flicker
or a restless jungle deer who slithers on leaves
a cobra/female in a darkened jungle hisses and sways
like my lusting eyes sliding over her body
the devadasi rubbing mud under her heels, exposes colors, black
black glittering eyes like lightning dance
and pearl-diamond jewelry flickers
in a tall, blue-black sky canopy, like stars and moon glimmering.

When I see
the fold of her slip taut under her arms
then my heart's flat beat
and my breath sharpens fast
when ripples flow through the long, loose, limber skirt
and its swirl collapses
every vein in my mind shudders
a melody of signs pours
coming forward, retreating, arrested
shuddering
carefully carefully she falls, falling
gently
fearful, hesitant, then with pleasure, fearlessly coming forward
let the hesitant boat of dharma roll
dancing,
dancing when she tires, tiring when there's confusion
it must steal my composure, my peace, my wisdom

then this sweet sight will dissolve
the shadows of the long stone pillar fold themselves around her
like crowding clouds gather lightning into their skirts.

*Prophecy from Another Time*[15]

After my life has come and gone, after my death perhaps
in a spring season
when a call returned drifts in
  my songs will be heard, once more, the world over!

*In the Blink of an Eye*[16]

How I love this woman
I walk past my house a little way, glimpse her, wish she were here.
Quickly, how quickly she eludes my glance
What should I believe, does she abhor me?
But this! She looked down so soon, so quietly.
What should I believe, does she know my longing?
And this? When our eyes meet, she shuts her door, and I, destitute, wander.
Never to see her again.
Well, yes . . . her friend emerged. Looked me over, went away.
What ought I think, did she come because she was asked?
What did I really witness: their laughter, graceful, sounded that moment
when in a quick turn of passion . . .
was it defeat exulting
or a spoor of courage?
What can I expect, what can I presume
does she despise me, or breathe yearning, if she hungers so
why must it take so long? If she hates me so
what must she imagine? Why tease me so,
endlessly? Yes,
I have news of her,
yes, this my love's prayer, absolute, sure, flawless gold its faith. Yes,
how I long
for that girl, who lives, so close to my house.

*The Clerk's Love Song (or: The Love Song of the Clerk)*[17]

My night spent,
all night I labor away at dreams and sleep
then, morning's mistress appears
I rise off my bed and wash.
Yesterday I had bought a slice of bread
and eaten half of it then
the rest is today's breakfast.

The world is painted in strange colors
the man who lives right in front of me, he has a woman at home
on my right is a single-storied house, now empty
the voluptuary who lives on my left, has a mistress at home
and among all this, there I sit, but . . . without you
I and you: I have every comfort, just missing the perfume of tangled hair
disentangled from breakfast, I slip out of the house
walk the road to the office,
on the way, the elegance of the town, a horse carriage, two cars,
children passing by toward school,
what can I say about horse carriages?
The cars are sparking lightning, how must I bear the arrows slung at me from carriages
in the time of similitude, this, the wealth pouring from the houses of proper gentry,
this, an illusion,
a mischief, an innocence,
but on the road, I walk, my fate unturned, sorrowful, sad
the sharp smile of electricity lighting up the carriages
the sweet modulations of conversation
this recognition hangs, waiting for me to come to it: does God have any compassion (in his heart)?
Everything lives here, but for you,
and my eyes don't even have the courage to cry, no tears.

The road cuts back and forth, the prison passes by,
perhaps I should lose my heart in work, someone grasps me,
I carry my heart slowly into the office,
my heart is simply innocent, foolish, a child—I give it away elsewhere,
and the river of work pulls me into its flow, my senses damped.
When half the day has angled by, lost,
the officer saunters in from home
summons me to his office, a servant called
he talks forwards and then sideways, but is quite without worth.
I tire of his words,

for a minute I come to my room to find a file,
a fire sparking my heart: were I also an officer
my house would be far from the town's dirt, the town's dusty streets,
and I'd have you,
but I am merely a munshi, you: queen of wealth, purveyor of fame
and this is the story of my desire, more seasoned than the earth.

*Strange Familiars*[18]

I took my tranquility on a walk
and chose my roads by their angled slant.
What I glimpsed I sighted from a tower's height.
The city's glory seen so, from here
to those places of rest, what do I imagine
holds those gestures of hell for me: jails, whorehouses, hospital.

Those places of rest bloom like the flowers of evil.
You know well, Satan, the cause of my discomfort.
You know well, this knowing: that I could not come here
eyes found on the road, alchemize
tears into flowers.

I, the old and worn heart, a hedonist
there, my faith tested, on arrival.
Far away, I thirsted, my heart's vagrancy.
Whose hellish beauty brings me to my youth.

My heart clings to you,
your familiarity, O dishonored city
dream that sleep, heavy with wet shadows
on your expanse bares the day's first light, a wave gathering
your body, clothed with the plain dress of night's color

prey and death-dealer, hunting the pleasures of their own forms/being
the blind never come, to the humility of their degraded familiars.

*Translation of Swinburne's "Ave Atque Vale"*[19]

O my brother
in the old season of your songs,

you saw those secrets, that grief, that anguish
which is denied us.
The harsh tautness of love's knife flame
at a place at night
where no one has dared breathe till now
the petals of sweet love's poisonous buds
bloomed for your delicate gaze.
No one else even glimpsed them.
The secret treasure of time's ripe fertility
its faults which have no astronomy
those things leached clean of happiness.
Two places, where with the eyes of a grieving soul
as it turns in sleep, turns from the dust motes
of strange dreams and weeps,
on each face you glimpsed a shadow so
you saw that what people gather in a garden
blooms only as thorn.

# APPENDIX B. WORKING TRANSLATIONS: ESSAYS, PROSE MUSINGS, MISCELLANEOUS POEMS

*How Songs Are Made*[1]

Waves of thought wash over me and carry me far away . . . to the left, the right, front, back, up, down.

Smoke spreads/swirls out in every direction. I don't recognize the shadows I see. I don't understand the melodies/songs I hear. My hands rise to touch them but fall back dangling without feeling. I am afraid. My soul tells me to get up, unravel myself from the upheaval.

My feet move forward but the earth doesn't slide back under them. But, beyond my sight, it clambers over the mountain and keeps going . . . slides on, doesn't stop. I recognize my helplessness . . . like a child cradled in its mother's lap, who feels only the lap-bed. All the things around me are no more than mist. And the child's laughing eyes know that the streams of nectar are not beyond recognition. And a voice had just called out and the tears just begun to flow when the nectar dripped. The child's thirst was sated, her hands began to pat and stroke, and at the same time, a sweet song was audible and the nectar dripping on [my] waving hands and feet could make [me] helpless. My hands and feet waved so long that I was unexpectedly overcome by exhaustion. Surges of shamelessness would dissolve the tiredness and call up sleep.

When the ripples of thought carried me, they took me so far that I began to think that women make songs. Sometimes they appear as seductive women, sometimes as ordinary women, and a man sings a song about one that is just about that one/remains that one's song, which draws everyone into its sweetness. And life's commotion moves on; the journey cannot be tiring. A play is continuously being produced. A play in which a mother says, "My child," and a sister says, "My brother," and a wife says, "My lord, my lover," and in each two-word phrase is the pleasure of a song. And whenever one is made, the person who hears them calls out, "Oh, one who makes all these, let the string of breaths swing on like this." Waves of thought bring one here. The earth moves forward under my feet, as I climb the mountain. My life is no longer in my grasp. The bonds from life after life break open.

Dimness is far away. To my right a flowing river hums. To my left, the gusting wind and bird calls make the jungle spread over the flowing maidan sing. In one direction the stream that falls off the mountain, in the other, blind waves rise off the sea, collide with each other. The sky spread out above them gathers all these voices into its lap and dissolves them. Its forehead wrinkles with power dripping like this. A half-open lotus then sways and rises. A ray of thunder calls out, "Who's saying that?" Even if anyone could say it they wouldn't be able to. No one says anything. The watchers' eyes shimmer with the show of magic. The leap/startled of lightning, "Look here/at me." My eyes keep shutting, they cannot see. Darkness on all sides, the kind of dark against which rays of light mingling eternally with one another create new shadows. And ears listen. Shimmer, shimmer.

*Miraji's Ghazals*[2]

From town to town the tourist wandered
and lost
the road to his house.
What belongs to me
what you own
he forgot
what was his and what was another's.

What he forgot, how he forgot
why ask about it.
Just think of it this way:
the cause isn't a sin;
he simply forgot.

How those days were
how those nights were
how were those words—the assaults.
My mind is a child
it forgot
the beautiful dream of love.

A ray peeped out from behind darkness
hesitated coyly.
I remembered
vaguely the outline,
but her face,
I forgot.

Roaming in search of memories
my heart
was so assaulted
happiness in sorrow, sorrow in happiness
this mysterious distinction
I forgot.

It's a question of a look
it's a question of a moment
breaths, a cord tied around a waist
when the light from one glance
dissolved
when the moment passed
I forgot.

It's not a question of understanding something
my mind is a pleasure-seeking
drunk
I drowned my head in rippling waves

the sea, however,
I forgot.

While laughing
while playing games
in conversations
color dissolved.
Although I had a heart
I forgot
my oozing wounds.

My life, which passes away,
my spent life has been spent.
When my heart took away my life
I spent my life
laughing
and forgot
to lament and cry.

Whoever you look at, in their heart
if there's a complaint
it's just this:
I remembered every single thing
but time forgot
us.

If anyone asks
Who said this,
tell them what's in your heart.
Miraji talked and repented
and then,
having talked,
forgot.

*The Fundamentals of New Verse*[3]

Some people have begun to call free verse in Urdu new verse. I am not among them. Some people, combining free verse and from the perspective of topics—women and workers—have begun to call that new verse. It's as though life's political, economic, or sexual aspects in their view are the unripe/unformed issues of new poetry. I don't say this either. In my view, measured writing can be called new verse in which a mode or method is constructed to describe, think about, or express some issue that leaves behind noisy/vocal effects. A new poet is someone who is distancing himself from the bonds of convention, who creates his individuality by revealing a felt thought or desire. Or else, he is an old one. And in that very way in the annals of Urdu poetry we find/learn about new poetry, from Nazir Akhbarabadi on. Even before Nazir, this sort of restless, fearless poet can be seen, one who attempted to walk a new road by any means. But from the point of view of society or atmosphere, he was not especially important. Therefore, having looked in every direction, we'll consider Nazir the exemplar of new poetry.

After Nazir, Ghalib is the kind of milestone, the effect of whose individuality is still evident. And we don't know how long it will be felt. After Ghalib the names of Hali, Azad, and Sail Merathi should not be taken in the same breath because they were subject to the pressures of the necessities of a time, on an intellectual plane that created a new desire for new inclinations from the widespread perspective of conventions and, moving away from the ghazal, empowered the *naẓm*. But this step of theirs was the sort of situation in which, instead of the gardens, a *būstāñ* of educational councils, they revealed ras to Urdu.

The needs of early humans were limited. Therefore, their poetry, too, walked on limited paths. Moreover one can say that their vision would only search for poetics within the circle of their own necessities. Sating himself with his soul mate, night, he found pleasure in moments of forgetfulness/repose, collecting food to fill his stomach and fear. Fear of the manifestations of nature and fear of enemies of the same species. The issues of poetry emerged from just these things. Early man's poetry is the gap/atmosphere stretched out between the parallel lines of fear and desire. As the stages of progress were traversed, and as they acquired the means for civilization and housing—the star of mankind's imagination having spread, and out of its illumined/fired up dust/cinders floating in splendor, becomes the Milky Way in the heaven of thought. The arrival of civilization and housing didn't just provide disciplinary satisfaction of desire and attraction, but after this the intellect began traveling on every type of creative or dividing and uniting path and, at the same time, began to wonder which point he would make his next destination. . . .

Art is the interpreter of many identities.[4] And identities put life on exhibition. It is obvious that nowadays our life definitely changes—if not every month, then every year. And it is not only that social and economic states have an effect on art and poetry, but on the intellectual plane too. Those Western ideas/thoughts have seemed to have an impact on literary and artistic *technae*, specially those which occasion custom/fashion; these, if one considers the issue of creativity, and looks at daily things/habits, have brought new modes.

In the first era, each thing was limited and fixed, and the stretch of speech was contained. And topics traveled the fixed circle of poetry. Along with this, the horizon/limit of intellect held [was painted in] only one color. In the new age, topics of speech birthed a breadth. Speech grew. New statues/idols came to be poured [in new molds]. And the intellectual horizon came to its desires through its colorful streams/rivers.

In the past five to seven years, the most attention-getting progress that has sprouted new stems is that of progress-loving (Progressive) theories. But if we take off from the metaphoric allusions/language of one of Faiz's titles/prefaces, we may say that dreams seem to have been disturbed/troubled by the excess of repairs/building. We want, as much as has been forbidden. [As much as has been forbidden, that much we want.] Under the circumstances, how can one know what is the real issue? The first, and most basic, error/mistake that the intellectual masters of this movement have made is that they believe that progressive-loving poetry is synonymous with participatory democracy. Rather than being enticed by the limits, their own horizons [of possibility], they remained the kind of people who only were limited by [only understood] the new form of literature: torment-loving literature. Instead let us define progress-loving literature as any form of literature which illuminates thought and compels us to take a step forward in the direction of any aspect of embodied/bodied/bodily life.

Today, science's inventors have brought each thing close to every other thing. But human beings are separated from each other. It's as though that early out of sight/evanescent thing is not around [no longer exists]. But the straightforwardness that was necessary for knowing one another put the depth of thought aside, for that depth no longer remains in anyone's constitution, or at the very least has begun to disappear. This is the reason that art, while coming closer to life, often remains distant from it. Earlier, too, this was the state of affairs in the present. But in another mode. Earlier in the royal palace/household of Urdu poetry, for a long time a bed of flowers had been laid. And on it the ghazal, a beautiful woman [having assumed the form of the ghazal], was sitting, adorned with the sixteen ornaments. The dwellers of the simile were employed in fanning the whisks of metaphor. The people who strolled in and out of the royal palace, the few carefully picked men could heat their hearts up and could bathe their eyes cool in the beautiful splendor of the restless beauty; and not just anybody had the courage to enter this aloof and untouchable gathering. Only those who had courtliness could go to the royal gathering, who were versed in the niceties of literature, who, listening to others, could make the appropriate sounds of praise, who would not sit at the feet of someone else. Nazir, Ghalib, Sharar. A few magicians of this sort came. They, using the help given them by the *rāg*, wanted to jell/coagulate into a new form. But their listeners were only able to hear the melodies/music of their time [familiar to them]. The invisible fetters that circled the ankles of those in the palace [and charmed evil away] could not be cut. [And life?] Life, strolling leisurely down the pathways, eating, drinking, laughing, speaking, saying her piece, listening attentively to others, reveling in her search for new paths, could not even step over the gilt threshold of that palace.

After this, having crossed seven seas, a besieging storm arose. The hurricane of Western culture, organization, and education struck. It picked up dried twigs and leaves. But in its own glory, it also brought rain to help new buds sprout. Now, step by step, new voices could be heard.

Some said: art should be brought closer to life.

Some began to say: we can't be goods carriers from our assets.

Some spoke out: we only know two things—integrity and freedom.

And the commotion of each one's music created a complication. A complication out of which new waves seethed. Which, having emerged, decided new stages for life's journey. But whose murkiness is like a forgotten goodness. The sort of forgetfulness in which only a few can see the right road and travel on it.

This is the quality of new poetry of that time. And the new poet is standing in the crossroads from which many roads emerge to the right, the left, in front, at the back. But he doesn't know fully on which road he has decided. What importance the trials of the past keep. For how long he has to stand in this way. To what extent the despairing [*iẓṭrār*] quality of the present age would remain with him. What road he has to walk on. And how much the dangers of the future would damage him.

The new poet makes the excuse of the profound allure of his world. But in truth he is merely erased/absorbed in one murky reflection [*ʿaks*] of his [own] nature. The old supports no longer remain around him on the strength of which, in the dilemmas of a domestic existence, people used to pass their entire life. He is now all alone and he is on a quest for support. Sometimes he understands the wrong things as a support. Sometimes even when he reaches a true support he doesn't know what happened. And the main reason for this is that [when] the structure/edifice has to be adorned, it has yet to be poured into its form. He is not fully aware of the state of these foundations.

And the causes of this upheaval begin in the murky [*mub-ham*] era of 1857. When from the point of view of social and political norms, earlier connections began to be dispersed and space was made for a new order. One could perhaps say this: that a gap of a few generations had already been established between the current young poets and those older/respected men. Who had seen that time of intellectual turmoil as a pulse. But history and genealogical [*naslī yādeñ*] memories coming together make the past era its proof; other than this, a person's intelligence is made by bringing together past, present, and future. The past molds his fundamental affairs. Present time investigates each movement of itself, and those very aspirations become intentions, and reach completion in the future, to make/render individuality visible.

When we bring the past of today's poets before us, from the political point of view, then along with the constricted ideas arising from the downfall/decay/failure of the government, we get the elements that increase the life of new political movements, and these were the intense suppressions of the first downfall. They, assuming a political cast, while setting one's nation/country in a contest/battle with the entire world, gave birth to new aspirations and created a desire for progress and freedom in all the clefts/branches of life.

When we consider the life of a poet from a social perspective, more than one issue emerges. As the gaps in/between cities disappeared, new education came. And the frog in the well began to think that there was a life outside his kind and his society, in which an unyielding space, by its depth, twists earlier ideas. Ease of [Leisure produced by] education and commerce introduced one to new presences [allowed one to tour new places], and the pictorial map of a domestic existence began to be erased.

Leaving the home, the frog began to feel increased alienation [loneliness/*tanhā'ī*]. That feeling, which grows and spreads in every direction, and in the process transforms the feelings of strength of those whose are constituted at the bottom [lowest]. Along with this, the new era brought with it a new speed. Where the footsteps of life sped up, and began to abbreviate life [offer its foreshortened or more concise version]. Everyone's intellect was biased toward the despair's texture [pleasure/*kaifiyat*], and tried to bring to fruition [completeness] their personal pleasures in whatever way was possible in the four moonlit nights [*cār din kī cāndanī*] available to them. So, abandoning deeply ordered contemplation, cursory views of everything became humanity's specialty. Superficiality became the norm. A lack of responsibility increased. New young poets began to be produced. The way one needs the thickness of knowledge to write poetry, the inclination toward this way came later. But this [knowledge] was rejected all at once, so that there was some agreement on the brevity/shortage of [*'ilm*] knowledge/discernment. [This loss/lack] is usually evident in the work of new poets. Although the experiments had not reached their culmination/conclusion, the claims of their exponents gave birth to their oppositions.

Domestic life was devastated, and with it came the tension of new desire.

These two things, desecration and desire, took form in different shapes and can be seen in the pen and the world/situation of each new poet.

Everyone could do with a few props [a little help] over the course of their life. In prior times, if one looks at the economic situation, what one sees are the old/established, formalized rituals and ways. But these did not stay on, and the era of competition arrived. In the past if one considered the point of view of different kinds of people, all of them had recourse to the stabilities/supports of domestic lives; a deep emotional comfort in their domesticity. That kind of collective soul is now gone. In its stead educational *nisvān* and cinema gathered together and revealed new avenues of pleasure. One has been given permission to view these avenues from a distance, but if you actually try to walk along them then you find yourself unable to complete your life. So this aspect, too, has remained unsatisfactory [thirsty].

The formal features of early poetry circled around fixity. These were obliterated or muted and hidden in a thick mistiness, and in the world of the temporal soul [*nafsā nafsī*] no new elements could be formed, this prop/help was available no longer. In this state, the new poet began to swerve/totter/flinch. This was the root/basic rule of the world, that whoever is beaten or has an accident, they must be pushed/shoved over by her [the world], so that they have the strength to refuse [*manāʿ ke bal kareñ*].

Therefore the shortage/dearth of change for the better is evident in some form in the poetry of new writers. This [shortage] is not the fault of new poetry. If there were a purpose, a benefit to be derived from education, then [new poets] would not even refuse those benefits.

New poetry is a linked [*masalsul*] experiment. It can be raw/deficient: every experiment has these [inadequacies]. But it also pays attention [gives importance] to its good qualities. Because rawness will ripen after a time of contemplative review, and the goodness will be enhanced, be greater than before, visible and complete.

But we will have to await this time with hope. A time when the warp and woof [nerves and sinews] of life's political, social, and personal dealings no longer need to be disentangled [set properly]. In that kind of time, we will hold onto an empathetic way of seeing [sympathetic sight-line], while paying close attention to this truth of new poetry—that, despite its expansive, extensive possibilities, it is still experimental. It is the kind of experiment for which it is both improper and as well as meaningless to hope for a quick/speedy culmination/resolution/sense of completeness, and whose future really promises a glorious vision/visionariness.

These successes or possibilities are in the hands of the new poets.

If they contemplate every side of every issue intently through their hearts, and pay careful attention to it, think hard upon it with affection and sincerity, and move forward with a collective heart or will, then whatever befalls them, the field [of possibilities] will sit within their grasp [will remain in their hands].

# GLOSSARY

*Aflātūn* Plato
*ā'inā* mirror
*'ālim, 'alīm, adīb* learned man, man of letters
*'amal* labor, action, effect, deed
*amrit* nectar
*añjalī* offerings
*anokhā* rare, uncanny
*'aql* reason
*ārzū* impossible desire
*asbāb* cause
*'āshiq* lover
*aṣl* real, root, origin
*aṣlīyat* truth, reality, pureness
*āvārā* vagabond, vagrant, traveler, alone person
*āzād* free
*bahū* daughter-in-law
*baqā* immortality
*bāṭin* exterior events
*beḳhudī* absorption
*bhaj* shared
*bhakta* devotee
*chārpai* bed
*darshan* seeing; *dekhnā* to look; *drsh ṣanskrit* to look
*devadarshan* gaze of the god or goddess
*ḍhañg* mode, form, style
*dīvān* collection of poems by a single author

*fanā* mortality, death
*fanā fi 'l-ḥaq* union with reality
*fann* craft or skill
*fikr o g̣haur* intellect
*gharānā* household, lineage of musicians or dancers
*gīt* song
*gopī* female herder
*gulistān* garden, rose garden
*guzarā hū'ā zamāna* past era
*ḥalqah-e arbāb-e ẕauq* circle of the men of taste
*ḥaqīqat parast* social realist
*ib-ham* allusiveness
*ijtamā'ī* social
*infirādī ḥāfiẓah* individual memory
*insānīyat-e arzū* human desires and needs
*ishq* love
*iṣlāḥ* correction, reform, revision
*iẓāfiyat* possibility of accrual
*jadīd* modern; *jadīdiyāt* modernist, modernity
*jān or sirr* higher soul
*jinsī* sexual
*jism* body
*josh* passion
*junūn* ecstatic madness of love
*kaifiyat* mood
*ḳhud 'arẓī* self-absorption, self-reflexive, reflective
*ḳhudī* personhood, Iqbal's notion of
*kināyāh* implication
*ma'āshī, iqtiṣādī* economic
*māddī* material
*mā'nī afrīnī* elaboration and reading of meaning
*maqāmāt* end, stages, places of rest
*mā'rifat* gnosis, mystical insight
*marśiyah* elegy
*maśnavī* narrative or reflective poem

*māẓī, hāl,* and *mustaqbil* past, present, and utopian future
*maẓmūn* poetic theme or proposition, topos
*maẓmūn āfrīnī* creating propositions
*mub-ham* murky, secret
*muḥabbat* love
*mukḥāṭab* reader, person addressed in literary work
*mushā'irā* a gathering at which poets read their verses
*nafs* carnal desire, lower soul, breath, moment, time
*naslī yāden̄* genealogical memories
*nayikā* beloved
*naẓar* looking, gaze; naẓariyah audience perspectives
*pardah nashīn* hidden behind the veil
*pīr* holy man; qalandars wandering holy men
*Plūtark* Plutarch
*pujārī* Brahmin priest
*qaṣīdah* ode
*qaum* community
*rekḥtī* a form of poetry in which women appear to speak to other women
*ruḥ* constituent of soul
*saramāyah* capitalism
*sharīf ādmi* moral man
*shi'r* two-line verse from ghazal, often treated as an independent unit
*shlokā* verse in ṣanskrit
*siyāsī* political
*swadeshi* of our own country
*tabdīl* change
*taḥrīk-e taraqqī* movement of progress
*takḥalluṣ* poetic name
*takḥayyul* human imagination, fancy
*taraqqī pasand* Progressives, progress loving
*taraqqiyāt* Progressive
*tārīkḥ* date, history
*ṭarīqah* sufi path
*tarjumān* translator
*taṣavvur* contemplation, imagination, idea, concept, term

*tāzagī* newness, freshness

*uslūb* way, style, method

*ustād* teacher

*yātrā/jātrā* ritualized, sometimes circular journey

*ẓāhir* exterior events, outside, open

*żāt* race, breed, caste, creed

## NOTES

### INTRODUCTION: JOURNEY TOWARD MIRAJI

1. "Āgahī dām-e shanīdan jis qadr cāhe bichā'e / muddā' 'anqā hai apne 'ālam-e taqrīr kā." Mīrzā Asadullāh Khān Ghālib, *Dīvān-e Ghālib* (Delhi: Educational Book House, 1981), 728.

2. Faiz and Rashid were Miraji's contemporaries—all three came into prominence in the 1920s and 1930s and engaged in discussions on poetry with each other. Faiz wrote the opening statement for Miraji's first book, *Mashriq o maghrib ke naghmeñ*, and Miraji and Rashid corresponded regularly about aesthetics and colonialism. Taken together, the three epitomize different poetic stances that work in tandem.

3. Miraji is a woman's name; though taking a poetic name was considered apropos for a poet, taking a name across gender was not.

4. For this book, all titles of poems, short stories, plays, and articles will appear within the text in their English translations (original titles will be used in the footnotes or appear after the English in parentheses); the titles of books, journals, and essays, however, will appear in their original language (translations will be given in parentheses).

5. As I will go on to discuss, my response to Miraji's poetry was not anomalous. Faiz, among others, was puzzled by it, his incomprehension at odds with the comfortable familiarity (to him) of Miraji's prose. This prose/poetry dichotomy echoes the simultaneous paradoxical ease and difficulty that one meets in oneself as a reader of Miraji's poetry.

6. "Classical" is of course a contested, constructed term, whose awkward history one only occasionally learns after being trained in it.

7. In an amusing essay, "The French Mistake," Nancy K. Miller describes in hilarious detail the kinds of mistakes a non-native speaker makes in awkward situations. Her slips are reminiscent of mine and gave me a vocabulary with which to

describe my own. See Miller, *Getting Personal: Feminist Occasions and Other Autobiographical Acts* (New York: Routledge, 1991).

8. For other discussions of comfort and discomfort under similar circumstances, see Stanley Fish, "Is There a Text in This Class?" and "How Ordinary Is Ordinary Language?" in *Is There a Text in This Class? The Authority of Interpretive Communities* (Cambridge, Mass.: Harvard University Press, 1980). See also Douglas Robinson, *The Translator's Turn* (Baltimore: The Johns Hopkins University Press, 1991).

9. Miraji's poetry falls into different incompatible modes. His ghazals and *gīt* are "scripted," as he puts it, for singing. They were sung on the radio in the 1930s and early 1940s, and their most recent incarnation is a pop version of the ghazal "Nagarī nagarī phirā musāfir," sung by Najma Rizvi. Miraji's ghazals and *gīt* are comprehensible because they are continuous with traditional forms, themes, and images. His *naẓm*, on the other hand, though they need to be read aloud, do not lend themselves to singing or to easy comprehension.

10. Ahmad is known in literary critical circles in the United States for his response to Jameson and for his recent book *In Theory: Classes, Nations, Literature* (London: Verso, 1992). His translations and transcreations of Ghalib's ghazals are collected in *Ghazals of Ghalib* (New York: Columbia University Press, 1971).

11. Slips in signification, reading him through the available categories of sexual deviance, were seemingly given factual credence by the balls. The oddness of the slips, continuous with those used on women writing in other sites (not on the subcontinent), mark cites of discomfort around gender. Gender, then, specifically reading poetry signed under a woman's name, produces slippages that are themselves incomprehensible if mapped onto one another.

12. Aijāz Aḥmad, "Mīrājī: Shaḳhṣiyat aur fann," *Saverā* 36 (May–June 1966): 5–39. Unless otherwise stated, all translations used in this book are mine.

13. The reason I have made this fairly obvious point explicit is precisely because something so ordinary—that people are complicated and paradoxical—seems to escape most of Miraji's biographers. They keep painting a portrait of him—that of the wild man—that is consistently and remarkably uniform and unhampered by paradox. I am not only interested in the content of the stories but also in the way that they come to function metonymically and stand in for the whole person. The "wild man" portrait became the popular and most widely circulated picture of Miraji, and often the *only* picture of him. See Chapter 1 for a longer discussion of this point.

CHAPTER 1: STORIES FROM A CHILDHOOD

1. From a story told by Shahid Ahmad Dihlavi, written for *Nayā daur* (New era). It had been told to him by a close friend of Miraji's, Yusuf Zafar. Dihlavi's version begins: "When I visited Pindi [Rawalpindi] some time ago, Miraji's close friend Yusuf Zafar Sahib narrated a strange incident to me. He had gone that year on the *haj*. He said . . ." *Shi'r o ḥikmat*, ed. Mughani Tabassum (Delhi: Educational Publishing House, 1987), 28.

2. "Żikr us parīvash kā, aur phir bayān apnā / ban gayā raqīb āḳhir thā jo rāzdān apnā." Ġhālib, *Dīvān-e Ġhālib*, 64.

3. I first encountered this information in an article written by Vajihuddin Ahmad, published while he was writing a dissertation on Miraji. This piece, "Sarguzasht-e Mīrājī," was published in *Shi'r o ḥikmat* (21–26) but has been reiterated in almost every chronological sketch of Miraji's life.

4. *Shi'r o ḥikmat*, between pages 54 and 55, has pictures of the house.

5. *Imperial Gazetteer of India*, 2 vols., Provincial ser. (Lahore: Aziz, 1979), 1: 101.

6. Anīs Nāgī, *Mīrājī: Ek bhaṭkā hu'ā shā'ir* (Lahore: Pakistan Books and Ladiri Sounds, 1991), 14. Nagi's position is a curious amalgam of early-nineteenth-century British versions of the antievolutionary immutability of the other, those who had no access to immediate power (working class, Indians) as seen in the work of Charles White and in Edmund Burke's exhortations to the working poor. This belief in immutability continued into the late nineteenth century in discussions of recapitulation that did not permit certain races to move out of their ontogenetic lot, and in accounts of innate criminality that told innateness from physical characteristics which linked criminals to primitives and animals. Accounts of Miraji's life narrated through his mental, psychological, and physical degeneracy rely implicitly on similar claims. See Stephen Jay Gould, *Ever Since Darwin: Reflections in Natural History* (New York: W. W. Norton, 1997), chaps. 27 and 28, for discussions on how insanity is substantiated, particularly in the work of Lombrosco.

7. Author interview with Mrs. Din, 10 September 1998.

8. "Ḳhāk pe bhī kūce kī ab apne lūtne dete tum nahiṅ, āh / yā ki hamāre ḳhātir kiyā kyā farsh bichāye jāte the." *Unkā 'ahd aur ishikīyah shā'irī* (Lahore: 1952), 97–99.

9. See Denzil Ibbetson, *Punjab Castes* (1916; repr., Delhi: B. R. Publishing, 1974). See also *Crime and Criminality in British India*, ed. Anand A. Yang (Tuscon: University of Arizona Press, 1985), as well as Raj Kapoor's 1951 film *Āvārā* (Bombay: R. K. Films), which portrays the life of a criminal and takes on questions of the law and its expectations of the immutability of someone born and bred in a criminalized world.

10. In Miraji's unpublished manuscript notes. The verse is Miraji's Urdu translation of an English translation of a *rubā'ī* from Omar Khayyam: "How sweet is mortal Sovranty—think some / Others—How blest the Paradise to come: / Ah, take the cash in hand and waive the rest / Oh, the brave music of a distant drum." *Rubaiyat of Omar Khayyam: A Critical Edition*, ed. Christopher Decker (Charlottesville: University of Virginia Press, 1997), 13, no. 12.

11. Mīrājī, "Nāmukammal sailf-porṭraiṭ," in *Mīrājī: Shakhṣiyat aur fann*, ed. Kumār Pāshi (New Delhi: Modern Publishing, 1981), 45–50, and in the reprinted edition as the foreword to the second edition of *Mīrājī kī naẓmeñ* (Lucknow: Nusrat Publishers, 1990), 14–20.

12. Miraji's translations folded the time of past into the time of the present.

13. "Peshīn go'ī / hamārī zindagī ke bād shāyad / ko'ī faẓl-e bahār ā'egī aisī / uṭhegī ko'ī ṣada-e bāzgusht aur / hamāre gīt ik duniyā sunegī." "Saifo," in *Mashriq o maghrib ke naghmeñ* (Songs from the East and from the West) (Lahore: Punjab Academy, 1958).

14. Ẓafar 'Alī Khān, "Bā'ykāṭ," in *Intikhāb-e zamīndār* (Lucknow: Uttar Pradesh Urdu Academy, 1988), 36–39; *Modern Review* 11, no. 4 (April 1912): 445–45; and no. 5 (May 1912): 541; "The Colonization of India" in May 1912, 457–84; and Sir H. H. Johnston, "The Rise of the Native," *Quarterly Review* (January 1910): 121–51.

15. Slavoj Žižek, *The Sublime Object of Ideology* (New York: Verso, 1989), 69–71.

16. For sentimentality and survival and its relationship to reiteration, or repetition of trauma, see Susan Stewart, "Coda: Reverse Trompe L'Oeil / The Eruption of the Real," in *Crimes of Writing: Problems in the Containment of Representation* (Durham, N.C.: Duke University Press, 1994), 273–90; Cathy Caruth, *Unclaimed Experience: Trauma, Narrative, and History* (Baltimore: Johns Hopkins University Press, 1996).

17. Lauren Berlant, *The Queen of America Goes to Washington City: Essays on Sex and Citizenship* (Durham, N.C.: Duke University Press, 1997). See also Berlant's more recent work on sentiment and sentimentality.

18. See Sir H. H. Johnston, "The Rise of the Native."

19. Žižek, *The Sublime Object of Ideology*.

20. Slavoj Žižek, "The Virtual as Real," in *The Plague of Fantasies* (London, New York: Verso, 1997).

21. Walter Benjamin, *Illuminations*, ed. Hannah Arendt., trans. Harry Zohn (New York: Schocken Books, 1978), 253–64.

22. See "Samuñdar kā bulāvā" (Call of the sea) and my discussion of it in Chapter 7.

23. Here, knowledge is like the mystification that attends the circulation of capital in discussions that link cotton and commodities (cotton as a commodity, cotton enabling commodification, etc.).

24. Why are Indian men barbaric? See Mrinalini Sinha's discussion on the Ilbert Bill controversy, chapter 1 of *Colonial Masculinity: The "Manly Englishman" and the "Effeminate Bengali" in the Late Nineteenth Century* (Manchester and New York: Manchester University Press, 1995).

25. The *Modern Review*, May 1912, describes the armed forces as the habitus of Muslims.

26. *Modern Review*, May 1912, 542.

27. Mīrājī, *Is naẓm meñ* (Delhi: Alami Press, 1944), and *Mashriq o maghṛib ke naghmeñ* (Lahore: Punjab Academy, 1958); Braj Narā'n Cakbast, *Intikhāb-e manẓūmāt* (Lucknow: Uttar Pradesh Urdu Academy, 1981); E. Powys Mathers, *Eastern Love*, vols. 1–3 (New York: Horace Liveright; London: John Rodker, 1933).

28. Certainly Powys Mathers's collection, which appeared to be one of Miraji's reference texts for pan-Eastern love lyric and which included Japanese and Korean poetry alongside South Asian verse, lent itself to these grouped configurations. But by the time Miraji wrote, "cultural nationalist" aesthetic questions posed in relation to painting/sculpture (Indian art) had already been linked to the history of Japanese aesthetics through Buddhism (among other lineages). The complex of Abdur Rehman Chughtai, Abanindranath Tagore, Okakura Kazuko (and his pan-Asian aesthetic promoted by Sister Nivedita, and his style of painting, wash, etc., promoted through exponents of the Bengal school) offered precursors who reconstituted the past through an efflorescence of style that Miraji might have availed himself of. In fact, some of Miraji's poetry seems like the lyrical, worded rendition of different styles of early-twentieth-century painting from Chughtai to Gagendranath Tagore (with the attendant negotiations with "Eastern-based" and "Westward-looking" aesthetic questions). Miraji might be fruitfully considered here alongside the Chayavad school of poetry, especially Nirala and Mahadevi Verma. See discussions by Tapati Guha Thakurta, *The Making of a New "Indian" Art: Artists, Aesthetics and Nationalism in Bengal, c. 1850–1920* (Cambridge, Eng.: Cambridge University Press, 1992); Partha Mitter, *Art and Nationalism in Colonial India, 1850–1922: Occidental Orientations* (Cambridge, Eng.: Cambridge University Press, 1994); Sister Nivedita, *The Complete Works of Sister Nivedita*, vol. III (Calcutta: Sister Nivedita Girl's School, 1967); Muḥammad ʿAdbur Reḥmān Cughṭā'ī, *Maqālāt-e cughṭā'ī*, ed. Shīmā Majīd (Islamabad: Markaz Khazati, 1987), for example, "Merā fann aur shāʿirī-e mashriq," 20–28.

29. "Aithans ke nām," in "Saifo," in *Mashriq o maghṛib ke naghmeñ* (Songs

from the East and from the West) (Lahore: Punjab Academy, 1958), 342. According to Miraji the poem was perhaps inspired by Sappho's compatriot Alcaeus's "Hubb-e vaṭan" (Love of one's homeland).

30. Mīrājī, *Mīrājī kī naẓmeñ* (1st ed., Delhi: Saqi Book Depot, 1944), 164–66. In the second, reprint edition of the book, 108–10.

31. Emmanuel Levinas, "The Face," in *Ethics and Infinity: Conversations with Philip Nemo*, trans. Richard A. Cohen (Pittsburgh: Duquesne University Press, 1985), 85–101.

32. See G. Bose, "The Genesis of Homosexuality," *Samiksa* 4, no. 2 (1950): 66–82, first published in *Proceedings of the Indian Psycho-analytic Society* (February 1926); also see Bose's article "A New Theory of Mental Life," *Indian Journal of Psychology* (January–July 1933): 147–57.

33. "Nagarī nagarī phirā musāfir ghar kā rāstā bhūl gayā / . . . kyā hai merā kyā hai terā apnā parāyā bhūl gayā," in Mīrājī, *Tīn rañg* (Pindi: Kitab Numa, 1968), 151.

34. For a more comprehensive account of local Kheda, Godhra, and Baroda politics of the time, see *Gujarat State Gazetteer* (Ahmadabad: Gujarat Government Publications Depot, 1989), 241–45. The accounts collected here are based on colonial ones from the *Bombay Presidency Gazetteer*.

35. The *Modern Review* ([March 1912]: 344) printed a thank-you notice for a remittance made to their fund for famine relief in Gujarat. It also mentions the ways in which the railways exacerbated famines, contributing to higher prices for food, provoked by an economy that transported the bulk of locally grown food away for export to other sites. Aruna Awasthi, *History and Development of the Railways in India* (New Delhi: Deep and Deep Publications, 1994), esp. chap. 5, 131, 155.

36. Quote from an interview with Miraji's brother 'Inayat' ullah Ḍār, in Aḥmad, "Sarguẓasht-e Mīrājī," 23.

37. P. S. A. Berridge, *The Story of the North Western Railway* (Newton Abbot, Eng.: David and Charles, 1969). See chap. 11, "The Lansdowne and Ayub Bridges," regarding all the tribulations of constructing the Lansdowne Bridge.

38. *Dalhousie's Minute: Railway Minute of the Governor General*, 20 April 1853. See also Dalhousie's minute for 4 July 1850, The National Archives, New Delhi.

39. Awasthi, *History and Development*, esp. chaps. 2–4.

40. *Illustrated London News*, 12 March 1864; *Calcutta Review* (1867); *Inspection Report of the East India Railway*, July 1865, East India Railway, National Archives of India, New Delhi.

41. J. N. Westwood, *Railways of India* (Newton Abbot, Eng.: David and Charles, 1974), 46.

42. Michael Satow and Ray Desmond, *Railways of the Raj* (New York and London: New York University Press, 1980), 17.

43. *Gujarat State Gazetteer*, "Mineral Wealth," 42–48; and *Gazetteer of India: Gujarat State, Vadodara District*, (Ahmadabad: Government Printing, Stationery, and Publications, 1979), 444.

44. *Gujarat State Gazetteer*, "Mineral Wealth," 46.

45. I am indebted to Kath Weston for helping me translate this line.

46. *Gujarat State Gazetteer*, "Mineral Wealth," 46.

47. Ghanshyām Joshī, *Pāvāgaḍh darshan* (Ahmadabad: Chirag Printers, 1998), 3.

48. *Shrī mahākālī mātājī* (Ahmadabad: Gaurav Publication, n.d.), 3–8.

49. Joshī, *Pāvāgaḍh darshan*, 3.

50. Leela Mayor, "Pavagadh and Champaner—A Tale of a Hill and a City: An Outline Treatment for a Documentary," faxed correspondence, 8 April 1998. Joshī, *Pāvāgaḍh darshan*, 50, 71–75.

51. "Tārīḳh kahatī hai dūr o rāz māẓī ke har ik lamḥe meñ ka'ī dāstāneñ haiñ! . . . aur phir sab taṣavvur aur sab ḳhyāl ḥāfiẓe meñ jā chupe yā raftā raftā tārīḳh ban gaye ya pānī kī ik būnd meñ bas gaye." Mīrājī, "Bāteñ: Kitāb-e pareshāñ" (The book of disquiet), in *ḳhayāl* (May 1949–); the beginning echoes "Bāteñ," from *Sāqī* (November 1944), reprinted in Jamīl Jālibī, ed., *Mīrājī: Ek muṭāla'h* (Miraji: A glance/perusal/study) (Lahore: Sang-e Masil Publications, 1990), 568–70.

52. Interviews with Leela Mayor, 10 January 1998, and Jayesh Patel, 11 January 1998; Joshī, *Pāvāgaḍh darshan*.

53. I take my lead from the questions provoked by Marghūb 'Alī in his introduction to the new edition of *Mīrājī kī naẓmeñ*: "Why only point to those attributes in Miraji and his work that seemed to be immediately visible and accessible?" Why not go to those things apparently hidden from the gaze, which were not necessarily even those that Miraji himself pointed out? Miraji's focus on obscurity might lead us to them, even though that movement might for a moment seem antithetical to Miraji's self-representations.

54. David Hardiman discusses Bhils who managed a portion of their livelihood by working as local enforcers. Hardiman also speaks to the production of tribal identity and a paradoxical sovereignty accorded to the Bhils through their participation in colonial spectacles, durbars, that attempted to transform them into acceptable forms of tribals. Hardiman points out that the Bhils of this region "were at best awkward participants in the ritual[s]." David Hardiman, "Power in

the Forest: The Dangs, 1820–1940," *Subaltern Studies* 8 (New Delhi: Oxford University Press, 1996): 89–147, esp. 107–12.

55. Miraji's most infamous poem, "Lab-e jū-e bāre" (Lip of a full river), circles around a woman peeing. See Appendix A for a translation.

56. See *Mashriq o maghrib ke naghmen.*

57. *Mīrājī: Shakhṣiyat aur fann*, 48.

58. Ibid., 49.

59. Ibid., 45.

60. Ibid., 45, 47.

61. See my discussion on "Devadāsī aur pujārī" (Devadasi and pujari) in Chapter 7.

62. Here Miraji explores the spaces where the fetish/fetishism (commodity fetishism and sexual fetishism) come together with visual registers from various poetic traditions. In the world of Miraji's childhood, the gaze he talks about, the forms of looking which he (as a writer describing the sexuality of a child) employs in the narrative, bring the ghazal into autobiography. The ghazal plays off resignification, resignifying body parts (the arch of an eyebrow), which then enter a metaphoric circle (archer, death dealer). In Miraji's work Urdu, Braj, and Sanskrit overlap, and all three turn to scenery, nature metonymizing as desire. This form of lingering looking, looking volunteers a lengthened temporality, stretches the time and space between seeing and touching, and lingers on the possibilities that to Miraji seem foreclosed by touch.

Cloth has by now, in the South Asian context, accrued a great deal of historical work around it. And some of this work haunts Miraji's desire told through cloth. Cloth, discussions of its worth and its designs flow forth when aesthetic desire is broached at the turn of the century, the early 1900s and late 1800s. Cloth becomes the object of fetishization. Nature, in these discussions of cloth, returns to a utopian, precolonial past, when cloth was not quite commodified, not quite produced as an industrial commodity, and circulated alongside mercantile capital as its trading pawn. In the struggles over cloth as the emblem of swadeshi and nationalism, this past is recalled in forms of cultural nationalism. Cloth is something literally stamped with the language of money and desire, and returned to its earlier forms of production, the artisanal communities. Though, in the exchanges where cloth (produced in factories) figures as central "thing" giving clothing in *darshan* (during marriages, childbirth, etc.), cloth sits uneasily in relation to earlier forms of circulation, production. Then there is, as always, Gandhi and his turn to the charka, weaving the idealized and desired national subject into being at the spinning wheel. Emma Tarlo, *Clothing Matters: Dress and Identity in India* (New

Delhi: Viking, 1996); Arjun Appadurai, ed., *The Social Life of Things: Commodities in Cultural Perspective* (Cambridge, Eng.: Cambridge University Press, 1986).

63. See Freud, *Introductory Lectures on Psychoanalysis*, ed. and trans. James Strachey (New York: W. W. Norton, 1977), 305, 348–49. Freud's tale of and event in the life of a man, a foot/shoe fetishist, whose incitement into their pleasures was occasioned when he sat on a stool by the "elderly, dried-up, plain-looking spinster," his governess. Her foot, which was not quite right that day, had been put on a cushion and cradled in a velvet slipper. Though her leg was "properly concealed" this kind of "thin, scraggy foot" became from that moment on the subject of the man's irresistible attractions, and the scene the node around which his fixations adhered. Miraji's tales promise similar incursions into sexuality, which may be the (always incompletely articulated) reasons why he is called a pervert by critics who write obsessively about his sexuality. But unlike this story of Freud's, which circles around "proper concealment," Miraji's visions of bodies are always in a state of improper concealment. In South Asia (as elsewhere) nature (as forest, wood, commodity) and cloth (as commodity) under colonial auspices begin to circulate in a slightly different regime of fetishization—that proposed by Karl Marx (*Capital*, [New York: International Publishers, 1979], 1: 71–94). I say "slightly different regime" because the forms of fetishization both nature and cloth come to bear actually bring together object as desired thing and object as commodity thing. For versions of these assignations between desire and commodification that are pertinent to this allusion see: Appadurai, ed., *The Social Life of Things*; Emily Apter and William Pietz, eds., *Fetishism as Cultural Discourse* (Ithaca, N.Y.: Cornell University Press, 1993); Anne McClintock *Imperial Leather: Race, Gender, and Sexuality in the Colonial Context* (New York and London: Routledge, 1995); and finally Žižek, *The Sublime Object of Ideology*. See also the extensive series of essays on art and cotton in the *Modern Review*, beginning with the swadeshi movement. They give just a tiny insight into the often rancorous discussions on art, aesthetics, desire, cloth, colonial hegemony taking place in South Asia (here primarily Bengal) that bring together cloth as commodity and cloth as object of aesthetic desire.

Though we do not know how much Miraji knew of Freud or Marx, we do know that the Jaico Paperback version of *Totem and Taboo*, published in the forties, was in a list of books Miraji marked off and that he wanted to read. I have the copy, and Akhtarul Iman told me that this wish list was one of many Miraji carried around.

64. Gail Minault, *The Khilafat Movement: Religious Symbolism and Political Mobilization in India* (New York: Columbia University Press, 1982).

65. See Minault's section on Urdu political poetry starting at page 154. See

"Iqbal's Contemporaries" in the second edition of Muhammad Sadiq's *A History of Urdu Literature* (New Delhi: Oxford University Press, 1964). Sadiq also mentions Khushi Muhammad Nazir's Hindi-inflected poetry, which presages some of Miraji's work. See Dr. Afẓal Aḥmad, *Cakbast: Jang-e āzādī kā ek mard-e mujāhid* (Lucknow: Milne Ka Patah, Ardi Khanah, 1975); Braj Narā'n Cakbast, *Subḥ-e vaṭan* (Allahabad, 1994); Muḥammad ʿAlī, *Kalām-e jauhar* (Delhi: Maktaba-e Jamia, n.d.); Hasrat Mūhānī, *Ek siyāsī Dāʿrī* (Dhuliya: Asliya Publications, 1977).

66. Ẓafar ʿAlī Ḳhān, *Bahāristāñ* (Lahore: Urdu Punjab Academy, 1937), 515.

67. Interview with Miraji's brother 'Inayat' ullah Ḍār, in Tabassum, ed., *Shiʿr*, 23. The essays were published by the Hind Printing Press, but the name of the collection is not known.

68. Shīmā Majīd, *Bāqeyāt-e mīrājī* (Remnants of Miraji) (Lahore: Pakistan Books and Ladiri Sounds, 1990), 5.

69. Very little is known about this "relationship" of Miraji's. The little I could glean about it came from letters he wrote to Bashir.

70. Tabassum, ed., *Shiʿr*, 76.

71. Nāgī, *Mīrājī*, 13–14.

72. Tabassum, ed., *Shi'r*, 23.

73. See the first part of Chapter 6 for an extended discussion on the stories and the politics of naming.

74. I have the manuscript version of this book, but it has also been published in a version edited by Shīmā Majīd, Mīrājī, *Sah ātishah* (Bombay: Rakhshanda Kitab Ghar, 1992), 27–29.

75. V. Aḥmad, "Sargużasht-e Mīrājī," 23.

76. Author interview with Akhtarul Iman, 12 January 1988.

77. Mīrājī, *Is naẓm meñ* (In this poem) (Delhi: Alami Press, 1944).

78. Nāgī, *Mīrājī*, 14.

79. "Vidyāpatī aur us ke gīt" (Vidaypati and his songs), in *Mashriq o maghrib ke naghmeñ*, 555–680. *Mashriq o maghrib ke naghmeñ* (Songs from the East and from the West) is the collection of Miraji's essays on non-Urdu speaking poets.

80. *Is naẓm meñ*, 4.

81. Miraji's supposed penchant for Hinduism (to the exclusion of Islam, Arabic, and Persian) is treated as an axis of analysis, but it is also called up as a problem—by Saqi Farooqi, for example. Though Farooqi believes Miraji to be one of the most innovative early exponents of *naẓm*, he feels that when Miraji moved over into Hindi he lost his edge. See Sāqī Fārūqī, "Naẓm kā safar: Mīrājī" (One journey of the *naẓm*: Miraji), in Jālibī, ed., *Mīrājī*, 345–53, esp. 353.

82. This was the second coming of swadeshi ("of our own country"); the first was preceded and gained volume during the swadeshi movement (1890s–1910s).

83. Sajjād Ẓahīr, "Pahalī kul hiñd kanfrains: 1936," in *Roshnā'ī* (New Delhi: Seema Publications, 1985), 97–99. All the information on the conference is from Ẓahīr's accounts and reports, published by the *Hindustan Times*, 9, 10, 11, 13, and 14 April 1936.

84. *Hindustan Times*, 9 April 1936.

85. Ibid., 11 and 12 April 1936.

86. Ibid., 14 April 1936 (report from Motinagar camp, Congress Special Service).

87. Ibid.

88. Folk "culture" had been revitalized, that is produced publicly as the terrain that enabled a return to the more natural rural (also produced as the land that had been gone over so many times that its contours were lost). This production of a folk as "re-vital" returned to some of the questions, concerns, and forms of speaking about value and commodification, as well as aesthetics, that had been initiated during the swadeshi period (and had been spoken about by British anthropologists in the late 1800s). See the *Journal of the Anthropological Society of Bombay* (1890) for samples of these discussions. Concerns with revitalization were concomitant with the PWA meeting in 1936. The PWA was accompanied by expanding socialist movements, revolutionary mushairas under Kaifi Azmi among Bombay workers; a consolidation of the right wing within Congress; an alienated Muslim League, sending out anti-Congress propaganda; the exacerbations of the Hindi-Urdu controversy particular to this time. Certainly all these found their ways, sometimes directly, sometimes obliquely, into the PWA's positions and into Miraji's writing. During the first phase of the Second World War, 1939–1942, Miraji wrote poetry directed at the war. He also commented on *naẓm* (N. M. Rashid's for example) that spoke to desiring forms of colonial territoriality which emerged in and through war. The genesis of the demand for Pakistan was in 1938–1939. Sikandar Hayat Khan, for instance, talks about Pakistan and his opposition to it in the Punjab assembly (while Miraji was in Lahore) in 1941. This period also saw the Cripps Mission and the bombing of Pearl Harbor.

89. The children treated Miraji as someone who could be taken for a woman. Their taunts made it clear that they did not assume he was a woman, but that he could generate confusion about his gender. This understanding of him, as a person who had the potential to gender-bend, is not one that has been explored before.

90. Shāhid Aḥmad Dihlavī, "Mīrājī: Shak̲h̲ṣiyat aur fann," in Kumār Pāshī, *Shak̲h̲ṣiyat aur fann*, 27–28.

91. Author interview with Akhtarul Iman, Bombay, 5 June 1988.

92. Dihlavī, "Mīrājī," 23.

93. Akhtarul Īmān, "Guftanī nā guftanī" (What should or should not be spoken), in Mīrājī, *Sah ātishah,* ed. Shīmā Majīd (Bombay: Rakhshanda Kitab Ghar, 1992), 13–25.

94. Ibid., 17–18.

95. Jālibī, ed., *Mīrājī,* 171–75.

96. "Guftanī nā guftanī," *Sah ātishah,* 15–16.

97. *Is naẓm meñ,* 106–10.

98. Muhammad Umar Memon offered readings of the essay (fax, 8 September 1992) that have been incorporated into my analysis.

99. Yūnus Jāved, *Ḥalqah-e arbāb-e ẓauq* (Lahore: Majlis Taraqqi-e Adab, 1984), 21–22.

100. Ibid., 24.

101. Ibid., 356.

102. Ibid., 40.

103. Ibid., 41.

104. M. R. Luthra, *Indian Broadcasting* (New Delhi: Publications Division, Ministry of Information and Broadcasting, 1986), 1–36; Partha Sarthi Gupta, *Radio and the Raj: 1921–47* (Calcutta: K. P. Bagchi, for the Centre for Studies in Social Sciences, 1995), 1–21.

105. Luthra, *Indian Broadcasting,* 37–49, 85–86; Gupta, *Radio and the Raj,* 23–25.

106. Luthra, *Indian Broadcasting,* 81–82; Gupta, *Radio and the Raj,* 26–29.

107. The opening programs from the Delhi station included: IBS orchestra, conducted by S. S. Niazi; ghazals sung by Master Faqiruddin; *tarañg*; a farce directed by K. M. Iftekharullah; news in Hindustani and news in English (Luthra, *Indian Broadcasting,* 95). The choices were skewed toward Urdu/Hindustani, perhaps because the broadcast area stretched from Lahore to Lucknow. But some people felt that the Delhi station was the private fiefdom of the Bokhari brothers, who inducted their old friends and favorites, mainly literati who wrote in Urdu/Hindustani.

108. Luthra, *Indian Broadcasting,* 92–94.

109. Ibid., 123.

110. Draft of letter written by Miraji to the news director of AIR Delhi, in *Shi'r,* 122–23.

111. The *Vanguard* (Delhi, 1942) presents complicated positions in relation to the "Quit India" resolution, since Hitler invaded Russia. That year saw a spate of interesting poetry, Marxist, and romantic (mystical/love lyric), written and published across South Asia. Some instances include: Jibananda Das, "Ajneya"; Banalatā Sen, *Ciṇtā* (which turned perhaps to D. H. Lawrence, whom Miraji had also

been translating); Mahadevi Verma, *Dīpashikhā*; Nirala, *Kukurmutta*; and Faiz Ahmad Faiz, *Naqsh-e faryādī*. Miraji wrote a piece for All-India Radio, hybridizing poetry/translations and music. The war broadcasts sent into the air forms of musical composition that were unmarked as hybrid. See David Lelyveld's work on the radio.

112. Dihlavī, "Mīrājī," 27–28.

113. Ibid., 27.

114. Vishvanandan Bhaṭnāgar, "Mīrājī merī naẓr meñ," in Tabassum, ed., *Shi'r*, 111–12.

115. Dihlavī, "Mīrājī," 29.

116. *Mīrājī ke gīt* (Lahore: Maktabah-e Urdu, 1943); *Gīt hī gīt* (Delhi: Saqi Book Depot, 1944); and *Mīrājī kī naẓmeñ* (Delhi: Saqi Book Depot, 1944).

117. See Jālibī, ed., *Mīrājī*, for "Bāteñ."

118. See ibid., 670; *Sah ātishah*, 107–20 ("Dillī meñ, 1942–46"); and *Bāqeyāt-e Mīrājī*, 100, 131, 134.

119. *Sah ātishah*, 114–15; *Tīn rañg*, 110–11. Miraji's manuscript of *Sah ātishah* is the place this poem appears in the manuscripts. It was probably added to *Tīn rañg* when the collection was edited and published after the poet's death. Maybe the version published in *Sah ātishah* was one that Miraji sent to *Jama'at* (Delhi) and then revised for the book. Like most of the poems in his manuscripts, this one has a note by it in the table of contents indicating where it had previously been published.

120. Bhaṭnāgar, "Mīrājī merī naẓr meñ," 112–13.

121. Dihlavī, "Mīrājī," 126.

122. Ibid., 127.

123. *Times of India*, 22 January 1946.

124. Ibid., 20, 21, 22, and 27 February 1946.

125. Ibid., 4, 6 April 1946.

126. Bhaṭnāgar, "Mīrājī merī naẓr meñ," 113–15.

127. Stephane Mallarmé, *Poems*, trans. Roger Fry, ed. and comm. Charles Mauron (New York: New Directions, 1951), 4. Mauron includes this "ironic" epigram, found among Fry's papers, in a footnote.

128. Sa'ādat Ḥasan Manṭū, trans., "Tīn gole" (Three balls), in Pāshī, ed., *Mīrājī*, 31; also published in *Ganj-e farishte* (Lahore: Maktaba Shur o Adab, n.d.), 79–100, and reprinted in Jālibī, ed., *Mīrājī*.

129. Ibid., 31–33. Manto uses the same words (*ib-ham* and *mub-ham*) to describe Miraji that Miraji uses as a category in which to place his poetry.

130. Miraji's readability and unreadability were located in two different texts—his prose was accessible and his poetry was not.

131. Manṭū, "Tīn gole," 32.

132. Faiẓ, "Ḥarf-e āg̱ẖāz" (Opening words), in *Mashriq o mag̱ẖrib ke nag̱ẖ-meñ*, 5–6.

133. Dilhavi's analogy for Miraji is of a crow trying to walk like a duck and in the process forgetting how crows walk while never being able to master duck walking.

134. The wild man represents an image of an ascetic. Both biographers concur in their use of the image, but do different things to it in relation to the real "historical" subject, Miraji. An ascetic for Manto and Ahmad is someone who eludes (repudiates) certain kinds of conventional characteristics; this is an appropriate anthropomorphic representation for someone like Miraji, who wrote difficult poetry.

135. Carlo Coppola, "Urdu Poetry, 1935–1970: The Progressive Episode" (Ph.D. diss., University of Chicago, 1975), 254–57. See Sajjād Ẓahīr, "Haiderābād aur ahamdābād kā kanfrains," in *Roshnā'ī* (New Delhi: Seema Publications, 1985), 360–91; author interview with Akhtarul Iman, 7 January 1988; also Īmān, "Guftanī nā guftanī" and "Mīrajī ke ākhirī lamḥe" (Miraji's last moments), in Jālibī, ed., *Mīrājī*, 171–75, for details not provided by his interviews.

136. *Sah ātishah*, 19; and "Mīrajī ke āxirī lamhe, 171.

137. See Chapter 6 for a copy of the frontispiece to the collection and a longer discussion on Mirabai, picked up again in Chapter 7.

138. See "Lessons of a Baud," in Mathers, *Eastern Love*, vol. 1.

139. See photo inserts between 64–65 of *Shi'r*. For another visual version of Miraji nearing his death, see Manṭo, "Tīn gole."

140. Īmān, "Mīrajī ke ākhirī lamhe." 172; author interview with Akhtarul Iman, 14 June 1988.

141. Author interview with Zoe Ansari, 19 May 1989.

142. Ibid., 3 January 1989.

143. Ibid.

144. For a more extensive discussion, see Chapter 2 in this book. See also Carlo Coppola's unpublished dissertation. Ismat Chughtai was charged with obscenity and brought to trial for her short story "Liḥāf"; the charges were dismissed.

145. Author interview with Akhtarul Iman, 14 June 1988.

146. This account is compiled from notes taken during all my conversations with Akhtarul Iman. The portrait of Akhtarul Iman describes him as I saw him at our first meeting.

147. Jacques Derrida, *The Gift of Death* (Chicago: University of Chicago Press, 1995), 41.

148. Ghālib, *Dīvān-e Ghālib*, 206.

149. Īmān, "Mīrajī ke ākhirī lamḥe," 173–75.

## CHAPTER 2: MIRAJI AND THE PROGRESSIVE WRITERS' ASSOCIATION

1. Slogan used by Akhtarul Iman to describe the Progressive Writers' Association, in interview with him, Bombay, 14 June 1988.

2. See Jāved, ed., *Ḥalqah-e arbāb-e ẓauq*.

3. I do not absolutely separate the Progressives from the modernists, because the work they did overlapped in substantive ways. If one wishes to separate them one has to elaborate and perhaps collapse or keep open the distinctions between *ḥaqīqat* and *taraqqi*, as well as the distinctions between *jadīdiyāt* and *taraqqi*. One also has to pose as necessary the isolation of form from content (but only in certain instances). Peter Gaeffke, writing about Ajneya, takes some of the influences on Ajneya into account, citing Valéry as one. On Ajneya's behalf, Gaeffke refuses the accusation that the poet is merely experimentalist: *nayī kavitā*, or new poetry, emerged from the formal and political questions asked by the *pratīgvādī* (Progressives). So, the particular form of modernism associated with *nayī kavitā* does not have to be nonpolitical. One instance of the fusion between Hindi Progressives and Urdu modernists (if one wishes to hold on to the differentiations between Hindi and Urdu, modernist and Progressive) is Upendranath Askh, who joined the Halqa under Miraji in the 1940s. Peter Gaeffke, *A History of Indian Literature: Hindi Literature in the Twentieth Century* (Wiesbaden: Otto Harrassowitz, 1978), 86–87.

4. See Ranajit Guha's essays in Ranajit Guha and Gayatri Chakravorty Spivak, eds., *Selected Subaltern Studies* (New York and Oxford: Oxford University Press, 1988), preface, 35–36, and "On Some Aspects of the Historiography of Colonial India," 37–44.

5. In practice they were somewhat like both colonial clubs and Urdu mushairas, where the members who attended were not just bound together by class or status (participation ensured a possible status) but through shared fantasies of what each member embodied and what "qualities" or ways of being had to be attended to in order to set up or enact principles of exclusion. These took on a certain cast if the clubs or groups were those whose members introduced new ones.

6. Luthra, *Indian Broadcasting*.

7. The language of diaspora, *pace* Homi Bhabha, is a language of nostalgic associations with a constructed tradition. For poets writing in Urdu (like Iqbal), the diasporic nostalgia is not just figured through geographic shifts within the Indian subcontinent but also in terms of a pan-Islamic transcultural heritage and the lost empire. In the poetry of Faiz, for example, this nostalgia for a lost "cultural tradition," with a past that was both left behind volitionally and as a condition of historical circumstances, is negotiated through the figure of a female beloved in

*nazm* like "Mujhse pahlī sī muhabbat mere meḥbūb na māñg." See Homi K. Bhabha, "DissemiNation: Time, Narrative, and Margins of the Modern Nation," in Homi Bhabha, ed., *Nation and Narration* (London: Routledge, 1990), 291–323.

8. Vinay Dharwadkar, writing about the formations of literature and vernacular in confluence with Orientalism, goes to Herder (romanticism) and early Enlightenment definitions of the literary to explore these formations. See "Orientalism and the Study of Indian Literatures," in Carol Breckenridge and Peter van der Veer, eds., *Orientalism and the Postcolonial Predicament* (Philadelphia: University of Pennsylvania Press, 1993), 155–85. See David Lelyveld's essay "The Fate of Hindustani: Colonial Knowledge and the Project of a National Language," in the same volume, 189–214; Michel Foucault, *Care of the Self,* vol. 1 (New York: Vintage Books, 1986); *Ethics: Subjectivity and Truth*, vol. 1, ed. Paul Rabinow, trans. Robert Hurley and others (New York: New Press, 1997); John Guillory, *Cultural Capital: The Problem of Literary Canon Formation* (Chicago: The University of Chicago Press, 1993), part 1, "Canonical and Noncanonical: The Current Debate"; part 3, "The Discourse of Value: From Adam Smith to Barbara Herrnstein Smith"; Gayatri Chakravorty Spivak, *Outside in the Teaching Machine* (New York and London: Routledge, 1993), 61–64, "Poststructuralism, Marginality," and *In Other Worlds: Essays in Cultural Politics* (New York and London: Routledge, 1988), 154–75, "Scattered Speculations of the Question of Value"; Pierre Bourdieu, *Distinction: A Social Critique of the Judgement of Taste*, trans. Richard Nice (Cambridge, Mass.: Harvard University Press, 1984). And of course, Marx. There is a vast literature on transformations of the canon, opening up the canon, institutional transformations in relation to practices in the United States.

9. Under Bentinck, in the 1830s, science was marked off as a different field of study with separate institutions that taught medical sciences, for example, and law clearly came to occupy a slightly different space than other forms of knowledge production (though it was still connected to them).

10. Lelyveld, "The Fate of Hindustani," 202.

11. It is necessary to hold onto the separation of the work from the writer who produces it, because the writer's personhood is not always based on the work. A work can be judged "immoral" while the writer is not. Certainly there are debates over where a writer falls in relation to work, or how a writer is produced in relation to work. See Foucault, *The Care of the Self.* Works often exceed the taxonomies used to categorize them; they spill out of the edges of taxonomic lists into the pressed-out spaces of the pleasurable that can not quite be contained or dissipated. Faiz's poetry is one instance of this circulation: his lyric detours into the space of pleasure.

12. Quoted in Sisir Kumar Das, *A History of Indian Literature 1912–1956* (New Delhi: Sahitya Akademi, 1995), 693.

13. Concern with poverty, realist representation, and folk literature predated the formation of the PWA in India; it was not new but part of a popular/populist literary trend. In Gujarati, for example, Jhaverchand Meghani wrote songs that resonated with Saurashtrian folk traditions; Umashankar's collection *Gaṅgotrī* (1934) contained socialist lyrics; "Koyā bhagat nī kaḍi vāñi ane garībanāñ gīto" (The bitter voice of Koya Bhagat and songs of the poor) was written by Sundaram in 1933. See Das, *A History of Indian Literature*, 88–89.

14. One strain of writing in Hindi that follows some of Miraji's concerns is Bacchan's, who wrote poems about the vagaries of desire and wine-enhanced pleasure, as well *gīt*-influenced lyrics; he also translated Omar Khayyam in 1935. However, the modernism (*jadīdiyāt*) supposedly initiated by Miraji and carried into a new disruption of the formal and thematic in recent years is probably more akin to *nayī kavitā* in Hindi; in both, newness is exemplified by unraveling of linear time and space, the exploration of language that engages with the intervals between word and thing, and metaphors that turn grammar slightly awry to produce suggestiveness or allusiveness (*ib-ham*), moving between "fantasy, dream, dialogue, image," as well as reiterating the "I" turned over and over in image to roll out or carefully delineate the shifting self. The more radical versions of this poetics metastasizes grammar, twisting and squeezing language, laying it down to bare the knife edges of rules, and turning semiosis against itself. Muktibodh is a well-known exponent, who like Miraji wrote journey poems, *mahākāvya*. See Peter Gaeffke, *A History of Indian Literature*. Gaeffke proposes Valéry, Lorca, Eliot as counterpoints, but the entire Symbolist movement might have served just as well. Twisting language has its precursors in the Indic tradition, most notably in the *ultī bāñsī* of Kabir. See ibid., 83–88.

15. Gene D. Overstreet and Marshall Windmiller, *Communism in India* (Berkeley: University of California Press, 1960), 432.

16. Ahmed Ali, "The Progressive Writers' Movement and Creative Writers in Urdu," in *Marxist Influences and South Asian Literature*, 1: 35–44. (East Lansing: Asian Studies Center, Michigan State University, 1974).

17. I believe that as the UPWA coalesced into a more sharply demarcated community and acquired more power there was more at stake in regulating literary activity. Also, it was clear that at this time the trajectories of communities were (confined to) unitary ones. Multiple perspectives and positions were not part of the vocabulary or discourse of community formation. Consequently, as the community formed, it ejected "inappropriate" definitions of the fields—literary and

political—that were considered integral to the community's identity. These fields then became narrower and more naturalized, and the definition of literature advocated by the UPWA became the "essential" core of literary activity. For "essentialism," see Diana Fuss, *Essentially Speaking: Feminism, Nature, and Difference* (New York: Routledge, 1989), 2.

18. See Kaifi Azmi's personal account of encountering the collection, and through it, meeting the Progressive movement for the first time. His story is told as a revelation: of the secret reading of *Añgāre*'s text, in a room, by a young man seated on the edge of his Maulavi Sahib's bed. Azmi, newly arrived from a small town and curious about what looked like a cryptic rendezvous, peeked into this room through a transom and saw this cabal (Maulavi laid out in bed, the boy sitting at his feet, and two or three other Maulavis huddled around the bed in chairs) in action. When the young boy emerged, Azmi asked him about the small book he was reading, and he darted in to recover it: it was revealed to be *Añgāre*. The play of revelation, secrecy, esoterica, and intimacy circling the "book" enacts in a curious palimpsestic way the drama around the book, investing it with the fervor of religious ritual that leaks into the prurience of a closeted sexual tryst. Quoted in the Hindi transliteration of *Añgāre*, from Kaifī ʿĀẓmī, "Maiñ aur merī shāʿirī," *Mʿaiyār (kaifī viseshāñk)* (special issue) (Delhi: Educational Publishing House, 1995), 90–91.

I do not mean to imply here that the concerns and issues espoused by various members of the PWA, which were also addressed in "manifestos" issued in the organization's name, emerged out of a vacuum; indeed, such issues as the politicization of literature had a long history. The beginning, or a first encounter, as in Azmi's remembrances, is not the origin of the politicization of literature.

For a short version in English of the connections between the stories in *Añgāre* (Lucknow: Sajjad Zahir, 1932) and the fiction of Premchand, see Leslie Flemming, *Another Lonely Voice: The Urdu Short Stories of Sadat Hasan Manto* (Monograph Series, vol. 18, Berkeley: Center for South and Southeast Asian Studies, University of California, 1979). For a more comprehensive account of affiliations between literary and political activity that focuses on poetry, see Carlo Coppola's dissertation, "Urdu Poetry, 1935–1970." For a substantive account of the publication of *Añgāre*, see the article by Coppola, "The Angare Group: The *Enfants Terribles* of Urdu Literature," in *Annual of Urdu Studies* 1 (1981): 57–69. Accounts by the members of "the group" in Urdu include two by Zahir: "Yādeñ," in *Indian Literature* 11 (1952): 22–56, appeared first in *Nayā adab* (January–February 1951); also, *Roshanā'ī*, 1st ed. (Delhi: Azad Kitab Ghar, 1959).

Many Urdu writers, including Miraji, trace the connections of the PWA back to the rebellion of 1857. Miraji's account of the PWA focuses (like Coppola's) on poetry and also locates its beginnings then, when power relations between the British and Indians were reversed. When I describe the "beginning" of the movement, I am referring to the situations considered integral to the initiation of the movement that appear in histories of it written in retrospect. For other Urdu accounts, see the comprehensive work by the Progressive critic Ḳhalīlur Raḥmān ʻĀẓmi, *Urdū meñ taraqqī pasand adabī taḥrīk* (Aligarh: Anjuman-e Taraqqi-e Urdu [Hind], 1972); see also ʻAlī Sardār Jāfri, *Taraqqī pasand adab*, 2nd. ed. (Aligarh: Anjuman-e Taraqqi-e Urdu, 1956); and Azīz Ahmad, *Taraqqī pasand adab* (Delhi: Caman Book Depot, n.d.).

19. There seems to be some uncertainty about the exact date when it was published. In his dissertation, Coppola says December 1931 or January 1932 (39); in his article, he says it was published in December 1932 (60). Leslie Flemming dates its publication as 1933. Since reaction to the volume appears to begin in early 1933 (several pieces on it were printed in journals and papers on 23 and 24 February), it was certainly published sometime prior to that date (Coppola, "The Angare Group," 60; ʻAlī, ed., *Añgāre*, 88, 89).

20. ʻAlī, ed., *Añgāre*, 97–99, 103. See also the notes outlining "offenses relating to religion and caste," on which this section of the penal code was based: Thomas Babbington Macaulay, *Miscellanies*, vol. 2 (Boston and New York: Houghton, Mifflin, 1900), 301–4; Ahmed Ali, "The Progressive Writers' Movement in Its Historical Perspective," *Journal of South Asian Literature* 8, nos. 1–4 (1977–78): 91. See also Ali, "The Progressive Writers' Movement and Creative Writers in Urdu."

21. "Āg dekho, Añgāre dekho aur pānī dekho." *Sarguzasht* (24 February 1933), repr. in K. ʻAlī, ed., *Añgāre*, 86–88.

22. Responses to *Añgāre* appear in the *Hindustan Times* (21 February 1933); in *Sac* (Lucknow, 24 February, 10 and 17 March, and 12 April 1933); in *Payām* (Aligarh, 5 March 1933), and in a play, *Āg khāyeñ*, by Mullah Shahadmi, published in *Ḳhashmaf nāmah* (10 February 1933). The group of authors is represented in the play as completely Anglicized. I discuss this point later in this chapter.

23. Coppola, "The Angare Group," 63. See also Khalid Ali's introductory essays on the collection.

24. Coppola, "The Angare Group," 63; also see K. ʻAlī, ed., *Añgāre*, 101–2. The original version of the editorial placed on the letters-to-the-editor page of the *Leader*, 5 April 1933, is much longer than those included in reprint editions of *Añgāre*. I have included extracts from the excised (central portion) of the letter, because it restores the polemical force of the original and offers the rhetoric deployed by the writers to supplement their argument.

25. One sphere that was considered private, according to the British, was religious or community activity.

26. Macaulay, *Miscellanies*, 302. Though Macaulay was referring here to "destroying or defiling places of worship, or of objects held sacred," the literal intent of his words could be turned to the less obvious violations of worship or belief, some of which he addresses in other places.

27. Ibid.; emphasis mine.

28. One of the few other instances of a ban enacted by the colonial regime against a publication by the PWA was the proscription of the journal *Kālim* (Speaker). This proscription was in part a reaction to the militantly antiwar stance of the writing by Progressives that was published in the journal at the beginning of World War II. I think that until this particular incident, much of the material attributed to the PWA was not explicitly and/or visibly anticolonial; thus it did not call attention to itself as subversive and was not proscribed.

29. A. Ali, "The Progressive Writers' Movement," 91.

30. *Hindustan Times*, 23 February 1933. The short article is based on a report from Lucknow written on 21 February.

31. I am indebted to Jeff Cox, whose question, "So why is this different?" asked when I was discussing this section of my chapter with him, led me to confront what was implicit in the reactions to *Añgāre*.

32. A. Ali, "The Progressive Writers' Movement," 93.

33. Coppola, "The Angare Group," 63.

34. See Kabīr, *Kabīr granthāvalī* (Allahabad: Sahitya Bhavan, 1985), and Shah Waliullah, *The Sacred Knowledge of the Higher Functions of the Mind*, trans. G. N. Jalbani (London: Octagon Press, 1982), as well as Shāh Vālī Ullagh, *Altafhīmāt alilahiy*, vols. 1 and 2 (Academy of Shahwali Ullah), 1114–76.

35. A. Ali, "The Progressive Writers' Movement," 77–78, 96.

36. Frances W. Pritchett, *Nets of Awareness: Urdu Poetry and Its Critics* (Berkeley: University of California Press, 1994), 43, 34, 38. See also Alṭāf Ḥusain Ḥālī, *Dīvān-e Hālī* (Delhi: Urdu Academy, 1991).

37. Although I do not have the space to explore it here, it would be useful to place the PWA in the context of other reform movements, especially in terms of their relationship to the colonial enterprise. The PWA was quite clearly not a conventional neocolonial elite group in the same way as the Bhadralok. For a history of the Brahmo Samaj, see David Kopf, *The Brahmo Samaj and the Shaping of the Modern Indian Mind* (Princeton, N.J.: Princeton University Press, 1979), 3–5.

38. *Journal of South Asian Literature* 22, no. 1 (Winter–Spring 1987) has a tribute to Rashid Jahan. Among the articles is one by Coppola and Sajida Zubair, "Rashid Jahan: Urdu Literature's First 'Angry Young Woman,'" 166–84. This issue contains translations of Jahan's work, which I will refer to later in this chapter:

"Sightseeing Trip to Delhi," "Behind the Veil," and "Woman: A One-Act Drama" (Dillī kī sair, Parde ke picche, and Aurat ek aikṭ kā Ḍrāmah). For the originals, see *Aurat aur digar afsāne* (Lahore: Hashmi Book Depot, n.d.).

39. It is quite clear, and I will deal with it more explicitly a little further along, that there were codes for "mimetic" representations. Certain scenarios were considered "authentic" portrayals of life and thus were "reflecting" life.

40. "Parde ke pīche: Ek aikṭ kā Ḍrāmaḥ," in K. ʿAlī, ed., *Añgāre*, 166.

41. Ibid., 169, 173.

42. Traffic in modernization occurs through women; so, although women need to modernize, men do not need to shift as long as there are some men who allow women access to the outside.

43. *Shia Conference Gazette*, 1 March 1933.

44. The four writers were depicted in lampoons as westernized "foolish heathens." See the play by Shahadmi, *Āg khayeñ*.

45. Ali's response to Rashid's excoriation of the obscenity in *Añgāre* is useful here; measuring Rashid's collection *Mawra* against *Añgāre* for "obscenity," Ali decides that Rashid is wrong in his assessment of *Añgāre*, because, after all, Rashid's poetry is so much more sexual. What the terms of the discussion make clear is that it is a circular conflict precisely because ascribing sexuality to a literary work is a mode for devaluing it. See K. ʿAlī, ed., *Añgāre*, 1977–78.

46. See Michel Foucault, "The Abnormals," in *Ethics: Subjectivity and Truth*, vol. 1. Abnormals were produced through institutions of "control, supervision, and distribution." The act/person distinction did not hold so completely in the case of colonial south Asia. Not all writers charged with deviant writing were considered deviant. The uneven terrain on which deviance and sexuality were distributed is closer in kind to Freud's descriptions in *Three Essays on the Theory of Sexuality* (New York: Basic Books, 1975). In the Indian instances one must consider the discrepancies between writers' characterizations of their own work and critics' readings of them. Disagreements between the two continued to inform discussions on sexuality and deviance. Childhood, too, another place where mechanisms of surveillance were put into effect, could not be scripted in quite the same way the Foucault suggests in his work. Though nationalism and the demand for a certain kind of believing working body trained from childhood forced childhood into becoming a place to be watched and thought about (witness Ismat Chughtai's novels and short stories), it never quite became the focus of extreme supervision, neglect, and interest.

47. Kenneth Ballhatchett, *Race, Sex, and Class Under the Raj: Imperial Attitudes and Policies and Their Critics 1793–1905* (New York: St. Martin's Press, 1980), 166.

48. On the threats instituted by interracial marriage, see ibid., 116–18.

49. Quoted in ibid., 10.

50. Ibid., 10.

51. Ibid., 162; also 10, 119, 120–21. Seduction and its dangers saturated the language of letters and minutes issued by military and medical authorities. Vagrant prostitutes, who crept in uncontrolled, and homosexuality were the focus of diatribes against unregulated desire. By the 1880s the body in danger was classed: working class. Upper-class infractions were addressed more frequently in the early 1800s. Like all such attempts at regulation, desire for control always exceeded the possibility of control, and people's practices continued to evade, leak through, and circumvent regulations.

52. Carla Petievich, "The Feminine Voice in the Urdu Ghazal," *Indian Horizons* 39, nos. 1–2 (1990): 25–42. See also C. M. Naim, "The Theme of Homosexual (Pederastic) Love in the Urdu Ghazal," in Muhammad Umar Memon, ed., *Studies in the Urdu Ghazal and Prose Fiction* (South Asian Studies, University of Wisconsin–Madison Publication Series, no. 5, 1979), 120–42. For another article in English on gender, sexuality, and the ghazal, see Tariq Rahman, "Boy Love in the Urdu Ghazal," in *Annual of Urdu Studies* 7 (1990): 1–21.

53. See Pritchett, 181, for this quote; also the original in Alṭāf Ḥusain Ḥālī, *Muqaddamaḥ-e shiʿr o shāʿirī*, ed. and intro. Waḥīd Quraishī (Lahore: Maktabah-e Jadid, 1953; repr., Aligarh: EMI, 1977).

54. Jürgen Habermas, *The Structural Transformation of the Public Sphere: An Inquiry into a Category of Bourgeois Society*, trans. Thomas Burger and Fredrick Lawrence (Cambridge, Mass.: Harvard University Press, 1989).

55. For a special selection on Ismat Chughtai, including an interview with Carlo Coppola, see *Mahfil* 8, nos. 2–3 (Summer–Fall 1972): 169–214. This special issue includes the translation of "Liḥāf" to which I refer in this chapter. For the original of the short story, see Chughtai's collection *Coṭeñ* (Aligarh: Educational Book House, 1982).

56. Ismat Chughtai, "The Quilt" (Liḥāf), *Mahfil* 8, nos. 2–3 (Summer–Fall: 1972): 195.

57. Ibid., 196.

58. My analysis is a quick reading of a fairly complex story. One of the issues I have not addressed is the mapping of incest onto a voyage of sexual discovery. The problems that this might cause in a reading of the story must be juxtaposed against marriage alliances, which are often made between two closely related partners.

59. The zenana was not always desexualized: it was often visited by intense speculation about the rambunctious (unhinging) sexuality of women. But by the mid-twentieth century this speculation had been muted, and certainly women

were not subjects permitted to explore in public the ramifications of their own sexuality.

60. For a more complete discussion of sexual encounters on either side of the peephole, see Chapter 6. Who opens up the peephole into the zenana and who gets to look at whom are important issues that come to play in this context. I will also explore the "politics" of looking in Chapter 6, when I talk about the construction of Miraji's biography.

61. See *Mahfil*, special issue on Chughtai.

62. Although the word "lesbian" is not strictly appropriate here because the relationship enacted between two women in this poetry has no counterpart in contemporary English, I have used the word for the lack of any other in English to suit my purpose.

63. Ismat Chughtai, interview with Carlo Coppola, *Mahfil* 8, nos. 2–3 (1972).

64. I discuss this in greater depth in the next chapter.

65. This seems an obvious point, but I will say again that because he (like Chughtai) questioned and reversed mainstream and marginal positions, he brought upon himself a much more virulent wrath than was deserved by a single, relatively powerless figure challenging a community.

66. Sajjād Ẓahīr, *Roshnā'ī*, 2nd ed. (New Delhi: Seema Publications, 1985), 27–28.

67. A mix of Progressives and other writers were slowly being edged out of the movement in the 1930s.

68. 'Āẓmī, *Urdū meñ taraqqī pasand adabī taḥrīk*, 96.

69. Author interview with Akhtarul Iman, 5 June 1988; see also Chapter 1.

70. For versions of the manifestos see the *Left Review* 2 (1936–37) and *Hans* (October 1936).

71. This article is in Akhtar Husain Raipuri's book *Adab aur inqilāb* (Bombay: National Information and Publishers, n.d.). It was also published in the Hindi monthly *Visvāmitra* (Friend of the universe) (April 1933) as "Sāhitya aur krāntī" (Literature and revolution).

72. His definition was much more broad-based than the explicitly political one used by the PWA. He defined progress as "change" of any kind. He felt the need to assert the primacy of the word in literary discourse and the necessity of using it to align himself as a critic with respect to it so that he could be read. He quite clearly included the Progressives in his perceived audience.

73. *Nayā adab* (April 1939) introduced the debate over the term "Progressive." The May 1939 issue discussed poetic vocabulary that was considered "traditional," as well as the relationship of traditional to contemporary poetry.

74. The Progressives tried to trim their rules to a single set and to construct a univocal system, whereas Miraji described a multivocal literary universe. Both the Progressives and Miraji, however, conducted their discussions using a common vocabulary.

75. The writing of "history" is not an untroubled process; even using the word "history" calls up a negotiation hedged in by colonial relationships. Meenakshi Mukherjee, in *Realism and Reality: The Novel and Society in India* (New Delhi: Oxford University Press, 1985), inadvertently alludes to this negotiation when she says that the writing of a historical narrative (i.e., the understanding of history as a delineation or enumeration of "real," temporally located facts) was a form of expression Indians learned from the British, occasioned by the spread of English education. Indeed, prior to this "influence," Indians wrote only myth. She does locate the "awareness of history" as a "relatively recent phenomenon even in the nineteenth-century west," and she does some very important work in tracking the effects of indigenous narrative forms on the novel and short story produced on the subcontinent (9, 38–54). Although as a reader I cannot deny European "influences," to discuss them in unidirectional terms unproblematized by the colonial situation is to reiterate the power relationships inherent in that situation. Historical narratives are fraught by the conviction associated with them that they convey, contain, or perhaps embody a sense of order and orderliness. In contrast, their nether image is constructed as myth.

76. See Rā'epūrī, *Adab aur inqilāb*.

77. Ibid., 14–16.

78. Ibid., 16.

79. Ibid., 36.

80. Marx, *Capital*, 1: 35–49.

81. Rā'epūrī, *Adab aur inqilāb*, 24–25.

82. Ibid., 17–18, 24.

83. See article by Stephen Greenblatt, "Towards a Poetics of Culture," in *The New Historicism*, ed. H. Aram Veser (New York: Routledge, 1989), 1–14.

84. This justification, as J. Cox has shown in his recent work, is not one limited or peculiar to the colonial enterprise; it was also used to sell the role of "missionaries" in Britain. But it assumes a particularly virulent strain in a colonial context precisely because of the specifics of the imbalance of power in this context. It is also important to note that even the missionary enterprise appeared to "secularize" its task. Eurocentric convictions that the decline of religion was a "natural" part of historical development affect readings of India that perceived (Hindu) India as a society where religion was integral to the socioeconomic structure (i.e.,

religion rules all of life, etc.); therefore India is considered "degenerate," which affects conceptions of the missionary program. Progress under this secularizing regime is written in terms of scientific and utilitarian assumptions about social organizations. This does not, however, detour the allegorical move.

85. See the introduction to Benita Parry's book *Delusions and Discoveries: Studies on India and the British Imagination, 1880–1930* (London: Allen Lane, 1972). Also see Sara Suleri, *The Rhetoric of English India* (Chicago: University of Chicago Press, 1992). For the fully rendered version, see the debates between Horace Hyman Wilson (as he defended Jones against Mill) and James Mill conducted in the additions to and the footnotes of *The History of British India* (10 vols., 5th ed., with notes by Horace Hyman Wilson [London: J. Madden, 1858]). Though Jones, Wilson, and Mill appeared to have very different agendas for the colonial enterprise, they come together in curious ways. One way is that all three agree on the primitive state of Indian science, which can only be alleviated through Western *technae*, education, and government. Javed Majid discusses the alliances implicitly struck between them, and their contractions, in *Ungoverned Imaginings: James Mill's The History of British India and Orientalism* (Oxford: Clarendon Press, 1992), 128–30.

86. See Hali, and Azad, for two versions of moments like these: for Hali, for example, early Arabia in the *Musaddas*. See also the ways in which classical (Hindu) India figures, and the ways in which Vedic India is used (as well as the differences between Jones and Max Muller) at different periods in a range of sources. Several instances are discussed at length in the collection edited by Kumkum Sangari and Sudesh Vaid, *Recasting Women: Essays in Colonial History* (New Delhi: Kali for Women, 1989).

87. See Macaulay, *Miscellanies*; also Gauri Visvanathan's (*Masks of Conquest: Literary Study and British Rule in India* [New York: Columbia University Press, 1989], esp. 123, 125) extensive discussion on the debates on education.

88. Āḳhtar Ḥusain Rā'epūrī, *Adab aur zindagī* (Bombay: National Information and Publishers, n.d.).

89. "'Aḥd-e javānī ro ro kāṭā pīrī meñ līñ āñkheñ mund / yā'nī rāt bahut the jāge ṣubḥ hu'ī ārām kiyā." Mīr Tāqī Mīr, *Kulliyāt-e mīr* (Karachi: Urdu Duniya, 1958), 105.

90. A. Ali, "The Progressive Writers' Movement in Its Historical Perspective," 96.

91. Partha Chatterjee, "History and the Nationalization of Hinduism," in *Social Research* 59, no. 1 (Spring 1992): 129. "The beginning was glorious . . . the cause of decline was Muslim rule."

92. Ra'epūrī, *Adab aur zindagī.*

93. Ibid., 29.

94. Ibid., 30.

95. See ibid., 27. See also the two editions of the "manifestos."

96. Ibid., 30, 32.

97. Chatterjee, in "History and the Nationalization of Hinduism," discusses the relationship of history to tradition to nationalism and the contrariness of valences of language in these instances.

98. See introduction to Bipin Chandra, *The Oppressive Present: Literature and Social Consciousness in Colonial India* (New Delhi: Oxford University Press, 1994), for a discussion on the pervasiveness of these positions in Indian literary negotiations from the nineteenth century through the twentieth, especially pages 10 and 11, which address hegemony and relationships to the state. See also Žižek, *The Plague of Fantasies*, 3–44, "The Seven Veils of Fantasy":

> "All humans have rights, *in so far as they truly are rational and free*" (author's italics), which implicitly excluded the mentally ill, "savages," criminals, children, women. . . . Fantasy designates precisely this unwritten framework which tells us how we are to understand the letter of the Law. And it is easy to observe today, in our enlightened era of universal rights, racism and sexism reproduce themselves mainly at the level of the phantasmic unwritten rules which sustain and qualify universal ideological proclamations.

99. Patricia Jeffrey, *Frogs in a Well: Indian Women in Purdah* (London: Zed Books, 1979).

100. Miraji's ms. fragment. The Blake poem is from *Songs of Innocence and of Experience, Shewing the Two Contrary States of the Human Soul* ([London]: William Blake, [1789–94]), Harry Elkins Widener Collection, Houghton Library, Harvard University, plate 44, verse 2.

101. Comments in *Hans* (July 1936).

102. Lata Mani, "Multiple Mediations: Feminist Scholarship in the Age of Multinational Reception," *Feminist Review* 35 (Summer 1990): 24–41.

103. "Previous research had made it possible to recognize a peculiar level among all those which enable one to analyze systems of thought—that of discursive practices. There one finds a type of systematicity which is neither logical nor linguistic. Discursive practices are characterized by the demarcation of a field of objects, by the definition of a legitimate perspective for a subject of knowledge, by the setting of norms for elaborating concepts and theories. Hence, each one of them presupposes a play of prescriptions that govern exclusions and selections." Foucault, *Ethics: Subjectivity and Truth*, 1: 11.

104. Akhtar Husain Rā'epūrī, *Adab aur zindagī* (Bombay: National Information and Publishers, n.d.), 20.

105. *Left Review* 2 (1936–37): 240.

106. Rā'epūrī, *Adab aur inqilāb*, 36.

107. See *Hans* (July 1936) for text of Premchand's speech before the PWA.

108. N. M. Rashid, interview with Carlo Coppola, *Mahfil* 7, nos. 1–2 (1971): 1–20.

109. Coppola, "Urdu Poetry, 1935–1970," 189.

110. See Gayatri Spivak, "Can the Subaltern Speak" in Cary Nelson and Lawrence Grossberg, eds., *Marxism and the Interpretation of Culture* (Urbana and Chicago: University of Illinois Press, 1988), 271–316; also another article by Spivak, "Subaltern Studies: Deconstructing Historiography," in Ranajit Guha, ed., *Subaltern Studies* 4 (New Delhi: Oxford University Press, 1994): 330–63; Dipesh Chakrabarty, "Invitation to a Dialogue," *Subaltern Studies* (New Delhi: Oxford University Press, 1994), 4: 364–76.

111. See Sajjād Ẓahīr, "Hindī, urdū, Hindustānī kā muṣlah" (The antidote to Hindi, Urdu, Hindustani), *Nayā adab* 3 (1944): 1–31. Zahir analyzes the Hindi-Urdu controversy as one piece of an imperialist strategy to divide and conquer. He advocates stretching out the commonalities between the two languages, learning to read and write both, and translating back and forth between scripts so that works are easily accessible in both. Also see Rā'epūrī, "Urdū zabān kā mustaqbil," in *Adab aur inqilāb*, 245–48.

112. Rā'epūrī, *Adab aur inqilāb*, 14.

113. Premchand, speech to the PWA, *Hans* (July 1936).

114. See Altaf Husain Hali, and Azad. For both nineteenth-century writers, the reform of poetry was inextricably woven with reform of society. Hali wrote at length about the two in Ḥālī, *Muqaddamah-e shi'r o shā'irī* (232): "Poetry changes with society, and its ability to excite emotions must be put to use for implementing social change (as hegemony). Poetry must be brought to simplicity: of its language and topics." Azad spent time ruminating on language as a transparent medium; he was also the initiator of photographic representations of poetic encounter in Muḥammad Ḥusain Āzād, *Āb-e ḥayāt*, 2nd ed. (facsimile of Lahore 1907 ed.; Lucknow: Ultar Prudesh Urdu Academy, 1982). Both Hali and Azad brought affect, emotion, desire to heel: either as something that incited writing and had to be conveyed to the reader and produced in the reader, or as something to be put to good use to implement change.

115. For historically rendered disquisitions on photography and its allegiances to colonial recording procedures and their requirements for fidelity, as well as its allegiances to the conventions of studio portraiture, and their requirements for

fantasy, play, as well as renditions of the real, see Christopher Pinney, *Camera Indica: The Social Life of Indian Photographs* (Chicago: University of Chicago Press, 1997).

116. See Mukherjee, *Realism and Reality.*

117. Miraji, "Farāns kā ek āvārā shā'ir: Cārls Bādla'ir" (An alien poet of France: Charles Baudelaire), in *Mashriq o maghrib ke naghmeñ*, 137–60; and the introduction to *Is nazm meñ*. The real for Miraji was not just reality, but something that moved back and forth between "reality" and the Lacanian "Real." Hence his turn to Baudelaire, as the poet who did not live in the cleanness of assured propriety, but who was constantly rent by failure, death, dirt, disease, trauma.

118. It is worth pausing to recollect Wordsworth's spots of time and Saree Makdisi's discussion of them alongside his elaborate analyses of British colonialism, in *Romantic Imperialism: Universal Empire and the Culture of Modernity* (Cambridge, Eng.: Cambridge University Press, 1998).

119. All these emotions are evoked by Raipuri in his essays. Some, however, like seduction, are parceled off into the past, and some, like loss and anguish, are recuperated for the present.

120. Miraji's metaphysical poetry travels through the mirror, to speak to its lineage as a Sufi image, as well as its necessary collaboration with the visual. In such poems, synaesthesia is, for Miraji, a "political" engagement with the visual.

## CHAPTER 3: MIRAJI'S RESPONSE TO THE PROGRESSIVES

1. Ghālib, *Dīvān-e Ghālib*, 132.

2. I use "avant-garde" not in its rigorously Russian sense, but with allusions to one particular discussion of the avant-garde that imbricates the avant-garde with the Russian socialist realists in ways that resemble Miraji's imbrications with the PWA. See Boris Groys, "The Birth of Socialist Realism from the Spirit of the Russian Avant-Garde," in John E. Bowlt and Olga Match, eds., *Laboratory of Dreams: The Russian Avant-Garde and Cultural Experiment* (Stanford, Calif.: Stanford University Press, 1996), 193–218. One pertinent commonality is that both Marxists and the avant-gardists placed the artist at the center of a life-building project, the former through economics and politics and the latter through aesthetics.

3. Henceforth "Shā'irī" (private collection; ms. with Akhtarul Iman). The essay is reprinted in Jālibī, ed., *Mīrājī*, 519–26. The following paragraph is from page 519 of Jalibi's compendium.

4. See also all the essays Miraji wrote on non-Urdu-"speaking" Indian writers

in *Mashriq o maghrib ke naghmeñ*. His analysis of historical evidence is as painstaking as his renditions of alternative readings. Of course, the point in both is to arrive at the apposite positions.

5. See Miraji's essay on Vidyapati as an example or his essay on Sappho.

6. It is worth noting here that some of the Progressives wrote for the Bombay movies, which were fairly widely circulated. The codification of cultural value for the movies is in terms of a language of criticism that valorizes "social realism," which has been attributed to the Progressives. Although the forms that "realism" takes are different in different contexts in the work of different writers, the general terms of its use remain the same. See Carlo Coppola's dissertation for a discussion of various manifestations of "social realist" poetry.

7. For a recent reassessment of the status of the subaltern in the face of critiques, see Sumit Sarkar, "The Decline of the Subaltern in *Subaltern Studies*," in *Writing Social History* (New Delhi: Oxford University Press, 1997), 82–108.

8. Although I speak here as though Miraji were a "composite author," I have in another place addressed the construction of a "him"; his biography, oeuvre, voice, gender, and name cannot be taken as static givens. So it is worth keeping in mind that even as a "figure" engaged in the production of certain narratives associated with him, the status of the "figure" is both settled and undermined by the ways in which he was and is read, including by me.

9. Vintage Said, flipped around to discuss representations of the colonizers from the perspective of the colonized; see Edward Said, *Orientalism* (New York: Pantheon Books, 1978). Rather than an analysis that takes one version of the "dominant" discourse as the default for discussion through which and in which colonized "others" are represented, I flip the direction of representation around to look for representations of the colonizers in the discourse of the colonized. This particular strategy has many exponents. For several versions based in colonial Bengal see the collection edited by Partha Chatterjee, *Texts of Power: Emerging Disciplines in Colonial Bengal* (Calcutta: Samya, in conjunction with Centre for Studies in the Social Sciences, 1996).

10. See Bhabha's categories of pedagogical and performative narrations of nationalist identity ("DissemiNation," 912). The performative (Miraji's discussions of his community) disrupts, disturbs, and renegotiates the pedagogical (his representations of the British). For other examples from the nineteenth century see Sudhir Chandra's work on Bharatendru Harishchandra, in *The Oppressive Present*. Chandra explores Bharatendru's shifting allegiances to the colonial state not as a linear teleology, but as a series of sometimes overlapping positions that move between valorization and critique. The same could be said of Altaf Husain Hali, and

certainly of the Progressives, or any person or group that called for modernization (without a trenchant critique), while either longing for the loss of a series of beliefs/practices or demanding nationalization and freedom from colonialism.

11. See Jāved, *Ḥalqah-e arbāb-e ẕauq*. The book attempts to provide an alternative story/history of the Halqa with a different view of the position of the "Progressives" that is in contention with the story that the author—Javed—says has become the authoritative one, introduced by Ali Sardar Ja'fri in his book *Taraqqī pasand adab*. That this author begins his account of the Halqa with the history as written by a major "Progressive" writer is some indication of the implicit power of these stories of members of this group in a particular period of Urdu literature; they provide the dominant narratives of the time.

12. This is a fantasy, a picture of unmediated power that circulates within a regime that (assumes [presumes?]) it occupies the unconditionally dominant place.

13. Mani, "Multiple Mediations."

14. Introduction to *Is naẕm meñ*.

15. See Edward Said, "Secular Criticism," in *The World, the Text, and the Critic* (Cambridge, Mass.: Harvard University Press, 1983), 31–54. Said talks about the move from filiative lineages—parental figures—to affiliative networks. Miraji makes the same move in his essay. For examples of South Asian literary filiative authorities see Visvanathan's information on the English curricula for schools in India, and Pritchett for Hali's evocation of Milton.

16. Writers in the United States, like Patricia Williams (*The Alchemy of Race and Rights* [Cambridge, Mass.: Harvard University Press, 1991]); Trinh-t Minh-ha (*When the Moon Waxes Red: Representation, Gender, and Cultural Politics* [New York: Routledge, 1991]); and Gloria Anzaldua (*Borderlands: La Frontera* [San Francisco: Spinsters/Aunt Lute Foundation Books, 1987]) are, with their shifting of the codes of what constitutes appropriate writing for a genre or violating genre guidelines, performing similar acts of resistance by their discursive activity, but I don't feel that they and Miraji can be mapped onto one another. The context of their activities is very different and so the product or the textures and content of the narratives is specific to the context and very different from Miraji's. But the forms of subversion they practice in the face of a controlling discourse and modes of representation are similar to Miraji's, and they provide an analogy for the kind of activity in which Miraji was engaged. Their activity fits Bhabha's category of the performative.

17. Miraji offers impropriety, improper men and women, to disturb the organizations of proper nationalist men created in the image of colonial heroism. Miraji's turn to desire/death as the sticky obscure place where work needs to be done to prepare people for the end of a colonial order brings eros/thanatos to a desire

for nation, nationalism, and the state. See his essays on Mallarmé, Baudelaire, and Sappho, in *Mashriq o maghrib ke naghmeñ.*

18. Walter Benjamin, "Theses on the Philosophy of History: XVI," in *Illuminations*, 262.

19. The tripartite division and three appellations for the stories are mine; in fact, the stories run together and the transitions between them are not explicit. I separated them because I saw them operating as variations on a repetitive theme, with each piece having repeating as well as diverging elements. I named them because of semantic strategies used in them that flagged narrative modes. The myth is marked by "first" (*ibtad[ā'ī]*). The historicist fable (appropos of Benjamin's distinctions) is marked by phrases like "in the past" and "crossed the seven seas," which come from a particular storytelling tradition. The materialist history, unlike the other two sections, follows the lineaments of Raipuri's/Hali's materialist histories and begins with a date (1857) and continues with terms like "economic/political" and "social."

20. Mill, *The History of British India*, book 2, chap. 9.

21. Rashid, interview with Carlo Coppola.

22. Rashid is also a useful reader for a reader like me because he attempts to read Miraji differently from the way various Progressive writers read him. So his reading gives me information on how far the reading practices endorsed by the PWA had become normal.

23. The myth is read as Freudian by Rashid, among others, but the details of the myth are far from "Freudian" or psychoanalytic; they are closer to a Hobbesian understanding of primordial relationships. But the use here of the word "Freud" here points to an awareness that Miraji's myth is a textual construct with connections to other narratives. Most psychoanalytic references made in conjunction with Miraji's work are made because there is no other available, easily accessible critical model for reading a narrative that attempts to depict emotional transactions in an unconventional form. The conventions for depicting emotional transactions between two individuals in this poetic tradition, I feel, rely on two possible models. One is the language of unrequited love that animates the ghazal and continues, in a modified form, to be used in twenty-first-century poetry, like in the poetry of Faiz, and even in some of Miraji's poems. The second is a sociocritical analysis of hegemonic sexual relationships. The comments of Rashid point to the dearth of the kind of generic mythic originary narrative of emotional transactions in the world for which Miraji writes.

24. See also John Guillory, *Cultural Capital*, on value and the relationship to "need," perhaps in tandem with "use."

25. The desire-fear dichotomy that establishes a dynamic of emotional attrac-

tion-repulsion is perhaps a more raw version of Jeremy Bentham's and, following upon him, Mill's *principle of sympathy and antipathy* and the field generated by both that partially organizes the principle of utility. Perhaps this conjunction between Miraji and Bentham is a fortuitous one, given the legacy of Utilitarians in the later discussion on education, but in any case, it is worth noting that this contrary movement becomes the guiding principle that pushes humans toward civilization. The transactions of desire/fear also have some relationship to Freud and through him to Lacan, specially desire/fear as the space of creative, imaginative, dream poetry.

See Jeremy Bentham, *The Principles of Morals and Legislation* (New York: Prometheus Books, 1988), 15–42, esp. 15. The discussion on sympathy/antipathy is conducted under the chapter "Of Principles Adverse to That of Utility." It is perhaps no accident that the footnotes on the previous page address colonial jurisprudence, and the imprudence of the "mischievous" system of British (judge-made) law that is laid down to replace "that bad system, of Mohametan and other native law." Bentham refers to Mill's history to describe in numerary terms the money extracted, stolen, and pocketed by the East India Company and its rule of law under Impey and Hastings: "*Let it but put money into our pockets, no tyranny too flagitious to be worshipped by us*" (emphasis mine).

26. The words *sundarī* (beautiful woman) and *singār* (decoration, decorated) call up associations to the *nāyik[ā]* (beloved), a figure who comes from a non-Islamic tradition of poetry. I am indebted to Carla Petievich for asking me about *nāyik[ā]*s and leading me to this connection.

27. Coppola, "Urdu Poetry," chap. 1.

28. The past, evoked here by Miraji, if it is brought into the now of a forming nation, is probably permeable, and if self-complete and self-circulating, at least hybrid.

29. Two quotes by Miraji from two different pieces substantiate this: "It is obvious that nowadays our life definitely changes if not every month, then every year"; and "Our lives are in constant change."

30. Jacques Lacan, *The Four Fundamental Concepts of Psychoanalysis: The Seminar of Jacques Lacan*, trans. Alan Sheridan (New York: W. W. Norton, 1981), book 11. Slavoj Žižek, *Looking Awry: An Introduction to Jacques Lacan Through Popular Culture* (Cambridge, Mass.: MIT Press, 1991). The movement of *fort-da* discussed first by Freud is particularly evocative of the kinds of leavings and exchanges enacted here.

31. In Tabassum, ed., *Shiʿr*, 77–79.

32. The passage I refer to is: "Filling his stomach, he found pleasure in moments of forgetfulness with his *hamdam* [soul-mate] night, collecting food to fill

his stomach and fear. Fear of the spectacles of nature and fear of *hamjins* enemies [enemies of the same species]. The issues of poetry emerged out of just these things. The first human's poetry is the intermediary space between the parallel lines of desire and fear" (Miraji, "Shāʿirī," 162).

33. The British become what I call *valorized other* in his narrative, conforming to other positive stereotypical representations of them in neocolonial texts.

34. E. B. Havel, the iconoclastic, idiosyncratic art historian who attempted to reconstitute Indian art in a sort of arts-and-crafts key (India needed both the village, pastoral artisan and classical art) during the swadeshi period, is renowned for his obsessive return to Indian architecture and the depredations wrought upon it by a foolishly violent civil service. Though the literalness of his obsessions have merit in themselves (witness the forms that rebuilding took, and the loss of crafts production under early industrial capitalism), it is important to remark on the metaphoric significance of them. It was precisely the architectural forms that colonialism took, which became the basis of his critique and lament (a later version can be found in: Ernest Binfield Havel, *Essays in Indian Art, Industry, and Education* [Madras: The Theosophist Office, 1910]); and one that was picked up by most writers who endorsed similar positions like Ananda Kentish Coomaraswamy and Alfred Chatterton. See Chatterton, "Industrial Education in India," *Calcutta Review* 228 (April 1902): 301–11.

35. See Nicholas Dirks, "History as the Sign of the Modern," *Public Culture* 2, no. 2 (Spring 1990): 25–32, esp. 29.

> Even as colonial theaters were fundamental to the development of modernity itself in the metropole, colonial contradictions help to reveal the cracks in modernity's mirror. At one level, colonialism is what modernity is all about. So perhaps it should come as no surprise that as we witness the struggles with modernity in historical representation throughout the world, colonial history and colonial anthropology seem to become reborn over and over again.

This quote is particularly apropos to the next section of this chapter, which deals with Baudelaire.

36. See Houston Baker, *Blues, Ideology, and Afro-American Literature: A Vernacular Theory* (Chicago: University of Chicago Press, 1987), 7, 200, 202. Both Miraji and Baker use the crossroads as an image to describe their condition because they both operate at multiple sites of power and in multiple positions. For both, the condition is "marked by transience," "its inhabitants are always travelers," and it is "polymorphous and multidirectional, scene of arrivals and departures, place betwixt and between (ever *entre les deux*)." But unlike Baker's, Miraji's description of the condition of someone at a crossroads is not a celebratory one.

37. "Shāʿirī," in Jālibī, ed., *Mīrājī,* 525.

38. See ibid., 7. The blues singer at the crossroads is described by Baker as a translator because he or she provides an "expressive equivalence for the junctures' ceaseless flux."

39. The essays were collected in *Mashriq o magḥrib ke naghmeñ* (Songs of the East and West).

40. Writers who represented the "white man" as a primitive.

41. My translation of Miraji's translation of a poem by Baudelaire (which Miraji may have seen in its English incarnation): "Cārls Baudelaʾir," in *Mashriq o magḥrib ke naghmeñ,* 161–89 (henceforth, "Cārls Baudelaʾir"), 184. This is one of the few poems that Miraji translates without offering a commentary or supplementary reading. The essay in an abbreviated form also appears in Jamīl Jālibī, ed., *Mīrājī: Ek muṭālaʿh* (Lahore: Sang-e Masil Publications, 1990), 501–18.

42. "Cārls Baudelaʾir"; an abbreviated version of the essay appears in Pāshī, ed., *Shakhṣiyat aur fann,* 12–137; "Bāteñ," in Jālibī, ed., *Mīrājī,* 567–85; Baudelaire was also included in Sheema Majid's collection and I have some of the work on him in manuscript.

43. "Cārls Baudelaʾir," 167.

44. Walter Benjamin, "On Some Motifs in Baudelaire," in *Illuminations,* 157–65.

45. "Bāteñ," in Jālibī, ed., *Mīrājī,* 569.

46. Ibid., 585, 567.

47. Benjamin, "On Some Motifs in Baudelaire," 157.

48. Elizabeth Mayes, "The Fantasy of Internalization in the Theoretical Imaginary," *Representations* 62 (Spring 1998): 100–110. Miraji takes on some of the places Mayes engages: mimicry (as something produced by colonial exigencies) and a turn from mimicry into internalization/possession. The question (which is produced in the uneven space-relations of capitalism) is how are both processes deployed and with what effects, given the valences accorded to either in this period?

49. Many of these introductory and necessary asides on Baudelaire, Miraji obviously garnered from Arthur Symons, whom he quotes. See Symons, *Baudelaire: Prose and Poetry* (New York: Albert and Charles Boni, 1926), and "Charles Baudelaire," in *Figures of Several Centuries* (London: Constable and Company, 1916), 310–15. This latter collection also includes a piece on Sarojini Naidu. Miraji takes information on Baudelaire directly from both books. Both were certainly available at public libraries in Bombay and seemed to be some of the most commonly circulated "informative" texts on the poet. Edna St. Vincent Millay, introducing her own (and George Dillon's) translations, is quite pointed about her evaluation of various translators, and Baudelaire attracted quite a few. She commends Swin-

burne, but calls the Arthur Symons version "shockingly inaccurate and misleading." Edna St. Vincent Millay and George Dillon, trans., *Flowers of Evil: From the French of Charles Baudelaire* (New York and London: Harper and Brothers, 1936). See Algernon Charles Swinburne, "Charles Baudelaire: *Les Fleurs du Mal*," *Spectator* (6 September 1862): 998–1000; and *William Blake: A Critical Essay* (New York: Benjamin Bloom, 1868).

50. This story goes against the grain of others that pose this journey as one that Baudelaire was forced to take by his stepfather.

51. Walter Benjamin, "The Task of the Translator: An Introduction to the Translation of Baudelaire's *Tableaux parisiens*," in *Illuminations*, 69–82; and "On Some Motifs," 155.

52. "Cārls Baudela'ir," 162.

53. See Tejaswini Niranjana, *Siting Translation: History, Post-Structuralism and the Colonial Context* (Berkeley: University of California Press, 1992); and Anuradha Dingwaney and Carol Maier, eds., *Between Languages and Cultures: Translation and Cross-Cultural Texts* (Pittsburgh: University of Pittsburgh Press, 1995).

54. Gayatri Spivak, *A Critique of Postcolonial Reason: Towards a History of the Vanishing Present* (Cambridge, Mass.: Harvard University Press, 1999), 153–56. For Malabar, Mauritius, and Reunion, Baudelaire circles toward land (through misnamed bodies) through a false cartography in the particular poems by him that Spivak discusses.

55. "Cārls Baudela'ir," 168–70.

56. Ibid., 168.

57. Ibid.

58. Ibid., 174.

59. Paul de Man, "Anthromorphism and Trope in Lyric," in *The Rhetoric of Romanticism* (New York: Columbia University Press, 1984), 239–62. I follow Miraji's deviation that takes Baudelaire on to a scene he never visits, by turning the possibility of anthromorphic (mis)reading to the service of biographical misreading, through the production of "obsession." See also de Man, "Lyric and Modernity," in *Blindness and Insight: Essays in the Rhetoric of Contemporary Criticism* (Minneapolis: University of Minnesota Press, 1983), esp. 184, about Mallarmé on Baudelaire, who "was for him [Mallarmé] a dark zone into which he could never penetrate"; and Jacques Derrida, *Specters of Marx*, trans. Peggy Kamuf (New York and London: Routledge, 1994), 154:

> Challenge or invitation, "encouragement," seduction encountering seduction, desire or war, love or hate, provocation of other ghosts: Marx insists on this a lot for there is a *multiple* of this sociality (there is always more than one com-

modity, more than one spirit, and even more specters) and ***number*** belongs to the movement itself, to the non-finite process of spectralization (Baudelaire invoked number very well in the anthill-city of modern capitalism—ghost, crowd, money, prostitution—and Benjamin likewise in his wake). For if no use-value can in itself produce this mysticality or this spectral effect of the commodity, and if the secret is at the same time profound and superficial, opaque and transparent, a secret that is all the more secret in that no substantial essence hides behind it, it is because the effect is born of a ***relation*** (ferance, difference, reference, and differ*e*nce), as double relation, one should say as double social bond.

60. "Cārls Baudelaʾir," 163–64.

61. Ibid., 169–70.

62. The poem is "Call" (*pukār*). I begin in the middle. The Urdu is as follows: "dil meñ nafrat kā añdherā / jab ki sab bañdh ho rāheñ / kaise g̣ham leke hai ātā." Ibid., 178.

63. Ibid., 172 ("Dark Song"; prose poem). "Uskī har bāt kāle rañg kī hai / voh to ruḥ-e shabānah dikhāʾī detī hai, ruḥ-e tīragī. Uskī āñkheñ guphāʾeñ banīñ jin kī gaharāʾī meñ asrār daraḳhshāñ haiñ, lekin in āñkhoñ kī nigāheñ bijalī kī ṭaraḥ banīñ ik camakārā jo rāt kī pardāh ko cīr de." This poem follows upon the previous one; the ellipsis indicates a break between poems. See Spivak, *A Critique of Postcolonial Reason*: "She remains the only 'thou' in the apostrophe that is not quite one: 'I am thinking of you.' The poet's self-deconstruction seems to be made possible by the metaphor of the powerful woman" (151)—here Kali/Jeanne Duval.

64. "Cārls Baudelaʾir," 182. This is my translation from Miraji's translation into Urdu of the original English. This poem gives voice and body to Miraji's poetics of translation. It is a much tauter, sparer rendition of anything that Swinburne was likely to have published and was probably based on one verse of the nine-page, eighteen-stanza elegy, "Ave Atque Vale." Swinburne's third stanza, the one that this translation resembles, reads:

Thou sawest, in thine old singing season, brother,
Secrets and sorrows unbeheld of us:
Fierce loves, and lovely leaf-buds poisonous,
Bare to thy subtler eye, but for none other
Blowing by night in some unbreathed-in clime;
The hidden harvest of luxurious time,
Sin without shape, and pleasure without speech
And where strange dreams in tumultuous sleep
Make the shut eyes of stricken spirits weep;

And with each face thou sawest the shadow on each,
Seeing as men sow men reap.

*The Complete Works of Algernon Charles Swinburne*, ed. Sir Edmund Gosse and Thomas James Wise (London: William Heinemann; New York: Gabriel Wells, 1925), 11: 44–51; 44.

CHAPTER 4: WHITHER MASCULINITY?

1. Epigram opening "Musāfir kī talāsh" (Search for a traveler), in the final section, "Kuch kahānī, kuch manẓir" (Some stories, some scenes), of *Pābañd naẓmen* (Rawalpindi: Kitab Numa, 1968), 140.

2. Manuscript version of *Sah ātishah*, the table of contents of which lists where poems were published. Miraji kept meticulous records of the journals where poems appeared, and incorporated those records into his manuscripts of books when he put them together.

3. *Mīrājī kī naẓmeñ*, 1st ed., 134–40, and Pāshī, ed., *Mīrājī*, 162–64. For a complete translation see this chapter and Appendix A (for two different versions). The poem is in the section from 1941 in the book and was written in Lahore. It is a *mub-ham* poem. For an explanation of *mub-ham*-ness, see Chapter 7.

4. Dedication to *Mīrājī kī naẓmeñ*.

5. Hali was particularly attuned to the multivoiced questions of translation. Although many critics have mentioned Hali's intimate concern with translation, its valences are worth returning to again.

6. See Pritchett, *Nets of Awareness*, chap. 2, "Beyond the Sea of Blood."

7. "Nauḥah-e dillī" (Lament for Delhi), reprinted in Narayani Gupta, *Delhi Between Two Empires, 1803–1931: Society, Government, and Urban Growth* (New Delhi: Oxford University Press, 1998).

8. Altaf Husain Hali, *Hali's Musaddas: The Flow and Ebb of Islam*, trans. Christopher Shackle and Javed Majeed (New Delhi: Oxford University Press, 1997), 151. Though this volume provides an excellent translation of these lines, I have chosen to translate them again because I wanted to include the multiple renditions of *ṭai*, going, traveling, as well as fixing or settling a dispute, which bring together travel and the law, and which seemed to be particularly apropos to this context, especially when connected to "treasure/wealth."

9. One of his own accounts of his life, in the first volume of *Kulliyāt-e nasr-e Ḥālī* (Hali's complete prose) (Lahore: Majlis Taraqqi-e Adab, 1968), turns from his job correcting Urdu translations from English works, to his growing kinship with English literature, to the subtle decline of the value of Persian in his eyes (339); also see Pritchett, *Nets of Awareness*. Hali followed up this movement (from translation,

through affinity, to effective separation) with information about the gatherings instituted by Mohammad Husain Azad under Colonial Holroyd, director of public instruction in the Punjab, where Hali recited a new kind of poetry (*maṡnavī*) on new topics like "the rainy season," "hope," "justice," and "patriotism."

10. I call Hali "incomplete" because he was not quite English enough in his tastes and his opinions, although he continually assessed his relationship to the question of what was of use in Englishness, and absorbed useful things from it through evoking their "value." Macaulay was seminal to Hali's interrogations. See Pritchett's skillful work on Hali for discussions on the ways he visited Macaulay as the arbiter of aesthetic information and aesthetic value.

11. *The Correspondence of Lord William Cavendish Bentinck*, ed. C. H. Phillips (Oxford: Oxford University Press, 1977), II: 1142 (henceforth *Bentinck*).

12. *Bentinck*, II: 525–26. I focus on Bentinck partially because his was the "reign" under which education policies of a certain sort, which were to continue and affect Indians like Hali, were discussed widely and implemented. I also concentrate on Bentinck because he was a reformer of a certain kind who took on questions about the social policy of legislating morality. Witness the extensive discussions on suttee: 10 April 1828, 10 November 1828, and 4 December 1829, Regulation XVII of the Bengal Code, which declared suttee illegal and punishable as a criminal offense; 19 December 1829, petition in support of suttee; 14 July 1830, Bentinck's response, which offers a claim of tolerance of religious belief while opening up the space between belief and reason/natural justice as one that falls within a legal jurisdiction. And also on thuggee: 6 April 1830, policy statement on thugee; 20 March 1832, 22 November 1832, 28 November 1832, 26 June 1833, and 16 April 1834.

Bentinck declared his allegiances to James Mill, though Mill himself was somewhat dubious about Bentinck's abilities: he saw Bentinck as "well-intentioned but not a very well instructed man." Orientalists on Bentinck's staff, like H. H. Wilson, concurred with Mill. Bentinck was someone, like Jones (discussed later), caught up between the paradox of transformation as decimation of a separate, autonomous clear-thinking other, and transformation as regeneration of an other who desperately needed the British to enable them to see morality through the lens of reason. Bentinck's note on "reform in India" is a remarkably candid, and confused elaboration of the paradoxes he seemed to struggle with: "[you] claim for the British system merit which it does not possess . . . [t]he great curse of our rule has been constant interference with the long established native systems of Indian society, and of the introduction of our own fancies and schemes, which coupled with our own ignorance, have desolated," and "general education is my panacea for the regeneration of India. The ground must be prepared and the jungle cleared away, before the human mind can receive with any prospect of real benefit, the seeds of improvement"("Reform in India," Ootacamund, 1 June 1834). Natives, for Bentinck, those recipients of his reforming zeal, were described in equally contradictory ways. On one hand, they are capable of a clear, pointed pragmatic understanding of what they need, and on the other hand, they need the British to show them how to actually read what they need: "The natives understand and appreciate the advantages of their own village system, and so they would the system of British government, if there were any system at all in it"; "if our rule is bad, as I believe it to be, let the natives have the means, through knowledge, to represent their grievances, . . . [i]f their own habits, morals or ways of thinking are inconsistent with their own happiness and improvement, let them have the means, provided by our greater intellignce, of discovering their errors." Bentinck sees some of the mercantile interests at the heart of British (mis)management: "The great object and end of all these innovations [that have desolated] was the increase of revenue." But what he does not want to see with the same occasional clarity is that perhaps all the "means, provided by our [perhaps not] greater intelligence" were liable to cause desolation, and were oriented toward the "increase of revenue" (1 July 1834).

Hali, and other variations of colonial mimic men, were produced at the junctions of these paradoxes; they were produced at the junctures of these ambivalences. It is no wonder, given the inconsistency of the site at which imitation (of the British by Indians) occurs, that the "imitation subverts the identity of that which is being represented"; Parama Roy quoting Homi Bhabha, *Indian Traffic: Identities in Question in Colonial and Postcolonial India* (Berkeley: University of California Press, 1998), 2. Parama Roy also explores much more complex, gendered, raced examples of indigenous mimicry, which form useful counterpoints to this discussion.

13. Visvanathan, *Masks of Conquest*, 33.

14. One early call that took the charter act in the direction that Bentinck wanted to take it, transforming the ground so as to "allure the natives to the study of European science and literature," assumed the form of organic metaphors of the grafting (synthesis) of European cultural and political organizations onto "native" soil. Paper by J. H. Harrington, 19 June 1814, quoted in *Adam's Reports on Vernacular Education in Bengal and Bihar*, quote from Visvanathan, *Masks of Conquest*, 173, note 15.

15. Before several of the education initiatives or policy statements that attempted to transform the direction education took in India, the money laid aside for education was substantially increased, sometimes in concordance with a renewal or renegotiation of the East India Company charter. In 1833 the grant for education made in 1813 was increased tenfold, and it was followed by Macaulay's

minute. In 1853 the outlay was probably augmented seven or eight times, though the original grant was supposed to be extended indefinitely, and it was followed by Sir Charles Wood's Dispatch of 1854. For a discussion, see the Rev. J. Johnston, *Abstract and Analysis of the Report of the Indian Education Commission with Notes and the Recommendations in Full* (London: Hamilton, Adams, 1884).

16. Visvanathan, *Masks of Conquest*, 24. Henry Montgomery, in the house debate, in Great Britain, *Parliamentary Debates*, (1813), 26: 830; Charles Grant, in Great Britain, *British Parliamentary Papers, 1831–32*, general appendix, "Observations on the State of Society Among our Asiatic Subjects," vol. 8: 10.

17. Maintaining peace when other parts of the empire were in a state of war or unrest; maintaining nature; or preventing famine that had haunted other provinces for three years; Warren Hastings, "The Address in His Defense, 2 June 1791," *The Impeachment of Warren Hastings: Papers from a Bicentenary Commemoration*, ed. Geoffrey Carnall and Colin Nicholson (Edinburgh: Edinburgh University Press, 1989), 23–28.

18. *British Parliamentary Papers*, 8: 20. Raising revenue, desolating regions to enable them to flourish—in the inimitable words of Warren Hastings.

19. Ibid.; see Visvanathan, *Masks of Conquest*, 26, for a disquisition on Grant and the process by which value is carved out as apart from a whole. See also Warren Hastings for a prolonged paean on his productive work.

20. Visvanathan, *Masks of Conquest*, 28. In "Transformations of Britain's Orient, 1785–1835" (in *Romantic Imperialism*, 117–21), Saree Makdisi divides Orientalism into two periods, which he sees as divided by an epistemic break. The first is "an Enlightenment discourse of otherness" (shared by Burke and Sir William Jones) and "a more properly modern and evolutionary one" (Mill, Macaulay). One piece of the difference is organized around how the other is portrayed. In the eighteenth century the other is immutable, unchangeable, radically different, and to be construed on its own terms, with the British accommodating to that difference. Later, especially by the late nineteenth century, the other had fallen under the "spell of difference" valued in relation to the self as the only self-present entity. Difference is devalued, produced as static and outside of history, parceled off into the past, and is to be transformed. As Makdisi himself is quick to suggest, such opposites are always rent by other discourses. And that is clearly the case with Jones's discussions on Indian knowledge in the eighteenth century. It is also the case that the other, who is supposed to be in place in the later nineteenth century, is produced as radically different (though the other was under erasure by a changing present, and paradoxically also situated in a static temporal past) in discussions by H. H. Wilson, as well by Denzil Ibbetson—both of whom returned to the

village/villagers, as multifarious, multiple sites of difference. See Denzil Ibbetson, "Address to the Fourth Annual Meeting, 26 February 1890," *Journal of the Anthropological Society of Bombay* (1890): 116–46, esp. 143–44.

21. Visvanathan, *Masks of Conquest*, 28.

22. Counterpose this, perhaps as a precondition, to Richard Burton's complex movement through knowledge and in tension with mimicry (double mimesis), explored so deftly by Parama Roy, in *Indian Traffic*, 30–33, "Oriental Exhibits." But Roy (31) also points to the opaqueness of the native, which makes it necessary to have them "known, categorized, fixed" (and, I would add, deciphered, in the above circuitry of knowledge), and uneasy links to their "permeability, malleability and lack of essence," which makes them perfect subjects (objects) for the process of double mimesis that Burton engaged. For the form of object-nessI refer to here see Roy's introduction, and Diana Fuss, "Interior Colonies: Frantz Fanon and the Politics of Identification," in Fuss, *Identification Papers* (New York: Routledge, 1995), 141–65.

23. O. P. Kejariwal, *The Asiatic Society of Bengal and the Discovery of India's Past, 1784–1838* (New Delhi: Oxford University Press, 1988).

24. See Sir William Jones's various "Charge[s] to the Grand Jury" in 1785 and in 1787; *The Works of Sir William Jones*, 13 vols. (London: Printed for John Stockdale, Piccadilly; and John Walker, Paternoster Row, 1807), 7: 8–32 (henceforth *Jones*). Jones shifts his evaluation of perjury (deceit) over the two texts. In the first, "though the information is not perfect," false evidence is clearly punishable under Hindu Laws; and for Muslims, "if they forswear themselves in regard to evidence already given, they cannot, except by divine mercy, escape misery in this world and the next"(*Jones*, 7: 19). By the second, Jones has revised his opinion entirely in the face of evidence; now Indians are likely to perjure, and in fact they seem to like to perjure and British officials need to do an enormous amount of work to get them to swear in court, through forms that might make legal lying difficult.

> Having spoken of the little credit, which I gave to the oath of a low native, I cannot refrain from touching upon the frequency of perjury; which seems to be committed by the meanest and encouraged by some of the better sort, among the Hindus and Muselmans [*sic*], with as little remorse as if it were a proof of ingenuity, or even a merit, instead of being, by their own express laws, as grievous a crime as man is capable of committing. I cannot name this offence without emotion; for (besides its natural enormity) it renders the discharge of our pubilck [*sic*] duty both difficult and painful in the highest degree; it is not in causes, where Hindus and Muselmans give evidence, that a fact is proved. (*Jones*, 7: 28–29)

25. "An Essay on the Poetry of the Eastern Nations," *Jones*, 10: 3359–60. See Makdisi's discussion of excess that I have drawn on (*Romantic Imperialism*, 108).

26. *Jones*, 7: 21: "to conciliate their affection, while we promote their industry, so as to render our dominion over them a national benefit."

27. For a few pertinent exegeses on knowledge gathering, translation, consolidation, capitalism, in this period, see Tejaswini Niranjana, *Siting Translation: History, Post-Structuralism and the Colonial Context* (Berkeley: University of California Press, 1992); Saree Makdisi, *Romantic Imperialism: Universal Empire and the Culture of Modernity* (Cambridge, Eng.: Cambridge University Press, 1998); and Bernard S. Cohn, *Colonialism and Its Forms of Knowledge: The British in India* (New Delhi: Oxford University Press, 1997).

28. *Jones*, 3: 13.

29. See David Arnold, *The Problem of Nature: Environment, Culture, and European Expansion* (Oxford; and Cambridge, Mass.: Basil Blackwell, 1996). See also Visvanathan, who speaks about the continuities between the two groups, especially in relation to science, and also addresses H. H. Wilson's claim that teaching Indians would enable the formation of a Trojan Horse who would transform the Indian polity from the inside. This, despite other arguments made by Orientalists engaged in this struggle that losing access to their knowledge would have detrimental effects on their sense of self-worth.

30. *Jones*, 3: 13; 14–15.

31. Ibid., 3: 19. See also Dipesh Chakrabarty, "Radical Histories and the Question of Enlightenment Rationalism: Some Recent Critiques of *Subaltern Studies*," *Economic and Political Weekly* (8 April 1995): 751–59. Chakrabarty addresses the relationship of science practiced under colonialism to its vilified other, religion. Jones draws a more complicated set of connections between science and the religions of the colonized, but science still stands paramount against forms of duplicity (read irrationality).

Jones's relationship to his own botanical adventures in the colonies is similarly fraught. He authorizes himself by placing himself in the lineage of Linneas, but he is a botanist with imperfect sight. Despite this, or perhaps because of this, Jones's instruments of measurement are, by his own account, unfailingly accurate. They produce sketches of botanical terrains that mediate between the local (Sanskrit, Ayurvedic, medical) versions and those seen literally by travelers encountering that terrain. Jones analogizes the botanist as a geographer who, "desiring to find his way in a foreign city or province, should never inquire by name for a street or a town, but with his tables and instruments, for a proper occasion to determine its longitude and latitude." The analogy hides a literal rendering of Jones's work. His work is to map, and to map in an appropriate temporality. What Jones's maps offer a traveler is a tourism handbook of science that will always circumvent local knowledge. As one reads Jones's botany, one reads the pleasure of seeing a splayed dissected body, its anatomical fineries, the subtle shading of veins and roots opened to sight and smell. Jones's work is a reminder of Hegel's master-slave dialectic; the aestheticized delectation of evisceration for knowledge that takes over the time-space of others. *Jones*, 5: 62–71. In Jones's work reason and taste do come together but they are coupled through the delights of a kind of sadism, where the other participates without a safety catch that assures his/her nondeath.

32. Charles E. Trevelyan's obviously Anglicist account of education, in *On Education of the People of India* (London: Longman, Orme, Brown, Green, and Longmans, Paternoster Row, 1838), discusses science education, anatomy, and medicine, inserted into Oriental institutions like the Calcutta Madressa (*sic*) and the Sanskrit College (7). Trevelyan assumes that though both he and his opponents might disagree on the relative merits of English versus Oriental literatures, they clearly concur on the question of science, "the comparative state of science in European and Asiatic countries might be too well known to admit of any dispute" (55).

33. For an exemplary, influential version see Mill, *The History of British India.*

34. *Bentinck*, II: 1241.

35. Ibid., 1261.

36. Ibid., I: 311.

37. Ibid., 311–12.

38. In 1833, the charter of the East India Company was renewed for twenty years, on condition that the company abandon its trade and permit Europeans to settle in the country. The governor-general's council was extended by one, by a "law member" who did not have to work for the company directly. A Law Commission was established to revise and codify the law. Macaulay was the first Law member and served as the first president of the commission. Bentinck covered the wide-ranging terrain of his policy initiatives sometimes at odds with London, and local officials, sometimes in harmony with them.

39. *Bentinck*, I: 77, 80, 144–45, 200, 201, 249, 299, 582; II: 587, 746–48, 5, etc.

40. Ibid., I: 38, 106, etc.

41. This paragraph was incited by a conversation with Lauren Berlant. See David Lloyd and Paul Thomas, *Culture and the State* (New York: Routledge, 1998); and Antonio Gramsci, *Selections from the Prison Notebooks of Antonio Gramsci*, ed. Quintin Hoare and Geoffrey Nowell Smith (London: Lawrence and Wishart, 1971).

42. The moral character of Indians was a subject that had taken tortuous paths that sometimes wound around the particular recommendations of colonial administrators and missionaries. For Johnston (*Abstract and Analysis*), who had an investment in religious education, educational practices that practiced religious neutrality taught "skepticism" that undermined native religious practices, and since these practices didn't replace skepticism with good biblical moral teaching, they obviously led to potentially immoral native-subjects. Johnston's presumptions about personal morality as something determined by circumstances had many adherents (Utilitarians like Mill, Anglicists like Trevelyan), who, however, followed different variations of the theme—that despotic practices molded character, certain kinds of texts inculcated moral positions, and so on. Obviously the corollary was that if whatever produced immorality was removed or transformed, the person's character would change too. But change required an assumption about the mutability of moral character. The question here was whether characters as they changed for the better moved toward an original purity (secular Platonism in Trevelyan [*On Education of the People of India*, 189–93]); away from original impurity (Johnston; and Alexander Duff, *New Era of the English Language and English Literature in India* [Edinburgh: John Johnston, 1837]); or toward something that was new and formed only by particular circumstances. In other words, according to this definition, moral character is mutable; there is no "basic" character. Everyone who addressed morality took on Oriental texts, texts that either offered something at odds with immoral practices (Jones; and Gottlieb William Leitner, "Report of the Committee Appointed to Examine Existing Standards of Examination of the Punjab University College," in J. P. Naik, ed., *Selections from Educational Records of the Government of India* [Delhi: For the National Archives of India by the Manager of Publications, Government of India, 1963], II: 262–73; see below); or were directly responsible for immoral practices (Kerr; see below), or mirrored (embodied) immoral practices (Mill). See Visvanathan, *Masks of Conquest*, 118–41.

43. *Bentinck*, 1: 524, quoting Sir Thomas Munro, who served under Hastings (1812–23); and Visvanathan, *Masks of Conquest*, 32, 44, 46. Character building through texts was opposed by groups of people who believed that education in a system ought not to assure a person a job in the system. To argue this point they proposed that labor—working in the system—built character; James Kerr (principal of Hoogly College), *A Review of Public Instruction in the Bengal Presidency from 1835–1852* (Calcutta: J. Thomas, Baptist Mission Press, 1852), part 1, 194–95. For character building through texts see ibid., 170. Kerr writes: "It may also be a point of honor with those natives who have received a good education, to be more trustworthy than the uneducated masses. It would give them more pain to be de-

tected in a falsehood or in any dishonest practice. A public feeling favourable to integrity is growing up among them" (ibid., 195).

44. Ibid., 170.

45. *Bentinck*, II: 1405.

46. Kerr, *A Review of Public Instruction*, part I, 171.

47. Ibid., 172.

48. Ibid., 10–14, 170–75.

49. Ibid., 175–77; esp. 177.

50. Ibid., 177.

51. Ibid., 150–51. Kerr quotes from a letter on education, written on 20 July 1843 by the lieutenant-governor at Agra, Colonel Sutherland.

52. Ibid., 148–49.

53. Ibid., 152.

54. James Thomason is depicted in his biography as a perfect example of an administrator. His aptness relies on a necessary distance from various British colonial masculine types and their desires toward the colonized. He is not versed in the colloquial like those who begin to turn native. He is not hearty and genial (bluff and red) with a personal knowledge of the locals. He is not loved by the natives because he has thrown himself into the project of saving them from pestilence, or by teaching/exhorting them or ministering to them. He is suave, bland, calm, undemonstrative, steadfast, and distant, ceaselessly expending energy on general welfare. His portrait in the opening pages of the book is of a slightly effeminate intellectual man. He is sitting half-turned, legs crossed, by a book, paper in hand; the Taj Mahal is in the background partly concealed by a wall. Thomason comes off as the ideal rational civil administrator, utterly beneficent, clean of all the messy desire (including that accompanying hypermasculinity) that incites work in the colonies. His rationality is beyond reproach. He is endorsed by an image that encapsulates the Indian past from the regions he administers, but he is not completely synonymous with that past. Sir Richard Temple, *James Thomason* (Oxford: Clarendon Press, 1893), 92–99, 171.

55. Rev. J. Johnston, *Abstract and Analysis*, 18–19.

56. Kerr, *A Review of Public Instruction*, part I, 185–87.

57. Ibid., 193; Visvanathan, *Masks of Conquest*, 89.

58. Bentinck asked to change the language of the courts from Persian to English, and was resisted somewhat. The resistance took the form of a curious tangle with Orientalism. Vernacular languages were suggested instead of English, in order to facilitate comfortable access for Indians, and it was suggested that the book versions of Hindu and Muslim law be dropped—not in favor of collected codifications of local custom, but in favor of the continually changing manifesta-

tions that custom took in the court. This, it was believed, would follow the British legal system of precedent and common law more closely than the current constructions of law on the subcontinent.

59. Kerr, *A Review of Public Instruction*, part 1, 195.

60. E. P. Thompson, *The Making of the English Working Class* (New York: Vintage Books, 1966), 607; Friedrich Engels, *The Condition of the Working Class in England*, trans. W. O. Henderson and W. H. Chaloner (1845; repr. of 1892 ed., Stanford, Calif.: Stanford University Press, 1968). The way that the fora for public discourse were used by the working class to enable its formation was also deployed by Bentinck's administration to enable the passage of the Minute on Education (*Bentinck*, 2: 1433).

61. See Thompson, *The Making of the English Working Class*, and Engels, *The Condition of the Working Class in England.*

62. See Kerr, *A Review of Public Instruction.*

63. "The Humble Petition of the British Indian Association, North-Western Provinces," 1 August 1867, *Selections from the Educational Records of the Government of India: Development of University Education, 1860–87*, ed. J. P. Naik (Delhi: National Archives of India, 1963), 11: 21–28. These members are writing from Aligarh.

64. Francis Robinson, *Separatism Among Indian Muslims: The Politics of the United Provinces' Muslims 1860–1923* (New Delhi: Oxford University Press, 1997), 34–47. Robinson, like Kerr in 1851, speaks of British resistance in the 1880s to the call for educational qualifications by such folks as the Board of Revenue, A. C. Lyall, district officers, and so forth. Some examples of the resistances included: a belief that the wrong person might get the job, that an officer might want to reward a subordinate, that few people applied from groups targeted for quotas. But according to Robinson (45–46), things did change.

65. See Fredrick William Thomas, *The History and Prospects of British Education in India* (Cambridge, Eng.: Deighton Bell, 1891), 86–89, for the figures announcing, with jubilation, the absorption, extinction, and destruction of indigenous schools. Thomas credits Thomason. For Thomas, the modern school has an advantage in that it is "better managed, liable to inspection, better taught, and with a wider curriculum." His is an ad hoc condemnation of local schooling that supports institutionalization of them, without any analysis of what these schools fostered. See F. Robinson, *Separatism Among Indian Muslims*, 35.

66. Thomas, *The History and Prospects of British Education in India*, 93–94; Rev. J. Johnston, *Abstract and Analysis*, 86–91. See David Lelyveld, *Aligarh's First Generation* (Princeton, N.J.: Princeton University Press, 1978), 83–101, for a discussion on why Muslims might not want to enter the educational system.

67. Thomas, *The History and Prospects of British Education in India*, 93–94.

68. Rev. J. Johnston, *Abstract and Analysis*, 86–87.

69. Ibid., 88–91.

70. Lelyveld, *Aligarh's First Generation*, 21.

71. Ibid.

72. Ibid., 23.

73. Ibid., 29.

74. Ibid., 30.

75. Ibid.

76. Ibid.

77. Carla Petievich, *Assembly of Rivals: Delhi, Lucknow, and the Urdu Ghazal* (New Delhi: Manohar Publications, 1992), 188.

78. Ibid., 26–37.

79. See Petievich, who explores the contiguities between what it meant to accrue value, worth, and morality in terms that brought nineteenth-century British constructions together with Indo-Islamic ones (through Persianizing) in the nineteenth century. Culture was a heavily contested term in Britain during that period. See Christopher Herbert, *Culture and Anomie: Ethnographic Imagination in the Nineteenth Century* (Chicago: University of Chicago Press, 1991). In Urdu the words for "culture" include *tahżīb*, from the Arabic *hżb*, prune, trim, clean, cleanse, polish, educate, which is close to the sixteenth- and early-nineteenth-century English cultivation or refinement of mind, tastes, matter. They also incorporate *tamaddun*, from the Arabic *mdn*, to found, build cities, urbanize, humanize, refine, which resonates with the more urban-bound notions of culture, a stage or type of intellectual development, the artistic side of civilization (perhaps), seen in Matthew Arnold's discussions of Hellenic *civitas*, a process of civilizing (perhaps also linked to the Urdu *markaz*, center or capital, linked to the Arabic *rkz*, plant, position, take place, naturalize [footstand, locality]—both suggesting "to establish" as well as the botanical, field metaphor "to cultivate").

Hali, in verse 8 of the *Musaddas*, uses *tamaddun*, *tamaddun kā us par paḍā thā nah sāyā*, "the shadow of civilization had not falled upon it" (*Musaddas*, 105). Here, Hali is describing what he thinks is the lawless, uncultivated (no fields), wild (jungles), multireligious situation in pre-Islamic Arabia. And civilization is precisely a form of *civitas* that has at its center the Holy Law.

80. See also Pritchett, *Nets of Awareness*, chap. 3, "Reconstruction," 31–59, for a more detailed account of Aziz's and Hali's complicated relationship with the British, who gave them both a forum and work after 1857.

81. Civilization, the apparatus of it, the languages of law and urbanity that gave it substance, the cultivated urban man, folded into a network of associations: all

were contested here, especially in relation to morality, and certainly in relation to the languages in which it took form. Arabic (as the language of religion and "tradition) had been hit hard, and Persian (as the language of law and political negotiation) had been supplanted, the legal systems were changing, and Urdu, as a vernacular, was given status as it had its value reassessed (or—more properly perhaps in the linguistic taxonomies of the British—assessed). Urdu was rife for refinement/enrichment, which put its worth and its refinement, especially its Persianized form, into jeopardy. A few British administrators spoke up for Urdu in the nineteenth century, among them M. S. Howell in 1868, who suggested that Urdu might be the right educational vernacular lingua franca for the Northwest Provinces (and picked over Hindi) because it was adaptable, flexible, and availed of a wider base of linguistic sources; and had been the language of the courts, intercourse, and business, and of general literature. Urdu might however still need translation into it. "Note by M.S. Howell, Esquire, stressing the importance of making the Indian languages as the media of instruction in schools and indicating the conditions essential for establishment of a Vernacular University for the North-Western Provinces and the Punjab," 28 November 1868, *Selections from the Educational Records* . . . , II: 73.

82. Lelyveld, *Aligarh's First Generation*, 68.

83. See Pritchett, *Nets of Awareness*, and Petievich, *Assembly of Rivals*.

84. Lelyveld, *Aligarh's First Generation*, 109–44. Certainly Sir Sayyid took up on filtration, Macaulay, and on the British discourses on science, but filtration (especially the Macaulayian kind, with its emphasis on a separate "class") suited the *ashrāf*. And by the time Sir Sayyid was writing, where he was positioned was very much in relation to his status as belonging to a certain "class," which had to be reiterated to establish his and the *ashrāf*'s privileged relation to education (in the vernacular and in English). "Class," as an expression, comes to the fore in British writings from this time in a very particular context (see earlier discussion of class), and also in relation to "culture." See Pritchett (*Nets of Awareness*, 153): the Viceroy gave Sir Sayyid a medal and a copy of Macaulay's work. Sir Sayyid is also consistently mentioned as the one exception to Muslim intransigence in the matter of education by British commentators on education. He is someone who is spoken of as understanding the programmatics of educational imperatives.

85. See Petievich's entire book (*Assembly of Rivals*) and Pritchett's book for discussions on the Delhi court and the Lucknow Nawabi, as well as in Bhopal.

86. Petievich, *Assembly of Rivals*, 144.

87. Hali, *Musaddas*, 105 (stanza 7).

88. The metaphors of this narrative return to the past echo those one finds in certain evocations of the "national" in this period. Hali finds precisely those kinds

of knowledge in his past that have to be inculcated through systems of British education. He brings together forms called for in a range of texts, but specially in Mill, *The History of British India*. Mill, however, does credit Islam with a particular sense of the historical, a sense missing in Hindus. See also Hegel.

89. *Musaddas*, 133–41. See esp. stanza 103 (141) which outlines all the *Garẓ-e fan*.

90. *Musaddas*, 193 (stanza 249).

91. Carlo Coppola, "Urdu Poetry, 1935–1970," 6. The Aligarh was Sir Sayyid's movement. See also regarding connections between Hali and Azad (134–39).

92. See Pritchett, *Nets of Awareness*, chap. 12, "Poetry and Morality," 169–83.

93. Hālī, *Muqaddamah-e shiʿr o shāʿirī*, 120–28. See Pritchett, *Nets of Awareness*, esp. 134–136 and 179, for elaboration of his "central theme" of the *Muqaddamah*.

94. See, esp., Pritchett, *Nets of Awareness*, 179, which is the source of the quote; see also Laurel Steele, "Hali and His *Muqaddamah*: The Creation of a Literary Attitude in Nineteenth-Century India," *Annual of Urdu Studies* 1 (1981): 10.

95. Hālī, *Muqaddamah-e shiʿr o shāʿirī*, 133.

96. Pritchett, *Nets of Awareness*, 149–50.

97. Coppola, "Urdu Poetry," 8.

98. Ḥālī, *Muqaddamah-e shiʿr o shāʿirī*, 140–41; Pritchett, *Nets of Awareness*, 180.

99. Coppola, "Urdu Poetry," 9.

100. The ghazal began to be treated as one of *the* modes through which the past was represented. By the time Miraji wrote, it is clear from his rhetorical style that this status was accepted as normal. Miraji uses the ghazal / woman as the allegorical figure representing the past. See the next chapter for a discussion of the ghazal / woman / past.

101. Hālī, *Muqaddamah-e shiʾr o shāʾirī*, 250–69.

102. Ibid., 127. Pritchett (*Nets of Awareness*, 163) addresses the issue of Hali's vexed relationship to the past, quoting Hali: "In fact, Hali notes two contradictory Arabic sayings on this subject: 'Earlier poets have left a great deal for later poets,' and 'Earlier poets have left nothing for later poets.' From these two sayings we should conclude, he says most interestingly, that 'earlier poets have left many incomplete things, so that later poets can complete them, but they have left for later poets nothing of which no example is already present'" (146).

103. Ḥālī, *Muqaddamah-e shiʾr o shāʾirī*, 127–38.

104. *Musaddas*, 179–85; "Mażhabī xayāl" and "ʿIlm," in Sar Sayyad Aḥmad Ḵhān, *Intiḵhāb-e maẓāmīn-e sar sayyad* (Lucknow: Uttar Pradesh Urdu Academy, 1983), 23–26, 27–29.

105. Although Hali and Sir Sayyid speak to the construction of a person, it is

clear that in this case the person is gendered male. Hali writes elsewhere about issues concerning women and in this venue speaks to the construction of a specifically female identity.

106. Ḥālī, *Muqaddamah-e shiʿr o shāʿirī,* 201, 202–3, 206. Saree Makdisi (*Romantic Imperialism,* 46–49) talks about Wordsworth's landscapes (nature) as framed by a subject in spatiotemporal grids; nature was viewed as scapes by a cognizant seer; value was given to a scene in the framing of it by a subject for whom that land was useless precisely because he was not concerned with extracting (nonaesthetic) value from it—resistance to modernization by rescuing from evolving scapes those that appeared to defy industrialization by remaining images (visual and temporal) that were the backdrops to the blurs of change.

107. Alṭāf Ḥusain Ḥālī, *Ḥayāt-e saʿādī* (Delhi: Maktaba Jamia, 1992). Pritchett (*Nets of Awareness,* 177–81) talks about Hali's analysis of the poetics of desire as something determined by the conventions of the language in which it was written and the time at which it was written (Persian and Urdu writes every kind of desire as between two men; Hindi and Braj write them as a woman in love with a man; Arabic as a man in love with a woman, and as something that must pay heed to moral claims of the age [poets of Iran and India will be judged according to law]).

108. *Musaddas,* 205 (verse 285).

109. Steele, "Hali and His *Muqaddamah,*" 22–23.

110. Ibid., 22.

111. See Pritchett, *Nets of Awareness,* part 1, "A Garden Now Destroyed," 1–59.

112. Ḥālī, *Muqaddamah-e shiʿr o shāʿirī,* 171.

113. See Emily Apter, "Ethnographic Travesties," in Apter, *Continental Drift: From National Characters to Virtual Subjects* (Chicago: University of Chicago Press, 1999). This invocation of realism stands quite precisely and quite imprecisely between my discussion of realism and the PWA in Chapter 2, and my closing, momentary return to realism at the very end of Chapter 7. Certainly anyone who studies colonialism must turn to realism, whether it be, as Apter points out, through the reality effects of the staged specularity of exhibitions (Timothy Mitchell, *Colonizing Egypt* [Berkeley: University of California Press, 1991]), or the stilled (and staged) specularity of colonial (and ethnographic) photography. See Pinney, *Camera Indica*; and Clark Worswick, *The Last Empire: Photography in British India, 1855–1911* (New York: Aperture, 1976). The Lacanian "Real" must haunt all such discussions; in Apter's words, "Intruding itself on the subject at a moment least expected, the real is that sudden and terrifying flash when the subject perceives the gaping hole in subjectivity tenuously papered over by denial" (258, note 1).

114. For other influences on the Progressives (Sir Sayyid, Iqbal, and the novel-

ist Nazir Ahmad, who wrote *The Bride's Mirror*), refer to Coppola, "Urdu Poetry."

115. Coppola, "Urdu Poetry," 615. One of the main differences between Hali and the Progressives that Coppola does not discuss is their respective notions of realism.

116. Ibid., 619.

117. Ibid., 415.

118. Much of what I say here is taken from readings of particular ghazals under the tutelage of my advisor, Professor Fran Pritchett. For a more detailed discussion, see Pritchett, *Nets of Awareness*, part 2, "Flowers on the Branch of Invention," 63–122, and 213 (for the way meaning is elaborated in ghazal and *naẓm/shi'r* and *shi'r angez*[?]).

119. "The Art and Craft of Poetry" and "The Mind and Heart in Poetry," Pritchett, *Nets of Awareness*, 91–105, 106–26.

120. Although many commentators use the critical vocabulary associated with describing the way an allegory works when they talk about this particular kind of doubled signification, they are loathe to actually call an allegory an allegory. Cf. Sadiq, *A History of Urdu Literature*; and Ralph Russell and Khurshidul Islam, *Three Mughal Poets* (Cambridge, Mass.: Harvard University Press, 1968), esp. the foreword.

121. In the case of a mushaira, it is also organized around a particular set of formal constraints with all the other *shi'r* recited in the mushaira as well as the "primal" *shi'r* that was used to set up the constraints. See Pritchett, *Nets of Awareness*, part 2, "Flowers on the Branch of Invention," esp. chap. 5, "Tazkirahs."

122. Kenneth Bryant, "Textual Obsessions: Conventionality in the Urdu Ghazal" (unpublished paper, 1986), 4.

123. For a sample discussion on Ghalib, see the preface to *Dīvān-e Ghạ̄lib*.

124. John T. Platts, *A Dictionary of Urdu, Classical Hindi, and English* (New Delhi: Oxford University Press, 1984), 95.

125. Muhammad Iqbal, *Secrets of the Self*, trans. Reynold A. Nicholson (London: Macmillan, 1920); *Poems from Iqbal*, trans. Victor Kiernan (London: Murray, 1955); *Notes on Iqbal's Asrar-e-Khudi*, ed. Arthur J. Arberry (Lahore: Muhammad Ashraf, 1959). "Aṣrār-e ḳhudī" was first read as an incomplete poem in the 1914 Lahore meeting of Anjuman-e Himayat-e Islam in Lahore. It was published in 1915.

126. I have chosen to focus on the later works of Iqbal, rather than discussing the development of his thought. For my purpose, which is to set Miraji in the context of his intellectual history, the way that Iqbal was understood is of paramount importance. See Muhammad Iqbal, *The Reconstruction of Religious Thought in Islam* (London: Oxford University Press, 1934). This collection of essays was first published in 1930 in Lahore by the Kapur Art Printing Works.

127. Whittemore, "Iqbal's Pantheism," in Waheed Querishi, ed., *Selections from the* Iqbal Review (Lahore: Iqbal Academy, 1983), 259.

128. See Reynold A. Nicholson, *The Mystics of Islam* (London: G. Bell and Sons, 1914), 39, 68; and Bo Utas, *A Persian Sufi Poem: Vocabulary and Terminology* (London and Malmo: Scandinavian Institute of Asian Studies, 1977), 169–73.

129. Iqbal, *Secrets of the Self*; Kiernan, trans., *Poems from Iqbal*, 16–17.

130. Iqbal, *The Reconstruction of Religious Thought in Islam*, 31–33.

131. Although *ḳhudī* has been here translated as "ego," I feel it is incompatible with Iqbal's use of the word, since ego carries with it Freudian connotations that are not present in Iqbal's *ḳhudī*. Ibid., 9, 180.

132. Ibid., 29.

133. Ibid., 36.

134. Ibid., 37.

135. Ibid., 38–39.

136. Whittemore, "Iqbal's Pantheism," 257–72.

137. For other discussions see Hafeez Malik, *Iqbal: Poet Philosopher of Pakistan* (New York: Columbia University Press, 1971), 251; and Naeem Ahmad, "Iqbal's Concept of Eternity," in Querishi, ed., *Selections*, 38.

138. Iqbal, *The Reconstruction of Religious Thought in Islam*, 284; Kiernan, trans., *Poems from Iqbal*, 93.

139. Kiernan, trans., *Poems from Iqbal*, 94.

140. M. Usman Ramz, "Iqbal's Philosophy of History," in Querishi, ed., *Selections*, 428–29.

141. Introduction to "Asrār-e ḳhudī," xvi; *Rumūz-e beḳhudī* (Enigmas of ecstasy).

142. *Letters of Iqbal*, comp. and ed. Bashir Ahmd Dar (Lahore: Iqbal Academy, 1978).

143. Muhammad Iqbal, *Shikwa and Jawab-e Shikwa, Complaint and Answer, Iqbal's Dialogue with God*, trans. Khushwant Singh (New Delhi: Oxford University Press, 1990).

144. Though Iqbal starts with certain givens that resonate with colonial representations, both Iqbal's production of self and his reproduction of his past served to untangle representations of his community from those that had been circulating. Temporality was precisely the place Iqbal needed to engage. In his discussion of the self (the self that formed the person in a community), Iqbal spent a fair amount of time in the essays disengaging time from space. He did this by suggesting that the kind of temporality he posed through the self was not one that could be rendered as a series of "nows" metaphorically stretched out on a string and therefore placed visually and in space. Iqbal divided the self into several pos-

sible versions that emerged under different conditions. The temporality of a series of nows was one that emerged when the appreciative self was placed in a "traffic" with the world of space and turned into an efficient self. He offered different possibilities for temporality, some allowing time to be stretched apart from space and not be merely spatialized, and space temporalized to enable the kind of temporality that rendered Indian Muslims static, produced them in the present as distant and relegated to a problem past. A *k̤hudī* in motion, whose very being was motion, and for whom time was inside itself and not prior, could hardly settle easily into the kind of static spacialized image that characterized colonial representations of the colonized (here I think Iqbal, like many other thinkers, resorts to Einstein to underscore his theoretical turns, when he actually meant Bohr/Heisenberg). Drawing the past into the present through the *k̤hudī bek̤hud* immersion in the *millat* keeps time moving in a way that halts attempts to draw it out into a linear historical timeline (Hegelian). See Johannes Fabian, *Time and the Other: How Anthropology Makes Its Object* (New York: Columbia University Press, 1983). Iqbal took on Bergson and worked against modernist representations of time. Iqbal is important for Mir̃aji, because he sets the terms for staging the political through the metaphysical. He stages the political through time, through the time of the present, by going to the "now" and reconstituting it in different ways. He rubs versions of the "now" against formulations of temporality that catch colonial subjects, and against formulations of temporality that allow them to slip.

145. Iqbal, *Shikwa and Jawab-e Shikwa, Complaint and Answer*, 88.

### CHAPTER 5: IN ILLUMINED SHADOWS

1. Ghalib, *Dīvān-e Ghālib*, 183.

2. Hali kept on trying to understand where he might put a Persian past that presented him endless ambiguities that he had to traverse: Did it allow kinds of immorality that were now illegal? Did it offer a simplicity of language of the kind he wanted for his compatriots? Was its poetry mired in unwieldy complexity? That British administrators were attempting to supersede Persian with English as the court language was probably tucked somewhere into Hali's tribulations. Arabic, and a certain reconstituted set of religious associations, was where Hali went to find a reasonable past. His explorations were fully consonant with other formations of nationalism at the time.

3. Iqbal's allegiances to Nietzsche and Hegel have been well documented.

4. Mīrāji, *Mīrājī kī naẕmeñ*, 134–40.

5. All these processes are depicted as being on a cognitive continuum.

6. Miraji's well-documented curiosity about Braj and Awadhi, the languages in which some bhakti poetry is written, can be seen through his translations of

Mirabai; in his *gīt,* written alongside "Traveler"; in the images that permeate other poems composed at the same time, like "Lab-e jū-e bāre"; and in his analyses in *Is naẓm meñ.* He also left behind notes about the lessons in Braj he took before he died.

Miraji's curiosity about Persian mystical poetry is evident from his translations of Omar Khayyam. Though the word for bird, *ṭā'ir,* which Miraji uses in this poem, is also seen in the ghazal; it is possible that Miraji was acquainted with Edward Fitzgerald's translation of Attar's work found in many libraries established in South Asia under British auspices. Miraji was certainly familiar with Fitzgerald's translations; he based his own Urdu versions of Khayyam on Fitzgerald's. In Miraji's notes verses from this English translation of Khayyam are accompanied by Miraji's Urdu ones: for example, verse 12 from the 1859 translation (Fitzgerald, trans., *Rubaiyat of Omar Khayyam,* 11). This interpolation raises the issue of Orientalist allegiances that Miraji had, or his turn to Orientalist translations to procure his past. These translations were often used as sources by him, but he diverted from their intent in certain ways. Firstly, Miraji's translations played havoc with "originals"; one could never turn the layers of transformations in translations back to any original that was recognizable as such if one used Miraji to begin that process. Secondly, by placing Orientalism, as in this poem, at the site of the loss and impossible recuperation of memory, Miraji made it hard for his translations to recover a past (that they seemed to offer simply) in any simple rendition.

That "Traveler" brought together bhakti and Sufism should be obvious to anyone who can read the allusions provoked by the language of the poem.

7. David L. Haberman, *Journey Through the Twelve Forests: An Encounter with Krishna* (New York and Oxford: Oxford University Press, 1994).

8. Annemarie Schimmel, *Islamic Literature of India* (Weisbadan, Ger.: Otto Harrassowitz, 1982); Nicholson, *The Mystics of Islam*; Margaret Smith, *The Sufi Path of Love* (London: Luzac and Company; 1931), 103.

9. Nicholson, *The Mystics of Islam,* 28.

10. Here, I am locating "Traveler" within one of the kinds of lyric to which it responds. I discuss the "self" as the "self" taken from Sufi poetry because of the connections between "self" and "journey," which are specific to Sufi poetry. Not all ghazals are Sufi; my discussion does not address non-Sufi verse.

11. Smith, *The Sufi Path of Love,* 58, 59.

12. Annemarie Schimmel, *As Through a Veil: Mystical Poetry in Islam* (New York: Columbia University Press, 1982), 264.

13. "Darkness" is also used in other contexts. For example, the beloved's hair is as dark as night.

14. Smith, *The Sufi Path of Love*, 64.

15. Utas, *A Persian Sufi Poem*, 135–41.

16. Smith, *The Sufi Path of Love*, 89.

17. Katherine Ewing, *Arguing Sainthood: Modernity, Psychoanalysis, Islam* (Durham, N.C.: Duke University Press, 1997).

18. Iqbal, *Secrets of the Ego*, trans. F. R. Tariq (Lahore: Islamic Book Service, 1977).

19. I discuss Iqbal here in counterpoint to Miraji. This section is to orient readers who do not have any familiarity with Urdu lyric and to give them some bases of comparison for Miraji.

20. Another translation is "one" and "second." I stay with "another" because it fits better with the context of the poem.

21. Schimmel, *Islamic Literature of India*, 118, 102; Ḥālī, *Dīvān-e Ḥālī*, 115–16.

22. Schimmel, *Islamic Literature of India*, 130–31.

23. *Ṭā'ir* recalls *Manṭiq-ut ṭā'ir*, the journey of the birds in Farīd ud-Dīn ʿAṭṭar's Persian mystical journey poem. In it a group of birds travel toward gnosis, traversing landscapes that throw up a variety of obstacles that the birds must surmount.

24. Note here the ironic implication of the juxtaposition of "leave your confusion behind" and the word used for secret—*mub-ham*—which is also used for obscured, esoteric, smoky. *Mub-ham* is also one of Miraji's identifying categories for his own poetry, and is one of a set of identifying categories in a chart Miraji draws on for several of his poems. For a more complete analysis of *mub-ham*, see Chapter 7.

25. An example of this kind of dissemination or dissolution can be seen in the unattributed Hindi verse cited by Schimmel (*Islamic Literature of India*, 289): "Put in some water, some salt— / when it dissolves, what shall it be called? Likewise Mustafa melted his self into God [*khudā*]. / When the self is dissolved whom could one call God?"

## CHAPTER 6: WHAT'S IN A NAME?

1. This is certainly the case in India. I cannot vouch for the situation in Pakistan, because I knew that most of the Pakistanis I have talked to about Miraji already knew of him.

2. I have even had to amend a slip made by a Pakistani woman well versed in eighteenth- and nineteenth-century ghazal. She assumed that Miraji was Mir Taqi Mir.

3. See Chapter 1 for stories.

4. This page was given me by Akhtarul Iman.

5. I have the only copy of this frontispiece. I am very grateful to Akhtarul Iman for presenting it to me along with copies of much of Miraji's unpublished work.

6. See Jacques Derrida, "Signature, Event, Context," in *Glyph* 1 (1977): 172–97, and *The Ear of the Other* (New York: Schocken Books, 1985), for discussions that interleaf with mine. Derrida does not, and perhaps cannot, speak to this particular configuration of a man taking a woman's name, or translating in that name, or work written in that name. See also Jonathan Goldberg, *Desiring Women Writing: English Renaissance Examples* (Stanford, Calif.: Stanford University Press, 1997), 85–87; and Yophie Prins, *Victorian Sappho* (Princeton, N.J.: Princeton University Press, 1999): "Introduction: Declining a Name," 3–22; "Afterlife in Translation," 40–51; and "The Double Signature," 80–87; Michel Foucault, "Language to Infinity," in Donald F. Bouchard, trans. and ed., and Sherry Simon, ed., *Language, Counter-Memory, Practice: Selected Essays and Interviews* (Ithaca, N.Y.: Cornell University Press, 1988), 52–67. Living on after death, life after death, life after life, all figure in Miraji's invocations of Mira, and of Sappho. This title page figures that movement.

7. Aḥmad, "Mīrājī: Shaḳhṣiyat aur fann."

8. Ḥusain, *Āab-e Ḥayāt*, 221; Farḥatullah Beg, *Dillī kī āḳharī shama*ʿ (New Delhi: Orient Longman, 1979); Ruth Vanita's essay on *reḳhtī* ("Rekhti Poetry," in Ruth Vanita and Saleem Kidwai, eds., *Same-Sex Love in India: Readings from Literature and History* [New York: St. Martin's Press, 2000], 220–28). It is probably no accident that Vanita has written on the nineteenth-century Sappho, Mira, and *reḳhtī*.

9. This is a common theme treated in feminist film theory. For one discussion see Teresa de Lauretis, *Technologies of Gender* (Bloomington: Indiana University Press, 1987). In the poem "Āñkh micholī" (In the blink of an eye), the lyric allows Miraji to open up a possible line of sight to Mira Sen, posed as a series of questions, beginning with "Kyā maiñ sochūñ?" (What should I think?), with speculative answers. Miraji cannot quite speak the other who is the object of his longing, but in lyric/fiction he can certainly attempt to bridge the gap between them. This gap, because it is never closed (Miraji never quite knows how Mira Sen feels), pushes Miraji's desire back at him, rather than pulling it forward to create Mira's desire as a certain thing. A hiatus in meaning and a hiatus in time are often exploited by ghazal *ḳhvān* (reciter), who want to stretch out, and linger on the impossibility of unrequited passion.

10. Except for the description of her in Aijaz Ahmad's article on Miraji, she is not specularized, that is, described as a visual object with visual details. Even Ahmad describes her as the antithesis of what he obviously considers is an appro-

priate visual object of desire—"She is dark and not even pretty." In Mrs. Din's story of Mira, she was not the antithesis of male desire. Rather, she was the embodiment of the beloved from ghazal: beautiful, alluring, someone who rendered hosts of men senseless and was available to none of them.

11. The idealized production of urban forms of bourgeoisie domesticity/publicness distributed gender unevenly, women confined (or behaving in public as though they were) and men free to wander. In the case of these stories, some produced gender to play out this form of domesticity, whereas others did not.

12. What do I do with the issue of mirroring: Sana' ullah Ḍār loves Mira, Mira is silent/silenced, Sana' ullah Ḍār becomes Mira. Sana' ullah reflects/mirrors Mira, who in turn has been made over so that he can reflect her (identification). What about the intersections with and differences from the mystic's tale, in which the lover of God at the moment of union is a mirror/heart, soul is a mirror which reflects the divine (ghazal)? In the mystic's tale, who is silent/silenced in order for the operation of mirroring to take place? The lover in this case stays male, and the beloved (God/boy/man/ambiguous) is also often male or not explicitly gendered. Is Miraji's a heterosexed inversion of a male/male poetic tradition?

Read this against Krishna bhakti, in which the archetypal lover is female (Radha), with Mira as her closest earthly incarnation, and the beloved Krishna is always male (see John Stratton Hawley, "Author and Authority in Bhakti Poetry," *Journal of Asian Studies* 47 [May 1988]: 279)—life after life he is true, but Mira is colored with the color of her Lord). So here the poet, if he is male and writing love lyric, shifts his position in the lyric to the feminine one in order to speak as Radha/*gopī*. As Radha, a male poet speaks in a particular conventional woman's voice. So is Miraji's story as intertextual with Mirabai's, a female-male drag version? What are the instabilities generated by holding these two—Urdu and Bhakti—against each other?

13. See V. T. Oldenburg, "Lifestyle as Resistance: The Case of the Courtesans of Lucknow," in *Feminist Studies* 16, no. 2 (Summer 1990): 259–88; Romila Thapar, "The Householder and the Renouncer," in T. N. Madan, ed., *Way of Life, King, Householder, Renouncer: Essays in Honour of Louis Dumont* (New Delhi: Vikas Publishing, 1982), 273–98.

14. See, for example, the Raj Kapoor film *Avārā*.

15. Oldenburg, "Lifestyle as Resistance," 23. As someone interpolated into twentieth-century Hinduism, as well as Islam, Miraji in these tellings moves somewhat uneasily between being a non-*sharīf ādmī*, an un-*grahasta* and a public-spirited, household-bound bourgeoisie man.

16. Stanley Fish discusses in great detail his own multiple role-playing and the conflicts inherent in this process in his book *Doing What Comes Naturally: Change*

*Rhetoric and the Practice of Theory in Literary and Legal Studies* (Durham, N.C.: Duke University Press, 1989), 30.

17. Prins, *Victorian Sappho*, 15.

18. Paul de Man, *The Rhetoric of Romanticism.*

19. Goldberg, *Desiring Women Writing*, 142. Miraji signs as a woman, and sometimes scripts the "I" in his poem through that signing, although he keeps the "Is" apart from his signature at other times. But if one reads, as I try to do in the next chapter, both those "Is" through the signature, one sometimes aligns desire across gender (while also reading that crossing as a differential reiteration of the same, thus aligning desire across different positions of the same gender).

20. For accounts of Mirabai that address this point, see *Songs of the Saints of India*, ed. John Stratton Hawley and Mark Jurgensmeyer (New York: Oxford University Press, 1988), and Parita Mukta, *Upholding the Common Life: The Community of Mirabai* (New Delhi: Oxford University Press, 1994). Hawley mentions evidence (however dubious) of early manuscript traditions for Mira, a Dākor manuscript (v.s. 1642, A.D. 1585); a Benares one (v.s. 1727, A.D. 1670); a poem attributed to her in the "oldest extant copy of the Banno edition of the *Ādī granth* (v.s. 1699, A.D. 1642), itself an ostensibly extant rendition of one from 1604, with its alternative recension containing a deletion where the poem might have been. (Hawley, "Author and Authority in Bhakti Poetry," 202, note 9). See ibid., 269–90, esp. 275–76. The manuscript variants of the corpuses of bhakti poets grow over time and continue to grow long after the poet's ostensible life. So, although the ever expanding work of a poet continues to be ascribed to him or her, it cannot have been composed by her. This opens up the collapse between the person signed into a poem and the person who did the signing, or between the ostensible author and the composer. What this points to, according to Hawley—and I concur—is an understanding of "authorship" as an umbrella under which many people of either gender could compose. It also highlights the importance of listeners'/readers' agreement not to open up the divide between author and composer. They had to accept that poems "signed by" and assigned to Mira were, in fact, Mira's. What, then, did it mean for Miraji to compose as Mira? Am I (i.e., G.P.: rhetorical) the audience that sanctions the collapse?

21. Parita Mukta speaks eloquently of this domestication, which is accompanied and perhaps facilitated by constituting Mira, from the nineteenth century on, as a possessive individualist self, as an autonomous poet who makes choices. The various productions of a Mira figure intersect with nineteenth-century politics around the amendations of vernacular languages, the death of rural practices, the rise of the bourgeoisie gendered subject, in texts like Gorardhanarama Tripathi, *The Classical Poets of Gujarat and Their Influence on Society and Morals* (Bombay:

Tripathi and Company, 1892). Gandhi formulates Mira as exemplary *bahū*, who exalts herself and wins over her husband through the force of her love. This Mira is reproduced in the 1945 Hindi version of a Tamil film, *Mīrā*, with M. S. Subbulakshmi singing *bhajan* that have been handed down in urban bhakti *bhajan melan* (author interview with Dr. Sunita Sharma [Bombay, 19 January 1998]). This film is one of a long list of films on the itinerant queen, made in 1921, 1932, 1933 (made by Debaki Bose after *chandīdās*), 1936, 1940, two in 1947, 1960, 1976, 1979, 1992, 1993. Both the Boses, Mīrā and Chandīdās, emphasized desire that troubled social conventions. If I were to attribute Miraji's Mira to a filmography, I would probably go to the Bose films because they were made at a time at which Miraji was also writing on Chandīdas, as well as on Vidyapati (on whom Bose made a film in 1937).

22. See Parita Mukta's elaborations of communities that formed around singing and sharing songs, which articulated this nexus. This kind of sharing alleviated the movements to produce Mira as a *figure*, as a person who made certain "choices," moral and immoral, appropriately political as well as politically suspect, that one sees in the *Manushi* issue on women *bhakta* (*Manushi* 50–52 [September–December 1989]). Mukta is trying to re-address the productions of personhood (post nineteenth century) that rely on possessive individualism (including those evoked by Gandhi) as a way of getting through to other formations around the figure, the voice, and the positions enabled by Mira.

23. Miraji's prose pieces on other poets reflect his own interests. Miraji's discussions of the poets he writes about, Baudelaire and Mallarmé for example, necessarily diverge from others' accounts of them and so look strange to anyone who has read them but does not know Miraji.

24. For a longer discussion of translation as mirroring, both as collapse into and as holding open the space between renditions, see Prins, *Victorian Sappho*. Is there a difference between the Sana' ullah–Mira story and Miraji's translation of Mirabai's work? Isn't it a similar move? But what are the exact mechanics of each move? Who performs the move: I, who read it, or Miraji?

25. See Goldberg, *Desiring Women Writing*; Derrida, *The Ear of the Other*; Prins, *Victorian Sappho*.

26. Mukta, *Upholding the Common Life*, chap. 10, "The Rainbird Thirsts"; also, interviews with women singers from Danilimda, Baroda, 20 June 1999.

27. Discussing Mira brings up the vexed, and pleasurable, place of the production of tradition italicized as a past in the present, especially in relation to nationalism and national formations. "Tradition" engages with rhetoric of anthropology, women's songs, and women's "traditions" in a troublingly sedimented, even if occasionally textured way. See Mukta (*Upholding the Common Life*) on temporality. Tradition could also be used in its nonitalicized, unmarked sense, as

a line of songsters who acknowledge the changes they craft as they sing for/as Mira, and in so doing, pull the past back into the present, stretching the moment in which they sing. See also de Man ("The Rhetoric of Temporality," in *Blindness and Insight*, 187–228), whose engagements with temporality have informed my readings, but who rarely brings gender in, and that too in moments only through Wordsworth.

28. Nābhādās, *Shrī bhaktamāl* (with "Bhaktirasabodhinī" commentary of Priyadas) (Lucknow: Tejkumar Press, 1969), for Mira stories. Priyadas' is an eighteenth-century commentary. See earlier note on manuscripts; also see Mukta.

29. Hawley, "Author and Authority in Bhakti Poetry," esp. 275–76.

30. See the preface to *Mīrājī ke gīt*. Is this move a logocentric one that privileges voice over writing, or a pragmatic one necessary for a culture in which transmission often occurs orally? At least one of the lyric traditions of Urdu, the ghazal, is written as well as recited and sung. See Pritchett on the ghazal; Peter Manuel (*Thumri in Historical and Stylistic Perspectives* [Delhi: Motilal Banarasidass, 1989]) on performances. All ghazals can be and are recited, but not all are sung. Many of the aficionados of the genre in the late twentieth and early twenty-first century are not "literate" in Urdu; that is, they cannot read it. So, for them the only access to the ghazal is through its performance.

For lyric genres that have gained ascendancy more recently, like the *naẓm*, the relationship between oral and written versions is more tenuous. But for Miraji, oral and written versions are inextricably woven together. Many of Miraji's poems that are not *gīt*, and not explicitly written for performance, still need to be oralized when they are read. They read very differently if read aloud. For example, it is easier to understand the mechanics of his poems orally, if his caesuras are oralized, and so on; this kind of information transforms the interpretive results.

31. Miraji's *gīt* were supposed to have been performed on the radio in Delhi in the 1940s while he worked at All-India Radio. The only records of their performance at AIR are a letter that Miraji wrote to AIR in which he says that his songs were performed at the station; his preface to *Mīrājī ke gīt*, where he says that the songs culled for the book had been performed on the radio; and through corroborations during some of the interviews I conducted. I have no other record of their radio performances, if there were any. Some of Miraji's ghazals have been performed, too. The performances of Miraji's ghazals that I have heard are those sung by Pakistani pop stars.

32. Self here becomes romantic creative genius, with allegiances to Hali's negotiations around poetry as "expressing some felt thought or desire." An author is given form through the objects of their creation, held in one's hand, reproducible as text printed mechanically. This kind of reproducibility, taken for granted with

the common circulation of printed material, disintegrates when the book literally disappears, becomes esoteric, is removed from circulation. Authorship authorized through the continuities of property that accrues to the name, in a tangible way through copyright, never quite comes into being such as when Miraji was writing, although copyright formed a piece of Macaulay's interventions in the British Parliament. In Miraji's case, reproducibility, reproduction might have one kind of substantiality, if one held to romantic (and in this case possibly masculinized) notions of person/poet/self. What one does with reproducibility is tangibly altered under several conditions that come into play here through gender: Miraji as male "I," reproducing Mira as female "I"; Miraji as female "I" reproducing Mira as female "I," body held at bay; Miraji singing alongside women who translate Mira into voice, compose Mira into lyric voice over more than one generation; Miraji putting into writing that is never seen, voice given to Mira.

33. All of these readings derive their power and authority from several assumptions that run together and run counter to the way I read these readings. The slippage, which is not questioned, between "each reading is the same as every other reading, so this is how it is, and everyone believes it to be so," and "this is the 'real' Miraji" permits the readings to hold and retain their authority.

### CHAPTER 7: READING GENDER, CHARTING THE OBSCURE

1. This, the first line of the first ghazal in Ghalib's *Dīvān* (29), forces one to read: word by word, syllable by syllable, in the metrical scheme given.

2. Shaiḵh Ibrāhīm Żauq, *Dīvān-e żauq* (Lahore: Atta Ram, 1933?).

3. As a reader of Miraji, Sadiq is fairly conservative. His sketches appear to present a modulated picture of Miraji.

4. The italicized portions in the 1947 edition of the Sadiq are not included in the second (1983) edition. All the additions in square parentheses and bold face are only present in 1983 edition. I will not include the entire article on Miraji from the 1983 edition, because it is much too long. Muhammad Sadiq, *Twentieth-Century Urdu Literature* (Karachi: Royal Book Depot, 1983), 219–26.

5. Muhammad Sadiq, *Twentieth-Century Urdu Literature* (1st ed., Bombay: Padma Publications, 1947), 76–78. This citation is for the complete piece on Miraji from the book. The 1983 version of the book says that the first edition was written in 1944.

6. The paradoxes of befuddlement continue to dog Sadiq's writing. Miraji is pathological and banal, obscure and arbitrary, but not quite obscure or arbitrary enough. Miraji "reverts to Hindu symbols that saturate the older tradition of Urdu poetry," which had been studiously discarded to bring it toward Persian. Miraji's preoccupation ostensibly places him in a direct allegiance with middle-class

(Hindu) morality. Perhaps Islamic nationalism would have been something that Sadiq believed (and rightly so) was anti–middle class, especially if that middle class was Hindu. But Sadiq is not addressing the conundrums offered by a figure like Miraji, who neither quite worked as a good middle-class Hindu man in the 1930s and 1940s, nor worked as a good middle-class Muslim man from the same time. Miraji's embodiment and body of writing created a frisson, *k̤halish*, in the production of national/nationalized male selves during that period, whether that production was secular, Hindu, or Muslim. His few allies, albeit difficult ones, in this endeavor were writers from the PWA and from the Halqa. Perhaps this is why he refused to leave either.

7. It is clear that for twentieth-century Urdu poetry both *āzād naẓm* (free verse) and *pāband naẓm* (foot-bound verse) are metrical (see Sadiq, *Twentieth-Century Urdu Literature*, 2nd ed.). Certainly for Miraji's poetry, the distinction between the two is couched in terms of unrhymed and rhymed verse. All Miraji's verse could be scanned into a loose meter. But foot-bound verse is usually understood as metrical and not necessarily rhymed. So I have left the difference between the two open.

8. In F. J. Steingass, *A Comprehensive Persian-English Dictionary* (1892; repr., Beirut: Librairie du Liban, 1970), 1152, the word *mub-ham* is translated as shut (door), occult, unknown, doubtful, obscure, uncertain, indeterminate, silent, dumb, unintelligible, anything prohibited; the agent, *mub-ham*, is one who shuts a door, who keeps concealed, who diverts anything. The root *b-h-m* in Arabic reads as: to make or to be obscure, dubious, unintelligible, *ib-ham* is obscure and *mub-ham* obscure, dark, cryptic, vague, abstract, ambiguous, as in abstract number.

9. I think of this "space" as the ellipsis in an originary narrative that goes on to become a totalizing narrative, which Homi Bhabha speaks of in *Nation and Narration* when he discusses the narrativization of "nation." I am also indebted to his discursive categories "pedagogical" and "performative" for my analysis of "change" in Miraji's essays.

10. This title can also be translated as "Oneness."

11. See Chapter 2 for a more extensive reading of both "his" responses and the Progressives' responses to their environment.

12. See Chapter 2.

13. This is how I use the chart as a way of ascribing reading positions.

14. See Appendix A for two versions of the English translation of "Traveler." For the most recent publication of the Urdu original, see *Mīrājī kī naẓmeñ* (2nd ed.).

15. Jacques Lacan, *The Ethics of Psychoanalysis, 1959–1960*, book 8 of *The Semi-*

*nar of Jacques Lacan*, trans. Dennis Porter (London: Routledge, 1992); *The Four Fundamental Concepts of Psychoanalysis, 1964*, book 9 of *The Seminar of Jacques Lacan*, trans. Alan Sheridan (London: Hogarth Press and the Institute of Psychoanalysis, 1977).

16. Ludwig Wittgenstein, *Tractacus Logico-Philosophicus* (London: Routledge and Kegan Paul, 1961), 74; no. 7: "What we cannot speak about we must pass over in silence." Miraji does not pass in silence what he cannot include in a chart; he speaks it and names it—*mub-ham*.

17. It is included in translation in Appendix A.

18. See the "private language" argument in Ludwig Wittgenstein, *Philosophical Investigations*, trans. G. E. M. Anscombe (Englewood Cliffs, N.J.: Prentice Hall, 1970), no. 269, especially nos. 275 and 380.

19. *Is naẓm meñ*, 21–22.

20. I use "gender" instead of "sex," because sex inevitably slides into a need to embody or give gender a body. The mechanism of gendering bodies, giving sex to bodies, the maleness and femaleness of bodies, circles tightly around the naturalness of biological determinants for gender and their congruences through heteronormativity. See Prins, *Victorian Sappho*; Goldberg, *Desiring Women Writing*; Lauren Berlant, *The Queen of America*; Michael Warner, "Sex in Public," *Critical Inquiry* 24, no. 2 (Intimacy Issue) (Winter 1998): 547–66; and Anne Fausto-Sterling, "The Five Sexes," *Sciences* (March–April 1993): 21–25. I want in this section to move away from that particular metonymic move into sexedness, and sex/sexuality. Gender in Miraji's work is sometimes embodied—given a body—and usually as a body characterized by female markers like breasts or certain types of clothing. In other words the body is coded, and the codes assign it a gender. Gender is also about the "I," the ways it is assigned gender through verbs, and the ways in which its gender is withheld by using verb forms that do not take a direct subject. Gender is about a recourse made to poetic conventions where the "I" has been allocated maleness, or to those where it has been allocated femaleness. Gender is also about the gender of nouns in a sentence, negotiated along their gendered axes or against them. I would like to deal with the codes, the literary markers, the system of agreements and repetitions through which gender is assigned, and then deal with the implications of these moves and mechanisms.

21. Foucault, *Ethics: Subjectivity and Truth*, vol. 1.

22. The word "cursive" comes from conversations I have had with my colleague Sabine Gölz. I use "cursive" not as an adjective that merely modifies script, but as a word that implies mobile or fluid. Cursive stands between discursive and cursor. I take "cursor" from computer terminology as the highlighted or marked portion of a conversation, oral/aural exchange, oralized work, or a written text. So

cursive positions are those that are highlighted or brought into the foreground, as well as those embedded in discourse.

23. Kath Weston, *Render Me, Gender Me: Lesbians Talk Sex, Class, Color, Nation, Stud Muffins . . .* (New York: Columbia University Press, 1996), chap. 7, "Me, Myself, and I," which uses renditions instead of intersections to talk about the multiplicity of differences and the ways they come together with gender.

24. *Us* = them/him/her/it; *kā* = of (masculine form).

25. *Sah ātishah*, 48. This poem was written between 1932 and 1942.

26. Tabassum, ed., *Shiʿr*, 76.

27. See Chapter 1 for a story told by Dihlavi about children who ran behind Miraji in Lahore, calling him, "baṛī mem . . ."

28. This is not particularly noteworthy when a poem follows conventions for writing as a woman, as in some Sanskrit lyric, or in Mira *bhajan*. But if those conventions are breached, for example carried over from another lyric tradition or if a woman's voice in the poem has no counterpart in local literary traditions, then the act of "writing as a woman" seems to flummox readers. For example: if one blends a nineteenth-century Mira with Urdu poetry written during the same period by someone like Ghalib, or blends Urdu Delhi Perso-Arabic poetics with earlier Deccani poetry. Hali, for instance, assigns certain conventions associated with gender and desire to particular "traditions," but his assignments occur on the terrain of nineteenth-century notions of cultural boundedness (which always seems to come apart even as he tries to hold it together), and the ahistorical (out-of-time) production of historical periodicity. Hali also resorts to particular notions about the "norm," the center, as that which was mediated through law (and eventually by morality).

29. I would like to register a caveat to my reading of Ahmad. Ahmad is incited by a scrupulously plangent concern that could be seen as feminist. He is troubled by the ways that bodies unhinge into pieces in Miraji's poetry, and what this kind of dismemberment might portend for a kind of violence against women. Like other such impulses, Ahmad's have their appropriate registers, even as they might be registered as troubling negotiations of sexuality. See Goldberg, *Desiring Women Writing*, and of course Judith Butler, *Gender Trouble: Feminism and the Subversion of Identity* (New York and London: Routledge, 1990).

30. *Mīrājī kī naẓmeñ*, 1st ed., 25–27.

31. By the time that Miraji wrote, the legislation criminalizing devadasis had been well under way for a little while and by 1938, four years after this poem was completed, the Madras legislature had amended the Suppression of Immoral Traffic Act of 1930. See Janaki Nair, *Women and Law in Colonial India: A Social History* (New Delhi: Kali for Women, 1996), 164–69. Miraji returned to the desiring

body of the courtesan as a site for knowledge production more than once, the last time, before he died, with his translation of the "Kuttanimatam" of Damodar Gupta; "The Lessons of a Bawd," from Mathers, *Eastern Love*, vol. 1. Malati, Damodar Gupta's heroine, is the center of the series of explorations on sexuality, and we hear her voice in the Powys Mathers and Miraji translations. But like the devadasi in this poem, her body is plotted as the seductive point of a reader's (and the recorder's) gazes.

32. The voiced call immediately collapses its texture/body, which is oral, into a visual field. Several other poems also play with the voice/visual dynamic. One example is "Call of the Sea," which also opens with a voiced call. This version of voicing, in "Devadasi and Pujari," subservient to visualizing, is different from that in "Call of the Sea," which is a self-reflexive call that speaks about calling: "Calling you again and again for years . . ."

33. Vaman Shivram Apte, *The Student's Sanskrit-English Dictionary* (Delhi: Motilal Banarsidas, 1982), 247, 258–59.

34. There are connections to *vrindāvan*, *yātrā*, and *kathā*. For a different turn towards *dṛsh*, slanted askance in relation to deconstruction, see Spivak, *A Critique of Postcolonial Reason*, 54. *Darshana* as philosophy does different work here, in this poem, in relation to reading, spoken through the visualization of "woman."

35. The use of *pavitra* could be read as Miraji's attempt to renegotiate the moral evaluation of sexual activity. It is possible that what is suggested here is that representations of sexual activity ought not to be treated as morally suspect, but as pure.

36. I have a copy of the manuscript given to me by Akhtarul Iman.

37. See Platts, *A Dictionary of Urdu, Classical Hindi, and English*, 743, for *ṣadā*; 1127, for *nidā*. See also William Edward Lane, *Arabic-English Lexicon* (London: Williams and Norgate, 1863–93; repr., Lahore: Islamic Book Centre, 1978), 1670 and 3030; and Steingass, *A Comprehensive Persian-English Dictionary*.

38. The translation follows Miraji's manuscript version of the poem.

39. Paul de Man, "Anthropomorphism and Trope in the Lyric," in *The Rhetoric of Romanticism*, 241. See Prins, *Victorian Sappho*, 21–22, 33. Personification has a different touch in this poem; it comes to be through difference, and vacillates between personification and abstraction from which questions about gender and authority flow. See also Barbara Johnson, *A World of Difference* (Baltimore: Johns Hopkins University Press, 1987), 45–47, and Peggy Kamuf, "Pieces of Resistance," in Lindsay Waters and Wlad Godzich, eds., *Reading de Man Reading* (Minneapolis: University of Minnesota Press, 1989), 136–54.

40. See Herman Rapaport, *Heidegger and Derrida: Reflections on Time and Language* (Lincoln: University of Nebraska Press, 1989), 104–5; logos as gathering and collecting other terms gathered together even as they fall away as one comes

to stand in for another. See also Blanchot, especially in Michel Foucault, "Language to Infinity," in *Language, Counter-Memory, Practice: Selected Essays and Interviews*, 58–59; the work of language is the body of language crossed by death in order to open this infinite space where doubles reverberate.

41. The poem leaves two questions unanswered until the end: who calls and who is being called? Since this poem speaks to the act of reading, I as a reader can interject myself both into these questions and into the positions opened up over the course of the poem. Then I stand in for the thing before the mirror, for the voice calling and the voice being called. Reflection and replacement go hand in hand, and turn the poem into a reflection of my concerns and an echo of my voice. Because the poem leaves itself available in this way for a reader its *mub-ham* status seems assured.

42. I have included a literal translation of the present progressive tense whenever it is used—in parentheses after the appropriate verb.

43. Rapaport, *Heidegger and Derrida*, 216; Emmanuel Levinas, *Ethics and Infinity*, and *Face to Face with Levinas*, trans. and ed. Richard A. Cohen (Albany: State University of New York Press, 1986), 21.

44. Hindi/Urdu allows women to speak in masculine verb forms—the masculine singular is the "default" gender used if the subject of a sentence is indirect (followed by a postposition). See beginning of the section "Return to and Convergence Upon Gender" for a more elaborate discussion of this point.

45. Jacques Lacan, *The Ego in Freud's Theory and in the Technique of Psychoanalysis, 1954–55*, book 2 of *The Seminar of Jacques Lacan*, trans. Sylvana Tomaselli (New York and London: W. W. Norton, 1991).

46. For "ironic consciousness" and its relationship to temporality see Paul de Man, "The Rhetoric of Temporality," in *Blindness and Insight: Essays in the Rhetoric of Contemporary Criticism* (Minneapolis: University of Minnesota Press, 1983), 187–228. "Irony," according to de Man, "divides the flow of a temporal experience into a past that is pure mystification and a future that remains harassed forever by a relapse within the inauthentic. It can know this inauthenticity but can never overcome it" (222).

47. See Chapter 2 for a longer exposition of Miraji's relationship to the Progressive writers who formed this movement.

48. Vazīr Āg̣hā, "Mīrājī: Dhartī pūjā kī ek misāl," in Kumār Pāshī, ed., *Mīrājī: Shaḳhṣiyat aur fann*, 141–219.

49. See discussions in this chapter on the ways that gender is assigned in Hindi/Urdu.

50. See Benjamin, "The Task of the Translator," and "Theses on the Philosophy of History," and Harry D. Harootunian, "The Benjamin Effect: Modernism,

Repetition, and the Path to Different Cultural Imaginaries," in Michael P. Steinberg, ed., *Walter Benjamin and the Demands of History* (Ithaca, N.Y.: Cornell University Press, 1996), 62–87.

EPILOGUE: ENTRANCES TO LIFE AND DEATH

1. Maurice Blanchot, *The Step Not Beyond*, trans. Lycette Nelson (Albany: State University of New York Press, 1973), 1.

2. Miraji, "Ābgīne ke us pār kī ek shām" (A night on the far side of the wine glass), line 22, unpublished notebooks.

3. Benjamin, "Theses on the Philosophy of History." This is a much quoted series of sentences; I quote it here to open historical materialism into that space between life, death, and afterlife that lingers on here from Benjamin's disquisitions on translation. See also Harootunian, "The Benjamin Effect."

4. Maurice Blanchot, *Awaiting Oblivion*, trans. John Gregg (Lincoln: University of Nebraska Press, 1997), 74–75.

5. Emmanuel Levinas, "Language and Proximity," *Collected Philosophical Papers*, trans. by Alphonso Lingis (Dordrecht, Boston, and Lancaster: Martinus Nijhoff Publishers, 1987), 104–5.

6. Emmanuel Levinas, "Love and Filiation," in *Ethics and Infinity*, 67.

7. See Ralph Russell's now well-known essay.

8. In Aijaz Ahmad, *Lineages of the Present: Political Essays* (New Delhi: Tulika, 1996), 191–92. See Harootunian, "The Benjamin Effect."

9. Ahmad, *Lineages of the Present*, 194–95. Certainly affect takes on the sifting softness, delusional mimicry, the accessibility of its late-twentieth-century retrievals, as Apter suggests. But here, in the vexed place-times of the colony, the questions of mimicry are augmented, and sometimes perceptibly, often almost imperceptibly sharpened through pain, anguish, loss, and grief. What does a ghost mirror, how does it come into sight as a phantom, vortexing its death through the things it moves in the world of "reality," as in Toni Morrison's *Beloved*? What does it mean for the imaginary of a child, that she must grow into her house with a phantom, the ghost of a child whose throat her mother had sliced open to save her from slavery?

10. Ahmad, "In the Mirror of Urdu," in *Lineages of the Present*, 195. Ahmad writes: "It [the mirror] is an old and rich metaphor, familiar enough to literary theorists, especially of the Marxist kind, but it is also a central metaphor in Urdu poetry and Ghalib has used it with nuances virtually infinite. For the outstanding feature of mirrors is that they are fragile things capable of rendering truth as well as illusion, but inordinately prone to blurring and breakage. They are humanly made, and they can reflect and render what human beings put in front of them for

the duration of time that is humanly determined. Mirrors are instruments of reflection, but also of erasure. A slight movement, and the image is altered, even erased. It is in the human act, mirrored in the mirror, that the act of reflection is done—or undone" (220).

11. Ghalib, *Dīvān*, 183.

APPENDIX A: BEVELED GLASS

1. *Mīrājī kī naẓmeñ*, 19–21. "Cal calā'o" is the opening poem of the collection. Translated with Kath Weston.

2. "Ūñcā mākān," *Mīrājī kī naẓmeñ*, 72–75.

3. "B'ād kā uḍāv," ibid., 99–101.

4. "Ras kī anokhī laḥreñ," ibid., 152–53.

5. "Samundar kā bulāvā," *Tīn rañg*, 127–30, and ms. (my translation follows the ms.).

6. "Taḥrīk," *Sah ātishah*, 48; ms. poem 10, *Pābañd naẓmeñ* (Rawalpindi: Kitab Numa, 1968), 52.

7. "Yagānagat," *Tīn rañg*, 147–49, and *Sah ātishah*, 256–59.

8. "Cheḍ," *Tīn rañg*, 110–11; also in *Sah ātishah*, 114, ms. poem 42.

9. "Yahūdī," *Tīn rañg*, 140–41; ms. of *Sah ātishah*, poem 49.

10. "Jātrī," *Mīrājī kī naẓmen*, 118–21.

11. "Ābgīne ke us pār kī ek shām," *Tīn rañg*, 142–48; ms. version, poem 1, in the *naẓm* section.

12. "Lab-e jū'e bāre," *Mīrājī kī naẓmen*, 80–83 (the title here is "Yak jū-e bāre"), poem 33 in the ms. version which I have followed; the poem is no. 31 and *yak* is *lab*.

13. "Pās aur dūr," miscellaneous ms.

14. "Devadāsī aur pujārī," *Mīrājī kī naẓmen*, 24–26, ms. version, poem 2.

15. "Peshīn go'ī." "Hamārī zindagī ke bād shāyad / ko'ī faẓl-e bahār ā'egī aisī / uṭhegī ko'ī sadā-e bāzgusht aur / hamāre gīt ik duniyā sunegī"; "Saifo," in *Mashriq o maghrib ke naghmeñ*.

16. "Āñkh micolī," *Sah ātishah*, 27–29, ms. poem 1.

17. "Klark kā naghmā-e muḥabbat," *Mīrājī kī naẓmeñ*, 124–26; poems from 1941.

18. "Ajnabī 'ishrateñ." My translation of Miraji's translation of a poem by Baudelaire (which Miraji probably saw in its English incarnation); in "Cārls Baudela'ir," in *Mashriq o maghrib ke naghmeñ*, 161–89, 184. This is one of the few poems that Miraji translates without offering a commentary or supplementary reading.

19. "Cārls Baudela'ir," 182.

## APPENDIX B: WORKING TRANSLATIONS

1. "Gīt kaise bante haiñ," *Mīrājī ke gīt* (Lahore: Maktabah-e Urdu, 1943), 7–10.

2. "Bhūl gayā," *Tīn rañg*, 151–53; ms. version, ghazal 1.

3. "Nayī shā'irī kī buniyādeñ"; ms.version; the essay is reprinted in Jālibī, ed., *Mīrājī*, 519–26.

4. This passage is from Jālibī, 521–23.

# BIBLIOGRAPHY

## ENGLISH-LANGUAGE SOURCES


Ahmad, Aijaz. *Lineages of the Present: Political Essays*. New Delhi: Tulika, 1996.

———. *In Theory: Classes, Nations, Literature*. New York: Columbia University Press, 1992.

———, ed. *Ghazals of Ghalib*. New York: Columbia University Press, 1971.

Ahmad, Aziz. *An Intellectual History of Islam in India*. Islamic Surveys, vol. 7. Edinburgh: Edinburgh University Press, 1969.

———. *Studies in Islamic Culture in the Indian Environment*. Oxford: Clarendon Press, 1964.

Ahmad, Naeem. "Iqbal's Concept of Eternity." In Waheed Querishi, ed., *Selections from the* Iqbal Review. Lahore: Iqbal Academy, 1983.

Ali, Ahmed. "Ahmed Ali: A Tribute." *Annual of Urdu Studies* 9 (1994): 6–56.

———. "Clouds Don't Come." *Journal of South Asian Literature* 22, no. 1 (1987): 189–92.

———. "The Progressive Writers' Movement and Creative Writers in Urdu." In Carlo Coppola, ed., *Marxist Influences and South Asian Literature*, 1: 35–44. Occasional Papers, no. 23. South Asia Series, East Lansing: Michigan State University, 1974.

———. "The Progressive Writers' Movement in Its Historical Perspective." *Journal of South Asian Literature* 8, nos. 1–4 (1977–78): 90–98.

———, ed. *The Golden Tradition: An Anthology of Urdu Poetry*. New York: Columbia University Press, 1973.

Alvi, Waris. Interview with Dr. Hiru Patel. Tape recording, Baroda, 6 April 1991.

Ansari, Zoe. Interviews with author. Tape recording, Bombay, 3 January and 19 May 1989.

Anzaldua, Gloria. *Borderlands: La Frontera*. San Francisco: Spinsters/Aunt Lute Foundation Books, 1987.

———. *Making Face, Making Soul = Haciendo Caras: Creative and Cultural Perspectives by Women of Color.* San Francisco: Aunt Lute Foundation Books, 1990.

Appadurai, Arjun, ed. *The Social Life of Things: Commodities in Cultural Perspective.* Cambridge, Eng.: Cambridge University Press, 1986.

Apte, Vaman Shivram. *The Student's Sanskrit-English Dictionary.* Delhi: Motilal Banarsidas, 1982.

Apter, Emily. "Ethnographic Travesties." In Apter, *Continental Drift: From National Characters to Virtual Subjects.* Chicago: University of Chicago Press, 1999.

Apter, Emily, and William Pietz, eds. *Fetishism as Cultural Discourse.* Ithaca, N.Y.: Cornell University Press, 1993.

Arnold, David. *The Problem of Nature: Environment, Culture, and European Expansion.* Oxford and Cambridge, Mass.: Basil Blackwell, 1996.

Askari, Muhammad Hasan. "A Novel by Ahmed Ali." *Annual of Urdu Studies* 9 (1994): 73–84.

Attar, Farid ud-Din. *The Conference of the Birds.* Trans. Afkham Darbandi and Dick Davis. Harmondsworth, Eng.: Penguin Books, 1984.

Awasthi, Aruna. *History and Development of the Railways in India.* New Delhi: Deep and Deep Publications, 1994.

Bailey, T. Grahame. *A History of Urdu Literature.* Calcutta: Association Press, 1932.

Baker, Houston. *Blues, Ideology, and Afro-American Literature: A Vernacular Theory.* Chicago: University of Chicago Press, 1987.

Bakht, Baidar, and Kathleen Grant Jaeger, eds. and trans. *An Anthology of Modern Urdu Poetry.* Delhi: Educational Publishing House, 1984.

Ballhatchett, Kenneth. *Race, Sex, and Class Under the Raj: Imperial Attitudes and Policies and Their Critics, 1793–1905.* New York: St. Martin's Press, 1980.

Barker, Muhammad Abd-al Rahman. *Classical Urdu Poetry.* Ithaca, N.Y.: Spoken Language Services, 1977.

———. *A Reader of Modern Urdu Poetry.* Montreal: McGill University, Institute of Islamic Studies, 1968.

Bedi, Rajinder Singh. Interview with Rajinder Singh Bedi. *Mahfil* 8, nos. 2–3 (1972): 139–58.

Benjamin, Walter. *Illuminations.* Ed. Hannah Arendt. Trans. Harry Zohn. New York: Schocken Books, 1978.

Bentham, Jeremy. *The Principles of Morals and Legislation.* New York: Prometheus Books, 1988.

Bentinck, William Cavendish. *The Correspondence of Lord William Cavendish Bentinck.* 2 vols. Ed. C. H. Phillips. Oxford: Oxford University Press, 1977.

Berlant, Lauren. *The Queen of America Goes to Washington City: Essays on Sex and Citizenship.* Durham, N.C.: Duke University Press, 1997.

Berridge, P. S. A. *The Story of the North Western Railway*. Newton Abbot, Eng.: David and Charles, 1969.

Bhabha, Homi K. "DissemiNation: Time, Narrative, and Margins of the Modern Nation." In Homi K. Bhabha, ed., *Nation and Narration*, 291–323. London: Routledge, 1990.

———. *The Location of Culture*. New York: Routledge, 1994.

Blanchot, Maurice. *Awaiting Oblivion*. Trans. John Gregg. Lincoln: University of Nebraska Press, 1997.

———. *The Step Not Beyond*. Trans. Lycette Nelson. Albany: State University of New York Press, 1973.

Bourdieu, Pierre. *Distinction: A Social Critique of the Judgement of Taste*. Trans. Richard Nice. Cambridge: Harvard University Press, 1984.

Breckenridge, Carol A., ed. *Consuming Modernity: Public Culture in a South Asian World*. Minneapolis: University of Minnesota Press, 1995.

Breckenridge, Carol A., and Peter van de Veer, eds. *Orientalism and the Postcolonial Predicament: Perspectives on South Asia*. Philadelphia: University of Pennsylvania Press, 1993.

Bryant, Kenneth. "Textual Obsessions: Conventionality in the Urdu Ghazal." Unpublished paper, 1986.

Butler, Judith. *Gender Trouble: Feminism and the Subversion of Identity*. New York and London: Routledge, 1990.

Caruth, Cathy. *Unclaimed Experience: Trauma, Narrative, and History*. Baltimore: Johns Hopkins University Press, 1996.

Chakrabarty, Dipesh. "Invitation to a Dialogue." *Subaltern Studies* 4: 364–76. New Delhi: Oxford University Press, 1994.

———. "Radical Histories and the Question of Enlightenment Rationalism: Some Recent Critiques of *Subaltern Studies*." *Economic and Political Weekly* (8 April 1995): 751–59.

Chandra, Bipin. *The Oppressive Present: Literature and Social Consciousness in Colonial India*. New Delhi: Oxford University Press, 1994.

Chatterjee, Partha. "History and the Nationalization of Hinduism." *Social Research* 59, no. 1 (Spring 1992): 120–30.

———. *The Nation and Its Fragments: Colonial and Postcolonial Histories*. Princeton, N.J.: Princeton University Press, 1993.

———. *Nationalist Thought and the Colonial World: A Derivative Discourse*. London: Zed Books, for the United Nations University, 1986.

———, ed. *Texts of Power: Emerging Disciplines in Colonial Bengal*. Calcutta: Samya, in conjunction with Centre for Studies in the Social Sciences, 1996.

Chatterton, Alfred. "Industrial Education in India." *Calcutta Review* 228 (April 1902): 301–11.

Chicago Cultural Studies Group. "Critical Multiculturalism." *Critical Inquiry* 18, no. 3 (Spring 1992): 530–55.

Chughtai, Ismat. "Amar Bel." *Journal of South Asian Literature* 22, no. 1 (1987): 193–200.

———. "Aunty Scorpion." *Annual of Urdu Studies* 8 (1993): 49–58.

———. Interview with Carlo Coppola. *Mahfil* 8, nos. 2–3 (1972): 169–88.

———. "The Quilt." *Mahfil* 8, nos. 2–3 (1972): 195–202.

———. "A Selection from The Realm of the Heart." *Annual of Urdu Studies* 8 (1993): 59–78.

———. "Two Hands." *Journal of South Asian Literature* 14, no. 2 (1981): 123–30.

———. "Wedding Clothes." *Mahfil* 8 (1972): 203–14.

Cohn, Bernard S. *Colonialism and Its Forms of Knowledge: The British in India.* New Delhi: Oxford University Press, 1997.

Coppola, Carlo. "Ahmed Ali (1910–1994): Bridges and Links East and West." *Annual of Urdu Studies* 9 (1994): 97–102.

———. "Ahmed Ali in Interview: An Excerpt from an Interview." *Annual of Urdu Studies* 9 (1994): 57–72.

———. "The Angare Group: The *Enfants Terribles* of Urdu Literature." *Annual of Urdu Studies* 1 (1981): 57–69.

———. "Premchand's Address to the First Meeting of the All-India Progressive Writers Association: Some Speculations." *Journal of South Asian Literature* 2, no. 2 (1986): 21–39.

———. "Urdu Poetry, 1935–1970: The Progressive Episode." Ph.D. diss., University of Chicago, 1975.

Coppola, Carlo, and Sajida Zubair. "Rashid Jehan: Urdu Literature's First 'Angry Young Woman.'" *Journal of South Asian Literature* 22, no. 1 (Winter–Spring 1987): 166–84.

Dalhousie, James Andrew Broun Ramsay. *Dalhousie's Minute: Railway Minute of the Governor General.* National Archives, New Delhi.

Daly, Barbara Metcalf. *Islamic Revival in British India: Deoband, 1860–1900.* Princeton, N.J.: Princeton University Press, 1982.

Das, Sisir Kumar. *A History of Indian Literature 1912–1956.* New Delhi: Sahitya Akademi, 1995.

De Lauretis, Teresa. *Technologies of Gender.* Bloomington: Indiana University Press, 1987.

De Man, Paul. "Anthromorphism and Trope in the Lyric." In *The Rhetoric of Romanticism*, 239–62. New York: Columbia University Press, 1984.

———. "Autobiography as De-Facement." In *The Rhetoric of Romanticism*, 67–81. New York: Columbia University Press, 1984.

———. "Lyric and Modernity." In *Blindness and Insight: Essays in the Rhetoric of Contemporary Criticism*. Minneapolis: University of Minnesota Press, 1983.

———. *The Rhetoric of Romanticism*. New York: Columbia University Press, 1984.

———. "The Rhetoric of Temporality." In *Blindness and Insight: Essays in the Rhetoric of Contemporary Criticism*, 187–228. Minneapolis: University of Minnesota Press, 1983.

Derrida, Jacques. *The Ear of the Other*. Ed. Christie V. McDonald, trans. Peggy Kamuf. New York: Schocken Books, 1985.

———. *The Gift of Death*. Trans. David Wills. Chicago: University of Chicago Press, 1995.

———. "Signature, Event, Context." In *Glyph* 1 (1977): 172–97.

———. *Specters of Marx*. Trans. Peggy Kamuf. New York and London: Routledge, 1994.

Dharwadkar, Vinay. "Orientalism and the Study of Indian Literatures." In Carol Breckenridge and Peter van der Veer, eds., *Orientalism and the Postcolonial Predicament*, 155–85. Philadelphia: University of Pennsylvania Press, 1993.

Dingwaney, Anuradha, and Carol Maier, eds. *Between Languages and Cultures: Translation and Cross-Cultural Texts*. Pittsburgh: University of Pittsburgh Press, 1995.

Dirks, Nicholas. "History as the Sign of the Modern." *Public Culture* 2, no. 2 (Spring 1990): 25–32.

Duff, Alexander. *New Era of the English Language and English Literature in India*. Edinburgh: John Johnston, 1837.

Engels, Friedrich. *The Condition of the Working Class in England*. Trans. W. O. Henderson and W. H. Chaloner. 1845. Repr. of 1892 ed., Stanford, Calif.: Stanford University Press, 1968.

Ewing, Katherine. *Arguing Sainthood: Modernity, Psychoanalysis, Islam*. Durham, N.C.: Duke University Press, 1997.

Fabian, Johannes. *Time and the Other: How Anthropology Makes Its Object*. New York: Columbia University Press, 1983.

Faiz, Alys. "Faiz Ahmad Faiz." *Journal of South Asian Literature* 10, no. 1 (1974): 123–30.

Faiz, Faiz Ahmed. "Faiz on Faiz." *Journal of South Asian Literature* 10, no. 1 (1974): 131–40.

———. Interview with Carlo Coppola. *Journal of South Asian Literature* 10, no. 1 (1974): 141–44.

———. *Poems by Faiz.* Trans. Victor Kiernan. London: George Allen and Unwin, 1972.

Farooqi, Saqi. "Hasan Kooza-gar." *Annual of Urdu Studies* 5 (1985): 3–19.

———. *A Listening Game.* Trans. Frances W. Pritchett. London: Lokmanya Press, 1987.

Farooqi, Muhammad Ahsan, N. M. Rashed, Wazeer Agha, and Saleem Ahmad. "The Future of the Ghazal." *Annual of Urdu Studies* 4 (1984): 1–24.

Faruqi, Shamsur Rehman. *The Secret Mirror: Essays in Urdu Poetry.* Delhi: Academic Literature, 1981.

Fausto-Sterling, Anne. "The Five Sexes." *Sciences* (March–April 1993): 21–25.

Finnegan, Ruth. *Oral Poetry: Its Nature, Significance, and Social Context.* Cambridge, Eng.: Cambridge University Press, 1979.

Fish, Stanley. *Doing What Comes Naturally: Change, Rhetoric, and the Practice of Theory in Literary and Legal Studies.* Durham, N.C.: Duke University Press, 1989.

———. *Is There a Text in This Class? The Authority of Interpretive Communities.* Cambridge, Mass.: Harvard University Press, 1980.

Fitzgerald, Edward, trans. *Rubaiyat of Omar Khayyam: A Critical Edition.* Ed. Christopher Decker. Charlottesville: University of Virginia Press, 1997.

Flemming, Leslie. *Another Lonely Voice: The Urdu Short Stories of Sadat Hasan Manto.* Monograph Series, vol. 18. Berkeley: Center for South and Southeast Asian Studies, University of California, 1979.

Foucault, Michel. *The Care of the Self.* Vol. 1. Trans. Robert Hurley. New York: Vintage Books, 1986.

———. *Ethics, Subjectivity, and Truth.* Vol. 1. Ed. Paul Rabinow. Trans. Robert Hurley and others. New York: New Press, 1997.

———. *Language, Counter-Memory, Practice: Selected Essays and Interviews.* Trans. and ed. Donald F. Bouchard, and ed. Sherry Simon. Ithaca, N.Y.: Cornell University Press, 1988.

Freud, Sigmund. *Introductory Lectures on Psychoanalysis.* Ed. and trans. James Strachey. New York: W. W. Norton, 1977.

———. *Three Essays on the Theory of Sexuality.* Ed. and trans. James Strachey. New York: Basic Books, Publishers, 1975.

Fuss, Diana. *Essentially Speaking: Feminism, Nature, and Difference.* New York: Routledge, 1989.

———. "Interior Colonies: Frantz Fanon and the Politics of Identification." In Fuss, *Identification Papers*, 141–65. New York: Routledge, 1995.

Gaeffke, Peter. *A History of Indian Literature: Hindi Literature in the Twentieth Century.* Wiesbaden, Ger.: Otto Harrassowitz, 1978.

*Gazetteer of India: Gujarat State, Vadodara District*. Ahmadabad: Government Printing, Stationery, and Publications, 1979.

Goldberg, Jonathan. *Desiring Women Writing: English Renaissance Examples*. Stanford, Calif.: Stanford University Press, 1997.

Gould, Stephen Jay. *Ever Since Darwin: Reflections in Natural History*. New York: W. W. Norton, 1997.

Gramsci, Antonio. *Selections from the Prison Notebooks of Antonio Gramsci*. Ed. and trans. Quintin Hoare and Geoffrey Nowell Smith. London: Lawrence and Wishart, 1971.

Great Britain. Parliament. *British Parliamentary Papers*. Vol. 8, *1831–32*.

———. Parliament. *Parliamentary Debates*. Vol. 26 (1813).

Greenblatt, Stephen. "Towards a Poetics of Culture." In H. Aram Veser, ed., *The New Historicism*, 1–14. New York: Routledge, 1989.

Groys, Boris. "The Birth of Socialist Realism from the Spirit of the Russian Avant-Garde." In John E. Bowlt and Olga Match, eds., *Laboratory of Dreams: The Russian Avant-Garde and Cultural Experiment*. Stanford, Calif.: Stanford University Press, 1996.

Guha, Ranajit, and Gayatri Chakravorty Spivak, eds. *Selected Subaltern Studies*. New York: Oxford University Press, 1988.

Guillory, John. *Cultural Capital: The Problem of Literary Canon Formation*. Chicago: The University of Chicago Press, 1993.

*Gujarat State Gazetteer*. Ahmadabad: Gujarat Print, Stationery, and Publications, 1989.

Gupta, Narayani. *Delhi Between Two Empires, 1803–1931: Society, Government, and Urban Growth*. New Delhi: Oxford University Press, 1998.

Gupta, Partha Sarthi. *Radio and the Raj: 1921–47*. Calcutta: K. P. Bagchi, for the Centre for Studies in Social Sciences, 1995.

Haberman, David L. *Journey Through the Twelve Forests: An Encounter with Krishna*. New York and Oxford: Oxford University Press, 1994.

Habermas, Jürgen. *The Structural Transformation of the Public Sphere: An Inquiry into a Category of Bourgeois Society*. Trans. Thomas Burger and Fredrick Lawrence. Cambridge, Mass.: Harvard University Press, 1989.

Hali, Altaf Husain. *Hali's Musaddas: The Flow and Ebb of Islam*. Trans. Christopher Shackle and Javed Majeed. New Delhi: Oxford University Press, 1997.

Hardiman, David. "Power in the Forest: The Dangs, 1820–1940." *Subaltern Studies* 8: 89–147. New Delhi: Oxford University Press, 1996.

Hardy, Peter. *The Muslims of British India*. Cambridge, Eng.: Cambridge University Press, 1972.

Harootunian, Harry D. "The Benjamin Effect: Modernism, Repetition, and the

Path to Different Cultural Imaginaries." In Michael P. Steinberg, ed., *Walter Benjamin and the Demands of History*, 62–87. Ithaca, N.Y.: Cornell University Press, 1996.

Hasan, Khalid. "Sādat Hasan Manto: Not of Blessed Memory." *Annual of Urdu Studies* 4 (1984): 85–96.

Hashmi, Alamgir. "Professor Ahmed Ali." *Annual of Urdu Studies* 9 (1994): 91–97.

Hastings, Warren. "The Address in His Defense." 2 June 1791. In Geoffrey Carnall and Colin Nicholson, eds., *The Impeachment of Warren Hastings: Papers from a Bicentenary Commemoration*. Edinburgh: Edinburgh University Press, 1989.

Havel, Ernest Binfield. *Essays in Indian Art, Industry, and Education*. Madras: The Theosophist Office, 1910.

Hawley, John Stratton. "Author and Authority in Bhakti Poetry." *Journal of Asian Studies* 47 (May 1988): 269–90.

Hawley, John Stratton, and Mark Jurgensmeyer, eds. *Songs of the Saints of India*. New York: Oxford University Press, 1988.

Herbert, Christopher. *Culture and Anomie: Ethnographic Imagination in the Nineteenth Century*. Chicago: University of Chicago Press, 1991.

Hill-Collins, Patricia. *Black Feminist Thought: Knowledge, Consciousness, and the Politics of Empowerment*. Boston: Unwin Hyman, 1990.

Ibbetson, Denzil. "Address to the Fourth Annual Meeting, 26 February 1890." *Journal of the Anthropological Society of Bombay* (1890): 116–46.

———. *Punjab Castes*. 1916. Repr., Delhi: B. R. Publishing, 1974.

Ikram, S. M. *Muslim Civilization in India*. New York: Columbia University Press, 1964.

Iman, Akhtarul. Interviews with author. Bombay, 7, 9, 12 January, and 5, 14 June 1988.

Iman, Sultana. Interview with author. 12 January 1988.

*Imperial Gazetteer of India*. 2 vols. Provincial ser. Lahore, Punjab: Aziz, 1979.

Inden, Ronald. *Imagining India*. Oxford: Basil Blackwell, 1990.

*Inspection Report of the East India Railway*. East India Railway. National Archives of India, New Delhi.

Iqbal, Muhammad. *Letters of Iqbal*. Comp. and ed. Bashir Ahmad Dar. Lahore: Iqbal Academy, 1978.

———. *Notes on Iqbal's Asrar-e-Khudi*. Ed. Arthur J. Arberry. Lahore: Muhammad Ashraf, 1959.

———. *Poems from Iqbal*. Trans. Victor Kiernan. London: Murray, 1955.

———. *The Reconstruction of Religious Thought in Islam*. London: Oxford University Press, 1934.

———. *Secrets of the Ego*. Trans. F. R. Tariq. Lahore: Islamic Book Service, 1977.

———. *Secrets of the Self.* Trans. Reynold A. Nicholson. London: Macmillan, 1920.

———. *Shikwa and Jawab-e Shikwa, Complaint and Answer, Iqbal's Dialogue with God.* Trans. Khushwant Singh. New Delhi: Oxford University Press, 1990.

Jahan, Rashid. "Sightseeing Trip to Delhi." *Journal of South Asian Literature* 22, no. 1 (1987): 131–32.

———. "That One." *Journal of South Asian Literature* 22, no. 1 (1987): 133–34.

———. "Woman: A One Act Drama." *Journal of South Asian Literature* 22, no. 1 (1987): 135–51.

Jeffrey, Patricia. *Frogs in a Well: Indian Women in Purdah.* London: Zed Books, 1979.

Johnson, Barbara. *A World of Difference.* Baltimore: Johns Hopkins University Press, 1987.

Johnston, Sir H. H. "The Rise of the Native." *Quarterly Review* (January 1910): 121–51.

Johnston, Reverend J. *Abstract and Analysis of the Report of the Indian Education Commission with Notes and the Recommendations in Full.* London: Hamilton, Adams, 1884.

Jones, William. *The Works of Sir William Jones.* 13 vols. London: Printed for John Stockdale, Piccadilly; and John Walker, Paternoster Row, 1807.

Kamuf, Peggy. "Pieces of Resistance." In Lindsay Waters and Wlad Godzich, eds., *Reading de Man Reading,* 136–54. Minneapolis: University of Minnesota Press, 1989.

Kapoor, Raj. *Avārā* (Vagabond). Bombay: R. K. Films, 1951.

Kejariwal, O. P. *The Asiatic Society of Bengal and the Discovery of India's Past, 1784–1838.* New Delhi: Oxford University Press, 1988.

Kerr, James. *A Review of Public Instruction in the Bengal Presidency from 1835–1852.* Calcutta: J. Thomas, Baptist Mission Press, 1852.

Khundmiri, S. Alam. "The *Musha'irah.*" *Annual of Urdu Studies* 3 (1983): 75–84.

Kiernan, Victor, trans. *Poems from Iqbal.* London: Murray, 1955.

Kopf, David. *The Brahmo Samaj and the Shaping of the Modern Indian Mind.* Princeton, N.J.: Princeton University Press, 1979.

Lacan, Jacques. *The Ego in Freud's Theory and in the Technique of Psychoanalysis, 1954–1955.* Book 2 of *The Seminar of Jacques Lacan,* trans. Sylvana Tomaselli. New York and London: W. W. Norton, 1991.

———. *The Ethics of Psychoanalysis, 1959–1960.* Book 8 of *The Seminar of Jacques Lacan,* trans. Dennis Porter. London: Routledge, 1992.

———. *The Four Fundamental Concepts of Psychoanalysis, 1964.* Book 9 of *The Seminar of Jacques Lacan,* trans. Alan Sheridan. London: Hogarth Press and the Institute of Psychoanalysis, 1977.

———. *The Four Fundamental Concepts of Psychoanalysis: The Seminar of Jacques Lacan.* Trans. Alan Sheridan. New York: W. W. Norton, 1981.

Lane, William Edward. *Arabic-English Lexicon.* London: Williams and Norgate, 1863–93. Repr., Lahore: Islamic Book Centre, 1978.

Latif, Khalid. "Ismat Chughtai." *Mahfil* 8, nos. 2–3 (Summer–Fall 1972): 189–94.

Lauretis, Teresa de. *Technologies of Gender: Essays on Theory, Film, and Fiction.* Bloomington: Indiana University Press, 1987.

Lawrence, Bruce, ed. *The Rose and the Rock: Mystical and Rational Elements in the History of South Asian Islam.* Durham, N.C.: Duke University, Programs in Comparative Studies on South Asia [and] Islamic and Arabian Development Studies, 1979.

Leitner, Gottlieb William. "Report of the Committee Appointed to Examine Existing Standards of Examination of the Punjab University College." In J. P. Naik, ed., *Selections from Educational Records of the Government of India,* II: 262–73. Delhi: For the National Archives of India by the Manager of Publications, Government of India, 1963.

Lelyveld, David. *Aligarh's First Generation: Muslim Solidarity in British India.* Princeton, N.J.: Princeton University Press, 1978.

———. "The Fate of Hindustani: Colonial Knowledge and the Project of a National Language." In Carol Breckenridge and Peter van der Veer, eds., *Orientalism and the Postcolonial Predicament,* 189–214. Philadelphia: University of Pennsylvania Press, 1993.

Levinas, Emmanuel. *Ethics and Infinity: Conversations with Philip Nemo.* Trans. Richard A. Cohen. Pittsburgh: Duquesne University Press, 1985.

———. "The Face." In *Ethics and Infinity: Conversations with Philip Nemo,* trans. Richard A. Cohen, 85–101. Pittsburgh: Duquesne University Press, 1985.

———. *Face to Face with Levinas.* Trans. and ed. Richard A. Cohen. Albany: State University of New York Press, 1986.

———. "Language and Proximity." In Alphonso Lingis, trans., *Collected Philosophical Papers.* Dordrecht, Boston, and Lancaster: Martinus Nijhoff Publishers, 1987.

Lloyd, David, and Paul Thomas. *Culture and the State.* New York: Routledge, 1998.

Luthra, M. R. *Indian Broadcasting.* New Delhi: Publications Division, Ministry of Information and Broadcasting, 1986.

Macaulay, Thomas Babbington. *Miscellanies.* Vol. 2. Boston and New York: Houghton, Mifflin, 1900.

Majid, Javed. *Ungoverned Imaginings: James Mill's The History of British India and Orientalism.* Oxford: Clarendon Press, 1992.

Makdisi, Saree. *Romantic Imperialism: Universal Empire and the Culture of Modernity*. Cambridge, Eng.: Cambridge University Press, 1998.

Malik, Hafeez. *Iqbal: Poet Philosopher of Pakistan*. New York: Columbia University Press, 1971.

Mallarmé, Stéphane. *Poems*. Trans. Roger Fry. Ed. and comm. Charles Mauron. New York: New Directions, 1951.

Mani, Lata. "Multiple Mediations: Feminist Scholarship in the Age of Multinational Reception." *Feminist Review* 35 (Summer 1990): 24–41.

"Manifesto of the Progressive Writers' Association." *Left Review* 11 (February 1936): 36–37.

Manuel, Peter Lamarch. *Cassette Culture: Popular Music and Technology in North India*. Chicago: University of Chicago Press, 1993.

———. *Thumri in Historical and Stylistic Perspectives*. Delhi: Motilal Banarasidass, 1989.

Marx, Karl. *Capital*. Vol. 1. New York: International Publishers, 1979.

Mathers, E. Powys. *Eastern Love*. 3 vols. New York: Horace Liveright; London: John Rodker, 1933.

Mayes, Elizabeth. "The Fantasy of Internalization in the Theoretical Imaginary." *Representations* 62 (Spring 1998): 100–110.

Mayor, Leela. "Pavagadh and Champaner—A Tale of a Hill and a City: An Outline Treatment for a Documentary." Faxed correspondence, 8 April 1998.

McClintock, Anne. *Imperial Leather: Race, Gender, and Sexuality in the Colonial Context*. New York and London: Routledge, 1995.

Meisami, Julie Scott. "Allegorical Gardens in the Persian Poetic Tradition: Nezami, Rumi, Hafez." *International Journal of Middle East Studies* 17 (1985): 229–60.

———. "Allegorical Techniques in the Ghazals of Hafez." *Edebiyat* 4 (1979): 1–40.

———. "Unity and Structure in a Ghazal of Hafiz: A Comparative Study." *Javadpur Journal of Comparative Literature* 14–15 (1976, 1977): 116–34.

———. "The World's Pleasance: Hafiz's Allegorical Gardens." *Comparative Studies* 5 (1983): 153–85.

Memon, Muhammad Umar. "A Storm in a Teacup." *Annual of Urdu Studies* 4 (1984): 101–6.

———. *Studies in the Urdu Ghazal and Prose Fiction*. Madison: South Asian Studies, University of Wisconsin–Madison Publication Series, no. 5, 1979.

Mill, James. *The History of British India*. 10 vols. 5th ed. With notes by Horace Hyman Wilson. London: J. Madden, 1858.

Millay, Edna St. Vincent, and George Dillon, trans. *Flowers of Evil: From the*

*French of Charles Baudelaire*. New York and London: Harper and Brothers, 1936.

Miller, Nancy K. *Getting Personal: Feminist Occasions and Other Autobiographical Acts*. New York: Routledge, 1991.

Minault, Gail. *The Khilafat Movement: Religious Symbolism and Political Mobilization in India*. New York: Columbia University Press, 1982.

Minh-ha, Trinh-t. *When the Moon Waxes Red: Representation, Gender, and Cultural Politics*. New York: Routledge, 1991.

Mirza, Khurshid. "Rashid Jahan: My *Āpābī*." *Journal of South Asian Literature* 22, no. 1 (1987): 152–57.

Mitchell, Timothy. *Colonizing Egypt*. Berkeley: University of California Press, 1991.

Mitter, Partha. *Art and Nationalism in Colonial India, 1850–1922: Occidental Orientations*. Cambridge, Eng.: Cambridge University Press, 1994.

Mukherjee, Meenakshi. *Realism and Reality: The Novel and Society in India*. New Delhi: Oxford University Press, 1985.

Mukta, Parita. *Upholding the Common Life: The Community of Mirabai*. New Delhi: Oxford University Press, 1994.

Naim, C. M. "The Theme of Homosexual (Pederastic) Love in the Urdu Ghazal." In Muhammad Umar Memon, ed., *Studies in the Urdu Ghazal and Prose Fiction*. Madison: South Asian Studies, University of Wisconsin–Madison Publication Series, no. 5, 1979.

Nair, Janaki. *Women and Law in Colonial India: A Social History*. New Delhi: Kali for Women, 1996.

Naqvi, Tahira. "Ismat Chughtai." *Annual of Urdu Studies* 8 (1993): 43–48.

National Archives of India. *Selections from the Educational Records of the Government of India: Development of University Education, 1860–87*. Ed. J. P. Naik. Delhi, 1963.

Nicholson, Reynold A. *The Mystics of Islam*. London: G. Bell and Sons, 1914.

Niranjana, Tejaswini. *Siting Translation: History, Post-Structuralism and the Colonial Context*. Berkeley: University of California Press, 1992.

Nivedita, Sister. *The Complete Works of Sister Nivedita*. Calcutta: Sister Nivedita Girl's School, 1967.

Oldenburg, Veena Talwar. "Lifestyle as Resistance: The Case of the Courtesans of India." *Feminist Studies* 16, no. 2 (Summer 1990): 259–88.

———. *The Making of Colonial Lucknow, 1856–1977*. Princeton, N.J.: Princeton University Press, 1989.

Parry, Benita. *Delusions and Discoveries: Studies on India and the British Imagination, 1880–1930*. London: Allen Lane, 1972.

Petievich, Carla. *Assembly of Rivals: Delhi, Lucknow, and the Urdu Ghazal*. New Delhi: Manohar Publications, 1992.

———. "The Feminine Voice in the Urdu Ghazal." *Indian Horizons* 39, nos. 1–2 (1990): 25–42.

———. "The Two-School Theory of Urdu Literature." Ph.D. diss., University of British Columbia, 1986.

Pinney, Christopher. *Camera Indica: The Social Life of Indian Photographs.* Chicago: University of Chicago Press, 1997.

Platts, John T. *A Dictionary of Urdu, Classical Hindi, and English.* New Delhi: Oxford University Press, 1984.

Prins, Yophie. *Victorian Sappho.* Princeton, N.J.: Princeton University Press, 1999.

Pritchett, Frances W. "Convention in the Classical Urdu Ghazal: The Case of Mir." *Journal of South Asian and Middle Eastern Studies* 3, no. 1 (1979): 88–97.

———. *Nets of Awareness: Urdu Poetry and Its Critics.* Berkeley: University of California Press, 1994.

———. "Orient Pearls Unstrung: The Quest for Unity in the Ghazal." *Edebiyat* 4 (1993): 54–69.

Querishi, Waheed, ed. *Selections from the* Iqbal Review. Lahore: Iqbal Academy, 1983.

Rahman, Tariq. "Boy Love in the Urdu Ghazal." *Annual Of Urdu Studies* 7 (1990): 1–21.

Ramz, M. Usman. "Iqbal's Philosophy of History." In Dr. Waheed Querishi, ed., *Selections from the* Iqbal Review. Lahore: Iqbal Academy, 1983.

Rapaport, Herman. *Heidegger and Derrida: Reflections on Time and Language.* Lincoln: University of Nebraska Press, 1989.

Rashid, N. M. Interview with Carlo Coppola. *Mahfil* 7, nos. 1–2 (1971): 1–20.

———. "N. M. Rashed's 'Safar Nama': Three Versions." *Annual of Urdu Studies* 5 (1985): 19–22.

———. "Nine Poems." *Mahfil* 7, nos. 1–2 (1971): 21–30.

———. "Poems from *Īrān meñ ajnabī*." *Annual of Urdu Studies* 5 (1985): 51–53.

———. "Poems from *Māwarā*." *Annual of Urdu Studies* 5 (1985): 49–50.

Robinson, Douglas. *The Translator's Turn.* Baltimore: The Johns Hopkins University Press, 1991.

Robinson, Francis. *Separatism Among Indian Muslims: The Politics of the United Provinces' Muslims 1860–1923.* 1964. Repr., New Delhi: Oxford University Press, 1997.

Rougemont, Denis de. *Love in the Western World.* 3rd ed. Princeton, N.J.: Princeton University Press, 1983.

Roy, Parama. *Indian Traffic: Identities in Question in Colonial and Postcolonial India.* Berkeley: University of California Press, 1998.

Russell, Ralph, and Khurshidul Islam. *Three Mughal Poets.* Cambridge, Mass.: Harvard University Press, 1968.

Sadiq, Muhammad. *A History of Urdu Literature.* 2nd ed. New Delhi: Oxford University Press, 1964.

———. *Twentieth-Century Urdu Literature.* 1st ed., Bombay: Padma Publications, 1947; 2nd ed., Karachi: Royal Book Depot, 1983.

Said, Edward. *Orientalism.* New York: Pantheon Books, 1978.

———. *The World, the Text, and the Critic.* Cambridge, Mass.: Harvard University Press, 1983.

Saiduzzafar, Hamida. Interview. *Journal of South Asian Literature* 22, no. 1 (1987): 158–67.

Sangari, Kumkum, and Sudesh Vaid. *Recasting Women: Essays in Colonial History.* New Delhi: Kali for Women, 1989.

Sarkar, Sumit. "The Decline of the Subaltern in *Subaltern Studies.*" In *Writing Social History,* 82–108. New Delhi: Oxford University Press, 1997.

Satow, Michael, and Ray Desmond. *Railways of the Raj.* New York and London: New York University Press, 1980.

Saunders, William. *A History of Medieval Islam.* London: Routledge and Kegan Paul, 1965.

Schimmel, Annemarie. *As Through a Veil.* New York: Columbia University Press, 1982.

———. *Islamic Literature of India.* Weisbadan, Ger.: Otto Harrassowitz, 1982.

Shackle, C., and D. J. Matthews. *An Anthology of Classical Urdu Love Lyrics, Texts, and Translations.* London: Oxford University Press, 1972.

Sharma, Sunita. Interview with author. Bombay, 19 January 1998.

Singh, K. Natwar. "Face of a Friend: Ahmed Ali 1910–1994." *Annual of Urdu Studies* 9 (1994): 103–6.

Sinha, Mrinalini. *Colonial Masculinity: The "Manly Englishman" and the "Effeminate Bengali" in the Late Nineteenth Century.* Manchester and New York: Manchester University Press, 1995.

Smith, Margaret. *The Sufi Path of Love.* London: Luzac and Company, 1931.

Spencer, Jonathan, ed. *Sri Lanka: History and the Roots of Conflict.* London and New York: Routledge, 1990.

Spivak, Gayatri Chakravorty. "Can the Subaltern Speak?" In Cary Nelson and Lawrence Grossberg, eds., *Marxism and the Interpretation of Culture,* 271–316. Chicago: University of Chicago Press, 1988.

———. *A Critique of Postcolonial Reason: Towards a History of the Vanishing Present.* Cambridge, Mass.: Harvard University Press, 1999.

———. *In Other Worlds: Essays in Cultural Politics.* New York and London: Routledge, 1988.

———. *Outside in the Teaching Machine.* New York and London: Routledge, 1993.

———. "Subaltern Studies: Deconstructing Historiography." In Ranajit Guha, ed., *Subaltern Studies* 4: 330–63. New Delhi: Oxford University Press, 1994.

Steele, Laurel. "Hali and His *Muqaddamah*: The Creation of a Literary Attitude in Nineteenth-Century India." *Annual of Urdu Studies* 1 (1981): 1–45.

Steingass, F. J. *A Comprehensive Persian-English Dictionary*. 1892. Repr., Beirut: Librairie du Liban, 1970.

Stewart, Susan. "Coda: Reverse Trompe L'Oeil / The Eruption of the Real." In *Crimes of Writing: Problems in the Containment of Representation*, 273–90. Durham, N.C.: Duke University Press, 1994.

Suleri, Sara. *The Rhetoric of English India*. Chicago: University of Chicago Press, 1992.

Swinburne, Algernon Charles. "Charles Baudelaire: *Les Fleurs du Mal*." *Spectator* (6 September 1862): 998–1000.

———. *The Complete Works of Algernon Charles Swinburne*. Ed. Sir Edmund Gosse and Thomas James Wise. London: William Heinemann; New York: Gabriel Wells, 1925.

———. *William Blake: A Critical Essay*. New York: Benjamin Bloom, 1868.

Symons, Arthur. *Baudelaire: Prose and Poetry*. New York: Albert and Charles Boni, 1926.

———. "Charles Baudelaire." In Symons, *Figures of Several Centuries*. London: Constable and Company, 1916.

Tarlo, Emma. *Clothing Matters: Dress and Identity in India*. New Delhi and New York: Viking, 1996.

Temple, Sir Richard. *James Thomason*. Oxford: Clarendon Press, 1893.

Thakurta, Tapati Guha. *The Making of a New "Indian" Art: Artists, Aesthetics, and Nationalism in Bengal, c. 1850–1920*. Cambridge, Eng.: Cambridge University Press, 1992.

Thapar, Romila. *Ancient Indian Social History*. New Delhi: Orient Longman, 1978.

———. "The Householder and the Renouncer." In T. N. Madan, ed., *Way of Life, King, Householder, Renouncer: Essays in Honor of Louis Dumont*, 273–98. New Delhi: Vikas Publishing, 1982.

Thomas, Fredrick William. *The History and Prospects of British Education in India*. Cambridge, Eng.: Deighton Bell, 1891.

Thompson, E. P. *The Making of the English Working Class*. New York: Vintage Books, 1966.

Trevelyan, Charles E. *On Education of the People of India*. London: Longman, Orme, Brown, Green, and Longmans, Paternoster Row, 1838.

Tripathi, Gorardhanarama. *The Classical Poets of Gujarat and Their Influence on Society and Morals*. Bombay: Tripathi and Company, 1892.

Utas, Bo. *A Persian Sufi Poem: Vocabulary and Terminology.* London and Malmo: Scandinavian Institute of Asian Studies, 1977.

Vanita, Ruth, and Saleem Kidwai, eds. *Same-Sex Love in India: Readings from Literature and History.* New York: St. Martin's Press, 2000.

Vendler, Helen. *The Music of What Happens: Poems, Poets, Critics.* Cambridge, Mass.: Harvard University Press, 1988.

———. *Soul Says: On Recent Poetry.* Cambridge, Mass.: Belknap Press, 1995.

Visvanathan, Gauri. *Masks of Conquest: Literary Study and British Rule in India.* New York: Columbia University Press, 1989.

Waliullah, Shah. *The Sacred Knowledge of the Higher Functions of the Mind.* Trans. G. N. Jalbani. London: Octagon Press, 1982.

Warner, Michael. "Sex in Public." *Critical Inquiry* 24, no. 2 (Intimacy Issue) (Winter 1998): 547–66.

Weston, Kath. *Render Me, Gender Me: Lesbians Talk Sex, Class, Color, Nation, Stud Muffins . . .* New York: Columbia University Press, 1996.

Westwood, J. N. *Railways of India.* Newton Abbot, Eng.: David and Charles, 1974.

Whittemore, Robert. "Iqbal's Pantheism." In Waheed Querishi, ed., *Selections from the* Iqbal Review. Lahore: Iqbal Academy, 1983.

Williams, Patricia J. *The Alchemy of Race and Rights.* Cambridge, Mass.: Harvard University Press, 1991.

Windmiller, Marshall, and Gene D. Overstreet. *Communism in India.* Berkeley: University of California Press, 1960.

Wittgenstein, Ludwig. *Philosophical Investigations.* Trans. G. E. M. Anscombe. Englewood Cliffs, N.J.: Prentice Hall, 1970.

———. *Tractatus Logico-Philosophicus.* London: Routledge and Kegan Paul, 1961.

Worswick, Clark. *The Last Empire: Photography in British India, 1855–1911.* New York: Aperture, 1976.

Yang, Anand A., ed. *Crime and Criminality in British India.* Tuscon: University of Arizona Press, 1985.

Zahir, Sajjad. "Visions of Paradise." *Journal of South Asian Literature* 22, no. 1 (1987): 185–88.

Zeno. "Professor Ahmed Ali and the Progressive Writers' Movement." *Annual of Urdu Studies* 9 (1994): 85–90.

Zizek, Slavoj. *Looking Awry: An Introduction to Jacques Lacan Through Popular Culture.* Cambridge, Mass.: MIT Press, 1991.

———. *The Sublime Object of Ideology.* New York: Verso, 1989.

———. "The Virtual as Real." In *The Plague of Fantasies.* London and New York: Verso, 1997.

NEWSPAPERS

*Bombay Chronicle*, 1941–46.
*Hindustan Times*, 1933–36.
*Illustrated London News*, 1862–64.
*Lahore Tribune*, 1912–15, 1936–38.
*Times of India*, 1943–46.
*Vanguard*, 1945.

SOUTH ASIAN–LANGUAGE SOURCES

Āg̣hā, Vazīr. "Mīrājī: Dhartī pūjā kī ek mis̄āl" (Miraji: An example of earth worship). In Kumār Pāshī, ed., *Mīrājī: Shaḳhṣiyat aur fann* (Miraji: Personality and work). New Delhi: Modern Publishing, 1981.

Aḥmad, Afẓal. *Cakbast: Jang-e āzādī kā ek mard-e mujāhid* (Cakbast: A crusader for the war of freedom). Lucknow: Milne Ka Patah, Ardi Khanah, 1975.

Aḥmad, Aijāz. "Mīrājī: Shaḳhṣiyat aur fann" (Miraji: Personality and work). *Saverā* 36 (May–June 1966): 5–39.

Aḥmad, ʿAzīz. *Taraqqī pasand adab* (Progressive literature). Delhi: Chaman Book Depot, n.d.

Aḥmad, Salīm. "Nayī naẓm aur pūrā ādmī" (New poetry and the total human). *Nayā daur* (New age) 27–28 (1962): 221–301.

Aḥmad, Vajihuddin. "Sarguzasht-e Mīrājī" (Miraji's story). In Mughanī Tabassum, ed., *Shiʿr o ḥikmat* (Poetry and knowledge), 21–26. Delhi: Educational Publishing House, 1987.

ʿAlī, Aḥmad. "Jadīd shaʿirī: Ek inṭervīʿū" (New poetry: one interview). *Nayā daur* (New age) 27–28 (1962): 182–89.

ʿAlī, Aḥmad, Rashīd Jahāñ, Maḥmūd ud-Ẓafar, and Sajjād Ẓahīr. *Añgāre* (Embers). Lucknow: Sajjad Zahir, 1932.

ʿAlī, Ḳhālid, ed. *Añgāre*. Delhi: Educational Publishing House, 1995.

ʿAlī, Muḥammad. *Kalām-e jauhar* (Jauhar's writings). Delhi: Maktaba-e Jamia, n.d.

ʿAskarī, Muḥammad Ḥasan. "Azād naẓm" (Free verse). In Askarī, ed., *Jadīd urdū adab* (New Urdu literature) (1975): 78–108.

Āzād, Muḥammad Husain. *Āb-e ḥayāt* (Water of life). 2nd ed. Facsimile of Lahore 1907 ed. Lucknow: Ultar Prudesh Urdu Academy, 1982.

ʿĀẓmī, Anjum. "Jadīd naẓm kā mafahūm" (Meaning of new verse). *Nayā daur* (New age) 27–28 (1962): 301–9.

ʿĀẓmī, Kaifī. "Maiñ aur merī shāʿirī" (Me and my verse). *Mʿaiyār (kaifī viseshāñk)* (special issue). Delhi: Educational Publishing House, 1995.

ʿĀzmi, Ḳhalīlur Raḥmān. *Urdū meñ taraqqī pasand adabī taḥrīk* (The movement of Progressives in Urdu). Aligarh: Anjuman-e Taraqqi-e Urdu [Hind], 1972.

Beg, Farḥatullah. *Dillī kī āḳharī shamaʿ* (The last mushaira of Delhi). New Delhi: Orient Longman, 1979.

Bhaṭnāgar, Vishvanandan. "Mīrājī merī naẓr meñ" (Miraji in my view). In Mughani Tabassum, ed., *Shiʿr o ḥikmat* (Poetry and knowledge), 111–15. Delhi: Educational Publishing House, 1987.

Cakbast, Braj Narā'n. *Intiḳhāb-e manẓūmāt* (Ordered selection of Chakbast). Lucknow: Uttar Pradesh Urdu Academy, 1981.

———. *Ṣubḥ-e vaṭan*. Allahabad, 1994.

Cugḥtā'ī, 'Iṣmat. *Coṭeñ* (Wound). Aligarh: Educational Book House, 1982.

Cugḥtā'ī, Muḥammad ʿAbdur Reḥmān. *Maqālāt-e cugḥtā'ī* (Articles of Chughtai). Ed. Shīmā Majīd. Islamabad: Markaz Khazati, 1987.

Dihlavī, Shāhid Aḥmad. "Mīrājī: Shaḳhṣiyat aur fann" (Miraji: Personality and work). In Kumār Pāshī, ed., *Mīrājī: Shaḳhṣiyat aur fann*. New Delhi: Modern Publishing, 1981.

———. In Mugḥanī Tabassum, ed., *Shiʿr o ḥikmat* (Poetry and knowledge), 28. Delhi: Educational Publishing House, 1987.

Faiẓ, Faiẓ Aḥmad. "Ḥarf-e āgḥāz" (Opening words). In Mīrājī, *Mashriq o magḥrib ke nagḥmeñ* (Songs from the East and from the West). Lahore: Lahore Academy, 1958.

———. "Mīrājī kā fann." In Mīrājī, *Mashriq o magḥrib ke nagḥmeñ*, 5–6. Lahore: Lahore Academy, 1958.

Fārūqī, Sāqī. "Naẓm kā safar: Mīrājī" (One journey of the *naẓm*: Miraji). In Jamīl Jālibī, ed., *Mīrājī: Ek muṭālaʿh* (Miraji: A glance/a perusal/a study). Lahore: Sang-e Masil Publications, 1990.

———. "Ṣirf cār shaʿir" (Only four poems). *Nayā daur* 27–28 (1962): 310–32.

Gḥālib, Mirzā Asadullāh Ḳhān [Ghalib]. *Dīvān-e Gḥālib* (Ghalib's collection). Ed. Malik Ram. 1969. Repr., Aligarh: Maktabah-e Ulfāz, 1981.

Ḥālī, Alṭāf Ḥusain. *Dīvān-e Ḥālī* (Hali's collection). Delhi: Urdu Academy, 1991.

———. *Ḥayāt-e saʿādī* (Life of Sadi). Delhi: Maktaba Jamia, 1992.

———. *Kulliyāt-e naṡr-e Ḥālī* (Hali's complete prose). Lahore: Majlis Taraqqi-e Adab, 1968.

———. *Muqaddamah-e shiʿr o shāʿirī* (Introduction to poetry and poetics). Ed. and intro. Vaḥīd Quraishī. Lahore: Maktabah-e Jadid, 1953. Repr., Aligarh, 1977.

Hassan, Nazia. "Mujhe cāhiye (Mīrājī)" (I want). London: EMI, n.d.

Husain, Intiẓār. "Shaḳhṣ aur shaʿir" (Person and poetry). *Ṣaḥīfāh* (Book) 12 (n.d.): 47–54.

Īmān, Akhtarul. "Guftanī nā guftanī" (What should or should not be spoken). In Shīmā Majīd, ed., *Mīrājī, sah ātishah* (With fire), 13–25. Bombay: Rakhshanda Kitab Ghar, 1992.

———. "Jadīd shā'irī" (New verse). *Nayā daur* (New age) 27–28 (1962): 170–76.

———. "Mīrajī ke ākhirī lamhe" (Miraji's last moments). In Jālibī, ed., *Mīrājī.*

Jāfri, 'Alī Sardār. *Taraqqī pasand adab* (Progressive literature). 2nd ed. Aligarh: Anjuman-e Taraqqi-e Urdu, 1956.

Jahāñ, Rashīd. *Aurat aur digar afsāne* (Women and other stories). Lahore: Hashmi Book Depot, n.d.

Jālibī, Jamīl. "Mīrāji ko samajhne ke liye." *Nayā daur* (New age) 41–44 (1967): 312–34.

———, ed. *Mīrājī: Ek muṭāla'h* (Miraji: A glance/perusal/study). Lahore: Sang-e Masil Publications, 1990.

Jāved, Yūnus. *Ḥalqah-e arbāb-e ẕauq* (Circle of the men of taste). Lahore: Majlis Taraqqi-e Adab, 1984.

Joshī, Ghanshyām. *Pāvāgaḍh ḍarsan* (A vision of Pavagadh). Ahmadabad: Chirag Printers, 1998.

Jur'at, Shaikh Qalañdar Baksh. *Unkā 'ahd aur ishikīyah shā'irī* (His special and love lyric). Lahore, 1952.

Kabīr. *Kabīr granthāvalī* (Kabir's poems). Allahabad: Sahitya Bhavan, 1985.

Khān, Sar Sayyad Aḥmad. *Intikhāb-e maẓāmīn-e sar sayyad* (Selections from the essays of Sir Sayyad). Lucknow: Uttar Pradesh Urdu Academy, 1983.

Khān, Ẓafar 'Alī. *Bahāristāñ* (Spring garden). Lahore: Urdu Punjab Academy, 1937.

———. *Intikhāb-e zamīndār* (Selections from *Zaminder*). Lucknow: Uttar Pradesh Urdu Academy, 1988.

Mahnāz. "Tum aur desh ham (Mīrājī)" (You and my country). London: EMI, n.d.

Majīd, Shīmā. *Bāqeyāt-e mīrājī* (Remnants of Miraji). Lahore: Pakistan Books and Ladiri Sounds, 1990.

"Manifesto of the Progressive Writers' Association." *Hans* (October 1935).

Manṭū, Sa'ādat Ḥasan. "Ganj-e farishte" (Treasury of angels). Lahore: Maktaba Shur o Adab, n.d.

———. "Tīn gole" (Three balls). In Kumār Pāshī, ed., *Mīrājī: Shakhṣiyat aur fann* (Miraji: Personality and verse). New Delhi: Modern Publishing, 1981. Also published in *Ganj-e farishte* (Lahore: Maktaba Shūr o Adab, n.d.).

Mīr, Mīr Tāqī. *Kulliyāt-e mīr* (Mir's complete works). Karachi: Urdu Duniya, 1958.

Mīr, Safdar. "Bayābān-e junūñ" (A description of madness). *Nayā daur* (New age) 27–28 (1962): 177–203.

Mīrājī. "Bāteñ: kitāb-e pareshāñ" (The book of disquiet). In *Ḳhayāl* (Thoughts) (May 1949–). Author's private collection, n.d.

———. "Broadcasting Rights in All Compositions (Past and Future) of an Author." Delhi: Educational Publishing House, 1945.

———. "Cārls Baudela'ir" (Charles Baudelaire). In *Mashriq o maghrib ke naghmeñ* (Songs from the East and from the West), 161–89. Lahore: Punjab Academy, 1958.

———. "Frontispiece of Mīrāñjalī." Author's private collection, n.d.

———. *Gīt hī gīt* (Only songs). Delhi: Saqi Book Depot, 1944.

———. "Gīt kaise banteñ haiñ" (How are songs made). In *Mīrājī ke gīt* (Miraji's songs), 7–10. Lahore: Maktabah-e Urdu, 1943.

———. *Is naẓm meñ* (In this poem). Delhi: Alami Press, 1944.

———. *Kulliyāt-e mīrājī* (The Complete works of Miraji). Ed. Dakṭar Jamīl Jālibī. London: Urdu Markaz, 1988.

———. *Mashriq o maghrib ke naghmeñ* (Songs from the East and from the West). Lahore: Punjab Academy, 1958.

———. "Mīrāji." Muḥammad Ḥasan ʿAskarī, ed., 178–87. Allahabad: Kitabstan, 1942.

———. *Mīrājī ke gīt* (Miraji's songs). Lahore: Maktabah-e Urdu, 1943.

———. *Mīrājī kī naẓmeñ* (Miraji's verse). 1st ed., Delhi: Saqi Book Depot, 1944; 2nd ed., ed. Marghūb ʿAlī, Lucknow: Nusrat Publishers, 1990.

———. Miscellaneous poems. Author's private collection, n.d.

———. "Nāmukammal sailf-porṭraiṭ" (Incomplete self-portrait). In Kumār Pāshī, ed., *Mīrājī: Shaḳhṣiyat aur fann* (Miraji: Personality and work). New Delhi: Modern Publishing, 1981.

———. "Nayī shāʿirī kī buniyādeñ" (The fundamentals of new verse). In Jamīl Jālibī, ed., *Mīrājī: Ek muṭālaʿh* (Miraji: A glance, a perusal, a study), 519–26. Lahore: Sang-e Masil Publications, 1990.

———. Notebook of translations (manuscript notebook). Author's private collection, n.d.

———. *Pābañd naẓmeñ* (Foot-bound verse). Rawalpindi: Kitab Numa, 1968.

———. *Sah ātishah* (With fire). Author's private collection, n.d.

———. *Sah ātishah*. Ed. Shīmā Majīd. Bombay: Rakhshanda Kitab Ghar, 1992.

———. "Saifo." In *Mashriq o maghrib ke naghmeñ* (Songs from the East and from the West). Lahore: Punjab Academy, 1958.

———. *Tīn rañg* (Three tones). Pindi: Kitab Numa, 1968.

———. Translations (on loose sheets of paper). Author's private collection, n.d.

Mūhānī, Ḥasrat. *Ek siyāsī Ḍāʿrī* (A political diary). Dhuliya: Asliya Publications, 1977.

Nābhādās. *Shrī bhaktamāl.* Lucknow: Tejkumar Press, 1969.

Nāgi, Anīs. *Mīrājī: Ek bhaṭkā hu'ā shā'ir* (Miraji: A poet who lost his way). Lahore: Pakistan Books and Ladiri Sounds, 1991.

Pāshī, Kumār, ed. *Mīrājī: Shakhṣiyat aur fann* (Miraji: Personality and work). New Delhi: Modern Publishing, 1981.

Rā'epūrī, Akhtar Ḥusain. *Adab aur inqilāb* (Literature and revolution). Bombay: National Information and Publishers, n.d.

Rāshid, N. M. "Jadīd urdū shā'irī" (Modern Urdu poetry). *Nayā daur* 27–28 (1962): 164–81.

*Shrī mahākālī mātājī* (The great mother). Ahmadabad: Gaurav Publication, n.d.

Tabassum, Mughanī, ed. *Shi'r o ḥikmat* (Poetry and skill / wisdom). Delhi: Educational Publishing House, 1987.

Thānvī, Shaukat. "Maiṅ Mīrājī ko nahīṅ jāntā" (I don't know Miraji). *Nūqush* 15 (1950): 89–90.

Valī allāh al dihlavī. *al-Tafhīmat al-ilāhiyah.* Hyderabad: Academy of Shah Hali Allah of Delhi, 1967–70.

Ẓahīr, Sajjād. "Haidarābād aur ahmdābād kā kanfrains" (The conferences at Hyderabad and Ahmedabad). In Ẓahīr, *Roshnā'ī* (Light), 2nd ed. New Delhi: Seema Publications, 1985.

———. "Hindī, urdū, hindustānī kā muṣlah" (The antidote to Hindi, Urdu, Hindustani). *Nayā adab* 3 (1944): 1–31.

———. "Pahalī kul hind kanfrains: 1936." (The first Indian conference: 1936). In *Roshnā'ī* (Light), 2nd ed., 97–99. New Delhi: Seema Publications, 1985.

———. *Roushnā'ī.* 1st ed. Delhi: Azad Kitab Ghar, 1959.

———. "Yādeṅ" (Memoirs). *Indian Literature* 11 (1952): 22–56.

Żauq, Shaikh Ibrāhīm. *Dīvān-e żauq* (Selections from Zauq). Lahore: Atta Ram, 1933.

# INDEX